WEBSTER'S WINE TOURS

FRANCE

Saulter, dancer, faire les tours
Et boyre vin blanc et vermeil
Et ne faire rien tous les jours
Que compter escuz au soleil

Rabelais (1494–1553)
Pantagruel, chapter 30

WEBSTER'S WINE TOURS
FRANCE

PHILIP and MARY HYMAN
ROSEMARY GEORGE M.W.
Foreword by OZ CLARKE

Prentice Hall Press
New York
and
Simon & Schuster
London

This edition published in the United States and Canada
in 1988 by Prentice Hall Press
A division of Simon & Schuster, Inc.
Gulf + Western Building
One Gulf + Western Plaza
New York, New York 10023

PRENTICE HALL PRESS is a trademark of Simon & Schuster, Inc.

Published in the United Kingdom by
Simon & Schuster Ltd
West Garden Place
Kendal Street, London W2 2AQ

Created and designed by
Webster's Wine Price Guide Limited,
5 Praed Street, London W2 1NJ

Copyright © Webster's Wine Guides 1988

Library of Congress Cataloging-in-Publication Data
Hyman, Philip.
  Webster's wine tours – France
  Bibliography: p.
  Includes index.
  1. Wine and wine-making – France – Guide books.
2. France – Description and travel – 1981 – Guidebooks. I. Hyman, Mary.
II. George, Rosemary. III. Title.
TP553.H94   1988   641.2′22′0944   87-30038
ISBN 0-13-008855-2

Editor: Fiona Holman
Deputy Editor: Ray Granger
Designers: Roger Boffey and Alison Leggate
Maps: Studio Briggs
Line illustrations: Joe Robinson
Wine consultants: Oz Clarke and Charles Metcalfe

Typesetting and reproduction by
SB Datagraphics, Colchester, England
Printed in Italy by Arnoldo Mondadori, Vicenza

CONTENTS

CONTENTS

How to Use the Book

Each regional chapter has five sections. There is an **Introduction** to the region and its wines.

Visiting the Vineyards includes suggested itineraries. Names of towns and villages along the routes are emphasized by bold type. Please note that the spelling of place names can vary in France; hyphens, especially, can disappear and reappear bewilderingly from sign to sign.

***Caves* and Vineyards to Visit** This section is in two parts. The first lists the more important producers who are easy to visit and gives brief location instructions. "Further *Caves* and Vineyards" lists additional suggestions, including those requiring more forward planning. Inclusion in this second list does not necessarily mean quality is any less high. Within each list the producers are listed alphabetically by village, and these villages are all plotted on the touring maps.

Sights A small selection of sights is given for each region to add variety to a wine tour. They have been chosen for their proximity to the wine routes, and represent just a fraction of the attractions France can offer.

Hotels, Restaurants and Where to Buy Wine This section selects a few hotels and restaurants offering interesting wines and menus, some further suggestions for pleasant places to stay and a few good wine shops. Some regions have one or more establishments singled out for extra attention at the beginning of the section. These are the authors' particular favorites.

Abbreviations (M) Merchant, (G) Grower, (C) Co-operative, (H) Hotel, (R) Restaurant, (W) Wine shop. *Credit and Charge Cards*: AE American Express, DC Diner's Club, MC Mastercard (Access), V Visa.

Conversions 8 kilometers = 5 miles; 2 hectares = 5 acres.

PREFACE

One of the great pleasures of travel is wine, and one of the great pleasures of wine is to drink it where it is grown and made. So the idea of a wine tour – a concept which is in any case well understood these days – does not really need much justification. It is, however, worth stressing that a wine tour need not by any means be wholly focussed on wine; indeed, the best wine-touring is extremely relaxed and unstructured, with wine-tasting and visits to *caves* and vineyards merely part of a rich mosaic of leisurely drives, sightseeing, fine views and lingering meals or picnics.

I have long had a clear idea of what kind of guide was needed to serve the wine-loving tourist: it must tell you where you can stay and where you can eat well; it must offer you routes that work and interesting distractions; it must enable you to plan in every way what is best for your style and your pace; and – of course – it must be a thorough source of information about where you can find and taste interesting wines.

No other country offers so many attractions to the wine lover on vacation as France, yet it also presents the greatest challenge because of the size and variety of its vineyard areas. We are very lucky in having access to the knowledge and expertise of the *Webster's Wine Guide* editorial team. Oz Clarke, Webster's main wine author, and Rosemary George, our associate editor and a Master of Wine, have reviewed and edited the wine information throughout the guide. Rosemary has also made a complete *rédaction* of the *Caves* and Vineyards to Visit sections following a recently completed tour of France. For the touring and planning information, we turned to Philip and Mary Hyman, who have lived in Paris for many years and translated some of the best known French chefs. The Hymans have driven and written up the suggested routes, the core of the whole guide; and their knowledge of French regional gastronomy was a crucial ingredient of the guide.

Preparing this guide has been a huge task. We hope that it will lead you to many wonderful experiences. Please share these with us and send us suggestions of your favorite hotels, restaurants and wines. And please read Oz Clarke's Foreword overleaf. His suggestions on how to approach different types of producer are vital to the enjoyment of your tour.

Have a great wine tour — and, please, don't forget to designate a driver who will not imbibe more than a glass or two en route.

ADRIAN WEBSTER

Publisher of Webster's Wine Guides

WINE TOURING by Oz Clarke

Calais is where you *can* start your wine tour. Honest! If you're coming from England you drive off the boat from Dover, negotiate the dismal industrial estate and the sludgy canal, and within 1km you'll see the sign – "Free Wine Tasting 200m on the right." No, I'll admit it; I haven't indulged myself in this remarkable act of cross-Channel generosity when I've hardly recovered from sea-sickness and the French Customs man, because it breaks two of my golden rules of wine-touring. Rule One is "Taste wines in the region in which they are grown." Calais is great at turnips and sugar beet but doesn't possess a single vine as far as I know. Rule Two "Only take notice of signs written in the native lingo." There's no French at all on this sign. So? So the whole operation is entirely set up to entrap unwary English-speaking tourists arriving in France, and the whole purpose of this guide is to avoid *that*.

France – once you've got past Calais – is an absolute treasure-house for wine lovers. Even within a couple of hours of Calais you find one of the brightest jewels of all – Champagne. When I'm touring France I still try to start with Champagne – dashing down the road to Laon, then cutting south into the hills above the Marne valley – simply so that I don't delay the thrill of seeing the first vineyard longer than necessary. If I can't make Epernay and Reims and the other Champagne towns, I go hell for leather to Paris on the autoroute, swing round the *periphérique* and as I turn onto the Autoroute du Soleil at the Port de Lyons I feel a surge of excitement to be heading south – only two hours' hard drive from Chablis. Another two hours and the road swoops down through a cleft in the hills – and there it is – Burgundy's great Côte d'Or! Savigny beneath me to the left, the hill of Corton rising just to the north. Beaune? The autoroute straddles her finest vineyards, and looking right there's Volnay, Pommard and the great whites of Meursault and Puligny-Montrachet.

Time to get off the autoroute and from here to the Spanish or Italian borders, the intrepid wine tourist should always aim to find the backroads, the little byways linking one village to another, too narrow and crooked to be of use to the juggernauts and hectic sunseekers. If you stay on the autoroute at Beaune, you will have experienced the Côte d'Or for precisely that half minute it takes you to speed across the narrow slope. But if you turn off at Beaune, circle the lovely walled town and then head north or south, the vineyards of these famous wines spread before you.

Let's say we go south. The vineyards flow right up to the edge of the town. In less than a kilometer, a small road forks right, dissecting the vineyards of les Epenots and heading for a small but world-renowned village – Pommard. Do you want to stop? To wander round, sit, have a coffee, then seek out the signs hanging above many of the doors – *Propriétaire Récoltant* – meaning these are the cellars of a grower in the famous vineyards surrounding the village, or you see the sign *Vente Dégustation* that means you are invited to taste in the hope that you'll buy.

But if you're not ready for that, there's no rush – drive on a little – or better still walk along the tiny tracks which run through the superb les Rugiens vineyards and into the tiny village of Volnay. Meursault is only a kilometer away across the sweep of vines, Puligny-Montrachet not much farther on again. These villages all have *Vente Dégustation* signs too, and perhaps the sun is rising high in the sky, perhaps it's getting a little near lunchtime. So pop into a cellar and in whatever French you can muster ask to taste. If you like the wines, buy a couple of bottles for lunch, thank the proprietor for his attention, and you'll just have time to saunter through the local *charcuterie* and *boulangerie* (the delicatessen and the bakers) for some paté, some cheese, an onion, a tomato or two, and a *baguette* and then climb up into the scrub above the Volnay Clos des Chênes vineyard or the Meursault Perrières or spread your picnic only yards from where your wine was grown. Later, as you doze happily in the heat of the day you can reflect contentedly that this beats *bifteck* and *frites* in a motorway "caff" somewhere near Lyon any day.

That's what touring the wine regions should be all about. Relaxation, winding down, not tearing about. It should be about taking your favorite villages or regions as a starting point, and relating the pleasure the bottles have given you at home with the physical fact of the wines, the valleys they grow in, the smell in the air as evening comes, the crunch of the gravel under your feet and the bustle and laughter of the local bar.

And it should be about seeking out the producers and growers. Some of them old and time-worn, guarded, suspicious of the outside world, some cheery-faced and open handed, free with their wine and eager for contact with their fans. Some will hardly be able to write yet will produce sublime wine – no one quite knows how, but their fathers were good too, and their fathers before them – and *they* couldn't write either. Others are snappily efficient, bright-shining with technical know-how and up-to-date ideas. Your bottles of Meursault, or Sancerre, or St Emilion, or Châteauneuf-du-Pape will always give you special pleasure when you have visited the vines and met the men and women whose lives are dedicated to producing them.

But you shouldn't just stick to your favorites. France has so many wines we've never had the chance to try – and what's a wine tour for if not to be just a little bit adventurous? You've drunk Sancerre, but what about Reuilly, or Quincy just down the road past Bourges? Châteauneuf-du-Pape we've all drunk, but what about Rasteau, or Gigondas? And Beaumes-de-Venise of Muscat fame? Turn left off the Orange-Carpentras road and you'll find all three, nestled under the giant bleached stumps of the Dentelles de Montmirail. Want to pack your bags? Want to head off into the sun? So do I. So let's lay down a few ground rules to make the whole adventure as much fun as possible.

Visiting Manners

The most important thing to remember if you're visiting small growers is that their livelihood is making and *selling* wine. Frequently these small estates are simple family affairs, with husband and wife or father and son or daughter working the vines, making the wine, and, if there's any time left over, coping with the odd visitor. But there are other things these people enjoy doing – like having a quiet lunch to themselves, like going to the café for a drink with their mates, like watching television for an hour – you know – normal human activities that we in our business and personal lives would regard as inalienable rights.

So a visit to this kind of grower is something of a privilege, and observance of certain etiquette will do you no end of good. First, few of them will speak any English, so a little time spent brushing up on your French or just learning the basic phrases of good-mannered small talk will immediately make you more welcome. After all, you don't enjoy attempting to communicate with bewildered non-English speakers – it's *very* tiring. In particular, a little knowledge of wine terms will allow you to discuss the object of your visit – the wines.

Second, remember growers are busy; a telephone call, or ideally a letter asking for a chance to visit is of tremendous value, even if not formally required. I know it's always absurdly difficult to understand French on the 'phone, but swallow your pride and keep at it. One thing that may often happen is the grower will say he's not free today but what about tomorrow? All he's doing is to see if you're really serious about a visit or are just passing through. If you say tomorrow's fine, he knows you're interested.

Of course, the best way to gain a welcome from a grower is to have a letter of introduction from a merchant. On my first trip I had this letter from Freddy Price of Dolamores which I used to wave about like a passport. It worked like a charm because they knew Freddy, and if Freddy said I was OK and interested they were happy.

With or without a letter of introduction, enthusiasm, keenness to learn and a respectful attitude to the grower and his art will work wonders. If the grower doesn't like you, why should he spend his time in your company? But if he starts to enjoy himself, and gets a bit of rapport going, he may well think – well, this isn't a bad way to spend an hour. He may think you're worth a taste of one or two of his more select barrels, especially if he thinks your remarks about his wines are shrewd and accurate (a little studious note-taking as you sip the wine is a good way of showing you're serious).

If you like the grower and like the wines – well, *buy* some. Don't think too much about the price, although it is worth knowing what the price would be back home, so that you can check you're not actually being charged *more*! Don't insist on its being a bargain. But remember you're not just buying the wine, you're buying the experience of visiting the cellars, you're buying the anecdotes and acquaintance of the grower, the stories to tell back home. So don't quibble too much on the price. And remember – if you don't like the wine, you don't have to buy any, despite any pressure that might be brought! If you buy wine at every cellar you visit your car is going to be so laden down within a couple of days there'll be no room for you and your luggage. Do any serious buying on the way home.

Tasting Tactics

If you're not used to spitting, now's the time to get used to it, because if you're driving a car and don't spit during tastings, you're going to become a danger on the roads and the French Drink-Drive laws are strict. Either take it in turns to be designated driver, or if you know that you just can't bear to spit out some particularly delicious little number – well, you'll just have to cut out wine at lunch or go and visit cathedrals until you've sobered up. Drinking's fun, and drinking good wine's even better. But leave the heavy session until the evening when the car is safely in the garage.

Sometimes, however, the grower will not spit out himself – this can be a particular problem in Burgundy. You should certainly ask politely where you can spit – he may have a spittoon, or he may be happy for you to spit on the floor. But if he looks ratty about spitting you'll just have to take very small mouthfuls and hand a half-finished glass back – which in Burgundy will usually be returned to the barrel! It's OK, wine's an efficient antiseptic! In many areas there will be tasting centers, large co-operatives or commercial houses which are well used to coping with crowds of visitors. This guide suggests only a few such places but in an area such as Champagne most of the top producers *are* well equipped to deal with visitors so their facilities should be taken advantage of. In Burgundy and Beaujolais there are various large houses – though by no means necessarily of the best quality – who organize tours of their cellars and tastings of their wines. There are also likely to be salesmen brandishing order-forms lurking at the exit – but I say again – if you didn't like the wine, don't buy it.

So the message of this guide really is – don't do anything which makes you feel bad – like buying wine you don't want, getting lost at nightfall, turning up at a cellar when it is closed – but also, don't do anything which makes the French feel bad. If we're guests in their country, we shouldn't behave thoughtlessly. This guide shows you the pleasures *and* the pitfalls with the intention of making your tour as enjoyable as possible, and ensuring that the locals cry *au revoir* as you leave – and mean it.

INTRODUCTION by Philip and Mary Hyman

Vineyards are so widespread in France that a traveler could not go very far without finding one. This guide is designed for wine lovers, those who ask "where are the vines?" before planning an excursion. France is a veritable paradise for them, with vines from the foothills of the Pyrenees to the valley of the Loire, from the Atlantic coastal plain east to the mountainous borders of Switzerland.

You might expect that driving through vineyards, like driving through pine forests or wheat prairies, could be boring and monotonous – not so. First, one is never simply "in the vineyards" in France. Though the neat rows of vines may look the same, the wines they produce are splendidly diverse. Great wines come from specific places and there is a real thrill in passing the rows of grapes that produce a Chambertin, a Margaux or a Côte Rôtie.

Mountains and rivers are the frequent companions of vineyards and rarely are grapes planted without a leavening of woods or orchards; even rose bushes are planted at the ends of rows of vines. This is not to say that vines are never to be seen spreading in all directions, covering hill and valley alike, but, perhaps because of the constantly varying patterns the rows trace across the landscape, monotony never sets in, and there is always the prospect of a fascinating new horizon just over the next rise.

Driving through the vineyards, enjoyable though it is, is but one aspect of wine-touring; tasting is another. Though the wine's birthplace is vital, the talents of the individual growers will produce enormous variation in the flavor of the wine and there is no better way to work out what's what than to talk, and taste, *sur place*; listening to growers, visiting their cellars and storing up memories that will add new dimensions to wine-drinking at home is an essential part of any wine-touring experience.

Finally, great wines are often associated with great cities; a trip to the vineyards can be the occasion to visit places such as Dijon, Reims, and Bordeaux and to discover a wealth of fine architecture, museums and good food as memorable as the *crus* that you are tasting. Even the smallest country town will present some timeless vignette of French provincial life to beguile the eye and heart of the traveler and many of the wine properties such as Château Giscours (below) are splendid buildings in their own right.

This book was designed to make discovering the vineyards, their wines, and their many attractions as easy as possible. The following pages give general advice about touring in France and complement the more detailed information about specific regions provided in the body of the book.

Bon Voyage!

INTRODUCTION

Planning Your Tour

Wine is made less than 100km from Paris; indeed, wine is made in Paris though the French capital can hardly be counted as a vineyard anymore. The closest wine-growing regions to the capital are Champagne, the Loire valley and the area around Chablis; any of these can easily be reached by car within a couple of hours' journey from Paris. Foreign visitors to France need only to carry a valid driving license from their home country – an international license is not required.

If you are visiting the more distant regions of France the train may be quickest method. Much of France is now more accessible from Paris thanks to the high-speed TGV trains. Lyon, the gateway to Beaujolais and the northern Rhône, is only a two-hour train ride from Paris, and Marseille and the wines of Provence only four hours away. If you rent a car in Paris you may simply "drop it off" in the region you are visiting before taking the train back to the capital, or you might take advantage of the French Railroad's (SNCF) facilities for shipping cars as they do baggage – you and your car will arrive at the same time.

There is also a well-developed domestic air network bringing all France's major cities within one or two hours of each other. Direct international flights can be made to Nice and Lyon as well as to Paris.

When to Tour

It is perhaps easier to say when not to visit the vineyards than when touring is most advisable. The time to avoid is around the harvest (late September and early October) since even the large houses find it hard to receive visitors then and small growers cannot even consider providing tastings at that time of year. From late October and November things settle down and the vineyards have a final flush of beauty as the vine leaves turn to bright gold before falling to the ground. In the winter months rain and cold can make driving a less than attractive prospect. The spring and early summer are much better times to visit. Do not be deterred by the fact that in the spring the vines have yet to produce their leaves; their gnarled black silhouettes are as striking as the lush greenery of summer. In July the roads are packed with Frenchmen on vacation and some roads (especially near the coasts) are so congested that touring becomes virtually impossible. In particular, keep off the roads during the "change over" weekend between July and August when a mad rush of eager August tourists meets the hordes returning from the July vacation. Put up in a nice country inn for the weekend.

Keep an eye on the calendar and avoid national holidays. In addition to Christmas, New Year and Easter these are May 1 (Labor Day); May 8 (Armistice 1945); May 12 (Ascension); May 22 (Pentecost); July 14 (Bastille Day); August 15 (Assumption); and November 1 (All Saints Day).

Driving the Routes

Each wine route in this book has been described with enough detail to keep you from losing your way. You will, however, benefit from having a detailed map of each region you plan to visit. The best maps are those produced by the IGN (Institut Géographique National); those with a scale of 1/100,000 are particularly recommended if you plan to do some exploring on your own. Otherwise the standard 1/250,000 Michelin maps are usually sufficient. A word of caution – in recent years the French have taken to renumbering many of their roads. In particular, some *routes nationales* (N prefix) have become *routes départementales* (D prefix). Some maps have not been updated.

In most of the wine regions official *Routes du Vin* exist. The itineraries in this book do not slavishly follow these routes, although on occasion the official route and the one recommended here do coincide. You are, of course,

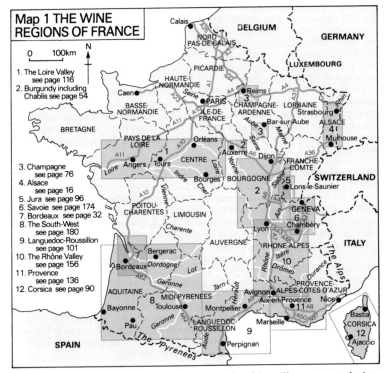

Map 1 THE WINE REGIONS OF FRANCE

0   100km   N

1. The Loire Valley see page 116
2. Burgundy including Chablis see page 54
3. Champagne see page 76
4. Alsace see page 16
5. Jura see page 96
6. Savoie see page 174
7. Bordeaux see page 32
8. The South-West see page 180
9. Languedoc-Roussillon see page 101
10. The Rhône Valley see page 156
11. Provence see page 136
12. Corsica see page 90

free to follow the official routes but generally this will mean wandering farther afield than if you had followed the *Webster*'s itineraries.

Do not let the length of the routes in this book deceive you; a route that is "only" 100km could take days to drive if you stop and visit a long list of growers. What's more, even in the best of driving conditions, many of these country roads cannot be traveled at high speeds; 50km an hour is a good average speed for many routes.

Hotels and Restaurants
A short list of hotels and restaurants is provided for each of the wine regions. Generally, one has the choice between staying in luxury establishments or opting for more modest accommodation and meals. For many of the regions, one or more restaurants have been singled out for an exceptional list of local wines and should not be missed.

A word should be added here about the use of the expression *nouvelle cuisine*. Since the early 1970s a tendency to juxtapose exotic and traditional ingredients, shorten cooking times, and lighten sauces has resulted in a "new way of cooking," or *nouvelle cuisine*. Certain ingredients have been adopted with enthusiasm by chefs throughout the country and some, like duck breast (*magret*), *foie gras* or raspberry-flavored vinegar, have become "standards" on menus. Obviously, not all restaurants have bowed to the trend but, increasingly, the choice is between restaurants offering *nouvelle* specialties and those with traditional regional dishes. On the whole, chefs today have greater freedom to experiment and exercise their imagination although, now that the initial shock-waves have passed, what was *nouvelle* is fast becoming *classique*. At its worst, *nouvelle cuisine* can be both bland and laughably pretentious, but at its best the taste of foods is intensified, the intelligence of the chef comes to the fore, and some astonishing harmonies are created.

PARIS FOR THE WINE LOVER

Paris itself needs no introduction: travelers have been spreading the word for centuries that this is a place not to be missed. One reason for visiting the city, however, is rarely evoked – Paris is the "Wine Capital of France." Just as Zola called the central market the "belly" of Paris, so Paris is the belly of France. Parisians have a gargantuan appetite for all the countryside can produce and wine is no exception. Though clearly the best place to taste the wines of any one region is in the region itself, the best place to sample the wines of all France is Paris.

Though wine shops and cafés abound, be forewarned that only a few are worth making a detour to visit and that the overall quality of "counter wines" is rather appalling. Nonetheless, numerous bistros offer good wines from the Loire and there is real excitement in the air every November 15 when Beaujolais Nouveau "arrives" – even the humblest café will acquire a barrel to satisfy the Parisians' thirst for this particular liquid.

Wine enthusiasts, however, will be pleased to find a growing number of wine bars which have spread throughout the city in recent years. As their name implies (they are called "wine bars" by the French as well), the English started the trend and now, in almost every district there is at least one of these establishments serving obscure "small" wines, such as the whites from Savoie or Jura, or "neglected" reds, particularly those of the Rhône, in addition to the usual assortment of wines from the Loire and Beaujolais. Some of these modest establishments also serve fine Bordeaux or burgundies by the glass, though, as a rule, you are generally better off ordering one of the regional wines the owner has proudly "discovered."

Given the proliferation of wine bars, the number of quality wine shops and some "sights" worth visiting one can easily plan several wine-related walks through the capital. The city also makes an excellent starting place for excursions to many of the vineyards, both near and far, described in the course of this book.

Paris is not simply a massive consumer of wines – it even produces them as well. There is a little plot of vines on the corner of the rue des Saules and the rue St Vincent, in the shadow of Sacré Coeur, which produces the wine of Montmartre. This is all that remains of the many vineyards that once covered the area.

The wines made in the vicinity of Paris were once the most sought after in France; today so little is produced it is considered strictly a curiosity. Attempts to revive wine-making in the near suburbs have, however, begun to attract attention: Suresnes is once again producing wine and vines have been planted at Issy-les-Moulineaux.

Restaurants, Wine Bars and Where to Buy Wine

The following is a list of shops, restaurants, and wine bars that offer exceptional selections of wines, often at reasonable prices. There is also a wine bookshop and a *boutique* offering a wide array of wine accessories for sale.

Jean-Baptiste Besse (W), 48 r. de la Montagne-St Geneviève, 75005. Tel: 43.25.35.80.
The "grand old wine merchant of Paris." In his cluttered hilltop shop, M. Besse unearths outstanding bottles from piles that only he can maneuver in. This is a place to come for specific wines rather than for idle browsing.

Carré des Feuillants (R), 14 r. Ca-stiglione, 75001. Tel: 42.86.82.82. Two Michelin stars. Reservations essential. Closed Sat–Sun. MC V
Regional wines, especially those from chef and owner Alan Dutournier's native South-West, are well represented and his wine list is full of "discoveries." The cuisine is imaginative and although only opened in 1986 this restaurant can be ranked among the best in Paris.

Caves de la Madeleine (W), Cité Berryer (25 r. Royale), 75008. Tel: 42.65.92.40. Closed Sat pm–Sun. AE MC V
Steven Spurrier, an Englishman, has turned this tiny shop into *the* wine shop of Paris. He is credited with democratizing wine-tasting through the lunches and more serious evening sessions at his Académie du Vin, just next door. Though the emphasis is on Bordeaux wines, Spurrier has done much to unearth and promote many "regional" wines from around the country.

A new addition to the Spurrier empire is **le Petit Bacchus (W,R)**, 13 r. du Cherche-Midi, 75006 Paris. Tel: 45.44.01.07. Closed Sun. AE V
A smaller selection of wines is offered than at the Caves de Madeleine though a counter for tasting and light lunches make a visit a pleasant detour.

L'Ecluse (R), 15 pl. de la Madeleine, 75008. Tel: 42.65.34.69. Closed Sun. AE V
This is one of five wine bars in Paris under the same ownership. Strictly for the lover of Bordeaux wines as no other wines are served. The young Bordeaux is well chosen. Light hot and cold dishes are well prepared.

L'Esprit et le Vin, 65 bd Malesherbes, 75008. Tel: 45.22.60.40.
No wine but a large selection of glasses, decanters and wine-related objects (some silly, some very useful). The wine-enthusiast's "gift shop."

Foire de Paris (late Apr. and early May).
A vast fair at the Porte de Versailles with an enormous number of wines to taste – many co-operatives are represented as well as individual producers. Foreign visitors are admitted free if carrying their passports.

Le Pain et le Vin (R), 1 r. d'Armaillé, 75017. Tel: 47.63.88.29. AE MC V
Three top chefs (Dutournier, Faugeron and Fournier) oversee the cooking and choose the wines. Traditional dishes with a *nouvelle* touch are served and there are good-value wines from little-known producers, especially in Burgundy.

Le Rubis (R), 10 r. du Marché-St Honoré, 75001. Tel: 42.56.04.60.
This is an old-fashioned *bistrot à vins* with all the noise, smoke and crowds one expects. Wines from the Beaujolais and the Loire Valley and "home cooking" – calf's head, sausages, salt pork with lentils, sandwiches and so on – attract crowds, especially at lunchtime. Very inexpensive. Come early or you won't get in.

Legrand Filles et Fils (W), 1 r. de la Banque, 75002. Tel: 42.60.07.12.
Lucien Legrand modestly offers a fine selection of generally inexpensive wines in his old-fashioned *épicerie* (grocery) near the Bourse. He has also opened a "cash and carry" extension of the shop in the Galerie Vivienne (no. 12). Both are worth visiting and the wines are excellent value.

Salon national des caves particulières (early November).
Several hundred large and small growers who bottle their own wine participate in this yearly fair.

Taillevent (R), 15 r. Lamennais, 75008 Paris. Tel: 45.61.12.90. Three Michelin stars. Reservations essential. Closed Sat–Sun, Aug and 1 week Feb. No cards.
Jean-Claude Vrinat's establishment is considered by many the finest cellar (and restaurant) in Paris. *Nouvelle cuisine* is prepared and there is an extensive wine list which is not particularly expensive. It is virtually impossible to secure a table unless booked weeks in advance, but once in Taillevent is one of the least intimidating of the great restaurants in Paris.

Caves Taillevent (W), 199 r. du fbg St Honoré, 75008. Tel: 45.61.14.09. Closed Sun–Mon am. V
Jean-Claude Vrinat has recently opened a wine shop around the corner from his restaurant. Fiona Beeston, formerly in charge of Legrand's cash and carry shop, and Jean-Claude Vrinat aim to make this a shop for "professionals," those really interested in wine, not only from France but from all over the world. The prices are as wide-ranging as the choice of wines.

La Tour d'Argent (R), 15–17 quai de la Tournelle, 75005. Tel: 43.54.23.31. Three Michelin stars. Reservations essential. Closed Mon. AE DC MC V
A grand restaurant in a penthouse with fine views across to Notre Dame. The wine list is one of the best in Paris and afterwards you can enjoy a *digestif* in the atmospheric cellars. Rare old bottles on the wine list and for sale in the boutique across the street. Good-value set menu at lunch.

Le Verre et l'Assiette, 1 r. Val-de-Grâce, 75005. Tel: 46.33.45.96.
Cookbooks upstairs and wine books (obviously) in the cellar. The largest selection of French wine books in Paris.

Willi's Wine Bar (R), 13 r. des Petits-Champs, 75001. Tel: 42.61.05.09. DC MC V
The best of the English-run wine bars – perhaps simply the best wine bar in Paris. Specializes in Rhône wines but offers a selection of fine (and inexpensive) wines from almost every region, as well as dishes both traditional and *nouvelle*.

Juvenile's (R,W), 47 r. de Richelieu, 75004. Tel: 42.97.46.49. Closed Sun. MC V
Lighter meals, snacks, and sandwiches around the corner from Willi's Wine Bar. A selection of wines to "take out" is offered as well.

ALSACE

If any province of France is *gourmand* it is Alsace. Wine is abundant, food is rich and plentiful, and the love of feasting is infectious. The people of Alsace seem to have insatiable appetites and unquenchable thirsts. This is not to imply that quantity counts for more than quality – you simply have the impression that wine is constantly flowing and platters of food and trays of pastry are everywhere you turn. This sense of prodigality is nothing new. One of the reasons this narrow strip of land has been coveted for centuries by both the Germans and the French is that it is extremely fertile. Vineyards now dominate the landscape but wheat fields were once common, cattle graze in the plains, and fruit trees still blossom everywhere. This wealth of natural resources means that Alsace has always been a densely populated region of France.

Great cities such as Strasbourg are few but villages of well-kept, half-timbered medieval houses with geranium pots on every windowsill line the roads. The people of Alsace like to congregate together and the isolated farmhouse, so common in other regions, is rare. Village life is animated and there are many feast days and festivals centered on food and wine.

It is often remarked that the food and wines of Alsace, and for that matter the people themselves, seem more German than French. This is simply not true. The abundance of German license plates on the roads testifies to the fact that there is something here one can not find *outre Rhin*; and indeed, the people still bitterly resent past German occupations and take any occasion they can to wave the French tricolor. Besides, though German wine and food are hardly known in France, the specialties of Alsace have traveled well and the green-stemmed glasses and *choucroute* (sauerkraut) of Alsace are now to be found throughout France. Alsace is unique, and the people have customs, a language and a history as distinctive as their wines.

The Wines of Alsace

Unlike virtually every other wine region in France, wines from Alsace have traditionally been identified by grape variety only. Indeed, there is still only one *appellation* for the entire region – Alsace. The best of these dry white wines (Alsace produces almost exclusively dry white wines) are made from "noble" grape varieties of which Riesling and Gewürztraminer are held to be the finest. Next come Muscat and Tokay-Pinot Gris, followed by Pinot Blanc, known in Alsace as Klevner and often confused with the Auxerrois Blanc. Sylvaner yields a rather hard and sharp wine, but, owing to its high yield, it remains popular. The planting of the pedestrian Chasselas, or Gutedel, is being discouraged although it is still used in making the Edelzwicker blend, popular as a table wine throughout the region.

In general, the wines are fruity and highly fragrant, dry and thirst-quenching. A little wine is vinified from the Pinot Noir, usually as a rosé or light red; it is light, pleasant and often served slightly chilled like the Pinot Noir from that other great white wine region, Champagne. A sparkling wine, which has its own *appellation* Crémant d'Alsace, is made from a mixture of grapes without any reference to them on the label.

In an effort to distinguish the quality of the region's wines, nearly 50 historically excellent, but only recently classified, vineyard sites have been designated *grands crus*. These wines can only be made from Riesling, Gewürztraminer, Muscat or Tokay-Pinot Gris and are easily identified by the mention *grand cru* on the label; as well as the name of the grape variety, the label mentions the locality in which the grapes were grown. These *grands crus* are not to be confused with names such as Réserve Exceptionelle and

Cuvée Exceptionelle which growers and merchants have traditionally used, without force of law, for their better wines.

Late-harvesting, especially of Riesling and Gewürztraminer, and occasionally of Pinot Gris or Muscat, produces Alsace's "late vintage" wines or *vendanges tardives*. Even better are the Sélections de Grains Nobles, made from even sweeter grapes affected by noble rot. These wines, made only in the best years, are truly exceptional and, like certain *grands crus*, merit aging, sometimes for quite extended periods.

In addition to the wines, do not neglect to taste the extraordinarily aromatic fruit brandies or *eaux-de-vie* – those made from plums (*prunes*), pears (*poires*), or raspberries (*framboises*) are outstanding.

Visiting the Vineyards

The vineyards of Alsace lie on a thin strip of land about 115km long but seldom more than 20km wide and are protected from the cold north-west winds by the Vosges mountains. With their picturesque medieval villages they provide the opportunity for one of the most enchanted wine tours in all of France.

Route One

Strasbourg to Colmar: 95 km

This route is essentially that of the Bas-Rhin, passing through such notable *grands crus* as Altenberg de Bergbeiten, Moenchberg, Wiebelsberg, and Kastelberg; it also enters the northernmost vineyards of the Haut-Rhin and the *grands crus* of Schoenenberg, Sporen, and Sonnenglanz before reaching Colmar, the wine capital of Alsace. Mutzig, the beer-producing capital of Alsace, is only 3km west of Molsheim. It is well worth visiting, especially around September 1 when the *fête de la bière* is held and free beer froths from the village fountain.

The Itinerary:

From **Strasbourg** take N4 to **Wangen**, then D142 south to **Westhoffen** and **Bergbieten**, where you meet the first *grand cru*, the Altenberg de Bergbieten. From Bergbieten, D275 leads through the vineyards to **Dangolsheim** and **Soultz-les-Bains**: once there, turn right on D422 to go to **Molsheim**.

Follow D422 out of Molsheim; shortly after the intersection with D392 turn right onto D35 in the direction of **Rosheim**. This extremely beautiful road climbs through the foothills of the Vosges to **Boersch**. On the way from Boersch to Barr, D35 passes through **Ottrot**, where one of the region's more interesting red wines is produced, and then **Heiligenstein**. The combination of vineyards and pine forests against a mountain backdrop makes for dramatic scenery.

From **Barr** follow D35 south; at **Mittlebergheim** D62 branches off right toward **Andlau**, one of the most attractive villages on the route and the home of three *grands crus*, Moenchberg, Wiebelsberg, and Kastelberg. On the slopes overlooking the town, just off D425, are the ruins of the Spesbourg and Andlau castles.

From Andlau take D425 to **Eichhoffen**, then turn right and continue south on D35 to **Nothalten** and **Blienschwiller**; just before Nothalten is the turnoff to Epfig, where several winemakers have their headquarters. Continue on D35 to **Dambach-la-Ville**. Between here and Colmar are the finest Riesling vineyards in Alsace. The next towns on D35 are **Scherwiller** and **Châtenois**; the latter has a perfectly preserved city gate dating from the 15th century. At **Orschwiller**, D35 becomes D1B and leads to **St Hippolyte**. This is the area with the greatest concentration of *grands crus*. In the stretch of a little over 20km that leads to Colmar, 20 major producers can be visited, as well as some of the most interesting Alsace wine villages. The first important one is **Ribeauvillé**, a beautiful little town and the site of an annual *Fête du Kugelhopf* in June. From there, follow D1B to **Zellenberg**, where D3B branches off right to **Riquewihr**, which remains much as it was 400 years ago; the town also boasts a large concentration of winemakers.

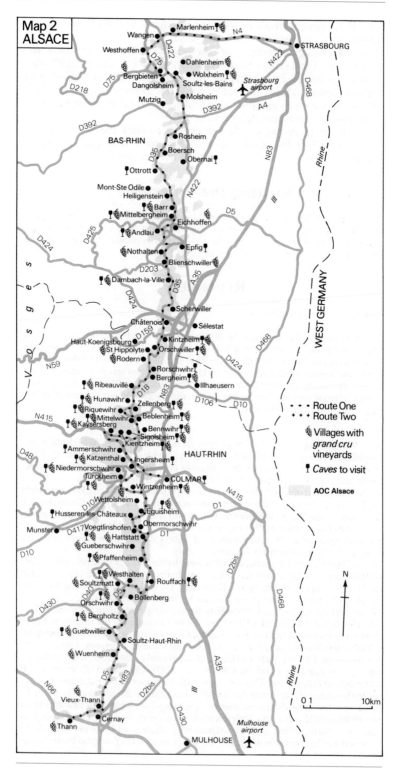

Map 2
ALSACE

Route One •••••
Route Two +++++
🍇 Villages with *grand cru* vineyards
🍷 *Caves* to visit
AOC Alsace

N

0 1   10km

Take D3 from Riquewihr to **Beblenheim**, then turn right on D1B as it curves around the mountains to **Kaysersberg**, tucked away in a narrow valley. The road passes through **Mittelwihr**, **Bennwihr**, **Sigolsheim** and **Kientzheim**, the headquarters of the Confrérie de St Etienne which oversees the quality of Alsace wines and has a wine museum in the town. From Kaysersberg, a sharp left turn on N415 leads through **Ammerschwihr** and then on to **Colmar**, the wine capital of Alsace.

Route Two

Colmar to Thann, about 80 km

The southern vineyards have their fair share of *grands crus*; Brand, Eichberg, Hatschbourg, Pfingstberg, Spiegel, Saering, Kitterlé, and Kessler are all here. Munster, where the famous cheese is made, is nearby, though one can discover the pleasures of ripe Munster with caraway seeds (*cumin*) in restaurants throughout the region.

The Itinerary:
Leave **Colmar** on D10 in the direction of **Turckheim**, home of the *grand cru* Brand; either make a detour and drive west on D10 through the mountains to **Munster** or drive through **Wintzenheim**, with its *grand cru*, Hengst, to **Wettolsheim**, which claims to be the oldest wine-producing area in Alsace; the Romans are said to have planted the first grapes here in the third century.

Just south of Wettolsheim is **Eguisheim**, perhaps the most photographed of Alsace villages; two *grands crus*, Eichberg and Hatschbourg, are found here. Leaving Eguisheim, take D14, a steep uphill road to **Husseren-les-Châteaux**, then follow D1 through **Voegtlinshofen**, where there are several good winemakers and **Obermorschwihr**. Turn right on N83 and either follow it into **Rouffach**, or make a slight detour along side roads to visit **Gueberschwihr** and **Pfaffenheim**, both surrounded by vineyards.

South of Rouffach, turn right on D18B to **Westhalten**, then left on D5 and D5II to **Orschwihr**, **Bergholtz** and **Guebwiller**. Though some excellent wines are produced further south, these towns represent the last enclave of *grands crus*, Orschwihr's Pfingstberg, Bergholtz's Spiegel, and Guebwiller's Saering, Kitterlé and Kessler. From Guebwiller, head south through **Soultz-Haut-Rhin** and on to **Cernay** on D5; from there D35 leads to **Thann** and the southernmost vineyards of the region. The end of this route makes a good starting point for an excursion into the Vosges mountains.

Caves and Vineyards to Visit

Alsace vineyards are often small, sometimes only a couple of hectares in size, often centuries old and divided among a multitude of owners (there are more than 10,000); nonetheless, the lone *vigneron* whose wines come strictly from his own vines is rarely encountered. Numerous co-operatives have been established in this century and their output is usually reliable, and sometimes outstanding. Most houses and co-operatives bottle wines from several grape varieties. Since legislation permits grapes to travel freely from one end of the region to the other, with the exception of the *grands crus*, one can never be sure where the grapes of a given wine were grown. Hence, the name and reputation of the producer is often more important than the name of the wine.

AMMERSCHWIHR, map 2

Vins d'Alsace Kuehn (G/M), 3 Grand-Rue, 68770 Ammerschwihr. Tel: 89.78.23.16.

The Kuehn family have been making wine here since 1675. Part of the buildings were destroyed in the fierce fighting of 1944 but the cellars survived, even providing shelter for the villagers and the statues from the local church. Their best wines are Gewürztraminer Cuvée St Hubert and Riesling Réserve Particulière.
Visiting hours: Mon–Fri 8–12, 1.30–5.30; open only until 4.30pm on Fri.
Location: In the center of the village.

ALSACE

Sick-Dreyer (G/M),
9 rte de Kientzheim,
68770
Ammerschwihr.
Tel: 89.47.11.31.

The Dreyer family has been growing grapes and making wines since 1750 and acting as *négociants* since 1950. Joseph Sick-Dreyer is an honorary officer of the Confrérie St Etienne, and Pierre Sick-Dreyer, the current head of the firm, is an active promoter of Ammerschwihr and the well-known Kaefferkopf vineyard. Their best wines are the Kaefferkopf Riesling and Tokay-Pinot Gris, made from late-harvested grapes.
Visiting hours: Mon–Fri 8–12, 1.30–6.30; Sat 8–12, 1.30–4.30.
Location: In the village.

ANDLAU, map 2
Domaine Fernand Gresser (G), 12 r. Deharbe, 67140 Andlau.
Tel: 88.08.95.83.

The domaine established an enviable reputation long before 1850, when its owner began to offer his wines under a vineyard name as Kastelberg Riesling – a highly unusual practice at that time in Alsace. The family's dedication to quality is maintained by the current owner, Marc Kreydenweiss, the great-grandson of Fernand Gresser. Their best wines are red Pinot Noir, and a Riesling Grand Cru Kastelberg.
Visiting hours: Mon–Tue, Thu–Sat, 9–12, 2–7.
Location: In the village, opposite the church.

BARR, map 2
Domaine Klipfel (G/M),
6 av. de la Gare, 67140 Barr.
Tel: 88.08.94.85.

Established in 1824, the domaine has 35 hectares of vines, including Clos Zisser. Its best wines are Riesling Kirchberg Grand Cru, a highly praised Tokay-Pinot Gris Freiberg, a Gewürztraminer Kirchberg and Pinot Noir Côtes de Barr.
Visiting hours: Feb–Nov daily, 8–12, 2–6; Dec–Jan by appt.
Location: In the town center.

BENNWIHR, map 2
Cave Co-opérative des Viticulteurs Réunis de Bennwihr (C),
3 r. du Gén.-de-Gaulle, 68630 Bennwihr.
Tel: 89.47.90.27.

Bennwihr was completely destroyed in 1940 and, faced with the formidable task of reconstruction in 1945, the local growers and winemakers decided to form a co-operative. The co-operative, which now vinifies grapes grown on 380 hectares of vines, has received widespread recognition for its quality. Today, it is an enormous modern establishment, with seven fermentation centers, and four large cellars stocking over 5 million bottles. It is well organized to receive visitors.
Visiting hours: Daily 9–11.30, 2–5.30.
Location: In the town center.

BERGHEIM, map 2
Gustave Lorentz (G/M),
35 Grand-Rue, 68750 Bergheim.
Tel: 89.73.63.08.

Gustave Lorentz is one of the best-known Alsace wine houses. It owns 30 hectares of vineyards, including 12 hectares in the *grands crus* of Altenberg and Kanzlerberg. The Riesling Cuvée Particulière and Grand Cru Altenberg are outstanding and the Gewürztraminer Cuvée Particulière and Grand Cru Altenberg are also good. The firm makes a fine late-harvested Gewürztraminer from grapes grown on a 2-hectare vineyard on a 16th-century estate outside the village of Riquewihr.
Visiting hours: Mon–Fri 8–12, 2–5; Sat 9–12.
Location: In the village center.

DAMBACH-LA-VILLE, map 2

Willy Gisselbrecht et Fils (G/M), 20 rte du Vin, 67650 Dambach-la-Ville. Tel: 88.92.41.02.

The house is well known in Alsace for its careful selection of grapes, grown either on their own 15-hectare vineyard or purchased from other growers. Their best wines are Riesling, Gewürztraminer Grand Cru Frankstein and Pinot Blanc.
Visiting hours: Mon–Fri 8–12, 1.30–6.
Location: On the S side of the village.

Louis Hauller (G), 92 r. du Mal.-Foch, 67650 Dambach-la-Ville. Tel: 88.92.41.19.

The family has been making wine since 1786, and as some members of the family were also coopers, making barrels for the trade, the Haullers have a traditional understanding of wood and its importance in maturing wines. The house makes virtually the full range of Alsace wines.
Visiting hours: Mar–mid Oct Tue–Sun, 8–12, 2–6.
Location: In the village.

Louis Hauller has its headquarters in a typical half-timbered Alsace house.

EGUISHEIM, map 2

Léon Beyer (G/M), 2 r. de la Première-Armée Française, 68420 Eguisheim. Tel: 89.41.41.05.

The Beyer family have owned vineyards at Eguisheim since 1580; and the present company was founded in 1867. They own a 20-hectare vineyard from which they make a range of outstanding wines, including the Cuvée des Comtes d'Eguisheim, a Gewürztraminer of great staying power and an elegant, steely Cuvée des Ecaillers Riesling.
Visiting hours: Jul–Aug daily, 9–1, 2–7; or by appt.
Location: In the village.

GUEBWILLER, map 2

Domaines Schlumberger (G), 100 r. Théodore Deck, 68500 Guebwiller. Tel: 89.74.27.00.

The domaine, the largest proprietor in Alsace, owns 140 hectares of vines which are planted on narrow terraces retained by 50km of dry stone walling. Of that total, 60 hectares consist of vineyards classified as *grands crus*: Kitterlé, Saering, Kessler and Spiegel. Schlumberger cultivates all the traditional grape varieties and makes a wide range of wines with an excellent reputation. The fermentation and cellar facilities are elaborate and extensive.
Visiting hours: Mon–Fri 9–5; closed Aug 1–15.
Location: At the N end of r. Théodore Deck (ask for the Domaine, otherwise you will be directed to the Schlumberger factory).

HUSSEREN-LES-CHATEAUX, map 2

Kuentz-Bas (G/M), 14 rte du Vin, Husseren-lès-Châteaux, 68420 Herrlisheim. Tel: 89.49.30.24.

The Kuentz family settled in Alsace around 1795 and in 1919 a daughter married a M. Bas, hence the name of the firm today. The present head is M. Christian Bas. The house owns 12 hectares of vineyards and produces a long list of highly reputed wines and especially good Rieslings.
Visiting hours: Mon–Fri 8–12, 2–6; Sat 8–12.
Location: On the Route du Vin.

INGERSHEIM, map 2

Cave Vinicole d'Ingersheim (C),
1 r. Clemenceau,
Ingersheim,
68000 Colmar.
Tel: 89.27.05.96.

This co-operative, one of the oldest in Alsace, was founded in the mid-1920s and its members own a total of 260 hectares of vineyards around Ingersheim, almost at the gates of Colmar. Production is relatively substantial, and the wines are generally good. They include rosé Crémant d'Alsace, a gold-medal winner at Mâcon, Pinot Blanc, Gewürztraminer, Tokay-Pinot Gris and rosé Pinot Noir.
Visiting hours: Apr–Oct Mon–Fri, 8–12, 1-30–7; Sat 8–12, 2–4; Sun 10–12, 2–4; Nov–Mar Mon–Fri, 8–12, 1.30–5.
Location: In the main street.

KAYSERSBERG, map 2

Mme Theo Faller et ses Filles (G),
Domaine Weinbach,
Clos des Capucins,
68240 Kaysersberg.
Tel: 89.47.13.21.

The Faller family owns 22 hectares of vineyards and is one of the most outstanding single proprietors in Alsace. Not only does Mme Faller, the widow of Theo Faller whose name appears on the basic wines, make a good Sylvaner and Pinot Blanc but her Rieslings, Gewürztraminers and Tokay-Pinot Gris, both the normal and late-picked wines, are superb and are worth aging for many years.
Visiting hours: Mon–Fri 8–12, 1–7; Sat–Sun by appt; no groups.
Location: On the Route du Vin.

KIENTZHEIM, map 2

GAEC Paul Blanck et Fils (G),
Domaine des
Comtes de Lupfen,
32 Grand-Rue,
Kientzheim,
68240 Kaysersberg.
Tel: 89.78.23.56.

Paul Blanck et Fils now own the 27-hectare vineyard which was formerly the property of the Counts of Lupfen. The wines are made according to modern techniques with controlled, low-temperature fermentation in stainless steel, though the *grand cru* wines are aged for a considerable time in the cellar. Marcel Blanck is one of the leading exponents of *grand cru* vineyards in Alsace and he fought hard to sell these wines as single vineyards.
Visiting hours: Mon–Sat 9–12, 2–7.
Location: In the main street.

MITTELWIHR, map 2

Edgar Schaller et Fils (G),
1 r. du Château,
68630 Mittelwihr.
Tel: 89.47.90.28.

Mittelwihr is called *le Midi* of Alsace with the warmest microclimate in the region. The family's main vineyard is located on *Mandelberg*, the Almond Hill, which is supposed to be the only place in Alsace where almonds will ripen. The best wines are Crémant d'Alsace and Riesling from the Mandelberg *cru*. Their Gewürztraminer, Muscat and Riesling are also good.
Visiting hours: Daily 8–7.
Location: On the Route du Vin.

PFAFFENHEIM, map 2

Cave Vinicole de Pfaffenheim (C),
5 r. du Chai,
Pfaffenheim,
68250 Rouffach.
Tel: 89.49.61.08.

Pfaffenheim was the first village in Alsace to organize a *sentier viticole*, a walk through the vineyards. The co-operative was organized in 1957 and quickly established a reputation for quality. In 1968 it merged with the co-operative at Gueberschwihr so that it now has a total of 200 hectares of vines. The best wines are Riesling, Gewürztraminer Grand Cru Goldert, Tokay-Pinot Gris, Pinot Blanc Schneckenberg and Hartenberger Crémant d'Alsace.
Visiting hours: Daily 8–12, 2–6; May–Sep open until 7pm.
Location: On N83.

Joseph Rieflé et Fils (G),
11 pl. de la Mairie,
Pfaffenheim,
68250 Rouffach.
Tel: 89.49.62.82.

This is a typical Alsace winegrower who pays meticulous attention to detail, an approach that has been followed for three generations. The best wines are Gaentzbrunnen Riesling, Bergweingarten Gewürztraminer and Tokay-Pinot Gris.
Visiting hours: Daily 8–12, 2–6.30; closed Jan–Feb and Sun am.
Location: In the village center opposite the *mairie*.

RIBEAUVILLE, map 2

Robert Faller et Fils (G),
36 Grand-Rue,
68150 Ribeauvillé.
Tel: 89.73.60.47.

The family operation, now headed by J.B. Faller, owns vines on the slopes of the Geisberg, Kirchberg and Trottacker. Its Grand Cru Geisberg Riesling is highly regarded and the Grand Cru Kirchberg de Barr Muscat is also good.
Visiting hours: Mon–Sat 8–6; Sun and hols by appt.
Location: In the main street.

RIQUEWIHR, map 2

Dopff 'Au Moulin' (G/M),
2 av. Jacques-Preiss,
68340 Riquewihr.
Tel: 88.47.92.23.

Dopff are one of the most important wine families of Alsace. Established in the 17th century, the house has developed from barrel-maker to wine broker to *négociant*. It is an extensive operation occupying several buildings on the outskirts of this well-preserved medieval town. As well as receiving visitors at its cellars it also provides tastings of its wines at the Hostellerie Au Moulin (open daily except Tue am and Wed). They produce a wide range of usually pleasant wines including the late-harvested Schoenenberg Riesling, Gewürztraminer, Tokay-Pinot Gris and Gewürztraminer Grand Cru Brand.
Visiting hours: Mon–Fri 8–12, 2–6; also Apr 1–Oct 31 Sat–Sun and hols 9–12, 2–6.
Location: At the entrance to the town.

Dopff et Irion (G/M), Château de Riquewihr,
av. du Gen.-de-Gaulle,
68340 Riquewihr.
Tel: 89.47.92.51.

This house, which operates on a large-scale from the 16th-century Château de Riquewihr, maintains high standards of quality but real individuality in the wines is sometimes lost by the size of the operation. It is a *négociant* and also owns 27 hectares of vines. Its best known wines are Riesling les Murailles and Muscat les Amandiers. The ordinary releases are pleasant but the most exciting wines are the Vendanges Tardives and Sélection de Grains Nobles.
Visiting hours: Mar–Oct daily, 9.30–7.
Location: In the town.

Hugel et Fils (G/M), 3 r. de la Première Armée Française,
68340 Riquewihr.
Tel: 89.47.92.15.

Founded in 1639, the house has been run by 12 generations of the same family, making it one of the oldest continuous wine-making establishments in Alsace. It acts as a *négociant* but also owns 25 hectares of vines, including a good part of the Sporen and Schoenenberg vineyards on steep hillsides above Riquewihr. Its wines are better known outside France than within since it exports 80 per cent of its production and in many parts of the world Hugel's normal-release wines are synonymous with Alsace wines. These are not the most interesting wines the firm produces. They have made a specialty of Vendanges Tardives and Sélection de Grains Nobles wines and were the first to make these on a regular basis in a good vintage.
Visiting hours: Mon–Thu 9.30–12, 2–5.30; also Jul–Sep Fri 9.30–12; remainder of the year by appt; groups by appt.
Location: In the main street.

ROUFFACH, map 2

Muré Clos St Landelin (G/M),
Carrefour RN 83,
rte de Soultzmatt,
68250 Rouffach.
Tel: 89.49.62.19.

The Muré family, who have been winemakers since 1630, obtain some extraordinary results with the grapes grown in their 16-hectare vineyard, the Clos St Landelin. This was first planted in the 8th century and is built up on a series of terraces supported by dry-stone walls. The Muré are both *négociants* and proprietors, but their most interesting wines come almost exclusively from their own estates. Their Clos St Landelin often produces remarkable wines including a Sélection de Grains Nobles. They make good *eaux-de-vie* too and also own Maison Pfister in Colmar (see page 30).
Visiting hours: Daily 8–12, 2–6; closed Jan–Feb Sun am.
Location: On N83.

SIGOLSHEIM, map 2

Pierre Sparr et Fils (G/M),
2 r. de la Première-Armée Française,
Sigolsheim,
68240 Kaysersberg.
Tel: 89.78.24.22.

This house has been run by eight generations of Sparrs since 1680. Though *négociants*, they also own 30 hectares of vines. The firm's basic wines are better than average; they also make fine Riesling from the Schlossberg and Altenberg vineyards, and Gewürztraminer from the Mambourg vineyard which, with Mittelwihr, is the warmest place in Alsace.
Visiting hours: Sep–Jul Mon–Fri, 8–12, 2–6; Sat 8.30–11.30.
Location: In the village.

WINTZENHEIM, map 2

Josmeyer et Fils (G/M),
76 r. Clemenceau,
Wintzenheim,
68000 Colmar. Tel. 89.27.01.57.

The Josmeyers own 13 hectares of vineyards and make wines from grapes purchased from growers who own a further 18 hectares in the villages of Wintzenheim and Turckheim. Jean Meyer is a meticulous winemaker and has established a reputation for high-quality wines, of which the best are a remarkably good Pinot Blanc and Auxerrois 'H' Vieilles Vignes (made from vines which are more than 25 years old), as well as good Riesling and Muscat.
Visiting hours: Mon–Fri 10–12, 2–5.
Location: In the village.

Domaine Zind-Humbrecht (G/M),
34 r. du Maréchal-Joffre,
Wintzenheim,
68000 Colmar. Tel: 89.27.02.05.

The family operation, currently headed by Léonard Humbrecht, uses grapes grown on 30 hectares of vines to make a wide range of single-vineyard wines, emphasizing their soil differences. A most exciting development has been their revival of the great Rangen vineyard, le Clos St Urbain at Thann in the far south of which they are the only owners. This is one of Alsace's steepest vineyards and the only one with volcanic soil. The Riesling from here is stupendous. They also have land in several other *grand cru* vineyards, including Brand at Turckheim.
Visiting hours: Mon–Fri 9–7; Sat by appt.
Location: On the corner of r. de la Petite Porte and r. du Mar.-Joffre.

ZELLENBERG, map 2

J. Becker (G/M),
2-4 rte d'Ostheim,
Zellenberg,
68340 Riquewihr.
Tel: 89.47.90.16.

The Becker family own 15 hectares of vineyard at Zellenberg, the former property of the Counts of Ribeaupierre, and have been selling wine since 1610. Their Gewürztraminer and Riesling are among the best, and the Muscat Grand Cru Froen is also good.
Visiting hours: Daily 8–6 (confirm visit at least one day in advance); closed during the harvest.
Location: Signposted in the village.

Further *Caves* and Vineyards to Visit

AMMERSCHWIHR, map 2
Caves Jean-Baptiste Adam (G/M), 5 r. de l'Aigle, 68770 Ammerschwihr. Tel: 89.78.23.21. Visiting hours: Mon–Sat 8–12, 2–6; groups by appt.
Fourteen generations of this family have made wine at Ammerschwihr. The firm is justifiably proud of its late-harvested Gewürztraminer, Tokay-Pinot Gris, Pinot Noir, including the Cuvée Jean-Baptiste, Pinot Blanc and Riesling Letzenberg.

ANDLAU, map 2
André Durrmann (G), 11 r. des Forgerons, Andlau, 67140 Barr. Tel: 88.08.26.42. Visiting hours: Mon–Sat 9–12, 2–7; closed Sep 1–15 and May 15–31.
Especially noted for its Grand Cru Wibelsberg Riesling, which can usually be aged for several years, depending on the vintage.

BARR, map 2
Maison Willm (G), 32 r. du Dr-Sultzer, 67140 Barr. Tel: 88.08.90.07. Visiting hours: Daily 8–12, 2–6.
The firm makes wines intended to be drunk young, as well as more sophisticated ones which are carefully aged in wood, such as the Riesling Kirchberg de Barr Grand Cru and the Gewürztraminer Clos Gaensbroennel. Maison Willm also makes the Klevner de Heiligenstein from the extremely rare Savagnin Rosé grape. Visitors passing through the gate will find an inner courtyard bright with flowers in summer.

BEBLENHEIM, map 2
Cave Co-operative Vinicole de Beblenheim (C), 14 r. de Hoen, 68980 Beblenheim. Tel: 89.47.90.02. Visiting hours: Daily 10–12, 2–6; closed Jul 15 for 3 weeks.
The Beblenheim vineyards established their reputation for quality as far back as the 16th century and the village has over 250 small growers. The large, modern co-operative tries to maintain this tradition and it makes a wide range of wines.

Bott-Geyl (G), 1 r. du Petit Château, 68980 Beblenheim. Tel: 89.47.90.04. Visiting hours: Daily 8–12, 1–7; closed Aug 10–Sep 10 for large groups only.
The Grand Cru Sonnenglanz Gewürztraminer is excellent.

BERGHOLTZ, map 2
Jean-Pierre Dirler (G), 13 r. d'Issenheim, Bergholtz, 68500 Guebwiller. Tel: 89.76.91.00. Visiting hours: By appt.
Founded in 1871 the firm makes good Pinot Blanc, Muscat, Sylvaner, and two highly regarded Rieslings, the Grand Cru Kessler and Grand Cru Spiegel.

COLMAR, map 2
Domaine Expérimental Viticole (G/M), 8 r. Kléber, BP 507, 68021 Colmar. Tel: 89.41.16.50. Visiting hours: By appt.
The experimental station, operated by the Ministry of Agriculture, makes an interesting Riesling and Gewürztraminer, both from late-harvested grapes. The 15th-century cellar is beneath an old convent in the center of town.

EGUISHEIM, map 2
Cave Vinicole d'Eguisheim (G), 6 Grand-Rue, 68420 Eguisheim. Tel: 89.41.11.06. Visiting hours: Daily 8–12, 2–6; Sun 10–12, 2–6.
This was one of the earliest Alsace co-operatives and is now the largest seller of the region's wines. The members own a total of 1,000 hectares of vines and production is as varied as it is extensive with good Pinot Blanc, a Riesling Armorié, Cuvée Schlossherr Tokay-Pinot Gris, a red oak-aged Pinot Noir and a Grand Cru Hatschbourg Gewürztraminer.

Paul Ginglinger (G), 8 pl. Ch. de-Gaulle, 68420 Eguisheim. Tel: 89.41.44.25. Visiting hours: Daily 8–12, 2–6.
The house makes a fine Cuvée Caroline Muscat, Cuvée des Prélats Tokay-Pinot Gris, Grand Cru Eichberg Gewürztraminer and Grand Cru Pfersigberg Riesling.

Bruno Hertz (G), 9 pl. de l'Eglise, 68420 Eguisheim. Tel: 89.41.81.61. Visiting hours: Mon–Sat and hols by appt.
This family firm has 5 hectares of vines and still uses wooden casks in the cellars. Their best wine is the Grand Cru Rangen de Thann Gewürztraminer, the grapes coming from a site identified as early as the 12th century as being exceptionally suited to the vine because of its thin, shallow volcanic soil and southern-facing slopes.

EPFIG, map 2

Domaine Ostertag (G), 87 r. Finkwiller, 67680 Epfig. Tel: 88.85.51.34. Visiting hours: By appt. The domaine makes good Sylvaner from vines near the Romanesque chapel of Ste Marguerite, while the grapes for its Grand Cru Moenchberg Riesling come from a ridge where vines have been grown since at least the 11th century.

HUNAWIHR, map 2

Cave Vinicole de Hunawihr (C), 48 rte de Ribeauvillé, Hunawihr, 68150 Ribeauvillé. Tel: 89.73.61.67. Visiting hours: Mon–Fri 9–12, 2–6; also Easter–Sep Sat, Sun, and hols 10–12, 3–7. Founded in 1954, this co-operative is one of Alsace's smallest (25 members) and is well known for the quality of its wines.

KATZENTHAL, map 2

GAEC Jean-Paul Ecklé et Fils (G), 29 Grand-Rue, Katzenthal, 68230 Turckheim. Tel: 89.27.09.41. Visiting hours: Daily 8–12, 1–7. Attractive wines include a good Sylvaner, a reliable Riesling, a Tokay-Pinot Gris which can age for up to 10 years, and a Crémant d'Alsace.

MARLENHEIM, map 2

Michel Laugel (G/M), 102 r. du Gen.-de-Gaulle, 67520 Marlenheim. Tel: 88.87.52.20. Visiting hours: By appt. The house was founded in 1889 and makes a wide range of Alsace wines, including a Pinot Noir from Marlenheim.

GAEC Mosbach (G), 10 pl. Kaufhaus, 67520 Marlenheim. Tel: 88.87.50.13. Visiting hours: Mon–Sat 8–12, 2–6; Sun and hols 9–12. The Mosbachs are an old wine-making family with an 18-hectare vineyard just outside Marlenheim. The Tokay-Pinot Gris and Gewürztraminer are good.

MITTELBERGHEIM, map 2

Emile Boeckel (G/M), 2 r. de la Montagne, Mittelbergheim, 67140 Barr. Tel: 88.08.91.02. Visiting hours: Mon–Fri 9–12, 2–5; Sat 9–12. Mittelbergheim is a beautifully preserved wine village and the biggest firm is Boeckel who make good Riesling Wibelsberg and Zotzenberg Gewürztraminer.

A. Seltz et Fils (G/M), 21 r. Principale,

Mittelbergheim, 67140 Barr. Tel: 88.08.91.77. Visiting hours: Mon–Fri 8–6; Sat, Sun and hols by appt. The domaine makes some good Alsace wines. Pierre Seltz studied at U.C. Davis in California and perhaps has a more broadminded view than many of his colleagues.

MITTELWIHR, map 2

Preiss-Henny (G/M), r. du Bouxhof, Mittelwihr, 68630 Bennwihr-Mittelwihr. Tel: 89.41.64.29. Visiting hours: By appt. The family firm cultivates 20 hectares of vines, including part of the well-known Mandelberg vineyard.

NIEDERMORSCHWIHR, map 2

Albert Boxler et Fils (G), 78 r. des Trois-Epis, Niedermorschwihr, 68230 Turckheim. Tel: 89.27.11.32. Visiting hours: By appt. The house makes a good Grand Cru Schlossberg Riesling, from a vineyard noted for the quality of its grapes in the 8th century.

OBERNAI, map 2

Union des Co-opératives Divinal (C), 30 r. du Gén.-Leclerc, 67210 Obernai. Tel: 88.95.61.18. Visiting hours: Mon–Thu 9–4; Fri 9–3. Created in 1964, Divinal is an association of co-operative wineries that produces a wide range of good wines.

ORSCHWIHR, map 2

F. Braun et Fils (G), 19–21 Grand-Rue, Orschwihr, 68500 Guebwiller. Tel: 89.76.95.13. Visiting hours: Mon–Sat 8–12, 2–7. The domaine produces a good range of wines including Pfingstberg Gewürztraminer, Riesling and Tokay-Pinot Gris.

ORSCHWILLER, map 2

Louis Siffert et Fils (G), 16 rte du Vin, Orschwiller, 67600 Sélestat. Tel: 88.92.02.77. Visiting hours: Mar–Dec daily, 9–12, 2–7. The house's highly rated Praelatenberg Gewürztraminer is made from grapes grown in a vineyard that existed in the 8th century.

OTTROTT, map 2

Edmond Vonville (G), 4 pl. des Tilleuls, 67530 Ottrott. Tel: 89.95.80.25. Visiting hours: By appt.
This family's most impressive wine is the Rouge d'Ottrott, vinified from Pinot Noir grapes and aged in oak.

PFAFFENHEIM, map 2

Pierre Frick et Fils (G), 5 r. de Baer, Pfaffenheim, 68250 Rouffach. Tel: 89.49.62.99. Visiting hours: Mon–Sat 8–7; Sun by appt.
The Frick family avoids using chemicals on its 7 hectares of vines and keeps chaptalization to the minimum. Its most outstanding wines are the Pinot Blanc, Tokay-Pinot Gris and Cuvée du Grand Bouteiller Gewürztraminer.

RIBEAUVILLE, map 2

Pierre Bott (G/M), 13 av. du Gen.-de-Gaulle, 68150 Ribeauvillé. Tel: 89.73.60.48. Visiting hours: Mon–Sat 9–12, 2–5.30 by appt.
The best wines are Riesling, Tokay-Pinot Gris and Gewürztraminer Réserve Personnelle.

Cave Co-opérative de Ribeauvillé (C), 2 rte de Colmar, 68150 Ribeauvillé. Tel: 89.73.61.80. Visiting hours: Daily 10–12, 2–5; closed Jan–Mar, Sat–Sun.
Founded in 1895, the co-operative is the oldest in France and enjoys a reputation for a wide range of good wines. Its specialty is the Clos du Zahnacker, first planted in the 9th century, which makes a good Tokay-Pinot Gris and Crémant d'Alsace from old vines.

Grands Vins d'Alsace Louis Sipp S.A. (G/M), 5 Grand-Rue, 68150 Ribeauvillé. Tel: 89.73.60.01. Visiting hours: Mon–Sat 8–6; Sun and hols 10–6.
The Grand Cru Kirchberg de Barr Riesling and Réserve Personnelle Gewürztraminer are good.

F.-E. Trimbach (G/M), 15 rte de Bergheim, 68150 Ribeauvillé. Tel: 89.73.60.30. Visiting hours: By appt; closed Aug.
This old firm is among the best in Alsace, and its wines include the Cuvée Frédéric Emile Riesling and Cuvée des Seigneurs de Ribeaupierre Gewürztraminer. It also owns the tiny Clos Ste Hune vineyard at Hunawihr which produces some of the best Alsace Riesling.

RIQUEWIHR, map 2

GAEC J.-J. Baumann et Fils (G), 43 r. du Gen.-de-Gaulle, 68340 Riquewihr. Tel: 89.47.92.47. Visiting hours: Daily 9–12, 2–6.
This house makes good Gewürztraminer and Riesling, as well as other wines.

RORSCHWIHR, map 2

Willy Rolli-Edel (G), 5 r. de l'Eglise, Rorschwihr, 68590 St Hippolyte. Tel: 89.73.63.26. Visiting hours: By appt.
There is an outstanding Riesling.

Rolly Gassmann (G), 2 r. de l'Eglise, Rorschwihr, 68590 St Hippolyte. Tel: 89.73.63.28. Visiting hours: Daily by appt.
One of the best Alsace producers with 18 hectares of vines at the foot of the Haut-Koenigsbourg. Their best wines are Riesling Réserve, Sylvaner Réserve, Tokay-Pinot Gris Réserve R.G. and Gewürztraminer Réserve.

SIGOLSHEIM, map 2

Co-opérative Vinicole de Sigolsheim (C), 12 r. St Jacques, 68240 Sigolsheim. Tel: 89.47.12.55. Visiting hours: Easter–Sep daily, 8–12, 1.30–6; remainder of the year, Mon–Fri 8–12, 1.30–6.
The co-operative, created in 1945, produces a wide range of wines, including a highly praised Pinot Blanc, Riesling Réserve, Tokay-Pinot Gris and a Sélection de Grains Nobles Gewürztraminer.

TURCKHEIM, map 2

Cave Vinicole de Turckheim (C), 16 r. de Tuleries, 68230 Turckheim. Tel: 89.27.06.25. Visiting hours: By appt.
This is one of the most consistently reliable co-operatives in Alsace. All its wines are good, but local conditions are particularly suited to Pinot Noir which is unusual in Alsace.

VOEGTLINSHOFFEN, map 2

Théo Cattin et Fils (G), 35 r. Roger-Frémeaux, Voegtlinshoffen, 68420 Herrlisheim. Tel: 89.49.30.43. Visiting hours: Mon–Sat 8–6; Sun and hols by appt.
The house produces several good wines, including the Cuvée de l'Ours Noir Gewürztraminer, which can be aged successfully.

WESTHALTEN, map 2
Maison Heim (G/M), 18 r. Soultzmatt, 68250 Westhalten. Tel: 89.47.00.45. Visiting hours: Mon–Sat 8–12, 2–6; Sun 10–12, 2–5.

The top wines at Maison Heim are the Zinnkoepflé Gewürztraminer, made from late-harvested grapes, Clos du Strangenberg Pinot Blanc and a Crémant d'Alsace La Dame Sans Gêne.

WOLXHEIM, map 2
François Muhlberger (G), 1 r. de Strasbourg, Wolxheim, 67120 Molsheim. Tel: 88.38.10.33. Visiting hours: Daily 9–12, 1–7.

At the northern end of the Alsace vineyards and in the nearest wine village to Strasbourg, this house produces fine Rieslings, particularly a Rothstein and the Grand Cru Altenberg de Wolxheim.

Sights

Alsace is a place of great natural splendor and many cultural riches. Many of the medieval wine villages, nestling in the foothills of the Vosges, are beautifully preserved, and the cities of Colmar and Strasbourg contain some fine museums with famous collections and well-maintained old quarters that are well worth exploring.

ANDLAU
The famous **Abbaye d'Andlau** was founded in 887 by the wife of Emperor Charles le Gros and most of the present building dates from the 12th century. North of the town are the châteaux of Haut-Andlau, restored in the 16th century, and of Spesbourg, largely destroyed in the 14th century. Both give splendid views over the Rhine valley.

BARR
The town of Barr has an attractive center. A wine fair is held here during the week of Jul 14 in the 17th-century city hall and a Fête des Vendanges (harvest festival) is celebrated on the first Sun in Oct.

An imposing 18th-century residence, **la Folie Marco**, houses a museum with a large collection of 18th–19th-century furniture, porcelain, and pewter. There is wine-tasting in the cellar. Open Jul 1–Oct 6.

COLMAR
Colmar is both a bustling city of 65,000 inhabitants and one of immense charm. The old quarter has narrow streets and houses with carved beams. The Quartier de la Krutenau, sometimes called **la Petite Venise**, is a well-preserved area of old houses lining the banks of the Lauch, and together with the recently restored Quartier des Tanneurs is ideal for casual strolling.

Colmar is an important center of the Alsace wine trade, and the wine festival held here in Aug is the most important in the region; les Journées de la Choucroute in the autumn also provide an occasion for tasting this regional dish in all its forms.

The **Musée Unterlinden**, housed in a 13th-century convent, possesses the world's finest collection of Alsace art, including the famous 16th-century painting of the crucifixion, the *Retable d'Issenheim* by Matthias Grünewald. A wine museum is located in one of the building's ancient cellars.

DAMBACH-LA-VILLE
This picturesque town retains its medieval walls, pierced by three gates, and many fine old, half-timbered houses. It is an important wine village and has a wine festival in the 1st half of Aug.

The **Château de Bernstein** which can be reached by a path from the town (about a two-hour walk) is a 12th–century castle in ruins, except for the well-preserved keep which gives a fine view of the Alsace plain below.

GUEBWILLER
A small town on the banks of the Lauch, Guebwiller lies at the entrance to one of the highest valleys in the Vosges, the Florival or Flower Valley. The **Musée du Florival** contains a collection of paintings, sculptures and archeology as well as local history displays.

HAUT-KOENIGSBOURG
This vast castle, the most important in the Vosges, stands on a hill with fine views over the Alsace plain. In 1901, the ruins were given to Kaiser Wilhelm II, whose zealous restoration has been criticized by some. Many of the private rooms within the triple circuit of walls can be visited.

HUNAWIHR

The owner of a stork farm east of the village is making a valiant attempt to repopulate the region with these birds, the symbol of Alsace; they used to nest on chimney tops throughout the area. Visits Mar 15–Nov 11, pm only.

KAYSERSBERG

This small wine town with a fine fortified bridge is the birthplace of Albert Schweitzer. His home is now a museum, open Mar 15–Oct 30.

KIENTZHEIM

This charming village still has its medieval fortifications and many old, attractive houses. There is a **Musée du Vignoble** in the remains of the old castle. The town is also the headquarters of the Confrérie de St Etienne, the wine association of Alsace.

KINTZHEIM

About 80 species of birds of prey are kept in the grounds around the ruins of the ancient castle, open Mar 15–Nov 11, pm only.

MOLSHEIM

A wine fair is held here May 1. **Le Metzig**, a fine Renaissance building built by the butchers' guild in 1554, is worth viewing, and there is a small museum where local wines can be tasted in the old cellar.

MONT STE-ODILE

One of the most popular sites in Alsace. The summit of the Hohenbourg, 761m high, has been occupied from the earliest times and is still partly enclosed by the remnants of a 10km-long prehistoric stone wall. Ste Odile, patron saint of Alsace, founded an abbey here in the 7th century. Though partly destroyed by fire in 1546, it was restored after the Revolution and nuns now operate a hostel in the buildings.

OBERNAI

One of the most fascinating small towns in Alsace with ramparts and a maze of narrow streets and small squares. Obernai is the birthplace of Ste Odile, patron of Alsace.

OTTROTT

On Sun, hols and Jul–Aug a small steam-powered train runs the 8km from Ottrott to Rosheim at 2.30 and 4.30, with one return trip at 3.30.

RIBEAUVILLE

This picturesque wine-making town annually stages one of Alsace's most colorful festivals, the Fife Players' Day, on the first Sun of Sep. Visitors are invited to sip wine, without charge, as it flows from the fountain in front of the **Hôtel de Ville**. There is also a local wine festival with free tastings on the last Sat and Sun in July, and a Fête du Kugelhopf is held in Jun.

RIQUEWIHR

By-passed by war and fashion, Riquewihr has remained much as it was in the 16th century. The town center is partly enclosed by walls and there are many fine buildings and ancient houses. In summer it can become overcrowded with visitors.

STRASBOURG

The capital of Alsace, and now one of the unofficial capitals of Europe, Strasbourg is a active modern industrial center that has managed to retain much of its former small-town charm. The Rhine, and thus the German border, is on the eastern edge of the city, while central Strasbourg itself is an island surrounded by another river, the Ill. The bridges across the Ill in the old part of town are very picturesque, as are the many old houses on its banks.

The 13th-century **Cathédrale Notre-Dame**, one of the most imposing in Europe, is built from pink sandstone. The sculptures on its tower and central façade are spectacular.

Strasbourg's important museums include the **Musée du Château des Rohan** (18th-century furnishings); the **Musée des Beaux-Arts** (French, German and Spanish paintings from the 16th to the 20th century); and the **Musée des Arts Décoratifs** (furniture, metalwork and porcelain), all in the **Château des Rohan**.

THANN

This is the oldest town in the southern part of the Alsace wine route. The **Eglise de St Thiébaut** is one of the finest Gothic buildings in the region.

Hotels, Restaurants and Where to Buy Wine

Alsace offers the visitor more opportunities to taste local specialties than any other province of France. Not only can you sample these in restaurants, but Alsace *charcuterie* is also famous, as are the pastries while the local version of the bistro, the *winstub* serves up simple dishes and jugs of wine at almost any hour of the day.

Winstube are the best way to introduce yourself to the wine and food of the province: *choucroute* (sauerkraut cooked in white wine and garnished with pork), and *flammekeuche* (onion tart) are standard fare as is *Edelzwicker* served by the jug. Too often, however, *winstub* fare is all some people encounter and this is a great pity. They may never discover the Alsace recipes for fish (particularly carp), snails, frogs' legs, or game. Local white asparagus is considered to be the best in France, as are the plums and apples from the many orchards that dot the countryside. The *kugelhopf* has become as much a symbol of Alsace as the storks; ask for it at breakfast time with coffee. Last but not least, Alsace is, with Périgord, one of the great *foie gras* provinces.

AMMERSCHWIHR (68770)
Aux Armes de France (R,H), 1 Grand-Rue. Tel: 89.47.10.12. Two Michelin stars. Reservations essential. Closed Wed–Thu lunch and 3 weeks in Jan. AE DC MC V

It's a blow to be what *was* the best restaurant in Alsace, but Pierre Gaertner and his son Philippe are certainly making the best of the situation. Their restaurant continues to be a favorite with the local population. The wine list is one of the best and most interesting in all Alsace.

ANDLAU (67140, Barr)
Au Boeuf Rouge (R), 6 r. du Dr-Stoltz. Tel: 88.08.96.26. Closed in Jan and end Jun. AE DC MC V
Old and charming.

Boutique aux Vins Catherine Lacoste (W), 12 r. Deharbe. Tel: 88.08.41.16. No cards.
One of the best *cavistes* in France with a fine selection of local and other wines.

COLMAR (68000)
Fer Rouge (R), 52 Grand-Rue. Tel: 89.41.37.24. One Michelin star. Closed 3 weeks Jan, 2 weeks Jul–Aug, Sun pm and Mon. AE DC MC V
Charming restaurant in an old Alsace house. Excellent cellar.

Maison des Têtes (R) 19 r. des Têtes. Tel: 89.24.43.43. Closed mid-Jan–mid-Feb, Sun pm and Mon. AE DC MC V
Delightful 17th-century restaurant.

Maison Pfister (W), 11 r. des Marchands. Tel: 89.41.33.61. Closed Jan–Feb Sun–Thu. AE DC MC V
Superb Alsace house and outstanding wines. Owned by the Muré family (see page 24).

Schillinger (R), 16 r. Stanislas. Tel: 89.41.43.17. Two Michelin stars. Closed Sun pm, Mon and Jul. AE DC MC V
Excellent regional dishes and creative *cuisine*.

Terminus-Bristol (H) and **Rendez-vous de Chasse (R)**, 7 pl. de la Gare. Tel: 89.23.59.59.(H) and 89.41.10.10. One Michelin star. (R) closed Jan 2-15. AE DC MC V
Luxurious and modern hotel. Traditional cooking with *nouvelle* touches.

EGUISHEIM (68420)
Le Caveau (R), 3 pl. du Château St-Léon. Tel: 89.41.08.89. One Michelin star. Reservations recommended. Closed Jan 15–Mar 1, Wed pm and Thu. AE DC MC V
Small, picturesque establishment which includes a cellar with tastings.

GUEBWILLER (68500)
Résidence les Violettes (R,H), Jungholtz (6km S by D5I). One Michelin star. Tel: 89.76.91.19. Closed 3 weeks in Jan. AE DC MC V
Quiet with traditional *cuisine*.

ILLHAEUSERN (68150)
Auberge de l'Ill (R), r. de Collonges. Tel: 89.71.83.23. Three Michelin stars. Reservations essential. Closed Feb, Jul 1–10, Mon pm and Tue. AE DC
With the only three-star restaurant in Alsace, the Haeberlin family has made Illhaeusern a regional gastronomic center. *Nouvelle cuisine* at its best.

KAYSERSBERG (68240)
Cellier de la Weiss (W), 11 r. Gén.-Rieder. Tel: 89.78.28.07. Closed Nov-Easter. No cards.
A good selection of local wines.

Residence Chambard (H,R), 11-13 r. du Gén.-de-Gaulle. Tel: 89.47.10.17. One Michelin star. (R/H) closed 3 weeks Mar and Dec 1–15. (R) closed Sun pm and Mon. AE DC MC V
Modern and comfortable, with good food and excellent cellar.

MITTELBERGHEIM
(67140, Barr)
Winstub Gilg (R,H), 1 rte du Vin. Tel: 88.08.91.37. Closed Jan 5–Feb 5, Tue pm and Wed. AE DC
Established in 1614, the house has a vast selection of the region's *grand cru* wines.

MOLSHEIM (67120)
Diana (H,R), 14 r. Ste Odile, pont de la Bruche. Tel: 88.38.51.59. AE DC MC V
Large, modern, comfortable and elegant.

OBERNAI (67210)
Duc d'Alsace (H,R), 6 r. de la Gare. Tel: 88.95.55.34. (R) closed Mon. AE DC V
A small friendly establishment.

Le Parc (H,R), 169 r. Gén.-Gouraud. Tel: 88.95.50.08. AE MC V
Large, country hotel with richly decorated rooms. Parkland setting.

OTTROTT-LE-HAUT (67530, Ottrott)
Beau Site (H,R), pl. de l'Eglise. Tel: 88.95.80.61. One Michelin star. (R) closed Sun pm. AE DC MC V
Good regional cooking and *nouvelle* specialties. Interesting Alsace Pinot Noir.

Hostellerie des Châteaux (H,R). Tel: 88.95.81.54. Closed Jan 15–Feb 15 and Tue in winter. MC V
Charming, quiet hotel. Good-value menus and good wines.

RIBEAUVILLE (68150)
Clos St-Vincent (R,H), rte de Bergheim. Tel. 89.73.67.65. One Michelin star. (R/H) closed Nov–mid-Mar. (R) closed Tue–Wed. MC V
Magnificent hotel in the middle of the vineyards. Relais et Châteaux.

Les Vosges (R,H), 2 Grand-Rue. Tel: 89.73.61.39. One Michelin star. Closed Dec–Mar. AE MC V
Modern with regional *cuisine*.

ROUFFACH (68250)
Château d'Isenbourg (H) and **Les Tommeries (R)**. Tel: 89.49.63.53. One Michelin star. V
Large, comfortable hotel in a park. One of the two dining-rooms is in a restored 13th-century cellar. Good wines.

ST HIPPOLYTE (68590)
Aux Ducs de Lorraine (H) and **Munsch (R)**, 16 rte du Vin. Tel: 89.73.00.09. Closed Jan 10–Mar 1, and Dec 1–15. AE DC V
Traditional hotel with views of the vineyards. Extensive menu.

SELESTAT (67600)
Edel (R), 7 r. des Serruriers. Tel: 88.92.86.55. One Michelin star. Closed Sun pm, and Tue pm and Wed in winter. AE DC MC V
Family cooking with good fish dishes.

The distinctive Alsace wine bottle and green-stemmed glass with a kugelhopf.

STRASBOURG (67000)
Buerehiesel (R), 4 parc de l'Orangerie. Tel: 88.61.62.24. Two Michelin stars. Reservations essential. Closed Tue pm and Wed, 2 weeks in Feb, Aug and Christmas. AE DC MC V
For many, the best restaurant in Strasbourg and set in a charming garden.

Chez Yvonne (R), 10 r. du Sanglier. Tel: 88.32.84.15. MC V
A highly regarded *winstub*.

Millésime (W), 28 av. de la Marseillaise. Tel: 88.36.59.65. Closed Sun–Mon. MC V
One of the region's most highly reputed *cavistes*.

Monopole Métropole (H), 16 r. Kuhn. Tel: 88.32.11.94. AE DC MC V
Modern hotel housed in a completely renovated old building near the station.

BORDEAUX

The fates of the city of Bordeaux and its neighboring wines have long been intertwined and their reputation owes much to the position of the city with its thriving port on the river Garonne, which combines with the Dordogne just north of Bordeaux to form the Gironde estuary. The English, who ruled here for 300 years in the Middle Ages, developed the trade in "Gascon" wines with countries of northern Europe which was for centuries Bordeaux's main market. Bordeaux's greatness was helped by two important natural factors: climate and soil. The proximity of the sea and the Atlantic Gulf Stream means the region has a temperate climate, and extensive pine forests between the sea and the vineyards bear the brunt of the winter rain and gales. The gravel banks along the Gironde provide perfect soil conditions for the vine.

The "gentlemen farmers" of the region, and in particular the Médoc, are relative newcomers; most of the "châteaux" were created in the 18th and 19th centuries when the wealthy Bordeaux *bourgeois* bought up small farms and grouped them together into larger units for practical purposes. These larger estates sold their wine under one name and were able to concentrate better on quality. The practice of calling these estates châteaux spread throughout the region and today there are nearly 4,000 of them. So, remember that even if the word "château" is on the label it does not necessarily mean a grand manorial estate. A modest house or even a farm shack will call itself "château" also. There are also a large number of co-operatives making wine for the many small growers in the lesser *appellations*, particularly in the Entre-Deux-Mers.

The Wines of Bordeaux

In the Middle Ages, Bordeaux was sold in barrels and drunk young in late November or December, much the same as Beaujolais Nouveau. The Bordeaux wines we know today evolved during the 17th century, the result of new techniques in vinification and innovations such as the use of bottles for aging and the perfection of corks (and cork-screws). It was also during the 17th and 18th centuries that the marshy land west of the Gironde was filled in to permit the planting of the Médoc vineyards that would later become the finest in the region. The role of the Bordeaux shippers was all important and the wine of Bordeaux was essentially theirs, rather than that of any particular estate. With the rise of the châteaux during the 19th century and the development of estate bottling, properties began to enjoy greater reputations, even though the shippers continued to handle the bulk of the wine transactions.

The importance of certain châteaux was permanently established in 1855 when a list was drawn up of the better wines according to price: first growths were the most expensive and fifth growths the least expensive. This classification influences opinion to this day, and when it was "revised" in 1973 there was only one promotion, Mouton-Rothschild which was granted first growth status – all the rest remained unchanged!

Although such famous names as Margaux are what normally spring to mind when Bordeaux is mentioned, many good, straightforward bottles of Bordeaux are also produced. Most of this wine is sold simply as AOC Bordeaux or Bordeaux Supérieur, though there are over 50 specific *appellations* used within the region. The wines differ greatly according to soil and micro-climate but, on the whole, relatively few grape varieties are used. Cabernet Sauvignon is the greatest of the red grape varieties and has found a perfect home in the Médoc. Merlot thrives in the conditions of St Emilion and is the next most important grape variety, followed by Cabernet Franc, Malbec and Petit Verdot. Sémillon and Sauvignon, with some Colombard and Muscadelle, are the most frequently grown grape varieties for whites. White Bordeaux is produced in much smaller quantities than red and only the sweet wines of Sauternes and Barsac, made mainly from Sémillon, can approach the reputation of the great reds; the great dry whites, particularly some from the Graves, have yet to obtain the recognition they deserve.

Visiting the Vineyards

The great land mass of Brittany jutting out into the Atlantic protects the region from the brunt of the prevailing north-west winds in winter and the sea breezes keep summer temperatures down so that the area enjoys a relatively mild climate.

On the whole, this is one of the more compact wine-growing areas to visit. The vineyards lie around the city on all sides, hence all of the recommended routes begin and end in Bordeaux, which is a delightful city. A walk around Bordeaux can include visits to shippers which will provide a good introduction to the workings of a profession that can claim much of the credit for making this city and its wine famous.

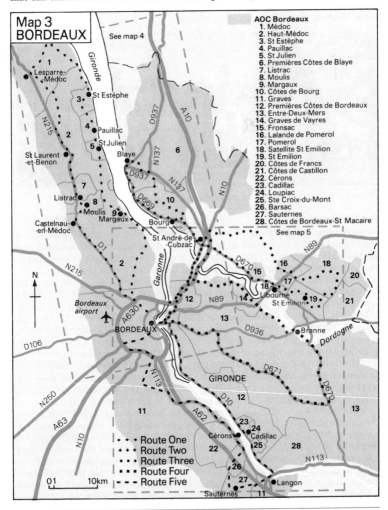

Map 3
BORDEAUX

See map 4

AOC Bordeaux
1. Médoc
2. Haut-Médoc
3. St Estèphe
4. Pauillac
5. St Julien
6. Premières Côtes de Blaye
7. Listrac
8. Moulis
9. Margaux
10. Côtes de Bourg
11. Graves
12. Premières Côtes de Bordeaux
13. Entre-Deux-Mers
14. Graves de Vayres
15. Fronsac
16. Lalande de Pomerol
17. Pomerol
18. Satellite St Emilion
19. St Emilion
20. Côtes de Francs
21. Côtes de Castillon
22. Cérons
23. Cadillac
24. Loupiac
25. Ste Croix-du-Mont
26. Barsac
27. Sauternes
28. Côtes de Bordeaux-St Macaire

See map 5

Route One
Route Two
Route Three
Route Four
Route Five

0 1   10km

Route One

Around the Médoc: 165km

Most of the famous châteaux of Bordeaux are in this area bordering the Gironde north-west of Bordeaux. It is divided into two zones; the north-western tip, the Bas-Médoc, whose wines use the *appellation* Médoc, and the southern section, closest to Bordeaux, the Haut-Médoc. In terms of wine, the Haut-Médoc is both the larger and the more prestigious of the two, and the village names read like a roll call of famous wines: Margaux, St Julien, Pauillac and St Estèphe all lie along the banks of the Gironde. Though the names might be impressive, the villages themselves are not, for the glory of the Médoc is not its villages but its châteaux, which vary greatly in size and style. Built for the most part in the 19th century, they range from the majestic Château Margaux to the exotic oriental-looking *chai* at Cos d'Estournel. Many of the properties are extensive, but there is still a surprising amount of land not being used for vines – a reminder that until it was drained and planted during the 17th and 18th centuries, the Médoc was a marshland totally unsuited for vineyards.

The Bas-Médoc produces many excellent wines and has the added appeal of providing the visitor with some spectacular views of the Gironde, notably from Château Loudenne a few kilometers north of St Estèphe. The drive back to Bordeaux from the Bas-Médoc passes through Listrac and Moulis whose much-improved "inland" vineyards, often in glades and clearings surrounded by forest, seem totally removed from their coastal neighbors only a few kilometers to the east, but the quality of the wines is improving with every vintage.

Château d'Issan is one of the oldest and most beautiful Médoc mansions.

The Itinerary:

From the center of **Bordeaux** follow the signs to the airport; once in r. de la Croix de Seguey, bear right onto av. de la Libération, then drive straight on until signs indicate a right turn to Pauillac on D2, and tell you that you are following the *Route touristique du Médoc*. Just before Blanquefort you pass the beautiful Château du Taillan.

The outer industrial suburbs of Bordeaux give way to countryside just after **Caychac**, where a sign points the way to Château Ségur off to the right. Watch for a right-hand turn toward **Ludon-Médoc** because the building to the right here is Château la Lagune, the first of Bordeaux's star properties on the route. The vineyards are on the right, then drive into a wood but do not miss the sign to Château Cantemerle, Macau's only classed growth, a fairy-tale castle set deep in the woods. Past the woods take a right fork through Macau, passing Château Maucamps, then continue on D209 past Château Dauzac and Château Siran into Cantenac. In **Cantenac** are the Prieuré-Lichine vineyards, with large signs inviting visitors to come and taste their wines 365 days a year – Christmas day included! Between Cantenac and Margaux is a sea of vines, with the majestic Château Palmer to your right in the hamlet of d'Issan.

At **Margaux** it is worth making a slight detour to the right to admire the beautiful Château, hidden from the main road by a long avenue of trees. Margaux has a large number of châteaux concentrated near one another, not spread out as in other parts of the Médoc. Continuing on D2 through **Soussans** and **Cussac**, the vines are once again interspersed with woods and crops; and for several kilometers after that you could be excused for thinking you weren't in a wine area at all. But the famous *appellation* of St Julien bursts onto the scene at Château Beychevelle, and from here to St Estèphe, the vines completely dominate the landscape. Some of Bordeaux's greatest

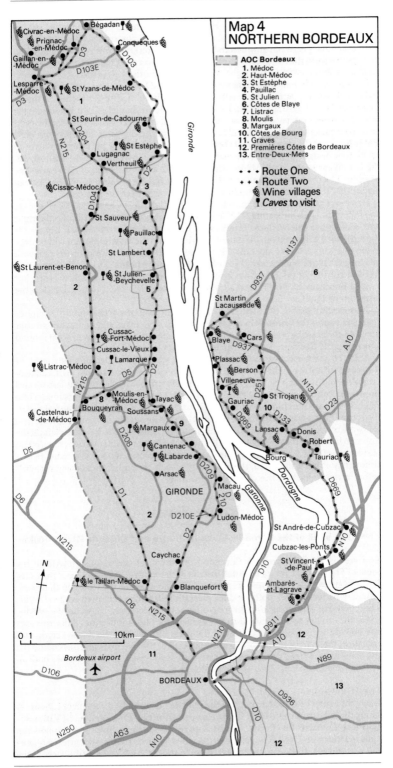

Map 4
NORTHERN BORDEAUX

AOC Bordeaux
1. Médoc
2. Haut-Médoc
3. St Estèphe
4. Pauillac
5. St Julien
6. Côtes de Blaye
7. Listrac
8. Moulis
9. Margaux
10. Côtes de Bourg
11. Graves
12. Premières Côtes de Bordeaux
13. Entre-Deux-Mers

• • • Route One
+ + + Route Two
Wine villages
Caves to visit

Civrac-en-Médoc
Bégadan
Prignac-en-Médoc
Conquèques
Gaillan-en-Médoc
D103E
D103
Lesparre-Médoc
St Yzans-de-Médoc
D3
St Seurin-de-Cadourne
Gironde
D204
St Estèphe
N215
Lugagnac
Vertheuil
D2
Cissac-Médoc
3
D104
St Sauveur
Pauillac
4
St Lambert
St Laurent-et-Benon
St Julien-Beychevelle
2
5
Cussac-Fort-Médoc
St Martin Lacaussade
N137
Cussac-le-Vieux
Cars
Lamarque
D937
Blaye
D937
Listrac-Médoc
Plassac
7
D5
D2
Berson
N137
Moulis-en-Médoc
Tayac
Villeneuve
A10
Bouqueyran
St Trojan
D23
Castelnau-de-Médoc
Soussans
9
Gauriac
N215
Margaux
D208
10
D133
D25
Cantenac
Lansac
Donis
Labarde
Robert
D5
Arsac
D209
Bourg
Tauriac
D1
GIRONDE
Macau
D669
2
D210
Garonne
Dordogne
D2
D210E
Ludon-Médoc
D6
Caychac
St André-de-Cubzac
N10
Cubzac-les-Ponts
N215
St Vincent-de-Paul
N
le Taillan-Médoc
Blanquefort
Ambarès-et-Lagrave
0 1
10km
D6
D10
D911
N215
12
A10
Bordeaux airport
11
N210
N89
BORDEAUX
D106
D936
13
N250
A63
N10
D10
12

châteaux, Branaire-Ducru, Ducru-Beaucaillou, Gruaud-Larose, and the trio of Léoville châteaux lie close to the road as it winds its way toward Pauillac. There is no visible boundary between St Julien and Pauillac, but you know you're in Pauillac when you pass between the two great châteaux, Pichon-Baron and Pichon-Lalande, and see Château Latour away to the right with its tower in the vineyards.

In Pauillac itself, follow the signs for *Centre Ville* and Lesparre; bear left at the square, right toward Lesparre, then left toward Château Lafite-Rothschild. Almost immediately after passing Château Lafite-Rothschild on your left, Cos d'Estournel, the first St Estèphe estate, appears straight ahead as the road twists left. At the next crossroads turn right still on D2, and follow it through the vineyards into the village of **St Estèphe**. Take the signs to *le port*; before actually reaching the port turn left across a small stone bridge along a winding marshy country road to **St Seurin-de-Cadourne**, the last village of the Haut-Médoc, then rejoin D2 in the direction of **St Yzans-de-Médoc**. The road overlooks the river, and on the right is the British-owned Château Loudenne, a beautiful pink building with good views over the Gironde.

Drive straight through St Yzans, following the signs to St Christoly. Then leave D2 and follow the signs indicating D103 and **Bégadan**, watching for a series of rapid right and left turns as you reach the intersection with D103E at **Couquèques**. Bégadan is the most northerly point on this tour of the Médoc and the most important wine village in the area with a good co-operative. It also has a lovely church with an open stonework bell tower. From Bégadan take D3 south to **Lesparre-Médoc**. To visit **Prignac-en-Médoc** turn right off D3 1.5km after **Civrac-en-Medoc**. In Lesparre, turn left toward Bordeaux on N215, then almost immediately left again to take D204 in the direction of Pauillac.

This western part of the Médoc is very different from the area around the famous châteaux nearer the Gironde in the Haut-Médoc. The towns and houses are prettier here and there are large stretches of forest, with a few concentrations of vines around Lugagnac, St Sauveur, Listrac-Médoc and Moulis-en-Médoc.

At the large intersection just after **Lugagnac**, watch for a faded sign indicating **St Sauveur** off to the right on D104. Drive through **Cissac-Médoc**, past Château Lamothe and through St Sauveur; at the intersection with N215 turn left toward Bordeaux, continuing straight through **St Laurent-et-Benon** with its interesting English-style gothic church. After St Laurent rejoin the N215. In **Listrac**, take a left turn onto D208 toward **Moulis-en-Médoc**, watching out for the beautiful white iron grillwork of the entrance to the Rothschild property, Château Clarke, on the left; at the stop sign in Moulis turn right onto D5 then, at the next major intersection, turn left on N215 toward Bordeaux. In **Castelnau-de-Médoc** bear left on the main road – although nothing is indicated, this is D1 which leads through farmland and orchards before arriving back in the center of Bordeaux.

Route Two

The right bank of the Gironde, Côtes de Bourg and Côtes de Blaye: 100km

This area is directly across the Gironde from the most prestigious growths of the Médoc. The Côtes de Bourg is a small district in the south of the region, and the Côtes de Blaye surrounds it and spreads northward. The wines of the Côtes de Bourg are generally better, though both produce pleasant reds which can often be good value. The vineyards bordering the Gironde offer some spectacular views of the Médoc across the estuary and the inland stretches make for pleasant driving. Since this area was making wine long before most of the great châteaux in the Médoc came into existence, there are some historic wine estates here, the two principal ones being the 16th-century Château Mendoce and the 18th-century Château de Barbe, both in Villeneuve and making good Côtes de Bourg.

The Itinerary:

Leave the center of **Bordeaux** across the Pont de Pierre in the direction of Libourne, taking the left turnoff onto D911 to go through **Ambarès-et-Lagrave**, **St Vincent-de-Paul**, **Cubzac-les-Ponts**, and **St André-de-Cubzac**; from there, follow the signs to **Bourg** on D669. The road is surrounded by vineyards, with scattered houses and few villages. In Bourg, the vines rise up to the right with a beautiful view of the

Dordogne on the left. Continuing on to **Gauriac**, the road passes the point where the Dordogne and the Garonne join to form the Gironde estuary; the drive from here, past the **Villeneuve** châteaux of Mendoce and Barbe which are both good Côtes de Bourg properties, through the Gallo-Roman town of **Plassac** and on to **Blaye** is quite spectacular.

In Blaye, a large resort town, the road passes right in front of the impressive *citadelle* built by Vauban in 1669. From the ramparts there are wonderful views across the Gironde to the churches of St Julien and Pauillac. Turn left onto D937 and bear right in the direction of Etauliers and Mirambeau. At **St Martin-Lacaussade**, turn right toward St Paul; a little way down the road, turn right onto CD133 toward **Cars**. Cross the railway, then turn left at the second crossroads to drive into Cars, up the hill and toward the church with its decoratively tiled roof, following the road around the village and back down onto the highway. Turn left onto D937, then right onto D251, following the signs to **Berson** through vineyards with very red earth.

Drive straight through Berson and **St Trojan**, then at **Tourteau** watch for a left-hand turnoff toward **Lansac** on D133; at the T-junction turn left, then almost immediately right to Lansac. Drive straight through the village to **Donis**, turning right onto D23 in the direction of Bourg before turning left on D133 through a mixture of vineyards, orchards and woods on a small country road to **Tauriac**. In the hamlet of **Robert** bear left at the fork in the direction of Tauriac. In Tauriac, turn right onto D133 toward Pont du Moron, then left onto D669 toward **St André-de-Cubzac**. From there, simply follow the signs to return to Bordeaux.

The magnificent Château la Rivière is also one of the best Fronsac properties.

Route Three

The right bank of the Dordogne – Fronsac, St Emilion and Pomerol: 130km

This route combines the picturesque region around Fronsac and St Emilion with the disappointingly featureless plateau of Pomerol that produces some of the world's greatest and most expensive red wines. St Emilion is a beautiful town perched on a hill, an island in a sea of vines that attracts tourists who may be only marginally interested in wine. Pomerol, however, has no real village center and every château stands apart in its vines. Even the church stands isolated.

The word "château" is used extremely loosely throughout this district, since virtually every wine producer feels obliged to elevate his home to "château" status. There are no grand buildings as in the Médoc. The properties, particularly in the St Emilion region, are very well signposted, with arrows pointing the way on roads that wind through woodlands and vines.

The Itinerary:
Leave the center of **Bordeaux**, crossing the Pont de Pierre in the direction of Libourne, then follow the signs to **Ambarès-et-Lagrave** and **St Vincent-de-Paul** on D911 and N10. The first vineyards can be seen just after leaving Ambarès. Continue across the Dordogne to **Cubzac-les-Ponts** and **St André-de-Cubzac**, then turn right on D670 to Libourne, after Bordeaux the most important wine center of the region. At first, D670 is a long, straight road through vineyards, fields and forest. At **Cadillac-en-Fronsadais** the land becomes hilly. More and more vineyards cover the hills and there is a lovely panorama approaching **St Michel-de-Fronsac** with Château la Rivière off to the left.

Continue on through **Fronsac**, a pretty town on the banks of the Dordogne, to **Libourne** where you must watch for a quick succession of signs; go over the bridge to pl. Jean Moulin and take the second turning right at the roundabout down the large allées R. Boulin toward the train station. At the roundabout in front of the station take the signs first toward **St Emilion**, then toward Montagne, then toward St Emilion on D117E which changes en route to D243. This road takes you past Château Figeac, one of the largest wine estates in St Emilion. Soon the tall church spire of St Emilion can be seen in the distance rising above the vines. St Emilion is the most enchanting wine town in this part of France and surrounding it are the steep slopes, or *Côtes*, which produce St Emilion's greatest wines. After visiting the town, drive on to the bottom of the hill looking up to the right at Château Ausone, the most famous château of the St Emilion *Côtes*, then turn left onto D245 toward St Laurent-des-Combes.

Driving through the vineyards, bear left at the fork a little way out of St Emilion, follow the signs toward St Etienne-de-Lisse, then turn left at the signpost indicating a list of châteaux including Destieux and Ferrand. Take this winding country road up onto the high vine-covered plateau, following the signs for **St Christophe-des-Bardes**; there turn right onto D130 toward **Parsac** and **Puisseguin**.

From here up to the plateau of **Pomerol** the scenery is breathtaking, the winding road falling and rising through the vineyards and bordered by tall houses with red tile roofs and there are occasional menhirs. After Puisseguin, follow the signs to **Lussac**, and on to **Montagne** on D122; in Montagne turn right toward Libourne on D244, then after **Corbin** follow the signs to the right to **Maillet**. At the first fork bear left toward **Néac**, left again at the road's end, then right toward **Chevrol** and N89. When you reach N89, a large main road though unmarked, turn left, then immediately right toward **la Lande-de-Libourne**. Wind through la Lande, turning right at the T-junction and then left toward St Denis-de-Pile, continuing over the railroad track, and straight on to D910, where you turn left.

At **les Billaux**, take the first large road to the right – a sign indicating **Galgon** will be visible once you have turned the corner. Drive through Galgon and **Caillon** on D18, then watch for a left-hand turn onto D10 toward **Périssac**. Continue on this road bordered by woods and vines, through **Salignac**, and across the railroad track to **St Antoine**, then follow the signs directing you to A10, and a quick return to Bordeaux.

Route Four

Entre-Deux-Mers and Graves de Vayres: 130km

South-east of Bordeaux, between the Dordogne and the Garonne, is a large scenic district known as Entre-Deux-Mers. The region makes for pleasant touring, with the vines growing amid farmlands, streams, and forest. Prehistoric dwellings and mysterious dolmens are reminders of ancient settlements. The Entre-Deux-Mers is the largest wine-producing *appellation* in Bordeaux and many of the wines sold simply as "Bordeaux" (white or red) or used by shippers for blending come from this region. The area is known mainly for its dry whites under the Entre-Deux-Mers *appellation*, though reds are gaining in importance (these can only be labeled Bordeaux or Bordeaux Supérieur).

The Graves de Vayres is a small area near Libourne, not to be confused with the famous Graves district south-west of Bordeaux, and has its own *appellation* for red and white wines.

The Itinerary:

From the center of **Bordeaux**, cross the Pont de Pierre, then follow the signs to Bergerac (after the large highway sign, watch for a side road to the right marked by a very small sign). Drive through **Fargues-St Hilaire** on D936, then turn right toward **Créon** and Sauveterre-de-Guyenne on D671; high-growing vines appear just before Créon. Créon is an old bastide town and the pretty valleys around the town have given the name "Petite Suisse" to the area. Drive through Créon and onto a wide, flat vine-covered plain on the way to **la Sauve** with its beautiful 11th-century Abbaye de la Sauve Majeure and the good Entre-Deux-Mers property of Château Thieuley.

Continue to **Sauveterre** on D671. In Sauveterre, turn left at the city gate and head north on D670 toward Libourne. Just before St Jean-de-Blaignac turn left on D18 toward **Branne**, then watch for another turning on the right, also toward Branne. The hills between Sauveterre and Branne provide a panoramic view of the vineyards as the road approaches St Jean and the beautiful Château de Blaignac.

In Branne turn left toward Bordeaux on D936 and right on D18 toward **Moulon** a little farther on. Continue on D18 through **Génissac**; at the T-junction turn right, then left onto N89, and right again onto D242 to **Vayres**. This is the end of the picturesque part of the route. From Vayres, a sprawling suburban town, simply follow the signs on D242 to **St Loubès** and **Ambarès**, and then the A10 to return to Bordeaux.

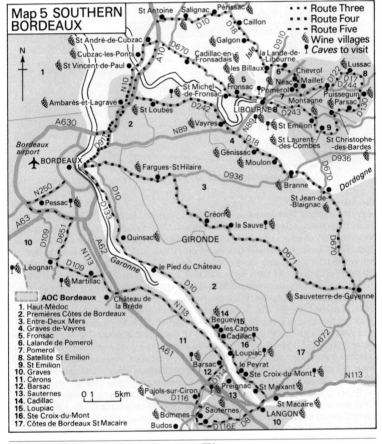

Map 5 SOUTHERN BORDEAUX

• • • Route Three
▪ ▪ ▪ Route Four
– – – Route Five
🍇 Wine villages
🍷 *Caves* to visit

AOC Bordeaux
1. Haut-Médoc
2. Premières Côtes de Bordeaux
3. Entre-Deux-Mers
4. Graves de-Vayres
5. Fronsac
6. Lalande de Pomerol
7. Pomerol
8. Satellite St Emilion
9. St Emilion
10. Graves
11. Cérons
12. Barsac
13. Sauternes
14. Cadillac
15. Loupiac
16. Ste Croix-du-Mont
17. Côtes de Bordeaux St Macaire

0 1   5km

Route Five

Graves, Sauternes and the Premières Côtes de Bordeaux: 125km

The vineyards of Graves are very close to Bordeaux – Haut-Brion, for instance, is surrounded by suburbs immediately to the south-west of the city. Both red and white wine are made throughout the Graves area; the whites can be the finest dry white wines in all Bordeaux.

Near the south-eastern end of the region is Sauternes, one of the prettiest areas to visit in all the Bordeaux region. The sweet wines of Sauternes and neighboring Barsac can only be produced if "noble rot," the *Botrytis cinerea* mold, develops on the grapes before harvesting. For this to happen there must be just the right amount of moisture and the proper temperature at vintage time, helped by the river Ciron, which flows through the area, and its low-lying valley. Across the Garonne three other *appellations* also make sweet wines from noble-rotted grapes: Ste Croix-du-Mont, Loupiac, and Cadillac. These rarely rival Sauternes though they can be excellent alternatives to the more expensive *crus* across the river. Many of these properties are now making ordinary dry white wines instead of the sweet wines which are much more expensive to produce.

Along the north bank of the Garonne, extending from Cadillac to Bordeaux, is the Premières Côtes de Bordeaux *appellation*. Both red and white wines are made here, and though the *appellation* has gained considerably in prestige the wines still represent good-value purchases.

Château Coutet, an excellent property, is one of two First Growth Barsac estates.

The Itinerary:

Leave the center of **Bordeaux** by r. de Pessac, cours du Maréchal Gallieni and av. Jean Jaurès to go toward Arcachon and **Pessac** on N250. This road takes you past Haut-Brion, the only château outside the Médoc to feature in the 1855 red wine classification. Most of the Classed Growths in Graves are near Pessac and Talence, close to Bordeaux, and around Léognan just to the south. After Pessac turn left on A630, toward Villenave-d'Ornon, and then right on D651 for **Léognan**. In Léognan turn left on D109, then follow the signs toward **Martillac**, driving through forest until well out of Léognan when the stony vineyards can be seen from the road. In Martillac, turn left toward Isle-St Georges and St Médard. At the intersection with N113 turn right, following the signs to **Langon** *par le R.N.* thereafter. This is a pleasant drive on a tree-lined road through vineyards and pastures all the way to **Barsac**. Drive through the village, then take D114 right toward **Pujols-sur-Ciron**; at the next intersection drive straight on and begin following the signs indicating the *Circuit du Sauternais* which twists through the vineyards, the Sauternes châteaux clearly indicated along it.

At the intersection after crossing the autoroute, continue straight on through Pujols, then turn left on D116 in the direction of Langon. The countryside is beautiful, with vines in all directions and a watermill as the road crosses the Ciron. On the other side of the river turn right for **Bommes**, then follow the signs to **Haute Bommes** and **Sauternes** on C1. At the next crossroads and in Sauternes, follow the *Circuit du Sauternais*; just before reaching the top of the hill in Sauternes, turn left onto an unmarked road opposite the sign indicating Budos and leading past the *Maison des vins de Sauternes*. From here, the route takes you to **Langon**, but when you reach the crossroads indicating D116E and Langon to the right, you might want to make a slight detour to glimpse the magnificent and world-renowned Château d'Yquem and its panoramic views over the valley. To do this, drive straight ahead across D116E and onto the unmarked dirt road that serves as the château driveway.

Back on D116E follow the signs to **Langon** onto D8, past Château Rieussec and the ruins of an old château on the hill to the right. Langon is another important town for the distribution of the region's wines. Go into Langon *Centre Ville*, then cross the Garonne on N113 toward Agen. At the roundabout on the other side of the bridge follow the signs indicating **St Maixant** and **Cadillac**. This road, D10, will take you all the way back to Bordeaux through some pleasant, gently rolling, vine-covered hills, the pretty little village of **le Peyrat** and the fortified towns of **Cadillac**, **les Capots**, and **le Pied du Château**, with some splendid views across the Garonne.

Bordeaux winemakers are generally not as willing or anxious to welcome visitors to their vineyards and cellars as producers in other parts of France. One cannot generalize, however, since growers in the Médoc, which teems with prestigious châteaux, are friendlier than those in the Graves and are more welcoming, surprisingly, than the little-known producers in the Entre-Deux-Mers. Nevertheless, travelers will find many estates and winemakers throughout the region displaying notices for *vente au détail* and *dégustation*. Their names may be unknown, but their wine can be surprisingly good from the standpoint of both taste and value.

BARSAC, map 5

Château Coutet (G), Barsac, 33720 Podensac. Tel: 56.27.15.46.

The estate, the largest in Barsac and one of the two Barsac First Growths, consists of 38 hectares of vines, which yield one of the best Barsac wines. The small attractive château incorporates the remains of a medieval castle. In exceptional years Château Coutet uses the best and richest grapes to make a special *cuvée*, Cuvée Madame, which is delicious but obviously diminishes the quality of the regular Coutet. There is also a dry white Graves, made from grapes containing too little sugar as well as from grapes from another nearby domaine, Château le Reverdon.

Visiting hours: Mon–Fri 2–6; appt. preferred.

Location: 1.5km S of Barsac.

BEGADAN, map 4

Château Latour-de-By (G), Bégadan, 33340 Lesparre. Tel: 56.41.50.03.

The attractive château run by Marc Pagès is on one of the highest ridges of the Bas-Médoc and has 72 hectares of vineyards. The château is named after the old beacon tower in the middle of the vineyards which was used as the By beacon light for ships in the Gironde in the middle 19th century. This Grand Bourgeois Médoc wine is of exceptional quality, with a particularly rich fruit flavor.

Visiting hours: Mon–Fri 8–12, 2–6; in winter Mon–Fri 8–12, 1.30–5.30.

Location: In the hamlet of By 1.5km N of Bégadan.

CADILLAC, map 5

Château Fayau (G), 33410 Cadillac-sur-Garonne. Tel: 56.62.65.80.

The Médeville family are owners of Château Fayau, consisting of 36 hectares of vines at Cadillac in the Premières Côtes de Bordeaux, as well as other properties in the *appellation* and in Graves. The estate makes a wide range of red and white wines under the Graves and Bordeaux labels, although when a sweet white wine is made it can carry the superior *appellation* of Cadillac and is one of the best-value sweet Bordeaux wines outside Sauternes.

Visiting hours: Mon–Fri 9–12, 2–6.30.

Location: Signposted in Cadillac.

CANTENAC, map 4

Château d'Issan (G), Cantenac, 33460 Margaux. Tel: 56.88.70.72.

At the heart of this ancient estate, now a Third Growth, is the 18th-century moated château, one of the most attractive in the Médoc. After a long period of neglect the late Emmanuel Cruse bought the property in 1945, renewed the 35 hectares of vines and spent the rest of his life restoring the château to its present glory. The estate started bottling its own wine in 1972. During the late 1980s the wine is rapidly becoming the new star in the Margaux *appellation* with its deep, powerfully scented flavor.

Visiting hours: Daily 9–12, 2–6.

Location: Just N of Cantenac.

Château Prieuré-Lichine (G),
Cantenac,
33460 Margaux.
Tel: 56.88.36.28.

As the name Prieuré suggests, vineyards were first planted on the property by Benedictine monks in the 16th century. When Alexis Lichine bought the property in 1951, it was in terrible condition and there were only 11 hectares of vines in production. He rebuilt and expanded the buildings and acquired more land and extended the vineyards so that they now amount to more than 60 hectares. The estate welcomes visitors and offers guided tours. This Fourth Growth Margaux is generally reckoned far above its classification and is one of the most reliable Margaux.
Visiting hours: Daily 9–6.
Location: In the center of the village, behind the church.

CUSSAC-FORT-MEDOC, map 4

Château Lanessan (G), Cussac-Fort-Médoc,
33460 Margaux.
Tel: 56.58.94.80.

Many Bordeaux estates have changed hands over the centuries with bewildering frequency and only a select few, such as Château Lanessan, have been kept in the same family for centuries. Over the centuries, this Cru Bourgeois Haut-Médoc estate has grown steadily in size and reputation and it now amounts to 264 hectares of which 40 are planted in vines. The vast estate stables have been converted into a comprehensive and fascinating carriage museum.
Visiting hours: (Cellars) May–mid-Nov daily, 9–12, 2–6; (Museum) Daily 9–12, 2–6.30; groups by appt.
Location: 3km N of Cussac.

LABARDE, map 4

Château Giscours (G), Labarde,
33460 Margaux.
Tel. 56.88.34.02.

This Third Growth estate has had its ups and downs since it was first documented in 1330 but since its purchase in 1952 by Nicolas Tari – it is now owned by his son Pierre – it has thankfully been in an upward curve. There are 80 hectares of vineyard surrounding the handsome Renaissance-style château, built in the mid-19th century. The Taris have restored the buildings and installed a reception center and dining-rooms. As part of their perfectionism a small lake has been dug at great expense to aid drainage of the vineyards.

During the 1970s and early 1980s this was one of the most exciting wines in Margaux but recent vintages, though good, have lacked a little sparkle.
Visiting hours: Mon–Fri 9–12, 2–5; appt preferred, and essential for groups.
Location: 1km SW of Labarde.

LISTRAC-MEDOC, map 4

Château Clarke (G), Vin. Edmond de Rothschild,
Listrac-Médoc,
33480 Castelnau-de-Médoc.
Tel: 56.88.88.00.
For visits: Cercle Oenologique du Clarke,
33480 Moulis-Médoc.
Tel: 56.88.84.29.

This Cru Bourgeois estate was first planted in vines by Cistercian monks in the 12th century and produced good wines for centuries. However, decline eventually set in and by the 1950s the property was derelict. Baron Edmond de Rothschild acquired the estate in 1973 and has completely replanted the vineyards, which now total 173 hectares. Investment in the property has been formidable. So far the vines are too young to judge the full potential of the wine, but the vintages of the mid-1980s have shown a big improvement.

Visitors should go to the Cercle Oenologique de Clarke from where they are taken on tours of the cellars. The Moulis reception center offers tastings and light meals.
Visiting hours: Jun 15–Sep 30 daily, 10–6; remainder of the year by appt.
Location: The Cercle Oenologique is in the center of Moulis.

MARGAUX, map 4
Château Lascombes (G),
33460 Margaux.
Tel: 56.88.70.66.

The property bears the name of its 17th-century owner, the Chevalier Antoine de Lascombes and is now owned by a British company, Bass-Charrington, who have spent vast sums on restoring the *chais* and the Edwardian château. This is a Second Growth Margaux, consisting of 98 hectares scattered throughout the *appellation* and is one the largest properties in the Médoc.
Visiting hours: Mon–Fri 9–12, 2–6; only until 5pm on Fri.
Location: In Margaux, between D2 and the railway.

The colonnaded chai at Margaux used for the first-year wines.

Château Margaux (G),
33460 Margaux.
Tel: 56.88.70.28.

The graceful porticoed mansion glimpsed at the end of a long avenue of trees must surely be one of the most famous sights in the world of wine. Château Margaux is now owned by the Mentzelopoulos family, who have been exemplary owners since 1977. No expense has been spared to restore the château and its surroundings to their original glory and a magnificent new underground *chai* was even built in 1982. After a long period in the 1960s and 1970s when First Growth quality was rarely achieved at Margaux, this heavenly fragrant wine is now enjoying a succession of brilliant successes as great as any in its entire history. The estate consists of 75 hectares and in addition to the Grand Vin Château Margaux, there is a second label, Pavillon Rouge du Château Margaux and an absolutely delicious, dry white Le Pavillon Blanc.
Visiting hours: Sep–Jul Mon–Fri, 10–12, 2–4, by appt; closed hols.
Location: Between the center of Margaux and the Gironde.

PAUILLAC, map 4
Château Batailley (G), 33259 Pauillac.
Tel: 56.59.01.13.

The name of this Fifth Growth estate has led many to speculate that a battle was fought on the site of the estate in the distant past. However, there is no proof either in archives or popular memory and the only battle Batailley is regularly involved in is the annual attempt to keep prices reasonable. The commune of Pauillac produces some of the most overpriced wines in France, yet Batailley is always extremely fairly priced. The estate centers on a handsome 18th–19th-century mansion set amid a fine park and is owned by the Castéja family who control many other Bordeaux estates. Vines cover about 50 hectares on high ground behind Pauillac. The wine, filled with delicious blackcurrant fruit and vanilla sweetness from the new oak barrels, is always ready to drink quite young, but does age extremely well over 10 to 15 years.
Visiting hours: Mar–Sep Mon–Fri, 8–12, 2–6; Oct–Feb by appt.
Location: On D206 2.5km S of Pauillac.

Château Lafite-Rothschild (G),
33250 Pauillac.
Tel: 56.59.01.74.

Given the fame of Château-Lafite-Rothschild – and the wealth of the Rothschild family – you might expect the château itself to be grander, whereas in fact it gives the impression of being a large, prosperous farm, rather than the Mecca for claret lovers world-wide. The château has a spacious terrace and vast cellars with fine arches and a fascinating collection of ancient bottles, the oldest dating back to 1797, which are stored in a separate cellar.

The First Growth wine, in the best years, has always been described as feminine because of its elegance, refinement and subtlety. Although the wine suffered somewhat of an eclipse in the late 1960s and early 1970s, it has since then been attempting to return itself to the peak of the claret pile with considerable, but not total, success.

Visiting hours: Write for appt at least 10 days in advance.
Location: Just off D2 3km N of Pauillac.

Château Latour (G), St Lambert,
33250 Pauillac.
Tel: 56.59.00.51.

The tower in the name of this First Growth estate is not the same as the one, restored and brightened up, that stands amid the vines. The original tower must have been one of the many built before or during the English occupation of the region in the Middle Ages to guard the Gironde estuary.

The British investment group, Pearson, acquired a majority share in Latour in the 1960s and undertook a vast renovation program. In the mix of grapes, Cabernet Sauvignon looms large – 80 per cent with 10 per cent each Cabernet Franc and Merlot – so that the wine is slow to open up, requiring many years of aging to reach its peak, but after 20 years or so it is a superb, rich mouthful, packed with blackcurrant and cedar flavors.

Visiting hours: Daily 9–12, 2–5, by appt; closed Aug, hols and Sep 25–Nov 10.
Location: Between D2 and the Gironde 2km N of St Julien.

Château Lynch-Bages (G),
33250 Pauillac.
Tel: 56.59.25.59.

The Lynch family came from Ireland and settled in Bordeaux in 1690. They bought the Bages property in 1740 and set about developing its vineyards. Lynch-Bages has been owned by the Cazes family since 1936 and is now exceeding its previous already considerable reputation. It was classified in 1855 only as a Fifth Growth but most would hold that it is now of good Second Growth standard. The property consists of 78 hectares and the wine produced is a classic and complete Pauillac, often a little sweeter and quicker to mature than other top growths. The second wine, Château Haut-Bages-Averous, is one of the best made.

There is a good view of the estuary and Pauillac from Lynch-Bages which is set back slightly from the Gironde on one of the highest parts of the *appellation*.

Visiting hours: Mon–Thu 9–12, 2–5; Fri 9–12, 1.30–4; appt preferred.
Location: Just S of Pauillac on D2.

Château Mouton-Rothschild (G),
La Baronnie, BP 32,
33250 Pauillac.
Office tel:
56.59.20.20. For appt
tel: 56.59.22.22.

There must be few people in the world of wine who have not heard of Mouton-Rothschild and it is a fascinating property to visit. There is also a Museum of Wine, with a unique collection of art objects associated with wine. Unfortunately, because it is so well known, there is a constant stream of visitors. While there is much that is interesting and appealing to see, the crowding and the occasionally defensive attitude of the beleaguered staff may put off some visitors, in which case they should seek out the lesser known châteaux in the neighborhood, at which the welcome may be somewhat

warmer and hordes of visitors a rarer event.

The property has belonged to the Rothschilds since Baron Nathaniel Rothschild bought it in 1853. The estate has steadily grown to include Château Mouton-Baronne-Philippe and Château Clerc-Milon, both Fifth Growth Pauillac estates. Mouton-Rothschild was only classified as a Second Growth until 1973 when it was finally upgraded to First Growth as a result of the frequently peerless quality of the wine and the flamboyant, obsessive one-man crusade by Baron Philippe to correct what he saw as a major slur on his great property. He was quite right; Mouton-Rothschild *is* a worthy First Growth. The property also makes Mouton-Cadet, Bordeaux's most successful branded wine.

Visiting hours: Sep–Jul Mon–Thu, 9–11.15, 2–4.15; Fri 9–11.15, 2–3.15; by appt.

Location: 2km N of Pauillac and signposted.

Haut-Brion, one of the most famous Bordeaux estates.

PESSAC, map 5
Château Haut-Brion (G),
Domaine Clarence
Dillon, BP 24,
33600 Pessac.
Tel: 56.98.33.73.

Pessac, once an isolated country village to the south-west of Bordeaux, has been engulfed by the city in its steady outward expansion. As a result, one of the world's best-known wines and its vineyards are now surrounded by urban development. Haut-Brion was the only non-Médoc red wine to be classed as First Growth in 1855. In 1953, when the Graves wines were classified, Haut-Brion was put at the head of the list as a matter of course. The ancient property has had many owners and it was once much more extensive than it is today, for it was broken up and sold piecemeal at the Revolution.

Now run by the Duchesse de Mouchy, whose American grandfather, Clarence Dillon, bought the estate in 1935, the Haut-Brion vineyards today amount to a total of 44 hectares, nearly all of which is devoted to production of the famous red wine. The rare white wine, from 50 per cent Sémillon and 50 per cent Sauvignon, is one of France's greatest white wines, equalling the finest of white burgundies in its luscious honeyed flavors and often excelling them in price!

The La Mission estate, almost opposite Haut-Brion, is under the same ownership and can be visited by appointment. The wine is more austere and a bit more reserved than the Haut-Brion, hefty rather than fragrant and rarely achieving Haut-Brion's heights. The former chapel attached to the château has magnificent stained-glass windows.

Visiting hours: Sep–mid-Jul Mon–Fri, 9–11, 2–5; appt preferred.

Location: On N250 between Bordeaux and Pessac.

POMEROL, map 5

**Vieux Château
Certan (G),**
Pomerol,
33500 Libourne.
Tel: 57.51.17.33.

Owned since 1924 by the Thienponts, a Belgian family, this well-known Pomerol estate is considerably larger than its more famous near neighbor, Château Pétrus, and has 13.5 hectares. In some years its wine is almost as good as Pétrus. There is a small, 17th-century château, one of the finest in Pomerol where the châteaux resemble at most manor houses rather than the grander versions of the Médoc.
Visiting hours: Daily by appt.
Location: In Pomerol at intersection of D121 and D245.

PREIGNAC, map 5

**Château de Malle
(G),** Preignac,
33210 Langon.
Tel: 56.63.28.67.

This lovely Renaissance château, a classified historical monument, is surrounded by a fine park with statues, terraces and even a small theater in the Italian style. The property is kept in immaculate condition by its owner, the Comte de Bournazel. The estate was classified in 1855 as a Second Growth Sauternes. Although it does sometimes produce wine of First Growth quality, it is in general on the lighter side, good but not ultra-luscious. Producing Sauternes has always been a risky business, since the "noble rot" will only develop if the conditions are just right and a couple of days' rain at the wrong moment can ruin the entire crop, so the estate has developed the dry wine side of the business under the name Chevalier de Malle for the whites and Château de Cardaillan for the reds.
Visiting hours: Thu–Tue 3–7; in Jul–Aug open from 10–7.
Location: On D125 just N of A62.

Château de Malle is one of the finest historical properties in the Bordeaux region.

ST EMILION, map 5

**Château Cheval-
Blanc (G),**
33330 St Emilion.
Tel: 57.24.70.70.

The wine of this First Great Growth is renowned throughout the world for its fine breeding and elegance, and marvelous depth of flavors. Though both Ausone and Figeac would want to argue the toss, Cheval Blanc is still the greatest St Emilion and has been owned by the Fourcaud Laussac family for several generations. In good years and bad there is a rich, ripe concentration of flavor which is of the top class. All aspirations of nobility at Cheval Blanc have gone into the wine rather than the architecture. The buildings – both the château and the cellars – are not majestic, but the small château is comfortable and the cellars and *chais* strictly functional. The property is reasonably sized in St Emilion terms with 36 hectares planted with 66 per cent Cabernet Franc and 33 per cent Merlot. The emphasis on Cabernet Franc is unusual in a region dominated by Merlot.
Visiting hours: Mon–Fri 9–11.30, 3–5, by appt.
Location: Off D245 between St Emilion and Pomerol.

ST JULIEN-BEYCHEVELLE, map 4

Château Beychevelle (G), St Julien-Beychevelle, 33250 Pauillac. Tel: 56.59.23.00.

The fine 18th-century mansion, separated from the Gironde by immaculate gardens, once belonged to the Duc d'Epernon, grand admiral of France. It was the custom for ships entering and leaving the estuary to lower their sails briefly as they passed the duke's residence and the command, *baisse-voile*, is supposed to account for the name, Beychevelle. Classified only as a Fourth Growth St Julien, it is easily Second Growth in quality. Although it seems quite quick to mature, in fact it benefits from aging as much as any St Julien and can be sublimely fragrant at 20 years old.
Visiting hours: May–Sep Mon–Fri, 9–11.30, 2–5.30; appt preferred.
Location: On S side of Beychevelle on D2.

ST MICHEL-DE-FRONSAC, map 5

Château la Rivière (G), la Rivière, St Michel-de-Fronsac, 33126 Fronsac. Tel: 57.24.98.01.

This is one of the best Fronsac properties and the beautiful Renaissance château, much restored in the 19th century, would seem more at home in the Loire valley than on the banks of the Dordogne. There are marvelous views of the surrounding hilly countryside from the château which is sited above the vineyards on a wooded slope. M. Jacques Borie, the owner of the estate, lives in the château with his family. The 44-hectare vineyards include 1 hectare of vines 115 years old, with vines 60 to 100 years old on another 9 hectares, and there is no question that the wine benefits massively from this high proportion of old vines.
Visiting hours: Mon–Fri 8–11, 2–5.
Location: On D670 in la Rivière.

ST YZANS-DE-MEDOC, map 4

Château Loudenne (G/M), St Yzans-de-Médoc, 33340 Lesparre. Tel: 57.41.15.03.

The elegant, pink, 18th-century château lies close to the banks of the Gironde and was bought by the Gilbey family in the 1870s. A Cru Grand Bourgeois, the property has 40 hectares of vineyards. Although the wine-making is taken seriously, the results are very gentle and soft and not typical of the Médoc. There is an agreeable white, rare for the Médoc, from equal parts Sauvignon and Sémillon, and sold under the Bordeaux Blanc *appellation*. Gilbeys are now part of the large International Distillers and Vintners group who have spent enormous sums on renovating the Victorian *chais*. The château is generally hospitable and will help visitors make arrangements to see other properties in the area.
Visiting hours: Mon–Fri 9.30–12, 2–4.30; appt for large groups.
Location: Off D2 1km S of St Yzans.

Le TAILLAN-MEDOC, map 4

Château du Taillan (G), le Taillan-Médoc, 33320 Eysines. Tel: 56.39.26.04.

Almost at the gates of Bordeaux, with the boundary between the Médoc and Graves *appellations* running through the estate, the château is an attractive 18th-century mansion with remarkable cellars and both are now classified as national historical monuments. The Cruse family have owned the property since 1806. The Grand Bourgeois estate makes a red Haut-Médoc and white Bordeaux Supérieur, the white sold under the name of La Dame Blanche. Horses are bred on the estate both for racing and hunting.
Visiting hours: Mon–Fri 8–12, 2–6.
Location: In the village center.

Further *Caves* and Vineyards to Visit

BARSAC, map 5

Château Nairac (G), Barsac, 33720 Podensac. Tel: 56.27.16.16. Visiting hours: By appt but not in harvest.

This Second Growth estate of 16 hectares is owned by an American, Thomas Heeter, and his wife, Nicole, a member of the Tari family who own Château Giscours and Branaire-Ducru in the Médoc. Their wine is excellent and above Second Growth standard.

CANTENAC, map 4

Château d'Angludet (G), Cantenac, 33460 Margaux. Tel: 56.88.71.41. Visiting hours: By appt.

Standards have dramatically improved at Angludet, particularly since 1961, when the present owner, Peter Sichel, began replanting and extending the vineyards. It is now one of the most exciting and fairly priced of all the 'non-classified' growths, and is always up to Classed Growth standard. The estate is well maintained and the park one of the most beautiful in the Médoc.

Château Palmer (G), Issan, Cantenac, 33460 Margaux. Tel: 56.88.72.72. For appt contact Maison Sichel, 19 quai Bacalan, 33028 Bordeaux. Tel: 56.39.35.29.

Château Palmer with its turreted roof is a well-known landmark in the hamlet of Issan. Although classified as a Third Growth, it frequently outperforms many of the First Growth estates and had a brilliant run in the 1960s and 1970s. Vinification is strictly traditional.

LABARDE, map 4

Château Siran (G), Labarde, 33460 Margaux. Tel: 56.88.34.04. For appt tel: 56.48.35.01. Visiting hours: Jul–Sep daily, 9–5; Oct–Jun Mon–Fri, 10–12, 2–5; Sat 10–5; Sun 1–5; appt preferred.

Château Siran has a pleasant park close to the Gironde where wild cyclamens bloom in the summer. It is ranked as a Cru Bourgeois Supérieur but it is generally accepted that the quality of this Margaux is far superior to that level.

LAMARQUE, map 4

Château de Lamarque (G), 33460 Lamarque. Tel: 56.58.90.03. Visiting hours: Nov–mid-Sep Mon–Fri, 9–12, 2–6.

The château is a marvelous medieval castle with towers and battlements and fine interiors and makes respectable Haut-Médoc. It is classified as a Grand Bourgeois estate and the present owners have undertaken extensive replanting of the vineyards.

LEOGNAN, map 5

Château Haut-Bailly (G), 33850 Léognan. Tel: 56.27.16.07. Visiting hours: Mon–Fri, preferably by appt.

This Classed Growth estate, situated on a high ridge on the left bank of the Garonne, makes one of the finest red Graves, being richer in flavor and gentler than most of its neighbors. There is no grand château at Haut-Bailly but a pleasant 19th-century house. The estate is owned by the Sanders family who also own other properties in Graves and Sauternes.

Château la Louvière (G), at Léognan. For appt contact Château Bonnet, Grézillac, 33420 Branne. Tel: 57.84.52.07. Visiting hours: By appt.

The vineyards were first planted as far back as 1550. Classified as a national historical monument the beautiful château of la Louvière is owned by André Lurton who owns several estates in Bordeaux. The red Graves Léognan is well regarded, while the white is one of the most exciting wines made in the region.

LIBOURNE, map 5

Château la Dominique (G), Société des Vignobles Dominique Pichon, BP 160, 33502 Libourne. Tel: 57.51.92.00. Visiting hours: Mon–Fri 9–6, by appt.

This is one of the best Classed Growths in St Emilion and the vineyards adjoin those of the great estate of Cheval Blanc virtually on the boundary between Pomerol and St Emilion; the wine made from the grapes blends the characteristics of the two *appellations* with the plump but minerally richness of Pomerol and the soft vanilla-tinged scent and flavor of St Emilion.

LISTRAC-MEDOC, map 4

Château Fourcas-Hosten (G), Listrac-Médoc, 33480 Castelnau-de-Médoc. Tel: 56.58.01.15. Visiting hours: Mon–Fri 8–12, 2–6.

The château stands opposite the church in the center of Listrac and has a pleasant wooded park at the rear. The 40-hectare estate is run by Patrice Pagès who also runs Château Fourcas Dupré nearby. This is an impressive Cru Bourgeois Listrac, a formidable wine that ages splendidly and bottles from 20 years ago are still in superb condition.

LOUPIAC, map 5
Château Loupiac-Gaudiet (G), Loupiac, 33410 Cadillac. Tel: 56.62.99.88. Visiting hours: By appt.
One of the best estates in Loupiac and making good wine with elegance and breeding, the château originally belonged to the 16th-century writer, Montaigne.

MARTILLAC, map 5
Château Smith-Haut-Lafitte (G), Martillac, 33650 la Brède. Tel: 56.30.72.30. For appt tel: 56.81.58.90. Visiting hours: By appt.
With 51 hectares, this is the most important estate in Martillac, and has long had a good reputation. It has undergone many improvements since the 1960s, including a brand new cellar housing up to 2,000 barrels. There is good red Graves and a delicious white Graves made entirely from Sauvignon.

PREIGNAC, map 5
Château Gilette (G), Preignac, 33210 Langon. Tel: 56.63.27.59. Visiting hours: Sep–Jul Mon–Fri, 8–12, 2–6.
Christian Médeville owns this tiny but interesting Sauternes property and uniquely ages his wines for 25 years or so in sealed concrete vats rather than in the normal wooden barrels. Production is necessarily limited, since the grapes used for this outstanding dessert wine are grown on only 4.5 hectares.

STE CROIX-DU-MONT, map 5
Château Loubens (G), Ste Croix-du-Mont, 33410 Cadillac. Tel: 56.62.01.25. Visiting hours: By appt.
Ste Croix-du-Mont makes the best sweet wines outside Sauternes, which it faces across the Garonne. Château Loubens is one of the best estates in the *appellation* and in good years the sweet wine is a lovely one of rare elegance. There is also a good dry white Bordeaux under the label Fleuron Blanc.

ST EMILION, map 5
Château Figeac (G), 33330 St Emilion. Tel: 57.24.72.26. Visiting hours: Mon–Fri, by appt.
This First Great Growth is one of the largest estates in St Emilion with 40 hectares of vines, and shares many of the qualities of the great Château Cheval Blanc. Owned by Thierry Manoncourt, Château Figeac is an elegant 18th-century residence with a fine park.

Château Monbousquet (G), 33330 St Emilion. Tel: 57.24.75.24. Visiting hours: By appt.
This very attractive château overlooking a small lake is on an estate of 30 hectares of vines on the flatter part of St Emilion near the Dordogne. The wines are always lighter from this soil, but Monbousquet can produce very fine St Emilion.

ST ESTEPHE, map 4
Château Cos d'Estournel (G), St Estèphe, 33250 Pauillac. Tel: 56.44.11.37. Visiting hours: By appt.
Cos d'Estournel, a Second Growth estate, is the top wine of St Estèphe. This is not the only reason for a visit as the *chai* is a fantastic oriental-looking building with pagoda turrets and arches overlooking the vineyards which stretch away toward Pauillac. It has been completely restored since damage in World War II.

ST JULIEN-BEYCHEVELLE, map 4
Château Langoa-Barton and **Château Léoville-Barton (G)**, St Julien-de-Beychevelle, 33250 Pauillac. Tel: 56.59.06.05. Visiting hours: By appt.
Château Langoa with its *cuvier* is one of the loveliest properties in the Médoc and is the home of the Barton family who came from Ireland in the 1820s. Léoville Barton has no château. The two estates are managed as one but the wines are harvested and vinified separately. Léoville-Barton, a Second Growth, is one of the best St Julien wines and Langoa-Barton, a Third Growth, is slightly lighter in style but still has the classic character of St Julien.

La SAUVE-MAJEUR, map 5
Château Thieuley (G), la Sauve-Majeur, 33670 Créon. Tel: 56.23.00.01. Visiting hours: Sep–Jul Mon–Fri, 8–12, 2–6, by appt; closed Aug 15–30.

Francis Courselle, who owns the 30-hectare Château Thieuley in the Entre-Deux-Mers, is one of the area's leading new winemakers and his dry Entre-Deux-Mers is well regarded.

TAURIAC, map 4

Cave Co-opérative de Tauriac (C), Tauriac, 33710 Bourg-sur-Gironde. Tel: 57.68.41.12. Visiting hours: By appt. There are various "château" wines at Tauriac, all good, and this co-operative can be regarded as one of the most impressive in Bordeaux, especially when new oak has been used on the wines.

VILLENEUVE, map 4

Château de Barbe (G), Villeneuve-de-Blaye, 33710 Bourg-sur-Gironde. Tel: 57.64.80.51. Visiting hours: By appt. Consisting of 56 hectares, the estate has a fine 18th-century château. In addition to Côtes de Bourg, there is a good Bordeaux Supérieur under the label Chapelle de Barbe.

Château Mendoce (G), Villeneuve, 33710 Bourg-sur-Gironde. Tel: 57.42.25.95. Visiting hours: By appt. This good Bourg estate is worth visiting for its château alone, one of the few medieval castles in the Bordeaux region.

Sights

The most famous sights in this region are the Médoc châteaux but not many of them allow visitors beyond their wine cellars. Although the town of St Emilion makes up for this, having become a tourist attraction in itself, most of the wine villages themselves are not very exciting despite their famous names. Visitors will find plenty to see, however, in Bordeaux, which is a remarkable and rather under-appreciated city, full of cultural and historical attractions. It is a convenient and comfortable base for exploring the famous vineyards nearby.

BLAYE

Vauban, the famous 17th-century military architect, was commissioned by Louis XIV to build the sprawling, well-preserved **Citadelle** that attracts visitors here today. With fine views overlooking the Gironde it contains a local history museum, and an extremely comfortable hotel and restaurant, La Citadelle (see page 52).

BORDEAUX

Bordeaux, the capital of Aquitaine and an important port, is one of the most exciting cities in France with elegant 18th-century architecture while the quays bordering the Garonne are an impressive sight. The **pl. de la Comédie** is the heart of the 18th-century city and is dominated by the colonnaded façade of the **Grand Théâtre**. Many of the elegant streets nearby are being carefully restored and contain the city's finest shops. The **Esplanade des Quinconces** facing the Garonne is one of the largest gardens in Europe.

Facing the cathedral is the **Hôtel de Ville**, behind which is a fine garden containing the **Musée des Beaux-Arts** and the **Musée d'Aquitaine**. In the nearby Hôtel de Lalande is the **Musée des Arts Décoratifs**, with a rich collection.

BOURG

There is a fine view of the Dordogne from the terrace near the church in the old town and from the **Château de la Citadelle**, a former summer residence of the archbishops of Bordeaux, which has a magnificent park.

To the east of Bourg near Prignac are the **Grottes de Pair-non-Pair** with prehistoric paintings of mammoths, bison and horses.

BUDOS

Just to the north of the village are the imposing ruins of a feudal castle built in the early 14th century by a nephew of Pope Clement V, who had been archbishop of Bordeaux.

CADILLAC

On a hill overlooking the Garonne, Cadillac was founded as a fortified village in 1280 and part of the ramparts still remain. There is a beautiful gateway onto the Garonne (**Porte de la Mer**) and an arcaded square. The huge **Château**, built between 1598 and 1620, is now the headquarters of the Connétablie de Guyenne wine society, which holds free wine tastings in the west wing of the château. A *vin nouveau* festival is held annually in Cadillac during Sep–Oct.

CHATEAU DE LA BREDE

This attractive moated castle was once the home of the 17th-century French statesman and philosopher, Montesquieu, and still belongs to his descendants. His room and the vaulted library with 7,000 volumes are still as they were when he lived at the château.

Montesquieu's home at la Brède.

CUSSAC-LE-VIEUX

Along with the citadel at Blaye, Vauban built **Fort Médoc**, still in good condition, to protect Bordeaux from attacks from the sea. From its ramparts there are fine views of the Gironde.

LIBOURNE

On the right bank of the Dordogne where it is joined by the river Isle, Libourne was once a fortified city and an important river port, though less so now. It is still a busy center of the Bordeaux wine trade.

ST EMILION

Perched on a steep hill overlooking the vineyards, St Emilion deserves its reputation as the most beautiful wine town in the whole region and it is hard to imagine that this peaceful, well-preserved town has had a long and bloody history, fought over by French and English, and Catholics and Huguenots. The narrow, winding streets are still encircled by medieval ramparts.

Not to be missed is the subterranean **Eglise Monolithe**, carved out of the hillside in the early 12th-century. From the **Château du Roi**, built by Henry III of England, there is a superb view of the surrounding vineyards which press close up to the town ramparts.

ST MACAIRE

Founded in the 12th century on the banks of the Garonne, this wine town has preserved many Gothic and Renaissance buildings, especially around the **pl. du Marché-Dieu**.

STE CROIX-DU-MONT

This pretty wine village lies on a cliff above the Garonne with the church and château on the highest part. There is a wine fair end Jul–beginning Aug.

VAYRES

The feudal château just outside Vayres was partly rebuilt in the 16th century and has an attractive garden sloping down to the Dordogne.

Hotels, Restaurants and Where to Buy Wine

Who would suspect that amid the vines dwell France's greatest shad enthusiasts or that the artichokes of the Médoc are as famous as its wines? Oysters from the bay of Arcachon (served here with hot pork sausage), sardines from Royan, lampreys caught in the Garonne, lamb from Pauillac and beef from nearby Bazas are all traditional fare. There are a good number of dishes *à la bordelaise* and, like their *bourguignon* counterparts, they usually involve making a red wine sauce – the most famous is *entrecôte à la bordelaise* (steak broiled over vine-cuttings and served with red wine sauce, shallots and bone marrow) and some insist that Cabernet cuttings give the best taste to the meat.

Château cookery has a reputation for being extremely simple, if not limited; the classic meal is freshly caught shad from the Gironde, grilled and served with a sorrel sauce and followed by a roast leg of lamb from Pauillac. More and more, however, Bordeaux is affirming its attachment to "the great South-West" and specialties such as *confit de canard* (salted and preserved duck) and *foie gras* are appearing on menus claiming to be typically *bordelais* (although wines from the South-West have made no such intrusion, Armagnac has replaced Cognac as the after-dinner brandy of choice). Many of the great regional specialties are only available or are at their best in the spring and early summer, by far the best time to visit the region.

With the exception of the *entrecôte*, hardly any of these preparations have a national reputation and most French people would be hard pressed to name a typically *bordelais* dish. The cooking of Bordeaux, in this respect, remains straightforward and simple and it relies almost entirely on the use of the best seasonal produce, often with little or no preparation.

There are two ways to serve great Bordeaux: in a crystal decanter with elegant food and surroundings, or, as in these two restaurants, poured from the bottle like any other wine, in a friendly atmosphere and with simple food.

Le Cellier Bordelais (R), 1 r. Porte de la Monnaie, 33800 Bordeaux. Tel: 56.31.30.30. v
The Cellier Bordelais, essentially a wine store with food, is a favorite with Bordeaux growers and shippers. There is no wine list and customers select their wines from the collection of over 50 that cover one of the walls. René Laffarge has chosen carefully and emphasis is on wines that are drinkable and of good value; great châteaux are often represented by bottles from what are normally considered the "poor" years, while less well known wines might be from better vintages. There is no more ceremony surrounding the uncorking of a Pétrus than a Côtes de Bourg – everyone clearly knows and appreciates the qualities of each.

The cooking is unpretentious and quite good; local products such as eel, shad, or lamb dominate. It is an enjoyable wine bar where the wines just happen to be fine Bordeaux.

La Tupina (R), 6 r. Porte de la Monnaie, 33800 Bordeaux. Tel: 56.91.56.37. Closed Sun and hols. AE V
Right around the corner and across the street at the Tupina, Jean-Pierre Xiradakis, whose Greek name conceals a true Gascon, is actively promoting the cooking of the South-West (which for him begins at Bordeaux). Though the famous *entrecôte à la bordelaise* is served here, *foie gras*, *confit*, and even *cassoulet* vie with it for space on the short menu.

Having toured the Médoc on foot (!) Xiradakis certainly knows the region and the wine list is full of his discoveries. More extensive than Le Cellier across the street, the selection includes some older bottles that are extremely reasonably priced. One shelf in the dining-room is lined with what is perhaps the finest collection of Armagnacs in the city.

Xiradakis believes that great Bordeaux should not be worshipped, simply respected and drunk with pleasure.

BARSAC (33720, Podensac)
Host. du Château de Rolland (R,H), on N113 S of Barsac. Tel: 56.27.15.75. AE DC V
An old Carthusian monastery situated in the middle of the vineyards. The rooms are comfortable and there are good-value menus.

BLAYE (33390)
La Citadelle (H,R), pl. d'Armes. Tel: 57.42.17.10. AE DC V
In the old citadel built by Vauban, this quiet establishment has its own small park, with a terrace and swimming pool. There are good views over the Gironde to the Médoc.

BORDEAUX (33300)
Badie (W), 62 allées Tourny. Tel: 56.52.23.72. MC V
This is one of Bordeaux's best stocked wine shops.

La Chamade (R), 20 r. Piliers de Tutelle. Tel: 56.48.13.74. One Michelin star. MC V
Reliable restaurant serves good food in a beautiful dining-room. Interesting wine list and impeccable service.

Clavel (R), 44 r. Charles-Domercq. Tel: 56.92.91.52. One Michelin star. Closed Sun–Mon. AE DC V
A Spaniard, Francis Garcia, oversees this restaurant which is one of the finest in Bordeaux. The cellar is excellent and his cooking, in the *nouvelle cuisine* style, has won him much praise. There is also a more modest bistro in the same building.

Dubern (R), 42 allées Tourny. Tel: 56.48.03.44. One Michelin star. Closed Sun. AE DC MC V
This establishment comprises wine bar, snacks and a prestigious dining-room all under one roof. The enterprising young chef, Christian Clement, serves audacious *nouvelle cuisine* dishes.

Ramet (R), 7-8 pl. Jean-Jaurès. Tel:
56.44.12.51. Closed Sat–Sun and 3 weeks
in Aug. One Michelin star. Reservations
recommended. V
One of the most popular and prestigious
addresses in Bordeaux, both for the
quality cellar and the *cuisine* of Jean
Ramet, Bordeaux's rising star. Specialties use ingredients from the South-
West. Good-value menu at lunch.

Grand Hôtel de Bordeaux (H), 5 pl.
de la Comédie. Tel: 56.90.93.44. AE
DC MC V
Near the center of the city, this hotel is
quiet and comfortable.

Hôtel des Vins (W), 106 r. Abbé-de-
l'Epée. Tel: 56.48.01.29. AE MC V
Center for tasting and buying Bordeaux
wines. Cellar visits organized to surrounding châteaux.

Normandie (H), 7 cours du 30-Juillet.
Tel: 56.52.16.80. AE DC MC V
Centrally located, comfortable and
friendly.

La Réserve (H,R), 74 av. du Bourgailh,
l'Alouette, 33600 Pessac. Tel:
56.07.13.28. Closed mid-Nov–Feb. One
Michelin star. AE DC MC V
Close to the Graves vineyards. Small
hotel with elegant dining-room, seasonal
menus and a good wine list.

BOULIAC (33270)
Le St James (R), 3 pl. Camille-Hostein.
Tel: 56.20.52.19. Two Michelin stars.
Reservations recommended. AE DC V
For many the finest restaurant in or
around Bordeaux. On a beautiful hill
overlooking the city, Jean-Marie Amat
serves dishes inspired by regional specialties (his *lamproie à la bordelaise* is
exceptional). There is a fine wine list and
a good-value fixed-price menu is served
both at lunch and dinner.

LANGON (33210)
Claude Darroze (R,H), 95 cours Gén.-
Leclerc. Tel: 56.63.00.48. Closed 2 weeks
Jan and Oct. One Michelin star. AE
DC MC V
Old, family establishment. Small menu
but excellent *cuisine* and a huge selection
of Bordeaux wines (308 to be precise) as
well as good burgundies and a superb
collection of Armagnacs. The wine list is
well organized by vintage and by price.

LESPARRE-MEDOC (33340)
La Mare aux Grenouilles (R), N on
N215. Tel: 56.41.03.46. AE DC V
An excellent cellar.

LIBOURNE (33500)
Loubat (H,R), 32 r. Chanzy. Tel:
57.51.17.58. AE MC V.
Comfortable traditional hotel. Excellent
selection of Bordeaux wines.

MARGAUX (33460)
Auberge le Savoie (R). Tel:
56.88.31.76. No cards.
Small, interesting restaurant with a huge
selection of Bordeaux wines.

Relais de Margaux (H,R), BP 5. Tel:
56.88.38.30. Closed Dec–Mar. One
Michelin star. AE DC V
Overlooking the Gironde and next door
to Château Margaux, this new
establishment is an excellent base for
touring the Médoc. The cellar is truly
exceptional with a wide range of Bordeaux wines at all prices. Visits to nearby
châteaux can be arranged with notice.

QUINSAC (33360, Latresne)
Robinson (R), 2km SE on D10. Tel:
56.21.31.09. Closed Tue, and mid-Nov–
mid-Mar. MC V
On the banks of the Garonne, this
restaurant serves regional *cuisine*.

ST EMILION (33330)
Auberge de la Commanderie (H,R),
r. des Cordeliers. Tel: 57.24.70.19. Closed
mid-Dec–mid-Jan, and (R) Tue. MC V
Pleasant and traditionally decorated
rooms.

Le Cellier des Gourmets (W), le
Castellot. Tel: 57.74.46.92. No cards.
A good choice of local wines.

Logis de la Cadène (R), pl. du
Marché-au-Bois. Tel: 57.24.71.40.
Closed Sun pm–Mon. Open for lunch all
year and also dinner Jul–Sep. MC V
Good-value traditional food.

Hostellerie de Plaisance (H,R), pl.
du Clocher. Tel: 57.24.72.32. Closed Jan.
AE DC MC V
Quiet establishment with luxurious
rooms overlooking the town and surrounding vineyards. Good wine list.

BURGUNDY

Burgundy is rural France as idealized by poets: rolling hills, timeless vineyards, grazing cattle, Romanesque churches and stone-built houses with colorful tiled roofs. It is a land of farmers and *vignerons* who live simply and there is little to suggest that this is some of the most coveted real estate in the world. The names of its towns and hamlets are known around the world because so many of them are the names of famous Burgundy wine. These cunning Burgundians know the world is watching them but they tend their grapes as though they were indifferent to their fame and, indeed, for the most part they are. The world may see Burgundy as a great wine region with famous growths; Burgundians, however, think in terms of tiny parcels and minuscule strips of land, and this explains both their modesty and their pride.

In Burgundy, you are constantly surprised by the beauty and variety of the landscape. Vines cover the plains and hills in all directions, then give way to large areas where no grapes grow, where cattle graze or trees bear fruit. Forests are never far from sight. Once a duchy extending north through Flanders and south along the Rhône, Burgundy is rich in man-made attractions. The dukes of Burgundy made Dijon a city of outstanding beauty, while Cluny, farther south, was one of the most powerful centers of medieval Christianity. The Hospices at Beaune, with its stunning multicolored roof, contrasts with the simplicity of the nearby small villages amid the vineyards.

As the French say, this is a place where *il fait bon vivre* (it is a pleasure to live). With its peaceful valleys, forests, and rivers, Burgundy is not only an eminently comfortable place but, like the wines which are produced here, hard to leave and impossible to forget.

The Wines of Burgundy

Today burgundy in the widest legitimate sense can come from one of six different growing areas: Chablis and the area around Auxerre; the Côte d'Or, made up of the Côte de Nuits stretching from Dijon to just north of Beaune and the Côte de Beaune, extending from the end of the Côte de Nuits south to Santenay; the Côte Chalonnaise which is a small group of vineyards south of Chagny; the Mâconnais which is a large area to the west and south of Tournus, extending beyond Mâcon; and the Beaujolais, the southernmost Burgundy vineyards which stretch from below Mâcon to just north of Lyon.

Burgundy wine means the Côte d'Or to most people; not surprising perhaps, since the wines from the Mâconnais and, even more so, from Beaujolais, rarely compare in quality with the great wines of the Côte d'Or. These two southern districts are much the larger geographically and consequently produce much more wine; the Beaujolais alone yields almost twice as much wine as all the northern vineyards combined.

Nowhere in France is the wine trade more complicated. Part of the reason lies in land ownership. The great monastic holdings were dismantled after the Revolution and sold off in tiny plots to the local peasants. The French laws of inheritance whereby every child has an equal share, and not just the eldest son, has meant that with the passage of time the plots became so small as to become uneconomic. The famous Clos de Vougeot, for example, which covers only 50 hectares, has 79 owners, some only with a few rows of vines.

There are five levels of *appellation* in Burgundy. Bourgogne is the overall regional *appellation* for red, white and rosé wines and Crémant de Bourgogne is for champagne-method sparkling wines. Reds are made from Pinot Noir and Gamay and whites from Chardonnay or Aligoté. Bourgogne Passetoutgrain is red or rosé made from a blend of Pinot Noir and Gamay and can be good. Next are the specific regional *appellations* – for example, "Chablis" covers all the less good vineyards in Chablis, and Hautes Côtes de Nuits and Hautes Côtes de Beaune cover the villages up in the hills behind the Côte d'Or.

Village *appellations* cover a single village only, such as Meursault or Gevrey-Chambertin. Sometimes vineyard names or *lieux dits* are used on the labels along with the village name. Then come the *premier cru* vineyards which are very specific sites and best of all are the *grand cru* vineyards found only in Chablis and the Côte d'Or. In Chablis the seven *grands crus* are huddled together on one slope above the town but in the Côte d'Or they are spread out between Gevrey-Chambertin and Vosne-Romanée and are all for red wines, except for a few white vines in Musigny. As always in Burgundy, the winemaker's name is all important and there are some *premiers crus* which reach the level of several *grands crus*.

Visiting the Vineyards

The following routes cover the six great wine-growing areas of Burgundy from north to south. Between Chablis in the north and Beaujolais in the south are the great vineyards of the Côte d'Or and the Côte Chalonnaise and the Mâconnais. Generally speaking, the farther south you go the more time is spent driving on twisting mountain roads and the more spectacular is the scenery. To see the real Burgundian countryside it is essential to get out onto the narrow country roads and often even the locals have to think twice before giving you directions on how to get to the next town.

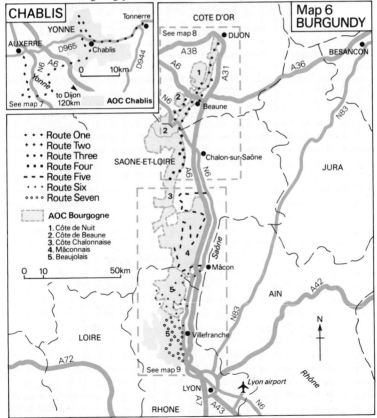

Route One

From Auxerre to Chablis: 70km

The region of Chablis is often called *l'Ile Vineuse* because the peaceful river valley of the Serein stands apart from the rest of the Burgundian vineyards. It produces a dry wine that has enjoyed an international reputation since the Middle Ages. Chablis is made only from the Chardonnay grape and production is divided, in ascending order of quality, into Petit Chablis, Chablis, Chablis *premier cru* and Chablis *grand cru*. The lesser wines are generally produced between Poinchy and Villy and around Courgis and the best *premiers crus* and *grands crus* between Maligny and Fleys. The seven *grands crus* are Blanchots, Bougros, les Clos, Grenouilles, les Preuses, Valmur and Vaudésir, all situated on a single sweep of hill above the town of Chablis and the Serein. The *premiers crus* are Montée de Tonnerre, Fourchaume, Mont de Milieu, Côte de Léchet, Montmains, Vaucoupin, les Fourneaux, Beauroy, Vaillans and Vosgros. Chablis is a rather sleepy place despite its famous name and the surrounding villages are relatively unspoilt.

Other wine-producing towns of the Yonne are Coulanges, Irancy and St Bris. From Coulanges come a light, fruity Bourgogne and sometimes Passetoutgrain; Irancy is noted for its rustic reds made from Pinot Noir and occasionally César (Côte de Palotte from the village of Cravant is the most outstanding *cru*) and St Bris makes a splendidly pungent Sauvignon de St Bris VDQS as well as some Chardonnay and Aligoté.

The Itinerary:

Leave Auxerre following the signs for Vaux, Avallon, and Lyon on D163. Passing through **Vaux**, follow the signs for Avallon, still on D163, then, after a short stretch on N6, turn right onto D463 toward **Escolives-Ste Camille** and left on D563 to enter the town. The rolling hills dotted with orchards give no indication that this is wine country. In Escolives watch for the sign indicating **Coulanges-la-Vineuse** and turn right when you see it. Vines now appear and there is a beautiful view of the surrounding countryside. Drive straight into Coulanges, bearing left and following the signs to **Vincelles** and **Vincelottes** on D85, then continue to the pretty village of **Irancy** on D38. Look for signs indicating **St Bris-le-Vineux** on the left, and take the road through the middle of the vineyards; turn left again at the T-junction to drive into the village.

Just inside St Bris, a hard right turn onto D62 will take you toward Chablis. Pass through **Chitry**, with its beautiful church, and continue on D62 which climbs through sparse vineyards as it approaches **Courgis**. After Courgis, the small town of Chablis can be seen in the valley in the distance; take the left fork to **Chablis**. On the hills that slope down immediately behind the town are the famous *grand cru* vineyards.

In Chablis turn left, following the signs toward Auxerre on D965; the **Milly** turnoff is to the left on D131 if you want to see growers there. At **Poinchy** bear right on D131

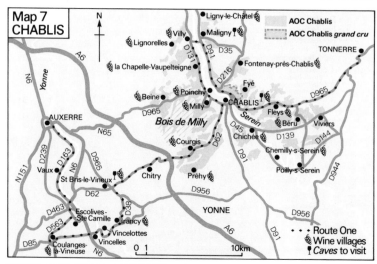

past the forest and along the Serein toward the villages of **la Chapelle-Vaupelteigne** and **Villy**. At Villy, turn right toward **Maligny** on D35; once there, follow the signs back toward Chablis on D91 past the *premier* and *grand cru* vineyards. This is the most beautiful stretch of vineyards in the region, with vines growing right down to the roadside. As you approach Chablis, either go straight into town, or continue left following D965 along the vineyards to **Fleys**. From Fleys, you can return along the same road into Chablis, or drive on to **Tonnerre** and thence south to Dijon and into the heart of Burgundy.

Route Two

The Côte de Nuits, from Dijon to Magny-lès-Villers: 40km

The Côte de Nuits begins at Marsannay, only a few kilometers south of Dijon. Though N74 is the fastest and busiest road between Dijon and Beaune, the following itinerary avoids it as much as possible and gives priority to country roads that enable you to see more of the vineyards. The names of the villages are those of the most famous wines in Burgundy: Gevrey-Chambertin, Morey-St Denis, Chambolle-Musigny, Vougeot and so on. Be sure to visit the château of the Clos de Vougeot or at least follow the example of one of Napoleon's generals who ordered his troops to salute as they passed it on their way to war.

Included in this route are the Hautes Côtes de Nuits, to the west of the Côte de Nuits, where good red wines and some excellent whites are made, particularly in Villers-la-Faye and Magny-lès-Villers while the scenery is positively sylvan.

The Itinerary:

In **Dijon**, follow the signs toward Lyon; watch for a sign indicating the *Route des Grands Crus* and **Chenôve** and **Marsannay-la-Côte** on D122, a small road that forks to the right off N74 just after it crosses the canal. As you approach Marsannay, vineyards appear on rugged hills, with vines growing down to the road, although generally speaking the best burgundies come from the vineyards on the *côtes* toward the tops of the hills. Continue through Marsannay and **Couchey** along D122, following the signs for the *Route des Grands Crus* to **Fixin**, where a sign proudly proclaims: "It is here that the great wines begin" (*Ici commencent les grandes appellations*). Continue on D122 through **Gevrey-Chambertin**, the largest village *appellation* of the Côte de Nuits, and **Morey-St Denis**. All along the road signs indicate specific *crus* or *appellations*; "Here Chambertin begins", "Here Chambertin ends", "Clos de la Roche", "Morey-St Denis, pride of the *grands crus*".

The road climbs up from Morey-St Denis on its way to **Chambolle-Musigny**, a pretty village at the top of a hill, then continues to **Vougeot**, famous for the walled vineyard Clos de Vougeot and the largest *climat* in Burgundy, and for the Confrérie des Chevaliers du Tastevin who hold banquets and tastings in the château.

The *Route des Grands Crus* then passes through **Vosne-Romanée**, which has five *grands crus*, some of the most famous and expensive wines in the world. After Vosne join N74 to enter the town of **Nuits St Georges**. Continue on N74 through **Comblanchien**, then turn right toward **Villers-la-Faye**, and the Hautes Côtes de Nuits. In the middle of Villers, turn left on D115J to **Magny-lès-Villers**, from which **Beaune** can be reached by way of routes D115C and N74, or continue on to **Pernand-Vergelesses** to explore the Côte de Beaune.

Route Three

The Côte de Beaune, from Magny-lès-Villers to Santenay: 65km

From the Côte de Beaune come the famous wines of Aloxe-Corton, Volnay and Pommard, as well as the extraordinary white burgundies of Meursault, Chassagne-Montrachet and Puligny-Montrachet. This route has spectacular views of vineyards, some stunning buildings such as the Château de la Rochepot with its spectacular tiled roof, and Beaune itself, the heart of the Côte d'Or and a delightful, bustling town with beautiful buildings, fascinating wine cellars and good restaurants.

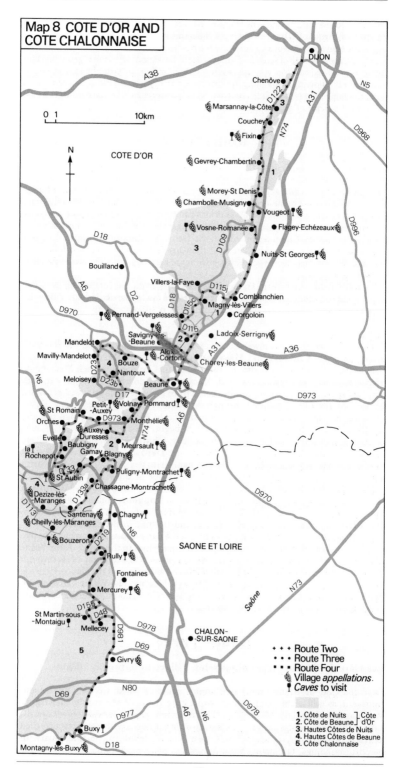

Map 8 COTE D'OR AND COTE CHALONNAISE

0 1 10km

N

COTE D'OR

DIJON

Chenôve

Marsannay-la-Côte

Couchey

Fixin

Gevrey-Chambertin

Morey-St Denis

Chambolle-Musigny

Vougeot

Vosne-Romanée

Flagey-Echézeaux

Nuits-St Georges

Bouilland

Villers-la-Faye

Comblanchien

Magny-lès-Villers

Corgoloin

Pernand-Vergelesses

Ladoix-Serrigny

Savigny-lès-Beaune

Aloxe-Corton

Mandelot

Chorey-les-Beaune

Mavilly-Mandelot

Bouze

Nantoux

Meloisey

Beaune

Petit-Auxey

Volnay

Pommard

St Romain

Monthélie

Orches

Auxey-Duresses

Meursault

Evelle

Baubigny

Gamay

Blagny

la Rochepot

St Aubin

Puligny-Montrachet

Dezize-lès-Maranges

Chassagne-Montrachet

Santenay

Chagny

Cheilly-lès-Maranges

Bouzeron

Rully

SAONE ET LOIRE

Fontaines

Mercurey

St Martin-sous-Montaigu

Mellecey

CHALON-SUR-SAONE

Givry

Saône

Buxy

Montagny-les-Buxy

+ + + Route Two
• • • Route Three
▪ ▪ ▪ Route Four
🍇 Village *appellations*.
🍷 *Caves* to visit

1. Côte de Nuits ⎤ Côte
2. Côte de Beaune ⎦ d'Or
3. Hautes Côtes de Nuits
4. Hautes Côtes de Beaune
5. Côte Chalonnaise

58

The Itinerary:
Magny-lès-Villers, north-west of Beaune, is the most southern village of the Hautes Côte de Nuits. From there, follow the signs for **Pernand-Vergelesses**, the first Côte de Beaune village. The road is narrow and twists through vineyards and pine woods before reaching a plateau with a magnificent view over the entire valley. In Pernand, a beautiful village whose church has a black and gold tiled roof, follow the road down the hill, turn left on D18, then left again on D115 which leads through **Aloxe-Corton**. Turn right on N74 toward Beaune, then follow the signs right toward **Savigny-lès-Beaune**. Follow the signs to the château to reach the center of the village. Return to N74 by the same road and then turn right for **Beaune**, the wine capital of Burgundy.

Having visited Beaune follow the signs *Toutes Directions* until you reach the turnoff indicating **Bouze**. This road is D970. Drive through Bouze, then take the side road to the left opposite the sign indicating Savigny; this tiny, twisting road will take you to **Mandelot** and provide beautiful views of the countryside on the way. Follow the road through the village, then turn left on D23, an uphill road through farmland and vineyards leading to **Mavilly**, where signs indicate Meloisey and the Hautes Côtes de Beaune. Just before Meloisey, turn left on D23B to **Nantoux**, then follow the signs right for Monthélie and Meursault. Watch for a left turn on D17 and follow it into **Pommard**, once apparently the site of a temple dedicated to Pomona, the Roman goddess of fruits. In Pommard, turn right on r. Charnot, then drive through the vineyards following the signs to Auxey-Duresses on D973.

This road bypasses Volnay up on its hillside before turning off right for **Monthélie**. Leave Monthélie bearing left down the hill, then cross D973 to **Meursault**. On the outskirts of Meursault, take a sharp right to go to **Auxey-Duresses**; from there follow the signs for Autun on D973 and then turn right on D17E to St Romain. Down the road from Auxey is the pretty little village of **Petit-Auxey**, from which you can see distant cliffs and a dramatic panorama. Leaving **St Romain**, take a left turn toward Ivry-en-Montagne, then follow the signs right to **Orches** on a twisting road that climbs to the top of the cliffs seen earlier, where there is a magnificent view of the valley. At Orches turn left, following the *Circuit Touristique* and the Hautes Côtes de Beaune through the villages of **Evelle** and **Baubigny**.

After Baubigny, the road dips down toward **la Rochepot**, passing in front of the impressive medieval château. At the junction indicating Autun, turn left on D33; this is the road to **St Aubin**, and once you have passed the trees it is worth stopping to admire the view of Château de la Rochepot and the valley.

Drive through St Aubin, then turn left on N6 and immediately fork left on the tiny road which leads through the vineyards to the small village of **Gamay**, where the road really begins to twist and turn. At the junction, turn right, then, at the stop sign, turn immediately left to head for the hamlet of **Blagny**. Once again you will have a magnificent view of the enormous expanse of the surrounding vineyards. From Blagny, the road dips sharply downward toward **Puligny-Montrachet** at the bottom of the hill. In Puligny follow the signs on D113A for **Chassagne-Montrachet**, crossing N6 on your way, then continue to **Santenay**.

Route Four

The Côte Chalonnaise, from Chagny to Montagny-les-Buxy: 45km

The Côte Chalonnaise is crammed into the hills and valleys between the Côte de Beaune and the Mâconnais and produces lighter red wines than its northern neighbor. Bouzeron, Rully, Mercurey, Givry and Montagny are the only villages to have their own *appellations* and the area makes some good red and white Bourgogne. The red wines are made mainly from Pinot Noir with some Gamay and those from Mercurey are generally the best. The whites come from Chardonnay and Aligoté and Rully has a good reputation, particularly for its Crémant de Bourgogne.

The Itinerary:
In **Chagny** follow the signs first to Cluny, then to Givry on D981; just outside Chagny, after crossing the railway track, turn right at the sign indicating *Bourgogne Aligoté de Bouzeron*, driving through the hills to **Bouzeron**, a sleepy little village.

After Bouzeron the road climbs through the vineyards and leads to **Rully**. Turn left at the Rully post office (PTT), then, at a roundabout with a large stone marker and a profusion of signposts, turn right into the center of the village. Leave Rully along this road then, after passing a church on your left, fork right onto a dirt road through the vineyards. A little farther on, the road is paved again as it approaches **Mercurey** at the bottom of the hill. Turn left on D978 at the T-junction, drive through the village, then turn right onto D155 at the sign indicating St Martin-sous-Montaigu.

Drive through **St Martin-sous-Montaigu**, bear left at the stone cross and follow the main road around to the left and down into the valley until you come to a left-hand fork indicating the way to **Mellecey**. Continue left on D48 through the outskirts of the village, then turn right onto D981 through **Givry** and on to **Buxy**. In Buxy follow the signs to Montceau onto D977, which runs through beautiful rolling hills to **Montagny-les-Buxy**. From here return to Buxy and follow D18 to **Sennecy-le-Grand**, the starting point of the route through the Mâconnais.

Château de Fuissé is one of the best producers of the famous Pouilly-Fuissé.

Route Five

The Mâconnais, from Sennecy-le-Grand to Mâcon: 130km

The Mâconnais lies between the Côte Chalonnaise and the upper Beaujolais and was until recently a predominantly red wine area using mainly Gamay and increasingly Pinot Noir. Its main claim to fame is Pouilly-Fuissé, an excellent white but usually overpriced. The Mâconnais is hilly and the vineyards mix with farmland and orchards in the north, giving way to rugged, flat-topped hills in the south near Milly-Lamartine and Pierreclos. This is a region of co-operatives and there are several good ones.

The Itinerary:
From **Sennecy-le-Grand**, take D18 into **Laives** and follow the signs first for **Lalheue** on D181, then for **la Chapelle-de-Bragny** on D6 and **Messey-sur-Grosne** on D147 past the beautiful 13th-century Château de Dordogne. From Messey, take D49 toward St Gengoux-le-National; you are now on the *Route du Mâconnais et du Beaujolais*. Follow the sign for Courtil and the *Route des Vins*, then take the first road you come to on the left; at the top of the hill continue on through **Bresse-sur-Grosne** and **Champigny-sous-Uxelles** to meet D215. Cross over D215 to **Chapaize** and in the village turn left onto D14 toward **Martailly-lès-Brancion** through spectacular hilly farmland. The vines reappear at Martailly; continue on D14, then turn right on D163 past **Gratay** to **Chardonnay** and **Uchizy**. At Uchizy turn right on D210 in the direction of Montbellet; after **Mercey** drive straight ahead toward Viré, turning left onto D106 at **Thurissey**. From **Viré** head south for Clessé; in **le Buc** turn right toward Péronne on D15 but watch for the left-hand Clessé turnoff onto D403bis. After passing through **Quintaine** you will reach **Clessé**; follow the signs indicating the *Eglises Romanes*, bearing right when leaving the village. Drive to **Lugny** on D103, the road twisting and turning through the woods.

In Lugny, which has a good modern wine co-operative, turn left on D82 through **Bissy-la-Mâconnaise** and on to **Azé**; at the junction with D15 turn right into Azé, then right again just outside the village to pick up D85, which will take you through **le Martoret, Igé, Verzé** and **la Roche-Vineuse**, where there is a beautiful view of the surrounding hills and the valley. Turn right in la Roche and follow the signs to

Berzé-le-Ville on D220. Just before the village is a stone cross on a wall; turn left here toward the Chapelle des Moines. At the bottom of the hill turn right, then left under the railway track to enter **Sologny**. The route here is only 5km south of Cluny via N79 and D980; and the town is worth visiting if time allows.

To continue on the route to **Milly-Lamartine**, look for a tiny dirt road called *la Rue* that forms a hairpin turn to the left just as you enter Sologny. At Milly, continue on the same road through the village, following the signs to **Pierreclos**; along here the vines grow right up to the roadside. At the bottom of the hill, turn left to drive into Pierreclos; go around the church, then turn right on D177 in the direction of **Vergisson**. Continue along this road as it twists and turns through woods into a beautiful valley where grapes grow up the sides of flat-topped hills.

From Vergisson follow the signs left on D117 to **Davayé** and Mâcon. Leaving Davayé, a sharp right onto D54 will take you into **Solutré** at the foot of the famous Roche de Solutré. Just past the church, an old sign on the side of a house on the left indicates the winding road to **Pouilly** and **Fuissé**; follow the signs for the *Circuit Pouilly-Fuissé*, then, in the middle of Fuissé, turn right on D172 for **Chasselas**. This road provides a very pretty view as you approach the village. From Chasselas go through **Leynes** on D31, then, before you reach Chânes, take the left turnoff onto D209 to **Chaintré**, another village in the Pouilly-Fuissé *appellation*. Continue on through **Vinzelles** to **Mâcon** by way of D169.

Route Six

Haut Beaujolais, from Mâcon to Villefranche: 125km

The Haut Beaujolais (upper Beaujolais) is where all the famous Beaujolais *crus* are found and most of the villages entitled to the *appellation* Beaujolais-Villages are here. High hills cut by valleys produce a variety of microclimates that explains, in part, the diversity of the wines produced here. The whole region is full of twisting country lanes, rolling hills and vineyards, but the circuit from Beaujeu to Quincié-en-Beaujolais is the most spectacular part of the route; it is also one of the most difficult to drive, given the conditions of the roads which vary from enlarged footpaths to narrow, paved roads. Road numbers are indicated poorly, if at all, so the traveler should be ready for some adventurous driving.

The Itinerary:
From **Mâcon** take N6 south to **Crêches-sur-Saône**. After the sign *Route des vins, droite au feu*, turn right at the next traffic lights toward **le Bourg Neuf** on D31. From there follow the signs for **St Amour**, the first Beaujolais *cru* on our route, then turn left through the vineyards to **Juliénas**. At the main junction in Juliénas, turn left toward Fleurie; at the next fork bear right, then follow the signs for Fleurie (don't miss the hard right turn at the next main junction). This winding uphill road goes through **les Deschamps** where signs point toward the *Route des Vins*, Chénas and Fleurie. In **Chénas**, a left turn takes you through the vines toward **la Chapelle-de-Guinchay**, turning right onto D166 at the next main intersection. As you enter la Chapelle watch for the right-hand road leading to **Romanèche-Thorins**. In Romanèche, bear right to follow the *Route des Vins* on D266 through **Moulin-à-Vent** with its famous windmill and houses with attractive tiled roofs. Then take the left fork and turn left again at the next main junction onto a winding road that leads to **Fleurie**.

From Fleurie, drive through **la Chapelle des Bois** to **Chiroubles**, set high on a hill with a magnificent view of the surrounding hills and vineyards. Leave Chiroubles by the same road you came in on and head for **Lancié** on D119. At Lancié, turn left toward the Pont de Thoissey on D86, then follow the signs to the right for **Corcelles-en-Beaujolais**; on the way to Corcelles you will pass the fine Château de Corcelles where Beaujolais-Villages is made. Turn right at the junction toward Beaujeu, then continue on D9 to **Villié-Morgon**, bearing left at the fork in the road, then left on D18 toward Belleville. Turn right, following the signs for **Morgon**, then left at the intersection in the village to rejoin D18 toward Belleville, driving past Château de Pizay, a hotel, restaurant and an excellent Beaujolais property all in one, on the left. Visit **Belleville**, the wine capital of Beaujolais, or turn right onto D37 to **Beaujeu**, the former capital of the Beaujolais area and a busy wine town.

Continue through Beaujeu, still on D37E; at **les Dépôts**, take a sharp left on D129 to **St Didier-sur-Beaujeu** where you bear left toward the Col de la Casse-Froide on a road that snakes through forests of fir trees with magnificent views of the surrounding hills. At the top of the hill, turn left onto a tiny road that winds through beautiful vineyards onto D9 to **Quincié-en-Beaujolais**. From Quincié, head first in the direction of Belleville, then turn right onto D43. Mt Brouilly is now on the left; every year on September 8 local winegrowers make their way to the chapel on the summit. The villages of **Brouilly, Odenas**, and **St Etienne-des-Ouillières** lie on or near D43 on the way to **Villefranche-sur-Saône**.

Route Seven

Bas Beaujolais: Villefranche to le Bois-d'Oingt and back: 115km

The wines of the Bas Beaujolais (lower Beaujolais) south of Villefranche are not as remarkable as those to the north, but the scenery is still spectacular. This is where most of the wine simply labeled Beaujolais or Beaujolais Supérieur comes from and much of this harvest now is made into Beaujolais Nouveau. This is a region of co-operatives and nearly every village has its own *caveau* with signs inviting you to come and taste the local Beaujolais.

Although the route is in the form of a loop, it is a long drive and the most spectacular scenery is in the first half. The route can therefore be shortened by leaving it at its southernmost point (Lozanne) and heading, for example, straight to Lyon.

The Itinerary:

In **Villefranche**, follow the signs north on N6 toward Mâcon, then to **Arnas** on D43. In Arnas turn left on D35 to **la Grange Perret** and **St Julien**. Continue on D35 and D19 until you reach the intersection with D49, then turn left toward **Vaux-en-Beaujolais**, the wine-making village used as a model for Clochemerle, in the novel of the same name by Chevalier. At Vaux, head for Lamure on D49E. At the junction with D504 turn left toward **Rivolet**, driving downhill through beautiful pastureland. Note the château of **Montmélas-St Sorlin** with its picturesque turrets off to the left, an island in a sea of vineyards. Just after Rivolet turn right onto D19, driving through **Cogny**, a pretty little village on the top of a rise, to **la Maladière**, where you turn right and then fork left onto D120 toward the attractive village of **Oingt**. In Oingt turn right, then, as you leave the village, follow D96 sharp right through **St Laurent-d'Oingt**. Immediately after crossing the railroad track, turn left toward Lyon on D485; stay on this road until the turnoff for **Châtillon**, unless making a detour to visit **le Bois-d'Oingt**.

In Châtillon with its château "of the golden stones" (*"des pierres dorées"*), turn left on D76, then take the second right and follow the signs on D70E and D70 toward **Charnay** where the houses are built of the same "golden stone" as the château. In Charnay follow D100 toward Morance. Continue on D100 until you reach a fork with large arrows indicating the main road to the left; leave D100 here and bear right driving downhill. At the bottom of the hill, turn right onto a small uphill road in the middle of the vineyards which leads to **St Jean-des-Vignes**. Continue over the hill, turning left at the first junction, then left again toward **Lozanne**. From Lozanne you can take D485 east until it meets N6 leading to **Lyon**. To return to Villefranche through the vineyards follow the signs toward **Chazay-d'Azergues** on D30 as you come into Lozanne; from Chazay follow the signs for **Morance** still on D30. The countryside gives way to a more suburban setting but this will change again.

Drive into Morance, take the left fork at the green metal cross and turn left again at the next junction. At **St Pierre** follow the signs for Charnay, but take the right fork toward les Beluises, then turn right at the next large road, D70, which takes you through lovely orchards. Continue on through **Lachassagne** toward **Pommiers**, turning left at the sign indicating *Pommiers (Bourg)*. Turn left after the parking lot, then right toward **la Grange Huget**, driving straight through the vineyards on a tiny road called the Chemin du Déo to the main road, D38. Turn right and drive past **Liergues** and **Gleizé** to **Villefranche**. Villefranche is only 25km by autoroute from the great gastronomic city of Lyon which, for most people, will be the place to end any visit to the Beaujolais.

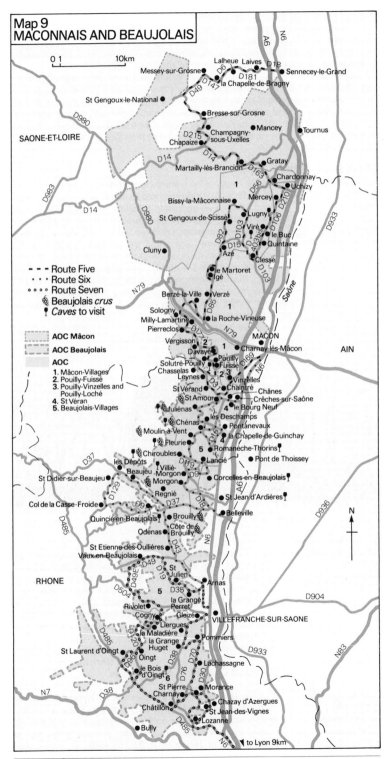

Map 9
MACONNAIS AND BEAUJOLAIS

0 1   10km

Lalheue Laives
Messey-sur-Grosne   Sennecey-le-Grand
D6   D18
D181
la Chapelle-de-Bragny
D49 D147
St Gengoux-le-National
D980
Bresse-sur-Grosne
SAONE-ET-LOIRE
Champagny-   Mancey   Tournus
D215   sous-Uxelles
Chapaize
D14
D14
Martailly-lès-Brancion   Gratay
D163
1   Chardonnay
D56   Uchizy
Bissy-la-Mâconnaise   Mercey   D706 D210
St Gengoux-de-Scissé   Lugny
D82 D103   Viré   le Buc
D983
D15   Quintaine
D14   Azé   Clessé
Cluny   le Martoret   D103
Igé
Berzé-la-Ville   Verzé
Sologny   D85
Milly-Lamartine   la Roche-Vineuse
Pierreclos   1
Vergisson   N79   MACON   AIN
2   1
Davayé   Charnay-lès-Mâcon
Pouilly-   D169
Solutré-Pouilly   Fuissé   N6
Chasselas   2 3
Leynes   Vinzelles
St Vérand   Chaintré
D3   Chânes
St Amour   Crèches-sur-Saône
4   le Bourg Neuf
Juliénas
Chénas   les Deschamps
Pontanevaux
Moulin-à-Vent   la Chapelle-de-Guinchay
Fleurie   4
Chiroubles   Romanèche-Thorins
5
les Dépôts   D119   Lancié   Pont de Thoissey
Beaujeu
D37   Villié-   D9
St Didier-sur-Beaujeu   Morgon   Corcelles-en-Beaujolais
D129   Morgon
Regnié   D37   St Jean d'Ardières
Col de la Casse-Froide   D9
D16   Belleville
D485   Quincié-en-Beaujolais   Brouilly
Odenas   Côte de
St Etienne-des-Oullières   Brouilly
Vaux-en-Beaujolais   D43
D49   St   D936
D46   Julien
D504   D19   Arnas
D35
5   la Grange
RHONE   Rivolet   Perret   D904
Cogny   Gleizé
Liergues,   VILLEFRANCHE-SUR-SAONE
la Maladière,
la Grange   Pommiers   D933
St Laurent d'Oingt   Huget
D20   Oingt   D38   Lachassagne   D30
le Bois   D76   N83
d'Oingt   6   Morancé
St Pierre   Chazay d'Azergues
N7   Charnay   St Jean-des-Vignes
Châtillon   Lozanne
Bully   D485   to Lyon 9km
N6

- - - Route Five
· · · Route Six
∘∘∘ Route Seven
🍇 Beaujolais crus
🍷 Caves to visit

AOC Mâcon

AOC Beaujolais

AOC
1. Mâcon-Villages
2. Pouilly-Fuissé
3. Pouilly-Vinzelles and
   Pouilly-Loché
4. St Véran
5. Beaujolais-Villages

N

A6   N6
D980
D933
D936
D904

Caves and Vineyards to Visit

In recent years a major change has occurred in the way that burgundies are made and sold. Traditionally, burgundies were made by the great shipping houses of Beaune who bought grapes from the many growers in the region with tiny parcels of land. The wines they bottled could be excellent but, from an early date, were blends that might have little or no relationship to the name on the label.

Some of the best wines in the region are still made by the great *négociants* but, nevertheless, individual growers are increasingly making and bottling their own wine and these are unquestionably the most interesting burgundies today. Although they often have parcels of land in several *appellations*, these small growers produce relatively very little wine, and since they are now doing much of the work they used to leave to the *négociants* they have little time for visitors; and a telephone call in advance is usually necessary and always polite.

ALOXE-CORTON, map 8

Château de Corton-André (M/G),
Pierre André,
Aloxe Corton,
21420 Savigny-lès-Beaune.
Tel: 80.26.44.25.

Pierre André is both a *négociant* who owns the Caves de la Reine Pédauque in Beaune and an owner of various parcels of land in some of Burgundy's leading vineyards. He is well aware of the rewards of good public relations, and both the château with its magnificent tiled roof at the edge of the tiny village of Aloxe-Corton and the modern complex at the entrance to the village near highway N74 are open to visitors.

Visitors are readily offered tastings and the chance to buy but if the firm's approach is somewhat touristy, it can also be recognized as an attempt to meet the public with an openness that might profitably be imitated by other Burgundian winemakers.

Visiting hours: Daily 10–6.
Location: Signposted in the village.

Château de Corton-André with its magnificent multicolored roof.

BEAUNE, map 8

Caves Exposition de la Reine Pédauque (M),
2 fg St Nicolas,
21200 Beaune.
Tel: 80.22.23.11.

Most visitors to Beaune driving around the boulevard just outside the town walls will pass la Reine Pédauque, a large stone building opposite Porte St Nicolas, one of the town's old gateways. Reine Pédauque is owned by Pierre André, who also owns Château de Corton-André (see above). The spacious cellars where the wines are stored are interesting to visit but the quality of la Reine Pédauque's wines is sometimes variable.

Visiting hours: Daily 9.00–11.30, 2–6; until 5.30 only from Oct–May; closed Jan 1, Nov 1 and Christmas.
Location: Opposite Porte St Nicolas.

Patriarche Père et Fils (M),
7 r. du Collège,
21200 Beaune.
Tel: 80.22.23.20.

Patriarche is one of the largest *négociants* in Burgundy and has its headquarters in a 17th-century convent. Their cellars are the largest in Burgundy and have become one of the most visited spots in Beaune. For 40 years Patriarche has been a major buyer of Hospices de Beaune wines at the famous annual auction in November and the cellars store a wide variety of wines, ranging in style and price from basic Aligoté to expensive *grands crus*. The Charmes-Chambertin, Volnay, Meursault Réserve Ste-Anne and Puligny-Montrachet are some of their better wines but the quality of the wines sold under the Patriarche label can be inconsistent.

Château de Meursault is one of Patriarche's domaines and makes good wines as well as being a beautiful property (see page 66).

Visiting hours: Mar–Dec 15 daily, 9.30–11.30, 2–5.30.

Location: In the center of town near the Hôtel de Ville.

BUXY, map 8
Cave des Vignerons de Buxy (C),
les Vignes de la Croix, BP 06,
71390 Buxy.
Tel: 85.92.03.03.

The Vignerons de Buxy are a good example of competent wine-making on a collective basis. Created in 1931, the co-operative draws on the output of 610 hectares of vineyards at the southern end of the Chalonnais region to make a wide variety of wines. Their best are the Aligoté, the white Montagny Premier Cru, the Mâcon Supérieur Rouge and the Bourgogne Pinot Noir. In the best vintages top vats of Pinot Noir are aged in oak barrels to give them added complexity. There are attractive cellars.

Visiting hours: Mon–Sat 8.15–12, 2–6.

Location: Next to the station on the rte de Chalon.

CHABLIS, map 7
Domaine Laroche (G/M),
22 r. Louis Bro,
89800 Chablis.
Tel: 86.42.14.30.
(Shop) 12 r. Auxerroise.

Domaine Laroche are one of the best *négociants* in Chablis and one of the most open-minded. New vinification methods are tried out here, including some aging in new oak barrels for both *grands* and *premiers crus* to give the wines more structure and weight.

Michel Laroche is the fifth generation to run the company whose headquarters and *caves* are in one of Chablis' finest old buildings, the Obédiencerie across the street from the church. Visitors, however, should go to the shop in the main street for tasting and purchase rather than the Obédiencerie. Apart from the experiments with oak barrels, the Laroche methods are among the most modern in Chablis. There are two modern plants in the nearby villages of Milly and Beines, and a small, more traditional cellar at Maligny.

As well as wines from the family's 81 hectares in Chablis, the *négociant* list is supplemented by wines from all the principal sites of Chablis, as well as from outlying vineyards of the Yonne. In 1985 Laroche became the owner of the 18-hectare estate Château de Puligny-Montrachet in the Côte d'Or.

Visiting hours: (Shop) Mon–Sat 9–12, 2–6; visits to Obédiencerie by appt.

Location: (Shop) In the main street.

CORCELLES-EN-BEAUJOLAIS, map 9
Château de Corcelles (G),
Corcelles-en-Beaujolais,
69220 Belleville-sur-Saône.
Tel: 74.66.00.24.

The fortified 15th-century Château de Corcelles is one of the most beautiful and best preserved in Beaujolais. The château is classified as a national monument and a great deal of restoration work has been carried out. The estate makes a light Beaujolais-Villages. Wines are matured in large oak casks in the attractive 17th-century *cuvier*.

Visiting hours: Mon–Sat and hols, 10–12, 2.30–6.30.

Location: Just N of Corcelles-en-Beaujolais on D9.

BURGUNDY

FUISSE, map 9

Château de Fuissé (G),
Marcel Vincent Père et Fils,
Jean-Jacques Vincent, Fuissé,
71960 Pierreclos.
Tel: 85.35.61.44.

Pouilly-Fuissé is the Mâconnais' most famous and most expensive wine, at its best producing delicious honeyed flavors, almost up to the standard of good Meursault. One of its best-known producers is the Château de Fuissé, run by Jean-Jacques Vincent, the fourth generation of the family to do so. The domaine has 20 hectares of vineyards, all planted in Chardonnay. M. Vincent makes three levels of wine: Pouilly-Fuissé Cuvée Première, Château Fuissé and Château Fuissé Vieilles Vignes made from vines over 20 years old. In a really ripe year this last wine is spectacular.

The domaine also makes a good St Véran, a neighboring *appellation* which can be as good as the best Pouilly-Fuissé at half the price.

Visiting hours: Mon–Fri 8–12, 1.30–5.30.
Location: On D209 between Pouilly and Chaintré.

MEURSAULT, map 8

Château de Meursault (G),
21190 Meursault.
Tel: 80.21.22.98.

Château de Meursault was originally built in the 15th century but considerably remodeled in the 18th and 19th centuries. It is a beautiful sight surrounded by its vineyards. The present owners are the Boisseaux family, who run the Patriarche firm of *négociants* in Beaune and since the mid-1970s they have restored the château and its outlying buildings. The magnificent cellars lie beneath the château and some were originally dug out by monks as long ago as the 12th century.

The domaine draws upon 8 hectares of vines to make a good Meursault which is highly suited to aging for a relatively long period. The Clos du Château de Meursault, a Bourgogne Blanc rather than a Meursault, is an elegant oaky wine.

Visiting hours: Daily 9.30–12, 2.30–6; closed 1st Sun of Nov.
Location: On N74 5km S of Beaune.

Château de Meursault, one of the most beautiful Côte de Beaune properties.

PERNAND-VERGELESSES, map 8

P. Dubreuil-Fontaine Père et Fils (G), Pernand-Vergelesses,
21420 Savigny-lès-Beaune.
Tel: 80.21.51.67.

Established in 1879, this domaine is the largest in the pretty village of Pernand-Vergelesses and owns a total of 20 hectares. Pierre Dubreuil is a well-known local figure and was mayor of the village for over 35 years. His son Bernard now runs the domaine.

The Ile des Vergelesses is Pernand's *premier cru* vineyard and the domaine's wine is a good example of the *cru* with deep color and a certain finesse. Dubreuil-Fontaine also owns the entire Clos Berthet vineyard and makes good red and white wines from it.

Visiting hours: Mon–Fri 9–12, 2–6.30; Sat 9–12.
Location: 7km N of Beaune by D18.

POMMARD, map 8

Château de Pommard (G), Jean-Louis Laplanche, 21630 Pommard. Tel: 80.22.07.99.

If you drive from Beaune to Pommard you cannot fail to see a beautiful white mansion on your left just before the village of Pommard. This is Château de Pommard, built in 1726 by an equerry of the king. Its current owner, Jean-Louis Laplanche, is a psychiatrist by training and a winemaker by preference. The domaine of 20 hectares is the largest single vineyard in Burgundy and is entirely surrounded by 2km of wall, a true Burgundian *clos*. The house's powerful style of Pommard has considerable strength and staying power.

Visiting hours: Mar 21–Nov 17 daily, 8.30–7.

Location: 3km S of Beaune on rte d'Autun (D973).

La ROCHEPOT, map 8

Centre Co-operatif de Diffusion et Vente (C), Château de la Rochepot, la Rochepot, 21340 Nolay. Tel: 80.21.71.37.

This visit combines seeing one of the prettiest châteaux of the region with tasting the local Hautes Côtes de Beaune wines. Château de la Rochepot and the little village immediately below it are tucked away in a valley at the southern end of the Hautes Côtes de Beaune *appellation*. The meticulously restored 17th-century château is in superb condition and has a typical Burgundian roof of multicolored tiles. Built in the 12th century it owes its name to the rocky eminence upon which it perches and to Philippe Pot, who was born in the castle in 1428. Pot served as ambassador for the Dukes of Burgundy and his fine tomb is at the Louvre in Paris.

Part of the château is open to the public and there is also a *caveau* organized by a group of local growers.

Visiting hours: (Château) Easter–Oct Wed–Mon, 10–11.30, 2–5.30; (Caveau) Jun–Aug when the château is open; Easter–May and Sep–Oct Sat–Sun only; groups by appt.

Location: N of the village of la Rochepot on D973.

RULLY, map 8

Domaine de la Renarde (G/M), Jean-Francois Delorme, r. de la République, Rully, 71150 Chagny. Tel: 85.87.10.12.

Rully has long been known as the home of a champagne-method sparkling wine made from Aligoté and Chardonnay which is now known as Crémant de Bourgogne. The village of Rully has been expanding its area under vine in recent years, mostly on the hillsides above the village.

Jean-François Delorme is one of the most energetic winemakers in the area and his estate now consists of 60 hectares of vineyards, mainly at Rully but also at Bouzeron, Givry and Mercurey. He makes a wide range of red, white and rosé wines, including an elegant white Rully les Varots. M. Delorme is the sole owner of the 18-hectare Varot vineyard, an unusual occurrence in Burgundy.

The label Delorme-Meulien is used for the *négociant* side of his business and these wines include good Crémant de Bourgogne, both white and rosé.

Visiting hours: Mon–Sat 8–12, 2–5.30.

Location: In the center of the village.

ST MARTIN-SOUS-MONTAIGU, map 8

Emile Voarick (G), le Bourg, BP 14, St Martin-sous-Montaigu, 71640 Givry. Tel: 85.45.23.23.

The *appellation* Mercurey includes wines from the village of St Martin-sous-Montaigu. Emile Voarick is a serious producer making consistently good wines. The grapes are grown on 50 hectares of vineyards divided between the Côte de Beaune and the Côte Chalonnaise and they are planted in Pinot Noir, Chardonnay and some Aligoté. Voarick is sufficiently progressive to harvest with machine but

keeps to more traditional methods of vinification. His Mercurey is well made. His red Givry and Bourgogne Rouge and his Crémant de Bourgogne are all good.
Visiting hours: Mon–Sat 8–12, 2–6.
Location: In the center of the village.

SAVIGNY-LES-BEAUNE, map 8

Domaine Chandon des Briailles (G), r. Soeur-Goby, 21420 Savigny-lès-Beaune.
Tel: 80.21.52.31.

The family has been established at Savigny since 1834 and the present owner is Comte Aymard-Claude de Nicolay. The 18th-century château is now classified as a historical monument. The domaine of 13 hectares includes vineyards in Pernand-Vergelesses and Aloxe-Corton as well as Savigny, and produces almost entirely red wines from Pinot Noir. The house displays its wines for sale in an 18th-century folly and the château has magnificent French gardens.
Visiting hours: Mon–Fri 9–12, 2–6.30; Sat–Sun by appt.
Location: In the village.

VILLIE-MORGON, map 9

Caveau de Morgon (C), le Bourg, 69910 Villié-Morgon.
Tel: 74.04.20.99.

A co-operative of growers from the Villié-Morgon area has set up an attractive tasting room in the magnificent vaulted cellars of an old 15th-century château. The Morgon made by the co-operative can be tasted and bought here and is a reliable example of the *cru*. There is a small zoo and playground in the public park surrounding the château to keep children amused while their parents enjoy a glass or two of wine. Unfortunately, the attractive setting in one of Beaujolais' best-known villages encourages many visitors at the height of summer, including scores of tourist coaches.
Visiting hours: Daily 9–12, 2–7; closed 1st 2 weeks Jan.
Location: In the public park.

VOUGEOT, map 8

Château de la Tour (G), Mmes Labet and Déchelette, Domaine du Château de la Tour, Clos Vougeot, 21640 Vougeot.
Tel: 80.62.86.13.

Clos de Vougeot, planted in the 12th century by the Citeaux monks and tended by them until the Revolution, has 50 hectares of vines divided between 79 owners, many of whom are proprietors of only a few rows of vines. However, the Domaine du Château de la Tour owns a grand total of 5.6 hectares and it is one of the few of the Clos de Vougeot proprietors to welcome visitors. Although the largest owner in the *clos*, the quality of the domaine's wine does not always live up to expectations.
Visiting hours: Apr–Oct daily, 10–12.30, 1.30–7; remainder of year by appt; groups by appt.
Location: Between the village of Vougeot and the Château du Clos de Vougeot.

Further *Caves* and Vineyards to Visit

BEAUNE, map 8

Maison Bouchard Père et Fils (M/G), au Château, BP 70, 21202 Beaune. Tel: 80.22.14. 41. Visiting hours: Sep–Jul by appt.
The house, founded in 1731, is one of the largest and most respected of Beaune *négociants* and also owns 92 hectares of vineyards, 71 of them *premiers* and *grands*

crus. Bouchard's headquarters are in a traditional old Burgundian mansion. Brand new cellars with a storage capacity of 1 million bottles have been built next to the beautiful old ones under the Château de Beaune. Bouchard Père is perhaps best known for its Domaines du Château de Beaune wines. After a few dicy years quality is now back in line.

Le BOIS D'OINGT, map 9
Vignoble Charmet (G), Pierre, Lucien et Jean-Marc Charmet, le Breuil, 69620 le-Bois d'Oingt. Tel: 74.71.64.83. Visiting hours: Mon–Sat 8–7.
If you want to have the essence of the fruity, juicy style of Beaujolais, Charmet is your man.

BOUZERON, map 8
Chanzy Frères (G), Domaine de l'Hermitage, Bouzeron, 71150 Chagny. Tel: 85.87.23.69. Visiting hours: Mon–Fri 8–6.
The Chanzy brothers cultivate a total of 30 hectares but their most highly rated wine comes from less than 1 hectare of the Mercurey *premier cru* Clos du Roy and the output is limited. There is also a particularly good Bourgogne Aligoté Bouzeron, a specialty of Bouzeron.

CHABLIS, map 7
La Chablisienne (C), 8 bd Pasteur, BP 14, 89800 Chablis. Tel: 86.42.11.24. Visiting hours: Mon–Sat 8–12, 2–6; also Jul–Aug Sun 8–12, 2–6.
La Chablisienne accounts for nearly one third of the production of all Chablis. All the *grands crus* except Valmur are represented, and growers bring their crop in the form of must which the co-operative then vinifies.

Simonnet-Fèbvre et Fils (M/G), 9 av. d'Oberwesel, BP 12, 89800 Chablis. Tel: 86.42.11.73. Visiting hours: By appt.
Simonnet-Fèbvre is a small but friendly operation with 5 hectares of vines. They also deal in a wide range of *crus* and make a good Crémant de Bourgogne, both white and rosé and a Bourgogne Rouge.

CHAGNY, map 8
Domaine de la Folie (G), 71150 Chagny. Tel: 85.87.18.59. Visiting hours: By appt.
This attractive domaine is owned by Messieurs E. and X. Noël-Bouton who make an excellent white Rully Clos St Jacques, one of the best white wines of the Côte Chalonnaise. There is also a good red Rully Clos de Bellecroix.

CHENAS, map 9
Domaine Champagnon (G), 69840 Chénas. Tel: 85.36.71.32. Visiting hours: Daily 8–7.

Louis Champagnon has 7.5 hectares of vineyards, mainly in Chénas and Moulin-à-Vent. The wines are packed with fruit and full of character and this is one of several estates responsible for the growing reputation of Chénas.

CHIROUBLES, map 9
La Maison des Vignerons (C), 69115 Chiroubles. Tel: 74.69.14.94. (*Caveau*)
La Terrasse de Chiroubles, rte du Col du Fut d'Avenas (3km W of Chiroubles on D18 in the direction of Monsols). Tel: 74.04.20.79. Visiting hours: Feb–Dec Mon–Sat, 10–11.45, 2.30–6.30; Sun 2–6.30.
This is one of many wine-tasting *caveaux* organized by local growers in the Beaujolais area. Chiroubles is the most remote of the Beaujolais *crus* and its vineyards stretch up into the hills. The view from La Terrasse, a Swiss-style chalet, is quite magnificent over the whole of Beaujolais and across to the Alps on fine days.

FIXIN, map 8
Philippe Joliet (G), Manoir de la Perrière, 21220 Fixin. Tel: 80.52.47.85. Visiting hours: By appt.
The domaine of 5 hectares makes a good Clos de la Perrière, which is Fixin's most famous *premier cru*.

FLEURIE, map 9
Cave Co-opérative des Grands Vins de Fleurie (C), le Bourg, BP 2, 69820 Fleurie. Tel: 74.04.11.70. Visiting hours: Mon–Fri 8–12, 2–6; Sat 8–12; *Caveau* visiting hours: Daily 9–12, 2–6.
This Beaujolais co-operative is well known for the high quality of its wines, including a delicious Cuvée Président Marguerite named after its director since 1946, Marguerite Chabert who is well known throughout Beaujolais.

JULIENAS, map 9
Cave Co-operative des Grands Vins (C), Château du Bois de la Salle, 69840 Juliénas. Tel: 74.04.42.61. Visiting hours: 8.15–12, 2–6. (*Caveau*) Le Cellier de la Vieille Eglise. Visiting hours: 9.45–12, 2.30–6.30; closed Nov 1, Christmas and New Year's Day.
The Juliénas co-operative has two tasting rooms, one at the Château du Bois de la Salle just outside the village and the second in an old, deconsecrated church.

LUGNY, map 9
Cave de Lugny (C), 71260 Lugny. Tel: 85.33.22.85. Visiting hours: Mon–Sat 8–12, 2–6.

The Mâconnais is a region of co-operatives and the one at Lugny is a good example and in the heart of the Mâcon-Villages area. It produces good Mâcon-Villages Lugny from Chardonnay and Mâcon Supérieur red and rosé from Gamay, as well as other wines.

MALIGNY, map 7
Domaine de l'Eglantière (G), Jean Durup, 4 Grande-Rue, Maligny, 89800 Chablis. Tel: 86.47.44.49. Visiting hours: Mon–Fri; closed hols.

There have been Durups at Maligny since the 15th century but Jean Durup has created a new estate, Domaine de l'Eglantière, and has also bought the medieval Château de Maligny which he is restoring. Some of his wine is sold under the label of Château de Maligny. He makes *premier cru* Chablis, including Fourchaume, and simple Chablis with successful results. His wine-making is modern and no oak is used.

MERCUREY, map 8
Antonin Rodet (M/G), Mercurey, 71640 Givry. Tel: 85.45.22.22. Visiting hours: Mon–Sat 9–6.

The Rodet family is well established as both grower and merchant in the heart of the Chalonnaise and is particularly noted for its red and white Mercurey Château de Chamirey, a property owned by the Marquis de Jouenne, Antonin Rodet's son-in-law who now owns the firm. The beautiful château cannot be visited but can be seen from the outside from the attractive 17th-century *cuverie* (to visit make an appointment with Antonin Rodet).

Now directed by Bertrand Devillard, Rodet are one of the few *négociants* to strive for quality rather than quantity of sales. They make outstanding Gevrey-Chambertin and Nuits St Georges.

NUITS ST GEORGES, map 8
Jean Chauvenet (G), r. de Gilly, 21700 Nuits St Georges. Tel: 80.61.00.72. Visiting hours: Daily 9–12, 2–6 except school hols.

A small producer, Jean Chauvenet makes a traditional, aromatic Nuits St Georges, rich in tannins and long-lived.

PERNAND-VERGELESSES, map 8
Domaine Rapet Père et Fils (G), Pernand-Vergelesses, 21420 Savigny-lès-Beaune. Tel: 80.21.50.05. Visiting hours: By appt.

The family has been active in wine-making since at least 1792 and their *premier cru* les Vergelesses is an outstanding product of that long tradition. Roland Rapet is now in charge.

PULIGNY-MONTRACHET, map 8
Domaine Etienne Sauzet (G), Puligny-Montrachet, 21190 Meursault. Tel: 80.21.32.10. Visiting hours: By appt.

The domaine makes a good Puligny-Montrachet but its *crus* les Perrières and la Truffière are among the best in the *appellation*. The *grand cru* Bâtard-Montrachet can be quite brilliant.

QUINCIE-EN-BEAUJOLAIS, map 9
Jean-Charles Pivot (G/M), Quincié-en-Beaujolais, 69430 Beaujeu. Tel: 74.04.30.32. Visiting hours: Mon–Sat; closed last 2 weeks in Aug.

The family domaine of 12 hectares makes good traditional and *primeur* Beaujolais.

ROMANECHE-THORINS, map 9
Château des Jacques (G/M), 71570 Romanèche-Thorins. Tel: 85.35.51.64. Visiting hours: By appt.

The Château des Jacques is a fine, turreted building with good views of the surrounding countryside, and its vineyards have always enjoyed an outstanding reputation. It is owned by the Thorin family, who have been making and selling wine in Beaujolais since the 11th century. Their Moulin-à-Vent is a formidable wine that improves with moderate aging. There are also 10 hectares of Chardonnay, vinified as Beaujolais Blanc and aged briefly in new oak casks. Most of Thorin's activities as a *négociant* are concentrated at the headquarters in Pontaneveaux.

ST AUBIN, map 8
Domaine Roux Père et Fils (G/M), St Aubin, 21190 Meursault. Tel: 80.21.32.92. Visiting hours: Mon–Sat by appt.

St Aubin is a small wine-making village up in the hills and has several conscientious producers, including Domaine Roux who make a good St Aubin la Chatenière Premier Cru and red Chassagne-Montrachet Clos St Jean.

ST BRIS-LE-VINEUX, map 7
Luc Sorin (G), 13 bis r. de Paris, 89530 St Bris. Tel: 86.53.60.76. Visiting hours: Mon-Sat.
The estate, run by Luc Sorin, is one of the most dynamic in the area. The Sauvignon de St Bris VDQS is excellent and other outstanding wines include a Bourgogne Aligoté Coteaux de St Bris.

ST JEAN D'ARDIERES, map 9
Château de Pizay (G), St Jean d'Ardières, 69220 Belleville-sur-Saône. Tel: 74.66.26.10. Visiting hours: Mon-Sat 8–12, 2–6, by appt.
Château de Pizay is a well-known estate in Morgon and makes one of the best examples of this Beaujolais *cru*, as well as some Beaujolais-Villages. The estate has a history of over 1,000 years and the 30 hectares of vineyards surround the attractive château with its square keep which is now a hotel and restaurant (see page 75).

SAVIGNY-LES-BEAUNE,
map 8
GAEC Simon Bize et Fils (G), 21420 Savigny-lès-Beaune. Tel: 80.21.50.57. Visiting hours: By appt.
The Bize wines are always some of the best in Savigny, and their price reflects this, but they are sometimes a little leaner than need be. The estate has been in the family for 150 years.

VIRE, map 9
Château de Viré (G), Cedex 2123, 71260 Lugny. Tel: 85.33.90.97. Visiting hours: By appt.
The attractive 16th-century château is also a domaine making good Mâcon-Viré. Hubert Desbois and his son François run the estate and the wines are distributed by Prosper Maufoux, the Santenay *négociants*.

VOLNAY, map 8
Domaine de la Pousse d'Or (G), Volnay, 21190 Meursault. Tel: 80.22.10.73. Visiting hours: By appt.
Gérard Potel, manager of the domaine, is one of the best-known winemakers in the Côte d'Or. His Volnay Caillerets Clos des 60 Ouvrées is particularly fine, but recent releases, though good, exhibit a slightly worrying thinness on the palate.

VOSNE-ROMANEE, map 8
Jean Gros (G), Vosne-Romanée, 21700 Nuits St Georges. Tel: 80.61.04.69. Visiting hours: By appt.
Vosne-Romanée has no fewer than seven *grands crus* and nine *premiers crus*, making it one of the top villages in the Côte de Nuits. Jean Gros' 14-hectare domaine is planted entirely in Pinot Noir and his finest wine is the Richebourg Grand Cru.

Sights

It is hard to imagine visiting Burgundy without taking an interest in its wines, but there is so much to see in this culturally rich area that wine-tasting need be no more than a pleasant diversion if so desired. The star attractions are the Romanesque churches, the medieval and Renaissance houses in Dijon and Beaune, or the old quarters of Lyon. Students of French literature can follow the *Route Lamartine* that winds through the Mâconnais countryside; and no medievalist can ignore the remains of the once-powerful Cluny abbey which attracts visitors from around the world.

AUXERRE
Strategically located on the Yonne, Auxerre was once a major trading center, and wine was shipped from here to Paris. The beautiful **Cathédrale St Etienne**, set on a hill dominating the old town, is a reminder of the town's former importance. The 13th-century stained-glass windows are particularly fine.

BEAUNE
Beaune is the heart of the world-famous Côte d'Or. The town has long been the wine-trading capital of the region and many merchants have their headquarters here with attractive old cellars, some of which can be visited.
 The auction of the new wine held in mid-Nov at the famous Hospices is a

BURGUNDY

The Hôtel-Dieu *with its Gothic architecture is the star attraction of Beaune.*

major event. The curious can taste newly pressed wine in a carnival-like atmosphere while the professionals keep a close eye on prices, the earliest indication of a vintage's "worth."

Beaune, although inevitably a great tourist attraction, still retains much of its charm and no visitor to Burgundy should miss it. The **Hôtel-Dieu**, centerpiece of the Hospices, is one of the symbols of Burgundy with its multi-colored roof and its courtyard with elaborately carved beams and gabled dormer windows. The Hospices functioned as a hospital up until 1971 and still includes a home for the elderly. Visit also the **Musée du Vin de Bourgogne**, which is housed in an interesting 16th-century building.

CHABLIS
The town of Chablis is small despite its famous name, with less than 2,500 inhabitants. Although it was damaged in 1940 by a bomb, there are still some attractive old buildings in the center.

CLUNY
Founded in 910 by Duke Guillaume of Aquitaine, the **Abbaye de Cluny** soon became one of the leading centers of medieval Christendom. Little now remains of the once-great abbey complex but there is an interesting **Musée Ochier** in the former abbot's palace, including 4,000 volumes from its once enormous library, along with modern plans and reconstructions.

DIJON
The most elegant city in the region, Dijon was once the capital of the ancient dukedom of Burgundy. The most impressive buildings are those surrounding the imposing **Palais des Ducs** which houses the excellent **Musée des Beaux-Arts**, one of the best outside Paris. The fascinating 15th-century ducal kitchens can also be visited. Behind the ducal palace are streets with old Renaissance houses and the fine Gothic **Eglise de Notre Dame**.

Dijon has an international gastronomic fair the first 2 weeks of Nov and a wine festival at the beginning of Sep.

LYON
At the confluence of the Rhône and the Saône, Lyon is at the southern end of the Beaujolais region and not far north of the famous northern Rhône *appellations*. The city has the largest population in France after Paris and has traditionally been its great rival, both commercially and culturally. With its *bouchons* (family-style bistros specializing in regional dishes) and the highest concentration of starred restaurants outside Paris (including the general area that surrounds the city), Lyon is a city where good food and wine are among the highest priorities and a source of much local pride.

The most interesting parts of the city are on the *presqu'île* separating the Saône and the Rhône, and on the west bank of the Saône in **Vieux Lyon** which has a stunning collection of Renaissance houses. An important textile center, Lyon has a **Musée Historique des Tissus** unrivaled in France. Both the **Musée des Beaux-Arts** and the **Musée Lyonnais des Arts Décoratifs** house outstanding collections of paintings, sculpture and furniture.

MACON
Mâcon is a flourishing commercial city and hosts an important fair of French wines in mid-May, after which the prize-winning wines have the right to a special sticker indicating which medal they were awarded. This is a major event, with up to 8,000 wines offered for tasting.

NUITS ST GEORGES
There is both a wine fair and auction on the Sun preceding Palm Sunday. The town itself is delightful and there are no crowds in the narrow streets lined with bright shopfronts and old stone façades.

TOURNUS
Tournus is an old city with a lovely location beside the river Saône and is a convenient and interesting stopping place between Dijon and Lyon. It has fine examples of Romanesque architecture, including the **Eglise St Philibert**, the best preserved Romanesque church in France. The **Musée Perrin-de-Puycousin** has interesting displays of Burgundian folklore.

VILLEFRANCHE-SUR-SAONE
Villefranche is the capital of Beaujolais and in Nov there is a Fête du Beaujolais which coincides with the release of the Beaujolais *primeur*.

VOUGEOT
The **Château du Clos de Vougeot** lies in the center of one of Burgundy's most famous vineyards. Members of the Confrérie des Chevaliers du Tastevin meet in the château for an elaborate dinner and wine-tasting as part of Les Trois Glorieuses in Nov.

Restored in the 19th-century, the château has a magnificent *cuverie* which has been turned into a wine museum.

Hotels, Restaurants and Where to Buy Wine

In 1560, a French chronicler recorded a Burgundian proverb "mieux vaut bon repas que bel habit" (a good meal is more important than fine clothes). This still holds true; though Burgundians shun ostentatious displays of wealth they support the greatest concentration of starred restaurants in all of France. Of course, the local inhabitants are not alone in frequenting these famous tables since the province is on one of the main north-south routes and is hence one of the most-visited of the French wine regions.

Visitors to Burgundy can discover both the creative cooking of three-star chefs as well as local specialties that are "farmhouse" cookery *par excellence*; snails in garlic butter, *andouillettes* (tripe sausages), a wide array of slicing sausages and, of course, *boeuf bourguignon*. The beef from the nearby Charolais district, the chickens from Bresse in the south-west of the region, and pork products from throughout Burgundy make for hearty dining at its best.

Though not strictly in Burgundy, Lyon is included here because of its links with Beaujolais just to the north – the Rhône, the Saône and "Beaujolais" are said to flow through the city. Characteristic Lyonnais *cuisine* is to be found in small restaurants called *bouchons*.

Hostellerie du Vieux Moulin (R,H), rte de Savigny, 21420 Bouilland. Tel: 80.21.51.16. One Michelin star. Closed Wed and Thu lunch, and mid-Jan. MC V
Bouilland is a hamlet in a deep valley only 16km from Beaune and the Hostellerie is run by a young couple, Jean-Pierre and Isabelle Silva. Mme Silva acts as *sommelier* and M. Silva is in the kitchen. The Silvas' wine list offers a fine selection of burgundies, and is revised frequently to reflect their latest acquisitions. The emphasis is on wines that are drinkable now rather than on famous vintages or rarities, though both can be found on their list.

In addition to the wines, the setting is idyllic – horses gambol across the road, a crystal clear stream runs past the window and the village is well located for touring the Côte de Beaune. The Silvas will arrange visits to growers if they feel you are serious about buying wines and not just looking for free tastings.

AUXERRE (89000)
Le Maxime (H,R), (H) 2 and (R) 5 quai Marine. Tel: (H) 86.52.14.19. (R) 86.52.04.41. (R) closed Wed, 3 weeks Dec and 10 days in Jun. AE DC MC V
Traditional hotel on the banks of the Yonne with regional cooking.

BEAUNE (21200)
Bistrot Bourguignon (R), 8 r. Monge. Tel: 80.22.23.24. Closed Mon. AE DC MC V
Excellent selection of burgundies from the best properties sold by the glass and accompanied by generous helpings of simple, regional food.

Les Caves du Couvent des Cordeliers (W), 6 r. de l'Hôtel-Dieu. Tel : 80.22.14.25. AE MC V
Tastings of Burgundian *grands crus* in the cellar of a 13th-century convent.

Jacques Lainé (R), 10-12 bd Foch. Tel : 80.24.76.10. One Michelin star. Closed mid-Oct–mid-Jun, Tue and Wed lunch. AE DC MC V
Excellent but pricy regional cooking.

Maison Denis Perret (W), 40 pl. Carnot. Tel : 80.22.35.47. AE MC V
Good selection of burgundies from the best vineyards and other wines.

La Poste (H,R), 1 bd Clemenceau. Tel : 80.22.08.11. Closed mid-Nov–Mar. AE DC MC V
Traditional hotel with fine view of the town walls. Good Burgundian cooking and a wide selection of regional wines.

CHABLIS (89800, Yonne)
Hostellerie des Clos (R,H), r. Jules Rathier. Tel : 86.42.10.63. One Michelin star. Closed Jan. AE DC MC V
Excellent base for touring the region, with modern rooms and a friendly welcome from M. and Mme Vignaud. Elegant dining-room with good seasonal food and wine list.

CHAGNY (71150)
Host. du Château de Bellecroix (R,H), 2km SE off N6. Tel : 85.87.13.86. Closed Wed and Christmas–Jan. AE DC V
A 17th-century château in a quiet park.

Lameloise (R,H), 36 pl. d'Armes. Tel : 85.87.08.85. Three Michelin stars. Closed Wed and Thu lunch and Dec 20–Jan 20. V
The Lameloise family run one of the best restaurants in the region in an old Burgundian house. Outstanding *cuisine* is served in elegant surroundings with a cellar directed by one of France's best *sommeliers*. Relais et Châteaux.

CHALON-SUR-SAONE (71100)
La Maison des Vins de la Côte Chalonnaise (W), promenade Ste Marie. Tel : 85.41.64.00. (R) 85.41.66.66. (R) closed Sun. No cards.
Wines from more than 26 villages are offered for tasting and sold at reasonable prices. There is a restaurant serving regional specialties.

St Georges (H,R), 32 av. Jean-Jaurès. Tel : 85.48.27.05. One Michelin star. AE DC MC V
The best restaurant in Chalon and the hotel rooms are modern and quiet.

CHENAS (69840)
Daniel Robin (R), aux Deschamps. Tel : 85.36.72.67. One Michelin star. Closed Wed, Sun–Thu pm, and Feb–mid-Mar. AE DC MC V
The Robin family makes an excellent Chénas which can be tasted at the restaurant. Traditional *cuisine*.

CHOREY-LES-BEAUNE (21200)
L'Ermitage de Corton (R,H), on N74. Tel : 80.22.05.28. One Michelin star. Closed Sun pm and mid-Jan–mid-Feb. (R) closed Mon. AE DC MC V
Excellent choice of burgundies and a restaurant of the same quality, with traditional *cuisine* prepared by André Parra. Comfortable rooms.

COLLONGES-AU-MONT-D'OR (69660)
Paul Bocuse (R), 50 quai de la Plage. Tel : 78.22.01.40. Three Michelin stars. AE DC V
Bocuse needs no introduction. A pilgrimage to what was once a humble family inn north of Lyon is now a must for gastronomes in the area.

DIJON (21000)
Chapeau Rouge (H,R), 5 r. Michelet. Tel : 80.30.28.10. One Michelin star. Reservations essential. AE DC MC V
The former stables of an ancient abbey are now a comfortable hotel and restaurant highly favored by locals. Excellent cellar.

La Cour Aux Vins (W,R), 3 r. Jeannin. Tel : 80.67.85.14. (R) reservations required. AE CD MC V
Wine-tasting and regional specialties.

Les Oenophiles "la Toison d'Or" (R), 18 r. Ste Anne. Tel : 80.30.73.52. Closed Sun and 3 weeks in Aug. AE DC MC V
A medieval residence restored with taste includes a small museum of Burgundian history and wine-making and a good restaurant serving regional *cuisine*. Good wine list.

FIXIN (21220)
Chez Jeannette (R,H), 7 r. Noiset. Tel: 80.52.45.49. Closed Thu and Jan. AE DC V
Small restaurant with regional cooking.

FLEURIE (69820)
le Cep (R), pl. de l'Eglise. Tel: 74.04.10.77. Closed Sun pm–Mon, except hols, and Dec. AE
A pretty situation opposite the village church and excellent local cooking.

GEVREY-CHAMBERTIN (21220)
Les Millésimes (R), 25 r. Eglise. Tel: 80.51.84.24. One Michelin star. Closed Tue–Wed lunch, and mid-Jan–mid-Feb. AE DC V
As the name of this family-run restaurant implies, the emphasis is on the wines. The restaurant has one of the best wine lists in Burgundy with over 1,000 wines! Fine setting in a tiny, vaulted cellar.

LYON (69000)
Léon de Lyon (R), 1 r. Pleney, 69001 Lyon. Tel: 78.28.11.33. Two Michelin stars. Reservations essential. Closed Sun–Mon lunch, and Dec 22–Jan 7. MC V
A favorite with the people of Lyon. Modernized versions of classic Lyonnais dishes and creative cookery by an attentive chef who respects the fine produce he uses. Good wine list including good-value Beaujolais and Côtes du Rhône served by the pitcher.

Le Garet (R), 7 r. du Garet, 69001 Lyon. Tel: 78.28.16.94. Reservations essential. Closed Sat–Sun, and mid-Jul–mid-Aug. MC V
Highly recommended *bouchon*. Tiny and noisy, but excellent Lyonnais specialties.

MACON (71000)
Hôtel Altea (H) and **le St Vincent (R)**, 26 r. de Coubertin. Tel: 85.38.28.06. (R) closed Sat and Sun lunch. AE DC MC V
Modern and comfortable hotel with a view of the Saône. Good restaurant.

La Maison Mâconnaise des Vins (W,R), 484 av. de Lattre-de-Tassigny. Tel: 85.38.36.70. Open daily 8–9. Closed May 1 and Christmas. AE MC V
Reasonably priced Mâcon and Beaujolais wines offered for tasting and sale. Regional specialties served.

NUITS ST GEORGES (21700)
La Côte d'Or (R,H), 1 r. Thurot. Tel: 80.61.06.10. Two Michelin stars. Closed Sun pm, Wed, and 2 weeks Feb and Jul. MC V
Small, modern and comfortable hotel. The restaurant concentrates on classic cooking. Fine cellar with good Nuits St Georges.

ST JEAN D'ARDIERES
(69220, Belleville)
Château de Pizay (H,R), on D69 between St Jean and Morgon. Tel: 74.66.51.41. (H,R) closed Feb. (R) closed Mon. AE DC
This 15th-century château with a beautiful formal French garden is in the middle of the Morgon vineyards. Good food, and swimming and tennis make this a delightful spot for visiting the surrounding Beaujolais countryside. The establishment is new but is rapidly making a name for itself.

SOLUTRE-POUILLY (71960)
Relais de Solutré (R,H), on D54. Tel: 85.35.80.81. Closed Dec–Feb. AE MC V
A family-run establishment and attractive restaurant with regional cooking. Fine views of the Beaujolais hills in the distance.

TOURNUS (71700)
Greuze (R,H), 1 r. Albert-Thibaudet. Tel: (R) 85.51.13.52. (H) 85.40.77.77. Two Michelin stars. Closed mid-Nov–mid-Dec. AE V
This is the "local" restaurant *par excellence* with rich, classic cuisine and good wines. The hotel itself is new.

VAUX (89290, Champs-sur-Yonne)
La Petite Auberge (R), 2 pl du Passeur. Tel: 86.53.80.08. One Michelin star. Closed Sun pm–Mon, hols, Dec 24–Jan 15, and first 2 weeks Jul. V
Small, charming country restaurant on the banks of the Yonne. *Nouvelle cuisine* with seafood specialties.

VILLEFRANCHE-SUR-SAONE (69400)
Château de Chervinges (H,R), 3km W on D38. Tel: 74.65.29.76. (H,R) closed Jan. (R) closed Mon. AE DC MC V
This is a luxurious hotel in the middle of the Beaujolais vineyards.

CHAMPAGNE

Champagne is neither one wine nor one region. Traditionally the province has been divided into three distinct areas: the arid and sterile plains west of Vitry-le-François called *la Champagne pouilleuse*; the strip of fertile rolling hills between St Dizier and Troyes known as *la Champagne humide*; and *la Champagne viticole*, mainly on the hills near Reims or in the Marne valley, where wine of quality has been produced since Roman times. The wines can be sparkling or still, dry or sweet, red, rosé or white; and few wines, and few regions, are and have been as varied.

Throughout Champagne are architectural wonders from the 12th and 13th centuries and many reminders that, at an even earlier date, Reims was the capital of a province extending east beyond the Rhine and south almost to Dijon. Because of its situation on one of the major north-south trading routes of medieval Europe, famous fairs were held in the region, at Bar-sur-Aube, Troyes and Provins; the strategic military and commercial importance of the region meant that periodically it became one large battlefield. Visitors to Champagne cannot help but be moved by the countless reminders of World War I; many of its major battles were fought in and around the Champagne vineyards.

Throughout the world, however, the word "champagne" calls to mind not battles, cathedrals, or fairs, but rather thick glass bottles full of that bubbling wine that heralds a celebration, launches a ship or toasts a bride – and to think that this gorgeous fizz comes from the most northerly vineyards of France.

The Wines of Champagne

Until the 17th century the wines produced in Champagne were still wines. Fermentation was halted by the chilly northern winters before the wine frothed and fizzed in the cask for a while before becoming flat again. The frothy spring wine was much appreciated, and the development of the *méthode champenoise* was all about harnessing and preserving this natural phenomenon.

Legend has it that it was Dom Pérignon, a Benedictine monk and cellarmaster at the Hautvillers abbey near Epernay, who invented champagne as we know it today in the late 17th century. He perfected the art of blending wines from different vineyards to produce a single *cuvée*; and he managed to preserve the sparkle in the wines, helped by two fairly recent innovations – stoppers made of cork bark from Spain and new, high-quality glass bottles from England. This bubbly wine became very popular at the courts of both France and England and the late 18th and early 19th centuries saw the rise of many of the great champagne houses we know today.

A second fermentation in a bottle posed several problems including removal of the sediment so that the resulting wine would not be cloudy when served. The wine had to be left on its lees for an extended period, anywhere from one to six years, before the sediment was removed – a task that was not effectively performed until the early 19th century when Nicole Barbe, the widow of the owner of a major champagne house, who subsequently became known as la Veuve Clicquot, perfected the system of *remuage* – placing the bottles almost horizontally in racks and regularly turning and tapping them, so that after a few months the bottles are vertical and the sediment from the second fermentation lies on the cork.

The same method is still used today, although many of the more modern champagne houses have introduced mechanical *giropalettes* which save on time and labor. The sediment is removed by *dégorgement* and each bottle is topped up by the addition of a small quantity of *liqueur*, a mixture of wine and sugar. The amount of sugar added determines the sweetness of the wine.

Most champagne is made from a blend of red and white grapes – Pinot Noir, Pinot Meunier and Chardonnay. It is almost always a blend of several vineyards and in the case of non-vintage champagne, of several years, which gives a consistent flavor and style. As well as vintage and non-vintage champagne many houses produce a flagship *cuvée* with exotic names and bottle designs.

Sparkling champagne is not, however, the only wine of Champagne. Still wines are made which are reminders of what champagne used to be. Their *appellation*, Coteaux Champenois, covers both reds and whites; the whites are made from white Chardonnay and the reds from Pinot Noir. These are pleasant wines, though generally not outstanding. There is a separate *appellation* for Rosé des Riceys, a still wine made from Pinot Noir planted in les Riceys in the southern area of Champagne. It is somewhat of a rarity, seldom appearing on wine lists even in the region.

Remuage by hand is still practiced by some houses but is labor-intensive and costly.

Visiting the Vineyards

The Champagne vineyards are the most northerly in France and over the centuries the *vignerons* have had to battle against the climate, as well as invading armies. If the climate is not particularly favorable, the composition of the soil is: the famous mix of Kimmeridgian clay and limestone, so prevalent in Champagne, also accounts for the qualities of the Chablis wine made to the south-east. Below the clay is a thick layer of permeable chalk that ensures good drainage, essential given the substantial rainfall.

The finest wines come from vineyards on the slopes of a large upland between Reims and Epernay, the Montagne de Reims. The relatively flat surface of this upland is heavily forested, but the slopes facing Reims and curving around to the south and east along the Marne valley are extensively planted in vines. A further slope extending southward from Epernay is called the Côte de Blancs, since it is planted principally in Chardonnay. The approved areas for vineyards are strictly demarcated and the wine villages are divided into *grand* or *premier cru* status. There are now 17 *grand cru* villages. The Montagne de Reims, the Marne valley and the Côte de Blancs are where the finest champagne grapes are grown but these areas represent only a small part of Champagne's vineyards which are scattered southward over a relatively large area.

Champagne is not one of France's most charming regions, but it would be unkind and untrue to describe it as bleak. It is a sea of billowy hills, heavily wooded in places but more often covered in open fields planted in grain, sugarbeets and other crops. The towns are usually in the valleys, protected from the winds that sweep across the open expanses. Except for their churches with picturesque pointed steeples that can be seen from afar, Champagne villages are generally undistinguished because of repeated devastation in the numerous wars fought in the area. Many of the best houses are survivors from the 1890-1910 period, the "golden age" when champagne was in great demand and business was flourishing.

The climate is decidedly cool and damp in Champagne, although summers can be uncomfortably hot and occasionally quite humid; late spring, summer and early autumn are the best times for touring.

Route One

From Reims to Ay around the eastern curve of the Montagne de Reims: 80km

This is the furthest north of the champagne vineyard areas and is mostly planted with Pinot Noir, the champagne grape which takes the longest to ripen!

The Itinerary:

Leave **Reims** on N51 (r. de Vesle) signposted for Soissons. At the roundabout in **Tinqueux** take the left-hand road, D380, toward Château-Thierry. After some flat farmland, vines will start to appear. Watch for a right-hand turnoff toward **Ormes** (D275); in Ormes when D275 turns toward Champigny, leave it and drive straight ahead on a country road through farmland toward a vine-covered hill. Approaching **Vrigny**, the next village, the vineyards come right down to the road; at the top of the hill, turn left onto D26 in the direction of **Pargny-lès-Reims**, continuing on D26 through the wine villages of **Jouy**, **Sacy**, and **Ecueil**. After Ecueil, D26 becomes the *Route de Champagne* with signs pointing toward **Chamery**; this stretch is a beautiful drive through the hills. Leaving Chamery, continue on D26 through **Nogent** and **Sermiers**. At the junction with N51 turn left into **Mont Chenot** and pick up the D26 at a right turn on the other side of the village. Follow the signs toward Verzy, through **Villers-Allerand**, **Rilly-la-Montagne**, **Chigny-les-Roses** and **Ludes** where Canard-Duchêne holds sway.

Leaving Ludes there is a large intersection: drive straight ahead toward Verzy. The next stretch of road, from **Mailly-Champagne** to **Verzy**, affords a magnificent view of the vineyards, made all the more picturesque by the large windmill perched on the side of the hill that leans toward Verzenay.

In Verzy, follow the signs indicating *Toutes Directions*, and then **Ambonnay**. At Ambonnay, take D19 to **Bouzy**, famous for its red Coteaux Champenois. From Bouzy a detour can be made south to Tours-sur-Marne where Laurent-Perrier are based, but to continue on the regular route, bear right (away from the sign indicating Tours-sur-Marne and Avize), following the *Route de Champagne*. This is a bumpy road surrounded by vineyards with stone markers by the roadside identifying the owners of the various parcels: Bollinger, Taittinger and so on. At the stop sign, follow the *Route de Champagne* taking you into **Louvois**; make a sharp left turn onto D9 toward Epernay and **Tauxières-Mutry**. Drive through Tauxières-Mutry and **Fontaine-sur-Ay**, whose church has a pointed steeple topped by a pretty ironwork motif with little bells. From Fontaine-sur-Ay, the road passes on its way to **Ay**, the third most important champagne town after Reims and Epernay.

Route Two

Along the Marne valley from Ay to Verneuil, then back to Epernay: 65km

The Marne Valley with its damper microclimate and clay soils suits Pinot Meunier, a crucial component of most champagne blends.

The Itinerary:

From **Ay** follow the signs for Reims and the *gendarmerie*, then head for **Dizy**; note the chalkiness of the soil along this stretch of road which is what makes it so excellent for vines. In Dizy, turn right on N51 toward **Champillon** and Reims; this is a winding uphill road with a beautiful view of the vineyards and Epernay in the valley to the left. In Champillon carry on up the hill to Bellevue if you wish to visit Le Royal Champagne (see page 88). At the first group of houses in Champillon, turn left on a small unmarked road just after a pedestrian crossing sign, driving downhill into town and straight past the church. Turn left toward Dizy and **Hautvillers**, driving through a small tunnel. At the stop sign, turn right toward **Cumières**, and follow the *Toutes Directions* signs before turning left again at the next sign indicating Cumières. Before reaching Cumières, the road passes through Hautvillers, a pretty village with wrought iron shop signs, and the site of the abbey where Dom Pérignon lived.

After Cumières, where some good Pinot Noir is produced, take D1 toward **Damery** and on to **Venteuil**; from just beyond Damery, Château de Boursault, built in 1848 for that famous widow Mme Clicquot, can be seen on the hill across the river. From Venteuil to **Châtillon-sur-Marne** is a lovely drive.

In the center of **Verneuil**, turn left onto D380 toward Epernay; cross the Marne, then turn left to Epernay on N3. The vineyards seem even more spectacular from this side of the river, especially **Troissy**, when the church steeple of **Mareuil-le-Port** is seen against the backdrop of the Montagne de Reims.

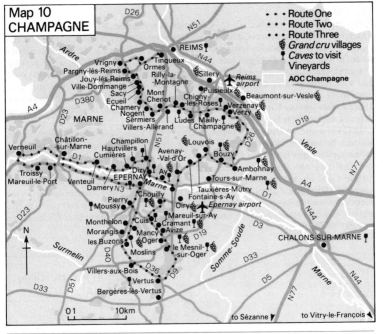

Route Three

The Côte des Blancs from Epernay to Chouilly by way of Vertus: 50km

The Côte des Blancs is planted mainly with Chardonnay which gives a lightness and more obvious fruit to blends dominated by Pinot Noir.

The Itinerary:
Leave **Epernay** on D51 in the direction of Troyes, then follow the signs for Sézanne. In **Pierry**, continue following the signs for Sézanne (and D51), and pass the Chouilly turnoff; then, at a large intersection of several roads, turn left onto the road opposite the sign pointing to Pierry (this is D10, which goes toward Avize, but the sign cannot be seen when coming from Epernay). At the next junction, turn right onto D40 and head for **Monthelon** on a small road with a very pretty view of the hills and vineyards. In Monthelon, start heading for **Morangis** and D210 then, almost immediately, follow the signs for **Mancy** on D40 and on through **Moslins** and **les Buzons**. At the large intersection after leaving les Buzons, turn left on D38 through **Villers-aux-Bois** to **Vertus**. The vines now disappear, giving way to forest and farmland, then suddenly reappear in a magnificent panorama as the road curves before Vertus.

From Vertus, a detour can be made south to **Bergères-lès-Vertus** on D9, but the main route is continued by turning left onto D9 in the direction of **le Mesnil-sur-Oger**. Just before reaching le Mesnil, leave D9 and take the left-hand fork through Mesnil and **Avize** on D10 which leads through **Cramant** to **Cuis**. Immediately after passing the sign indicating that you are entering Cuis, take a hard right onto the small road toward **Chouilly** – you will see the sign only after turning the left-hand curve. The drive from Vertus to Chouilly winds through vineyards and ends with a striking view of the little church of Chouilly. Drive through Chouilly, then, at the D3 junction turn left to head back toward **Epernay**.

Route Four

Bar-sur-Aube to les Riceys, by way of Bar-sur-Seine: 55km

This route covers the little-known area of the Aube in the south of Champagne. Much of its production is blended into the champagnes of Reims and Epernay, but the Aube is well worth visiting for its lovely remote countryside.

The Itinerary:

Bar-sur-Aube is reached from **Châlons-sur-Marne** by way of **Vitry-le-François** and **Brienne-le-Château** (the latter town, where Napoleon trained at the military academy, is famous today for its *choucroute*, usually considered a specialty of Alsace). The vineyards begin just north of Bar-sur-Aube on N19, after passing Arsonval. Once in Bar-sur-Aube, head toward Bar-sur-Seine on D4, a pleasant road that winds through hills and valleys dotted with well-kept stone houses, very different from those in the northern Champagne towns, and not unlike those of Burgundy. Shortly after leaving **Couvignan** to the south is a particularly beautiful view of the hillsides and vineyards.

As D4 approaches **Bar-sur-Seine**, there are many vineyards planted high on the hill just below the fringe of forest. Coming into Bar, go around the roundabout following the signs for *Autres Directions*, then take a left turn onto N71 toward Dijon and Châtillon-sur-Seine. After passing **Merrey-sur-Arce** on the left, watch for a turnoff right toward les Riceys on D452. This road passes through the vineyards around **Polisot** and **Polisy** before reaching **les Riceys**, famous for its rosé. From les Riceys, the southernmost point of the *Route de Champagne*, either travel north to the historic city of Troyes, or south toward Tonnerre and the vineyards of Chablis, the gateway to Burgundy and the south of France.

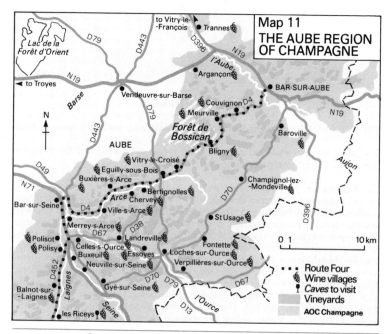

Caves and Vineyards to Visit

At Epernay, Châlons-sur-Marne, and especially at Reims, a visit to the cellars of one of the great champagne houses is one of the principal tourist attractions. These cellars, dug by Romans excavating chalk for road construction, were simply considered oddities until champagne became the sparkling wine we know today and the great champagne houses were formed in the late 18th and early 19th centuries. Since champagne, unlike almost every other wine, is aged in bottle for up to six years and since the *pupitres* or racks used in the course of making the wine take up so much space, immense cellars are indispensable; as chance would have it, the former Roman chalk mines proved perfect places for making and aging this special wine.

Cellars and bottle stocks are larger here than anywhere else in France: Möet and Chandons's stocks amount to 84 million bottles, and both Piper-Heidsieck and Mercier have installed miniature trains to transport visitors through the kilometers of cellars below ground.

Well aware of the promotional value of these cellars, the big houses, called *négociants-manipulants*, have gone out of their way to make visitors welcome. In many respects, Champagne is a paradise for the tourist interested in wines and wine-making. The champagne method is a complicated one, with numerous steps involving the use of exotic equipment and procedures that nearly everyone finds fascinating. A visit to one of these large cellars is a must.

In addition to the large champagne houses there are, in almost every village, small producers – approximately 600 in total – who make and sell champagne under their own labels. These winemakers, generally referred to as *récoltants*, rely entirely on grapes from their own vines and their wines are therefore much more subject to variation than those of the large houses who can buy grapes throughout the region. The sophistication involved in making champagne, the ability to combine different grape varieties, different *crus* and eventually to have a supply of vintages for mixing, gives the big houses a definite edge, so, contrary to the rule in most other regions, the better wines are generally those produced by the big houses rather than the lone *récoltant*, at least insofar as the sparkling wines are concerned. This is less true of the Coteaux Champenois, however, and in good years the wines from certain small producers can rival those of their giant competitors.

EPERNAY, map 10

de Castellane (M),
37 r. de Verdun,
51200 Epernay.
Tel: 26.55.15.33.

Founded in 1890, the company has always functioned as a *négociant* and has no vineyards of its own, purchasing the grapes that it presses and vinifies itself. The house is traditional in its use of wood casks but now has some stainless-steel vats. The building is a distinctive one and can be seen from many parts of Epernay. De Castellane produces a good range of wines, including red and white Coteaux Champenois in some years and a new product, Vicomte de Castellane, which is a blend of traditional champagne products: marc, ratafia, Fine Marne and Vieux Vins de Champagne.
Visiting hours: May 1–Oct 15 daily, 10–12, 2–6.30.
Location: From av. de Champagne take r. d'Alsace and turn right into r. de Verdun.

Mercier (G/M),
73 av. de Champagne,
51200 Epernay.
Tel: 26.54.75.26.

Now part of the Moët-Hennessy group, Mercier has vast premises in Epernay. The firm was founded in 1858 by Eugène Mercier, who is credited with popularizing champagne in France and throughout the world by smart promotion and advertising. The Merciers, who are still active in the company, have traditionally held an important place in the social and political life of Epernay. The cellars hewn from the chalk beneath the headquarters extend for a distance of 18km and visitors are taken through them in small electric trains.
Visiting hours: Mon–Sat 9.30–12.00; Sun and hols 2–4.30; closed Christmas and New Year.
Location: At the Châlons end of av. de Champagne.

Moët & Chandon (G/M), 20 av. de Champagne, 51200 Epernay. Tel: 26.54.71.11.

Founded in 1743 by Charles Moët, the firm expanded considerably under the management of his grandson, Jean-Rémy Moët. Jean-Rémy was succeeded by his son Victor and his son-in-law, Pierre Gabriel Chandon, at which time the firm's name was changed to Moët et Chandon. The family is still involved in the operation, which, however, is now part of the Moët-Hennessy–Louis Vuitton group. The firm's cellars

CHAMPAGNE

are vast (28km) and production is enormous, about 18 million bottles annually. Moët & Chandon own 461 hectares of vineyards in both *premier* and *grand cru* villages, as well as buying in grapes. Their leading champagne, Cuvée Dom Pérignon, was first sold in 1936 and is made from 50 per cent each Pinot Noir and Chardonnay.

Visiting hours: Apr–Oct Mon–Fri, 9.30–12.00, 2–4.30; Sat 9.30–12, 2–5; Sun and hols, 9.30–12, 2–4. Nov–Mar Mon–Fri, 9.30–12, 2–5.30.

Location: Enter av. de Champagne from pl. République and Moët are the first set of *caves* on the right.

de Venoge (M),
30 av. de Champagne,
51200 Epernay.
Tel: 26.55.01.01.

De Venoge owns no vineyards but buys in the grapes to make its wines, the output amounting to a respectable 1.4 million bottles annually. Most of de Venoge's champagnes are sold as Buyer's Own Brand wines. The company's headquarters are one of the most attractive in Epernay's "Champagne Row" and have been extensively refurbished since the mid-1980s.

Visiting hours: Mon–Fri 10–12, 2–6; Sat, Sun and hols by appt.

Location: Between Perrier-Jouët and Pol Roger.

LUDES, map 10
Canard-Duchêne (G/M), BP 1,
1 r. Edmond Canard, Ludes,
51500 Rilly-la-Montagne.
Tel: 26.61.10.96.

The house, founded in 1868, is now owned by the Veuve Clicquot group. Total output amounts to 3 million bottles annually and grapes are bought in from the Aube, the Marne valley and the Côte des Blancs as well as from their own 17 hectares. Canard-Duchêne produces a wide range of wines in its modern, well-equipped premises.

Visiting hours: Sep–Jul daily, 9–11.15, 2–4.

Location: In the center of the village.

MAILLY-CHAMPAGNE, map 10
Champagne Mailly-Champagne (C),
BP 1, Mailly-Champagne,
51500 Rilly-la-Montagne.
Tel: 26.49.41.10.

When World War I finally ground to a halt in 1918, the vineyards of Champagne were in pitiable condition. The growers faced an enormous task of reconstruction; and at Mailly-Champagne many of them decided to group together. They founded a co-operative in 1929 that now has 70 members with a total of 70 hectares of vines, all within the *grand cru* village of Mailly-Champagne. The co-operative's Brut Réserve and the Vintage Brut, sold in an 18th-century-style bottle, are both made from 80 per cent Pinot Noir.

Visiting hours: Apr–Sep daily, 9–11, 2–5; Oct–Mar Mon–Fri, 9–11, 2–5.

Location: At the entrance to the village.

REIMS, map 10
G. H. Mumm (G/M), 34 r. du Champ-de-Mars,
51100 Reims.
Tel: 26.40.22.73.

The family of Mumm originated in West Germany at Rüdesheim in the early 19th century. Peter Arnold de Mumm founded the firm in 1827 and his son lent his name to the company. The company was confiscated after World War I as the Mumms had never sought naturalization and sold at auction. Mumm Cordon Rouge, the firm's big seller, was first made in 1876 and now has an international reputation. The giant Canadian company Seagram is now a major shareholder.

Visiting hours: Mon–Fri 9-11, 2–5; closed hols; groups limited to 12 persons.

Location: Off pl. République.

Piper-Heidsieck (M), 51 bd Henri-Vasnier, 51100 Reims. Tel: 26.85.01.94.

There are three champagne houses in which the name of Heidsieck appears. Florenz-Louis Heidsieck settled in Champagne in 1777 and founded a champagne company in 1785. His three nephews, whom he had taken into the firm, divided the business among them at their uncle's death and formed separate operations, all of which still exist. Piper-Heidsieck dates from 1834. Visitors see part of the firm's 12km of cellars from an electric train and it was one of the first firms to use mechanical riddling with *giropalettes*.

Visiting hours: Mar 31–Nov 11 daily, 9–11.30, 2–5.30; remainder of the year, Mon–Fri 9–11.30, 2–5.30; closed hols.

Location: Near bd Pasteur.

Pommery (G/M), 5 pl. du Gén.-Gouraud, 51100 Reims. Tel: 26.05.05.01.

Pommery's premises are the Champagne equivalent of Disneyland with pinnacles and turrets. They are built on top of 19km of limestone Gallo-Roman galleries, many of which are decorated with carvings of vineyard scenes by the 19th-century Reims sculptor Navlet. The company, now owned by BSN, the giant French food group, has over 300 hectares of vineyards, many in *grand cru* villages. The prestige *cuvée* Louise Pommery is named after Mme Louise Pommery who is credited with having popularized *brut* champagne around 1860.

Visiting hours: Nov 1–Mar 15 daily, 9–11, 2–5; remainder of the year, Mon–Fri 9–11, 2–5; Sat–Sun 10–11.30, 2–5; closed Dec 20–Jan 2.

Location: On pl. du Gen.-Gouraud.

Taittinger C.C.V.C. (G/M), pl. St Nicaise, 51100 Reims. Tel: 26.85.45.35.

The original company of Fourneaux, founded in 1734, was one of the first champagne houses. Pierre Taittinger bought the company after World War I and built it up to become one of the most prestigious of all. The cellars at pl. St Nicaise are in Roman quarries and contain the crypt of the St Nicaise abbey, which was destroyed during the Revolution.

The firm's reputation for quality is based on special *cuvées* that are among the best produced. The new Vintage Collection was launched with the 1978 vintage and has an original bottle shape for each vintage, designed by a famous artist. The vintage Comtes de Champagne Blanc de Blancs is made from 100 per cent Chardonnay and a rosé version is also made. Taittinger owns 250 hectares of vines, most of them in *grand cru* villages and these provide nearly 50 per cent of its needs.

Visiting hours: Mar–Nov daily, 9–11, 2–5; Dec–Feb Mon–Fri, 9–11, 2–5.

Location: Pl. St Nicaise is at the S end of bd Victor-Hugo.

Veuve Clicquot-Ponsardin (G/M), Office: 12 r. du Temple, 51100 Reims. Tel: 26.85.24.08. *Caves:* 1 pl. des Droits de l'Homme.

The widow Clicquot was left at the age of 27 to run her husband's company which she did with persistence and independence of mind and spirit. The firm she inherited, founded by her husband's father in 1772, was facing ruin because of the English blockade during the Napoleonic wars. However, she succeeded in getting a shipment of 10,000 bottles to St Petersburg and in 1815 she beat her competitors in placing her wines back on foreign markets. She is also credited with perfecting the process of *remuage*. The company is one of the leading producers in the region with an annual output of about 7 million bottles and makes champagne of a consistently high quality.

Visiting hours: May–Jul and Sep–Oct Mon–Fri, 9–11.15, 2–5; Sat, Sun and hols 2–5; remainder of the year by appt.

Location: Next to av. du Gen.-Gouraud.

Further *Caves* and Vineyards to Visit

AMBONNAY, map 10
Secondé-Prevoteau S.A.R.L. (G/M), 2 r. du Château, Ambonnay, 51150 Tours-sur-Marne. Tel: 26.57.01.59. Visiting hours: By appt; possibility of meals also.
M. Prevoteau owns 12 hectares of top Ambonnay vines and is proudest of his red Ambonnay Coteaux Champenois, which he makes by the *barrique perpétuelle* technique in which older wine is combined with younger in the cask in a never-ending process.

AVIZE, map 10
Michel Gonet (G), 196 av. Jean-Jaurès, 51190 Avize. Tel: 26.57.50.56. Visiting hours: By appt.
Michel Gonet is descended from a long line of Champagne winemakers. That tradition and experience show in his *premier cru* Blanc de Blancs.

Jacques Selosse (G), r. Ernest-Vallé, 51190 Avize. Tel: 26.57.53.56. Visiting hours: By appt.
This small, traditional house is now run by Anselme Selosse, who makes highly regarded classic champagne.

AY, map 10
Ayala (G/M), 2 bd du Nord, 51160 Ay. Tel: 26.50.13.40. Visiting hours: Mon–Fri 9-11, 2–5, by appt; closed hols and Aug.
Established in 1860, Ayala is a traditional firm and makes good-value, straightforward champagne, including a Vintage Brut.

J. Bollinger (G/M), 16 r. Jules-Lobet, BP 4, 51160 Ay. Tel: 26.50.12.34. Visiting hours: Mon–Fri by appt; closed hols and Aug.
Founded in 1829 by Jacques Bollinger the firm is still run by his descendants. It is one of the most traditional of Champagne winemakers and strict adherance to the highest standards has ensured its continuing success. It owns 140 hectares of vines in the finest areas of Champagne.

Deutz & Geldermann (G/M), 16 r. Jeanson, 51160 Ay. Tel: 26.55.15.11. Visiting hours: Mon–Fri by appt.
Established in 1838, the house is still managed by a direct descendant of the founder. Tradition is closely followed at Deutz and there are good-quality vintage champagnes.

Gosset (G/M), 69 r. Jules-Blondeau, 51160 Ay. Tel: 26.55.14.18. Visiting hours: By appt.
This is Ay's oldest wine house – it was founded in 1584. Now run by Albert Gosset, the firm enjoys a good reputation. Gosset believes in aging its wines for much longer than most houses before releasing them for sale.

BOUZY, map 10
Barancourt (G/M), BP 3, Bouzy, 51150 Tours-sur-Marne. Tel: 26.57.00.67. Visiting hours: Mon–Fri 8–8; closed hols.
Barancourt is an old name in Bouzy but this is a new house, founded only in 1969 by three young cousins, all sons of *vignerons*. They began with only a few hectares of vines and a well-defined intention of emphasizing *cru* as opposed to blend. From their current 72 hectares, 40 per cent in *grand crus* at Bouzy and Cramant, the cousins make good quality champagne.

Georges Vesselle (G/M), 16 r. des Postes, Bouzy, 51150 Tours-sur-Marne. Tel: 26.57.00.15. Visiting hours: Mon–Fri 8–6.
In the village of Bouzy where winemaking is the most important activity, the mayor is a *négociant-manipulant*, as well as being manager (*administrateur*) of three major Champagne firms, Mumm, Heidsieck-Monopole and Perrier-Jouët, and an owner of a vineyard of 17 hectares entirely within the village of Bouzy. He makes good Champagne Brut and red Coteaux Champenois Bouzy.

CHALONS-SUR-MARNE, map 10
Albert le Brun (G/M), 93 av. de Paris, 51000 Châlons-sur-Marne. Tel: 26.68.18.68. Visiting hours: By appt.
The firm, founded 125 years ago by Léon le Brun at Avize, makes good-value champagne, including excellent Blanc de Blancs Brut.

Joseph Perrier Fils et Cie (G/M), 69 av. de Paris, BP 31, 51000 Châlons-sur-Marne. Tel: 26.68.29.51. and 26.68.16.04. Visiting hours: By appt.
One of the leading houses in Châlons today is Joseph Perrier, founded in the late 18th century, whose wines are made in the extensive Roman cellars below the firm's headquarters.

CHAMPILLON, map 10

Gérard Autréau de Champillon (G), 15 r. René-Baudet, Champillon, 51160 Ay. Tel: 26.51.54.13. Visiting hours: Mon–Sat 9–12, 2–5; closed 2 weeks in Aug.

M. Autréau owns vineyards at Ay, Champillon and Chouilly and produces a *premier cru*, non-vintage Champillon that is unusual for the preponderance of Pinot Meunier (80 per cent).

CHIGNY-LES-ROSES, map 10

Société Civile d'Exploitation Champagne Cattier (G), 6 r. Dom-Pérignon, Chigny-lès-Roses. Tel: 26.03.42.11. Visiting hours: Mon–Fri 8–12, 1–5 by appt.

The Cattier family have been winemakers at Chigny since 1763. The standard non-vintage *brut* is highly regarded, as is the Clos du Moulin Brut.

Jules Lassalle (G), 21 r. des Châtaigniers, Chigny-lès-Roses, 51500 Rilly-la-Montagne. Tel: 26.03.42.19. Visiting hours: By appt.

Mme Lassalle and her daughter now run the firm, which owns *premier cru* vineyards at Chigny. They make a good rosé champagne.

CHOUILLY, map 10

R. & L. Legras (G/M), 10 r. des Partelaines, Chouilly, 51200 Epernay. Tel: 26.54.50.79. Visiting hours: By appt.

The Legras have been *vignerons* for two centuries. Their best champagne is the vintage Cuvée St Vincent.

CRAMANT, map 10

Bonnaire-Bouquemont (G), 105 r. du Carrouge, Cramant, 51200 Epernay. Tel: 26.57.50.85. Visiting hours: Sep–Jul Mon–Fri, 8–12, 2–6 by appt.

One of the leading growers in the Côte des Blancs, André Bonnaire makes his wines in modern premises.

CUIS, map 10

Pierre Gimonnet et Fils (G), 1 r. de la République, Cuis, 51200 Epernay. Tel: 26.55.12.54. Visiting hours: Mon–Sat 8–12, 2–6; closed Aug 15–Sep 15.

The firm, owned by M. Michel Gimonnet, has 20 hectares of vines at Cramant, Cuis and Chouilly and makes good vintage and non-vintage champagne.

DIZY, map 10

Jacquesson et Fils (G/M), 99 r. du Col.-Fabien, Dizy, 51200 Epernay. Tel: 26.53.00.66. Visiting hours: By appt.

Bought by Jean Chiquet in 1974, the company makes elegant champagnes which are generally highly respected.

EPERNAY, map 10

Boizel (M), 14–16 r. de Bernon, 51200 Epernay. Tel: 26.55.21.51. Visiting hours: Mon–Fri 8–12, 2–6; closed 3 weeks in Aug.

The firm, founded in 1834 and still owned by the same family (the present owner is Mme Roques), makes champagnes which are well made and excellent value.

Gratien, Meyer, Seydoux et Cie (G/M), 30 r. Maurice-Cerveaux, 51201 Epernay. Tel: 26.54.38.20. Visiting hours: By appt.

Founded in 1864, the house is noted for its strict adherence to traditional practices and wines are kept in wood. The champagnes are sold under the Alfred Gratien label, and include elegant vintage wines.

Perrier-Jouët (G/M), 24–28 r. de Champagne, BP 3, 51201 Epernay. Tel: 26.55.20.53. Visiting hours: Mon–Fri 8–12, 2–5 by appt.

Founded in 1811, and now owned by Seagram, Perrier-Jouët enjoys a fine reputation based on their non-vintage Grand Brut.

Pol Roger et Cie (G/M), 1 r. Henri-Lelarge, 51200 Epernay. Tel: 26.55.41.95. Visiting hours: Mon–Fri by appt.

This was Sir Winston Churchill's favorite champagne and he even called one of his racehorses Pol Roger. Pol Roger own a total of 70 hectares in both the Marne valley and the Côte des Blancs and make one of the finest vintage pink champagnes.

MAREUIL-SUR-AY, map 10

Champagne Philipponnat (G/M), 13 r. du Pont, BP 2, Mareuil-sur-Ay, 51160 Ay. Tel: 26.50.60.43. Visiting hours: Mon–Fri; appt for groups.

The Philipponat family have been in Ay since the 16th century but their champagne house was not founded until 1912. It is now owned by the firm of Gosset.

Philipponnat has 12 hectares of

vineyards, including the highly reputed Clos des Goisses overlooking the Marne au Rhin canal, which yields an excellent vintage champagne.

Le MESNIL-SUR-OGER, map 10
SA des Champagne de Salon (G/M), le Mesnil-sur-Oger, 51190 Avize. Tel: 26.50.53.69. Visiting hours: By appt.
Most champagne makers offer a range of products but Salon makes only a Cuvée "S," a vintage Blanc de Blancs made only in good years. The careful application of the proper technique ensures good acidity, which means the wine ages well.

MOUSSY, map 10
Paul Gobillard (M), Château de Pierry, BP 1, Pierry, 51200 Epernay. Tel: 26.54.05.11. Visiting hours: By appt; closed 3 weeks in Aug.
The Gobillard family have been making champagne for more than a century and now own the nearby Château de Pierry.

REIMS, map 10
Besserat de Bellefon (G/M), allée du Vignoble, BP 301, 51061 Reims. Tel: 26.36.09.18. Visiting hours: By appt; closed Aug.
Methods at Besserat de Bellefon are modern and the wines are excellent and on the light side, but little known abroad.

Heidsieck & Cie Monopole (G/M), 83 r. Coquebert, 51100 Reims. Tel: 26.07.39.34. Visiting hours: Mon–Fri by appt; closed hols and Aug.
The well-known company was bought by Mumm in 1972 but the two houses operate independently. Heidsieck's own vineyards, amounting to 110 hectares, provide almost one third of their needs. The firm owns the historic windmill at Verzenay which is used for receptions.

Charles Heidsieck (M), 3 pl. des Droits de l'Homme, 51100 Reims. Tel: 26.85.03.27. Visiting hours: Mon–Thu by appt; closed hols and Aug.
Charles-Camille Heidsieck, a member of the wine-making family, founded his own firm in 1851. He was the "Champagne Charlie" of George Leybourne's famous music-hall song, acquiring the name when he toured the United States in flamboyant style. Rémy Martin, the Cognac firm, now own Charles Heidsieck.

Krug Vins Fins de Champagne S.A. (G/M), 5 r. Coquebert, BP 22, 51051 Reims. Tel: 26.88.24.24. Visiting hours: Mon–Fri by appt.
Since the firm's establishment in 1843 by Johann-Joseph Krug of Mainz, it has enjoyed an enviable reputation for the finest quality and deliberately limits its production. Krug owns only 15 hectares of vines, 1.87 being in the famous Clos du Mesnil, which gives a Blanc de Blancs that is offered only in the best years in numbered bottles and features among the great champagnes.

Lanson Père et Fils (G/M), 12 bd Lundy, BP 163, 51100 Reims. Tel: 26.40.36.26. Visiting hours: Mon–Fri by appt; closed hols.
The company is one of the oldest houses in Champagne and is now owned by BSN, the giant French food group who also own the champagne house of Pommery. Its standard champagne, the non-vintage Black Label Brut, is famous worldwide and about 6 million bottles of it are produced each year.

Louis Roederer (G/M), 21 bd Lundy, BP 66, 51053 Reims. Tel: 26.40.42.11. Visiting hours: Mon–Fri am by appt.
The presence of Roederer on the wine lists of the world's leading restaurants is a proof of its quality and reputation. It is now a public company and owns 180 hectares of vines in the leading villages. The most prestigious *cuvée* is the Cuvée Cristal, a vintage wine named after Tsar Alexander II who had his orders filled in crystal bottles. Today it is bottled in clear glass with a cellophane wrapping to protect the wine from daylight.

Ruinart (G/M), 4 r. des Crayères, BP 85, 51053 Reims. Tel: 26.85.40.29. Visiting hours: Mon–Fri by appt.
The oldest of the champagne houses, Ruinart was founded in 1729, only 14 years after the death of Dom Pérignon. The cellars, with their magnificent Roman chalk quarries, are now a national monument. Today Ruinart is owned by the Moët-Hennessy group and produces a series of quality champagnes.

Les RICEYS, map 11
Pascal Morel (G), 93 r. Gén.-de-Gaulle, 10340 les Riceys. Tel: 25.29.10.88. Visiting hours: By appt; closed 2 weeks in Aug.
Rosé des Riceys is an unusual and

interesting rosé made only in this particular village and in minute quantities. It is rarely found outside the region. M. Morel owns a small vineyard of 5 hectares, and produces only a limited amount of wine, about 3,500 bottles of Rosé des Riceys annually. The color is deeper than usual, and the wine can age well.

TOURS-SUR-MARNE, map 10
Domaine Lamiable (G), 8 r. de Condé, 51150 Tours-sur-Marne. Tel: 26.58.92.69. Visiting hours: by appt. Jean-Pierre Lamiable makes a series of fine champagnes from *grand cru* vineyards.

Veuve Laurent-Perrier (G/M), Domaine de Tours-sur-Marne, 51150 Tours-sur-Marne. Tel: 26.58.91.22. Visiting hours: Mon–Fri by appt; closed hols and Aug.

The company was founded in 1812 by Eugène Laurent, whose widow, Emilie Perrier assumed direction of the firm, and the name was changed to Veuve Laurent-Perrier. Today, the champagne is called simply Laurent-Perrier.

The current owner of the firm is Bernard de Nonancourt. Laurent-Perrier is and always has been a dynamic company and was one of the first to sell to the United States. The firm makes a wide range of champagnes.

Sights

Though major cities such as Reims, Troyes or Châlons-sur-Marne all have impressive buildings dating back hundreds of years, the most moving of all are the modest monuments in almost every village to soldiers of World War I.

BAR-SUR-AUBE
On the banks of the Aube, this small, attractive country town is surrounded by wooded slopes and vineyards.

BAR-SUR-SEINE
A pretty town with some Renaissance houses. The **Eglise St Etienne** has fine old stained-glass windows.

CHALONS-SUR-MARNE
The former Gallo-Roman city of Catalaunum, Châlons is a thriving industrial center and was an important center of the champagne trade in the 19th century, though less so now. Despite its growth, it has preserved many fine buildings, especially of the 17th–18th centuries. The 12th-century **Eglise Notre-Dame-en-Vaux** with its **Musée du Cloître** contains a remarkable series of stained-glass windows dating from the 15th and 16th centuries. Also worth visiting is the **Cathédrale St Etienne**.

EPERNAY
In the middle of the vineyards, Epernay is where many of the most famous champagne houses have their cellars, and **les Caves de Champagne** are indeed the town's principal attraction. There is also an interesting **Musée du Champagne et de la Préhistoire.**

HAUTVILLERS
Hautvillers, on the southern slope of the Montagne de Reims, offers superb views of the surrounding vineyards. Its Benedictine abbey was the residence and "laboratory" of Dom Pérignon (1638–1715), who is credited with inventing champagne as we know it. Dom Pérignon's tombstone is in the sanctuary.

Hautvillers abbey

REIMS
Many of the most important champagne houses have their headquarters and cellars at Reims, the capital city of Champagne. These are concentrated in the Champ de Mars section to the north of the city center and along the slope of the Butte St Nicaise to the south-east.

Reims is also the site of one of France's

most famous cathedrals, the **Cathédrale Notre-Dame**. Though seriously damaged during World War I, it has been restored to much of its former Gothic splendor. Begun in 1211, it was for centuries the place where French kings were traditionally crowned. Many of these kings are buried nearby in the **Basilique St Rémi**.

Also worth a visit are the **Musée St Denis**, with its late 15th-century paintings by the Cranachs; the **Hôtel Musée le Vergeur**, devoted to the history of Reims and also boasting an exceptional series of Dürer engravings; and the **Salle de Guerre** where the German surrender was signed on May 7 1945 – the room has been left as it was on that momentous day.

Balloon excursions over Reims, Eper-nay and the villages and vineyards around the Montagne de Reims are organized each summer by the Champagne Air Show, 15 bis pl. St Nicaise, 51100 Reims. Tel: 26.82.59.60.

Reservations can be made in the United States by contacting Autoventure, 920 Logan Building, Seattle, WA 98101. Tel: (206) 624-6033.

VERTUS

This wine town is one of the most charming of the Côte des Blancs with narrow, irregular streets and numerous fountains. The Romanesque **Eglise St Martin**, built in the 11th century, has been restored following heavy fire damage in 1940.

Hotels, Restaurants and Where to Buy Wine

Champagne is where the famous *potée champenoise* (boiled pork and vegetables) and the *pieds de porc St Menehould* (breaded pigs' feet) are made, but these dishes are not considered "gastronomic" and people will insist that regional specialties don't exist here. No one serves the ham of Reims any more and the *pain d'épice* (spice bread) for which that city was famous has all but disappeared. Troyes proudly continues to produce vast quantities of a famous tripe sausage (*andouillette*) but on the whole, regional specialties are few and far between. Today, what is called a "regional specialty" is sometimes no more than the result of the chef adding a glass of champagne to whatever he is preparing, but some such creations have nonetheless become widely accepted: the *fricassée de poulet champenoise* (chicken in cream and champagne sauce) is a case in point.

A visit to this region is the perfect occasion to discover the variety of champagnes available and to experiment with them in combination with different foods. Nowhere are champagnes so reasonably priced, and most restaurants have a long list of excellent wines in the 150- to 200-franc category. Ideally, you would have dry champagne (*brut*) as an aperitif, a vintage champagne with fish, a *cuvée speciale* with chicken, veal or sweetbreads, a red Côteaux Champenois with cheese, and a bottle of *demi-sec* champagne with dessert.

Finally, at least one meal should end with a glass of Marc de Champagne, a brandy made from the residue of the pressed grapes. *Marcs* are extremely aromatic, but they can be "rough," representing perhaps the only link that exists between the champagne houses of today and the peasant traditions of the past that have all but disappeared.

Le Royal Champagne (R,H), 51160 Champillon-Bellevue (6km N of Epernay by N51). Tel: 26.51.11.51. One Michelin star. Closed Jan. AE DC MC V A marble plaque informs you that "Napoleon ate here" and the owner of this once modest inn does not want you to forget its military associations: crossed rifles and swords, and chandeliers in the form of battle flags decorate the dining-room. All this is overshadowed by the view of the vineyards from the dining-room, and the stupendous wine list. Over 130 champagnes are listed in a thick ring binder.

All the important *cuvées* are represented, as are some older bottles, such as a 1914 and a 1928 Moët & Chandon (both priced at 700 francs).

The cooking is straightforward and enjoyable; regionalism makes an appearance in the form of an excellent *fricassée de poulet au champagne* although, for the most part, the dishes are in a classic mode, with marginal concessions to *nouvelle* trends. One is likely to hear much talk of champagne at surrounding tables, since this restaurant is a favorite with the big houses in Châlons and Epernay.

AMBONNAY (51150, Tours-sur-Marne)

Auberge St Vincent (H,R), r. St Vincent. Tel: 26.57.01.98. DC MC
Small and inexpensive. Good-value menus.

BAR-SUR-AUBE (10200)

Le Commerce (H,R), 38 r. Nationale. Tel: 25.27.08.76. Closed Jan. AE DC MC V
A small attractive hotel in the center of town. Restaurant used by locals.

BERGERES-LES-VERTUS (51130, Vertus)

Mont-Aimé (H,R), 4 r. de Vertus. Tel: 26.52.21.31. Closed in Jan. AE DC MC V.
Quiet and simple. Menus at all prices.

CHALONS-SUR-MARNE (51000)

Angleterre (H) and **Jacky Michel (R)**, 19 pl. Monseigneur-Tissier. Tel: 26.68.21.51. AE DC MC V
Pleasant and quiet, this restaurant is often cited by locals as the best in Châlons, both for its excellent cellar and the quality of the cooking.

Aux Armes de Champagne (R,H), 51460 l'Epine (7km E by N3). Tel: 26.68.10.43. One Michelin star. DC MC V
This restaurant has a growing reputation and the cooking tends toward the adventurous *nouvelle* style.

EPERNAY (51200)

Les Berceaux (H,R), 13 r. des Berceaux. Tel: 26.55.28.84. AE DC MC V
A comfortable hotel with English owners. Good choice of champagnes, many of which are served in the wine bar attached to the restaurant.

La Briqueterie (H,R), rte de Sézanne, Vinay, 51200 Epernay (7km S on N51). Tel: 26.54.11.22. One Michelin star. AE MC V
Quiet and comfortable with garden. Excellent service and magnificent cellar.

Champagne (H), 30 r. E.-Mercier. Tel: 26.55.30.22. AE MC DC V
Modern and near the champagne cellars.

Yag (W), 38 r. Henri-Dunant. Tel: 26.51.72.40.
A good wine shop, despite its name.

Le MESNIL-SUR-OGER (51190, Avize)

Le Mesnil (R), 2 r. Pasteur. Tel: 26.57.95.57. AE DC MC V
Cheerful service and elegant. Large list of champagnes.

MONTCHENOT (51500, Rilly-la-Montagne)

Auberge du Grand Cerf (R). Tel: 26.97.60.07. One Michelin star. AE MC V
Excellent service and cellar.

REIMS (51100)

Assiette Champenoise (R), 40 av. Paul Vaillant-Couturier. Tel: 26.04.15.56. One Michelin star. AE DC MC V
Inventive and light *cuisine*. Excellent service and cellar.

Boyer "les Crayères" (H,R), 64 bd Henri Vasnier. Tel: 26.82.80.80. Three Michelin stars. Reservations essential. Closed Christmas and New Year. AE DC MC V
Sixteen luxurious rooms and apartments in a 19th-century château, set in a large garden. No doubt the region's most talked-about chef and the only one to have earned three Michelin stars. *Nouvelle* to the extreme, Boyer indulges in flights of fancy that may not be to everyone's taste. Wines are reasonably priced but dinner can be expensive.

Le Chardonnay (R), 184 av. Epernay. Tel: 26.06.08.60. Closed Sun pm, 10 days in Feb and 2 weeks end Jul. One Michelin star. AE DC MC V
Simple *cuisine* and friendly service.

Le Florence (R), 43 bd Foch. Tel: 26.47.12.70. One Michelin star. AE DC MC V
Elegant, and good champagne list.

Hôtel de la Paix (H,R), 9 r. Buirette. Tel: 26.40.04.08. AE DC MC V
Comfortable establishment with garden and swimming pool. Good-value menus.

La Vinocave (W), 43 pl. Drouet-d'Erlon, Tel: 26.40.60.07. MC V
An extensive selection of wines.

SILLERY (51500)

Relais de Sillery (R), 3 r. de la Gare. Tel: 26.49.10.11. MC V
Charming inn with good-value menus.

CORSICA

The island of Corsica, a mountain range rising sheer from the sea 175km from the French coast, has stronger historical ties with the Italian peninsula than with France and officially became part of France only in 1768; three months later its most famous son, Napoleon Bonaparte, was born in Ajaccio. Corsica has not always been as attractive a place for the tourist as it is today. The eastern shore was dangerously infested with malaria-carrying mosquitos which were not eradicated until after World War II. Both the landscape and the population have changed dramatically since then. Thousands of displaced Frenchmen resettled here in the late 1950s and 1960s following independence in Algeria, and invested heavily in two crops, grapes and tangerines. Tourism and wine now produce most of the island's income and the rest comes from the orchards where vast quantities of tangerines and kiwi fruit are grown.

Getting to Corsica is relatively simple nowadays. There are regular car and passenger ferry services all year round from the mainland; sailings are from Marseille or Nice, with additional crossings from Toulon in the summer. There are also daily flights from Paris, Marseille and Nice. Tourists are warmly welcomed by the islanders and invited to discover the diversity and natural beauty of what they proudly call the *Ile de Beauté*.

The Wines of Corsica

Though Corsica has one of the oldest wine-making traditions in Europe, the influx from Algeria greatly expanded the area under vine, but sadly in areas not suitable for viticulture, so that many of these vineyards have now been pulled up. The area under vine now amounts to 10,000 hectares. Serious producers have concentrated on the traditional grape varieties and have improved their vinification methods so that Corsican wines now have some individual character and quality, with a unique island flavor.

Grape varieties found throughout the south of France are also cultivated on Corsica; they include Grenache, Cinsaut and Carignan. However, it is the island's indigenous varieties that give the better wines their distinctive character. The Nielluccio, for example, is used to make one of the island's best reds in the Patrimonio *appellation*. The Sciacarello, used especially in the wines of Sartène, gives body and character to wines meant to be aged. The Vermentino makes good white wines when harvested early.

Patrimonio was the first *appellation* on the island. Now Vin de Corse is the regional *appellation* with local names added – Patrimonio, Coteaux d'Ajaccio, Figari, Sartène, Porto-Vecchio, Coteaux du Cap Corse or Calvi. The proportion of *appellation* wines is on the increase, and there is also a delightful-sounding Vin de Pays l'Ile de Beauté.

Visiting the Vineyards

The vineyards of Corsica spread inland from the coast all around the island. The scenery is spectacular, with craggy mountains rising out of the sea while the interior is cut by narrow isolated valleys. Be warned, however, that this is wild country; the highways are frequently narrow and there are usually more curves per kilometer than the traveler can count. Swift journeys are impossible in Corsica, with the possible exception of that between Bonifacio and Bastia on the eastern seaboard where the road is quite good and straight.

Corsica can be uncomfortably hot and crowded in high summer while in winter storms and high winds make visits to the interior difficult. Spring is changeable, while early summer or fall are almost always delightful and by far the best times to visit the island.

Route One

From Bastia to Calvi around Cap Corse: 180km

The Itinerary:

This is a very long day's drive, so break the journey at St Florent, a seaside town, if you don't want to be too exhausted. From **Bastia**, take D80 along the coast through a succession of small ports and narrow inlets around Cap Corse. Scattered vineyards, mainly at Rogliano on the northern tip, produce red, rosé and white wines all eligible for the *appellation* Vin de Corse-Coteaux du Cap Corse.

Seven kilometers south of **Nonza**, on the western side of the peninsula, is **Patrimonio**, home of the island's finest wines. To visit the area, take D81 eastward to the **Col de Teghime**, then D38 as far south as **Oletta**, and D82 to **St Florent** on the coast. If you prefer not to drive this extremely tortuous but beautiful inland route, simply continue westward along the coast on D81 from Patrimonio to St Florent.

From St Florent, D81 winds westward to the sea near **Ogliastro**. Shortly before it meets N197, the road enters the vineyards of the Vin de Corse-Calvi *appellation*. Continue right along the coast on N197 through **l'Ile-Rousse**, an appealing resort town, to **Calvi**. Alternatively, if you have the time, turn left on N197 to go inland to explore **Corte**, the ancient capital of the island.

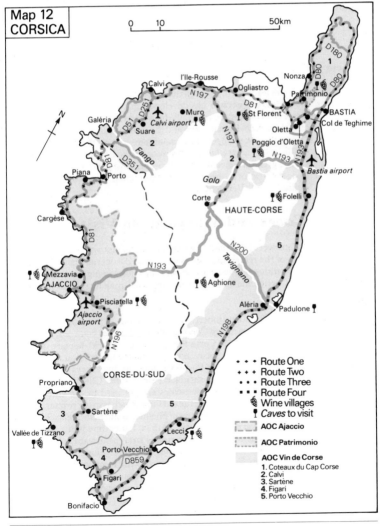

Route Two

Calvi to Ajaccio: 160km

From **Calvi**, take N197, then bear right on D251 to the hamlet of **Suare**, then right on D51 in the direction of Galéria; do not go into Galéria but continue on D351 and D81 to **Porto**. The Calvi production area ends just south of the point where the highway crosses the river Fango. Near Porto the vineyards of the Ajaccio *appellation* begin; continue on D81 through **Piana** and **Cargèse**, along the coast and through the mountains to **Mezzavia** and **Ajaccio**, a lively port.

Route Three

From Ajaccio to Bonifacio: 140km

Leave **Ajaccio** on N193, drive past the airport, then turn right on N196 and drive through the mountains to the seaside resort of **Propriano**. Continue on this road to the medieval town of **Sartène** which has lent its name to another Vin-de-Corse *appellation*. From there N196 leads through the small *appellation* of Vin de Corse-Figari to **Bonifacio**, an old fortress-port on a cliff-lined peninsula where there are good views of Sardinia in the distance.

Route Four

Bonifacio to Bastia: 180km

From **Bonifacio**, N198 leads north through the vineyards of the Vin de Corse-Porto-Vecchio *appellation*. **Porto-Vecchio** has developed in recent years as one of the island's leading resorts. N198 can be taken all the way back from here to Bastia. At **Aléria**, the ruins of the Greco-Roman town and the museum are worth visiting. The many vineyards along the lower slopes of the mountains and on the coastal plain are part of the overall Vin de Corse *appellation* or produce Vin de Pays l'Ile de Beauté. The area claims the island's greatest concentration of co-operative wineries, some of which have concentrated their efforts on Cabernet Sauvignon and Chardonnay, in preference to Nielluccio and Vermentino.

Caves and Vineyards to Visit

A small number of growers (less than 1 per cent) control almost 20 per cent of the vineyards and much of the remaining land is worked by co-operatives. Experiments with both new and traditional grape varieties and the efforts being made to improve overall quality make Corsica one of the most exciting wine-making regions in France.

LECCI, map 12
Domaine de Torraccia (G),
Lecci, 20137 Porto-Vecchio.
Tel: 95.71.43.50.

Christian Imbert, the owner, is one of the most enthusiastic proponents of Corsican wine and makes good red, white and rosé Vin de Corse Porto-Vecchio. His 35-hectare domaine lies on hills between the sea and the inland mountains about 10km north of Porto-Vecchio and the vineyards have been created out of shrubland since 1966. Chemical fertilizers, herbicides and pesticides are not used in the vineyards.

His best wine is the red Oriu which is made primarily from the Corsican varieties of Nielluccio and Sciacarello. The wine is warm and tannic with a fruity bouquet, capable of moderate aging. The rosé is straightforward, pleasant and undemanding and should be drunk young. The dry white from Vermentino goes well with local seafood while the standard red is made from the island's indigenous varieties, with some Syrah for greater complexity.
Visiting hours: Mon–Sat 8–12, 2–7; closed hols.
Location: 1km N of Lecci.

MEZZAVIA, map 12

Domaine Comte Peraldi (G),
chemin du Stiletto,
20167 Mezzavia.
Tel: 95.22.37.30.

The estate has 40 hectares of vineyards which are well situated on the ridge of the Mezzavia, overlooking the Gulf of Ajaccio from the north-east. It is an old property but the owner, the Comte de Poix, is also looking to the future. The vineyards have been replanted since 1966. The different varieties – Nielluccio, Sciacarello, Vermentino, Grenache, Cinsaut and Carignan – are vinified separately, then blended together to make a variety of wines. The red Coteaux d'Ajaccio, made from 60 per cent Sciacarello, is a powerful wine with a bouquet of tobacco and red fruits that can usually be extensively aged. The count is experimenting with aging his red wines in oak *barriques* bought from Beaune.
Visiting hours: Mon–Sat 8–12, 2–6; open until 7pm in summer.
Location: 3km S of Mezzavia on N194.

PATRIMONIO, map 12

Clos de Morta Maio (G),
20253 Patrimonio.
Tel: 95.37.08.27.

The domaine's fine white, made entirely from Malvoisie, is pale yellow with greenish highlights, a floral bouquet and a balanced fresh flavor. The wine is made from grapes grown on a 6-hectare vineyard owned by Antoine Arena, who comes from an old Corsican family.
Visiting hours: Daily 7–7.
Location: In the center of the village.

PISCIATELLA, map 12

Clos Capitoro (G),
rte de Sartène,
Pisciatella,
20166 Porticcio.
Tel: 95.25.19.61.

Part of the 20-hectare property run by the Bianchetti family is within the *appellation* Vin de Corse-Coteaux d'Ajaccio, while the rest is covered by the *appellation* Vin de Corse. The red Ajaccio Clos Capitoro is the best wine, with a good flavor and a bouquet of tobacco and vanilla. It is a substantial wine which can be aged for up to a decade. Jacques Bianchetti believes wine should be handled with velvet gloves!
Visiting hours: Mon–Sat 8–12, 2–6; groups by appt.
Location: Signposted from Pisciatella.

Further *Caves* and Vineyards to Visit

AGHIONE, map 12

Domaine du Listincone (G), Aghione, 20270 Aléria. Tel: 95.56.13.89. Visiting hours: By appt.
The domaine's Muscat, a Vin de Pays l'Ile de Beauté, is good. Although sweetish, it has a dry finish that makes it particularly pleasant when served, well-chilled, as an aperitif.

FOLELLI, map 12

Domaine de Musoleu (G), Folelli, 20213 Castellare di Casinca. Tel: 95.36.80.12. Visiting hours: Mon–Sat 8–12, 3–7.
The domaine on the edge of the coastal plain is owned by Charles Morazzani, and produces red and rosé Vin de Corse. The rosé has benefited from modern

technology and goes well with local *cuisine*, particularly charcuterie. The red is a warm and supple wine.

MURO, map 12

Clos Réginu (G), 20225 Muro. Tel: 95.61.72.11. Visiting hours: Mon and Wed–Sat 8–12, 4–7.
The 24-hectare domaine, owned by Michel Raoust, is in the middle of nowhere, high up in the mountains and there are wonderful views on the way. He grows a wide variety of grapes – Grenache, Nielluccio, Sciacarello, Malvoisie, Barbarossa, Syrah, Carignan, Cinsaut and Ugni Blanc – to make wines in the *appellation* Vin de Corse-Calvi. There is a small, well-equipped cellar with stainless-steel vats and a few

wooden barrels. The Blanc de Blancs, made from Malvoisie, is dry and fragrant, and best drunk in its youth. Both the red and rosé are supple, perfumed wines.

PADULONE, map 12
Cave Co-opérative d'Aléria (C), Padulone, 20270 Aléria. Tel: 95.57.02.48. Visiting hours: By appt.
The co-operative winery is on the shores of the Mediterranean near Aléria. Its most interesting wine is the Réserve du Président, a red Vin de Corse made mainly from Syrah and Nielluccio.

POGGIO-D'OLETTA, map 12
Domaine Leccia (G), 20232 Poggio-d'Oletta. Tel: 95.39.03.22. Visiting hours: Mon–Sat 8–6.
The estate makes a good red Patrimonio from grapes grown on 20 hectares altogether. The owner, Yves Leccia, now uses Nielluccio as well as some Grenache to make a supple wine with a peppery nose and rich flavors. He also makes an excellent white Patrimonio, a rosé and a perfumed Muscat *vin doux naturel*. The

estate is off the beaten track, with a small, neat cellar outside the village of Oletto.

ST FLORENT, map 12
Domaine Dominique Gentile (G), Olzo, 20217 St Florent. Tel: 95.37.01.54. Visiting hours: By appt.
The 16-hectare domaine produces red, rosé and white wines within the Patrimonio *appellation*. There is also a sweet red wine, called Rappu, which is the most individual wine of the estate. It is made from overripe grapes, aged in wood and bottled after three years.

VALLEE DE TIZZANO, map 12
Domaine d'Ariale (G), Vallée de Tizzano, 20100 Sartène. Tel: 95.77.00.27. Visiting hours: Jun–Oct Mon–Sat, 8–12, 4–7.30; Nov–May by appt.
The 21 hectares of vines were planted in 1963 by J.-A. Mosconi. Half the domaine is used to make an interesting red Vin de Corse-Sartène that is fruity and supple with an attractive bouquet and flavor.

Sights

The tourist visiting Corsica will discover the remains of Greek and Roman settlements, medieval villages and striking fortifications, small churches and chapels. These, together with the natural wild beauty of the island and the varied coastline, make it an ideal vacation spot.

AJACCIO
The capital of Corsica, Ajaccio could be called the "town of the Bonapartes": the house where Napoleon was born can be visited; there is a **Musée Napoléonien** in the Hôtel de Ville and statues of the little corporal throughout the town.

There are other things to see in Ajaccio, however, such as its 16th-century cathedral, and **pl. Mar.-Foch**, a palm-shaded square which is the town's social center.

ALERIA
In an area of large lakes and long sandy beaches, Aleria was once a Greek colony later occupied by the Romans. The Roman city has been excavated and visitors can see the remains of many buildings. Many of the artifacts found are in the **Musée Jérome Carcopino**.

BASTIA
Founded by the Genoese in 1380, Bastia is the largest and most lively port in Corsica. The center of the city's bustling social life is the **pl. St Nicolas**, where everyone seems to gather in bars and cafés in the early evening. A visit to the **Musée d'Ethnographie Corse** gives an excellent insight into Corsican life, from ancient times to the present.

BONIFACIO
The town is spectacularly situated on top of a narrow peninsula at the southernmost tip of Corsica. From the old town, a maze of narrow alleys and massive walls perched high above the sea, there are views across the sea to Sardinia. Excursion boats make regular trips around the peninsula. The port and new quarter around it are the liveliest parts of Bonifacio.

CALVI

This pleasant little port has two distinct parts: the fading grandeur of the 15th-century citadel on top of a rocky promontory, and **la Marine**, the harbor and nearby busy tourist beaches ringed by pine forests and mountains.

The ancient citadel of Calvi.

PORTO-VECCHIO

The port, now a popular resort, was founded by the Genoese in 1539. However, its growth was impeded until the 20th century by the unhealthiness of the area, where malaria was endemic. Part of the Genoese fortress has survived.

ST FLORENT

The old town in a picturesque bay is a warren of narrow streets and small flower-decked squares around the Genoese citadel.

SARTENE

This inland town is perched high up in the mountains with views of the sea. The **quartier de Santa Anna** is typically old Corsican.

Hotels, Restaurants and Where to Buy Wine

Corsican cooking relies on the use of humble products specific to the island, such as chestnut flour, goat's meat, fresh sheep's milk, and wild pig. The dark, powerful Corsican reds are at their best with the dark meat stews popular on the island while the rather unusual whites can be served with either fish or poultry.

AJACCIO (20000)

Côte d'Azur (R), 12 cours Napoléon. Tel: 95.21.50.24. Closed Sun, and mid-Jun–mid-Jul. AE DC V
Fish dishes and some interesting Patrimonio white wines. Good-value menus.

Hôtel Fesch (H), 7 r. Fesch. Tel: 95.21.50.52. AE DC MC V
Traditional hotel in the center of town.

BASTIA (20200)

Chez Assunta (R), 4 pl. Fontaine Neuve. Tel: 95.31.67.06. Closed Sun and Jan. AE DC MC V
Fish dishes; *nouvelle* and local specialties well served in a converted chapel.

Pietracap (H), Pietranera, 20200 Bastia (2km N on D80, then 1km from D80). Tel: 95.31.64.63. AE DC MC V
Large rooms with balconies in quiet, comfortable modern hotel.

CALVI (20260)

Grand Hotel (H), 3 bd Prés.-Wilson. Tel: 95.65.09.74. AE DC MC V
Fine old hotel with superb views. Six apartments.

Restaurant Ile de Beauté (R), quai Landry. Tel: 95.65.00.46. One Michelin star. Closed Sep–May. AE DC MC V
Good fish dishes, local wines and fine views over the harbor. Probably the best restaurant on the island.

PORTO-VECCHIO (20137)

Restaurant Lucullus (R), r. Gén.-de-Gaulle. Tel: 95.70.10.17. AE DC MC V
Small, interesting bistro with large, unpretentious menu. Good local wines.

U Stagnolu (R,H), rte Cala Rossa, 20137 Porto-Vecchio (7km NE by N198 and D468). Tel: 95.70.02.07. Closed Sep–Apr. AE DC MC V
Rooms, studios and apartments with kitchenettes. *Pension* only in season.

PROPRIANO (20110)

Lido (R,H). Tel: 95.76.06.37. AE DC V
Seafood specialties. *Demi-pension* obligatory in season.

Hôtel Miramar (H,R), rte de la Corniche. Tel: 95.76.06.13. Closed Nov–Easter. DC
Large, luxurious, finely furnished rooms in modern hotel overlooking the sea.

JURA

The Jura, like much of eastern France, was for a long time part of the Dukedom of Burgundy and did not become French until 1678. It is mostly wild, mountainous country, physically more akin to Switzerland than France. Vines have been grown here since Roman times, on the gentler slopes in the west of the region. The area was badly devastated by phylloxera at the end of the nineteenth century, and most of the replanted vineyards today lie between Arbois and Lons-le-Saunier.

The Wines of Jura

The regional *appellation* is the Côtes du Jura, which covers whites, reds and rosés as well as *vin jaune*, Jura's most characteristic wine. Specific *appellations* are Arbois (best for red wine), Château-Chalon (exclusively for *vin jaune*) and l'Etoile (exclusively for white wine). Local grape varieties dominate throughout the region and the wines are distinctly different from those in any other part of France.

The whites, which are the best wines, are made from Chardonnay or the local Savagnin grape and often have a sherry-like taste that is most concentrated in the famous *vin jaune*, made from ripe Savagnin grapes and aged at least six years in wooden casks before bottling. It has a deep golden color and nutty bouquet and flavor and will appeal to all sherry lovers. The other Jura specialty is *vin de paille*, a rare, and hence expensive, sweet wine made from overripe grapes which were dried originally on straw mats, hence the name, and now by hanging up the bunches in well-ventilated rooms to concentrate the sugar.

Reds and rosés are generally less impressive than the whites, though rosé made from the local Poulsard grape can be quite elegant; and reds, customarily made from the local Trousseau grape, with or without the addition of some Pinot Noir, yield sturdy wines that can age well.

Recommended Route

From St-Amour north to Arbois : 105km

The vineyards of the Côtes du Jura begin in the south around **St Amour**. From St Amour take N83 north toward Lons-le-Saunier; after **Beaufort**, which is better known for its cheese than for its wines, the vines steadily increase in number. From the peaceful town of **Lons-le-Saunier**, continue on N83 in the direction of Poligny through the vineyards of **l'Etoile**, which is an important but small white wine *appellation*.

In **St Germain-lès-Arlay**, turn either left to **Arlay** on D120 to visit two good growers, Jean Bourdy and Château d'Arlay, or right on D120 to **Voiteur**, where there is a left turn onto D5, a narrow road that winds up the steep hills to **Château-Chalon**, a tiny mountain-top village famous for *vin jaune*.

After visiting Château-Chalon take D5 back down the hill; at the first hairpin bend, a narrow road leads off to the right. This is D57E1, which winds its way north among vineyards and forests through **Menétru-le-Vignoble** to **Passenans**. From Passenans, D101 leads back to N83. Turn right on N83 to go to the wine-making town of **Poligny**, one of the most charming in Jura and the center of the Comté cheese industry; continue on N83 to **Arbois**, the picturesque wine capital of the region with an *appellation* of its own. (If you wish to visit growers at Pupillin, between Poligny and Arbois, take a turning to the right at **Buvilly** and then left to **Pupillin**.) The area around Arbois is heavily planted in vines but only a short distance to the north, after **Montigny-lès-Arsures**, the vineyards stop and the Jura wine route ends. At Montigny-lès-Arsures, Lucien Aviet at the Caveau de Bacchus makes some excellent wines. Salins-les-Bains, another delightful Jura town, is only 6km to the north-east by N83 and D105.

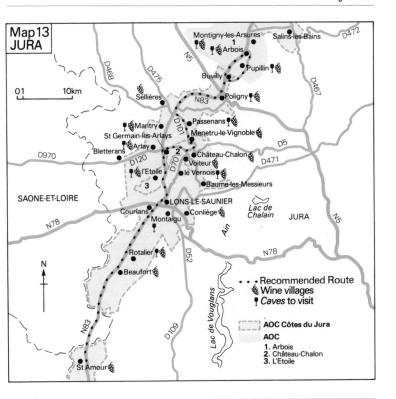

Map 13
JURA

0 1   10km

Montigny-les-Arsures
1
Arbois
Salins-les-Bains
Pupillin
Buvily
Sellières
Poligny
Passenans
Mantry
Menetru-le-Vignoble
St Germain-les-Arlays
Bletterans
Arlay
2
Château-Chalon
l'Etoile
Voiteur
le Vernois
3
Baume-les-Messieurs
SAONE-ET-LOIRE
LONS-LE-SAUNIER
Lac de Chalain
JURA
Courlans
Conliège
Montaigu
Ain
Rotalier
Beaufort
Lac de Vouglans
N
St Amour

• • • Recommended Route
🍷 Wine villages
🍷 *Caves* to visit

- - - AOC Côtes du Jura
AOC
1. Arbois
2. Château-Chalon
3. L'Etoile

Caves and Vineyards to Visit

Vineyards which covered 20,000 hectares as recently as the late 19th century, cover no more than 1,500 today. Co-operatives (called *fruitières vinicoles* here) are important. Polyculture has tended to disappear as people have made the choice between vines, wheat or cows and in recent years vineyards have been grouped into larger units.

ARBOIS, map 13
Henri Maire (G/M),
les Tonneaux,
r. de l'Hôtel-de-Ville, 39600 Arbois.
Tel: 84.66.12.34.

Henri Maire is the Jura's largest winemaker, and after Pasteur, the best known *fils d'Arbois*. He has done much to promote the region and to revive the quality and the reputation of its wines, especially *vin jaune*. His properties, totaling 400 hectares of vineyards, 300 in production, center on the attractive town of Arbois, in the middle of which he has set up a "hospitality complex" for visitors. The white Arbois of the Domaine de la Grange Grillard, established in the 16th century, is excellent, as is his *vin jaune*.
Visiting hours: Daily 8.30–5.
Location: In the center of town.

ARLAY, map 13
Jean Bourdy (G/M), Arlay,
39140 Bletterans.
Tel: 84.85.03.70.

This firm, now run by Christian Bourdy, is one of the great producers of Château-Chalon and also makes an excellent *vin jaune* under the Côtes du Jura *appellation* from its 5-hectare vineyard at Arlay, as well as red, white and rosé Côtes du Jura. The date 1781 on the wall of the cellar marks the beginning of the Bourdy family's involvement in the region's wine-making.
Visiting hours: Daily 9–8.
Location: Signposted in the village center.

Château d'Arlay (G/M), Arlay, 39140 Bletterans. Tel: 84.85.04.22.

The château, with its Restoration furnishings, is elegant, and has nice gardens. The 27-hectare vineyard, owned by Comte Renaud de Laguiche, produces excellent wines and is undoubtedly the best Jura property. The most intriguing is the rosé Côtes du Jura Cuvée Corail which is a blend of five varieties; the reds are the indigenous Poulsard and Trousseau, plus Pinot Noir, and the whites are Chardonnay and the indigenous Savagnin. The estate also makes red and white Côtes du Jura and a rich and superbly scented *vin jaune*. Sales hours: Mon–Fri 9–12, 2–6. Cellar visits: Jul–Aug daily, 10–12, 2–6; closed Sun am.
Location: 7km from Arlay on the road to Bletterans, and signposted.

MONTIGNY-LES-ARSURES, map 13

Lucien Aviet (G), Caveau de Bacchus, Montigny-lès-Arsures, 39600 Arbois. Tel: 84.66.11.02.

Lucien Aviet is one of the characters of Arbois; he names his vats not after vineyard plots, but after his best customers! The red Cuvée des Géologues, made from Trousseau, is a fine wine of considerable strength with a bouquet that needs some bottle age to develop fully. The Cuvée des Docteurs, made entirely from Poulsard, is a fine and delicate wine and benefits from moderate aging. M. Aviet's *vin jaune* is excellent, too, and is the perfect accompaniment for mature local Comté cheese. There are white wines as well, made from Chardonnay and Savagnin. The domaine covers a total of 5 hectares.
Visiting hours: Daily by appt.
Location: 3km N of Arbois.

Rolet Père et Fils (G), au Caveau des Capucins, pl. de l'Hôtel-de-Ville, Montigny-lès-Arsures, 39600 Arbois. Tel: 84.66.00.05.

The Rolet family's vineyards cover a total of 48 hectares which makes their property the second largest wine estate in the Jura. They make good wines of all types. Their *vin jaune* has balance, richness and aromatic length, while their two red Arbois, made from Pinot Noir and Trousseau respectively, both reflect the characteristics of the grapes and demonstrate the quality of Arbois. The rosé made from Poulsard is a substantial wine that gains flavor from aging. The Rolets also make very reliable whites from Chardonnay and Savagnin, as well as a red Côtes du Jura.
Visiting hours: (Sales only) daily 9–12, 2–7. Cellar visits by appt.
Location: Opposite the Hôtel de Ville.

Further *Caves* and Vineyards to Visit

ARBOIS, map 13

Jacques Forêt (G), 44 r. de la Faïencerie, 39600 Arbois. Tel: 84.66.11.37. Visiting hours: Daily 8–12, 2–7.

On his 13 hectares of vineyards, Forêt cultivates Trousseau and Pinot Noir for his red wines and Chardonnay and Savagnin for the whites. All his wines are of high quality, especially the finely scented Arbois rosé, which, like all Jura rosé, is deep pink in color, with the depth of flavor, weight and ability to age of a red wine. The red Arbois is a complete wine that also lends itself to aging in bottle and the Chardonnay has a pronounced bouquet and flavor. There is also a rounded Chardonnay Savagnin blend and a champagne-method sparkling wine.

Fruitière Vinicole d'Arbois (C), 2 r. des Fossés, 39600 Arbois. Tel: 84.66.11.67. Visiting hours: Daily 8–12, 2–6.

The co-operative was founded in 1906 and is one of the oldest wine co-operatives in France. Its members cultivate 400 hectares of vines between them, which is a sizeable production for the region. However, there is a very strict selection of grapes, resulting in some excellent wines. The best is the sparkling Côtes du Jura, a fresh and lively wine that makes an excellent aperitif. The still white Arbois Grande Sélection has a good bouquet. Aging in bottle is recommended for the red Arbois Cuvée Vieilles Vignes but the rosé Vigne-St-Jean should be drunk young. Naturally, they also make a *vin jaune*, which is very aromatic, with a perfume of walnuts and almonds.

L'ETOILE, map 13
Château l'Etoile (G), l'Etoile, 39570 Lons-le-Saunier. Tel: 84.47.33.07. Visiting hours: Mon–Sat 8–7.
This estate, run by J. H. Vandelle et Fils, is one of the two principal producers of the tiny *appellation* of l'Etoile. The château sits on a hilltop, with 20 hectares of vines tumbling down the steep hillsides. The *vin jaune* has an attractive bouquet of hazelnuts and vanilla with a long, lingering finish. The l'Etoile is a fine white wine, as is the champagne-method sparkling wine.

Domaine de Montbourgeau (G), l'Etoile, 39570 Lons-le-Saunier. Tel: 84.47.32.96. Visiting hours: Daily; appt preferred.
The 7-hectare domaine, owned by Jean Gros and his daughter Nicole, is the other principal producer of l'Etoile and it has an excellent reputation. They make *vin jaune* and a rich *vin de paille* from partly dried grapes that is the traditional regional accompaniment to *foie gras*.

MANTRY, map 13
Gabriel Clerc et Fils (G), Mantry, 39230 Sellières. Tel: 84.85.50.98. Visiting hours: By appt.
This small domaine makes sparkling wine from Pinot Noir and red, white and rosé Côtes du Jura. The fruity rosé is particularly good.

MONTAIGU, map 13
Cellier des Chartreux de Vaucluse (G), 11 pl. Rouget-de-Lisle, Montaigu, 39570 Lons-le-Saunier. Tel: 84.24.24.30. Visiting hours: Daily by appt.
The 12th-century vaulted cellar, once used by a monastic community, is now owned by P. and F. Pignier, who make a fine white Côtes du Jura that is delicate

and aromatic, as well as a rich, mouth-filling *vin de paille*.

MONTIGNY-LES-ARSURES, map 13
Roger Lornet (G), Montigny-lès-Arsures, 39600 Arbois. Tel: 84.66.09.40. Visiting hours: Daily pm or by appt.
The red Arbois produced by Roger Lornet is among the best of the *appellation* and requires considerable aging in bottle to mellow. The white can also be laid down for as much as five years in most vintages. M. Lornet and his son cultivate 8 hectares of vines divided between several small, scattered vineyards. Vinification varies according to grape varieties, which include Trousseau, Chardonnay, Savagnin, Poulsard and a little Pinot Noir.

PASSENANS, map 13
Grand Frères (G), Passenans, 39230 Sellières. Tel: 84.85.28.88. Visiting hours: Daily 9–12, 1.30–7.
The white Côtes du Jura is the best of the domaine's wines with its bouquet of almonds and long-lingering flavor. There is also a *vin jaune*, a red Côtes du Jura and a dry sparkling Chardonnay, all made in the modern cellars.

POLIGNY, map 13
Caveau des Jacobins (C), r. du Collège, 39800 Poligny. Tel: 84.37.14.58. Visiting hours: Mon–Sat 9–12, 1.30–6.30; Sun 10–12.
The co-operative, which has set up a retail sales outlet in a deconsecrated church in the center of Poligny, makes red, white and rosé Côtes du Jura.

PUPILLIN, map 13
Désiré Petit et Fils (G), Pupillin, 39600 Arbois. Tel: 84.66.01.20. Visiting hours: Daily 8–8.
The village of Pupillin distinguishes itself from others in the Arbois *appellation* with a mention on the label. Désiré Petit and his son Gérard have 12 hectares planted with the five Jura grape varieties, and as well as Pupillin they make a little Côtes du Jura. The fact that their 1978 Vin Jaune Arbois was selected for the 50th anniversary celebrations of the INAO (the Institut National des Appellations d'Origine) is indicative of the quality of their wines.

ROTALIER, map 13
Domaine du Château Gréa (G),
Rotalier, 39190 Beaufort. Tel:
84.25.05.07. Visiting hours: Mon–Sat 9–
12, 2–7; groups by appt.
This is an old domaine, dating from 1679.
The owner, Pierre de Boissieu, uses
traditional grape varieties and traditional
vinification methods. There is a wide
range of Côtes du Jura wines.

Le VERNOIS, map 13
Pierre Richard (G), le Vernois, 39210
Voiteur. Tel: 84.25.33.27. Visiting
hours: By appt.
Pierre Richard has a small domaine and is
dedicated to the quality of his wines. His
family have been at le Vernois since the
early 16th century. His champagne-
method sparkling wine is one of the best
in the area.

Sights

There is an unhurried pace to life in the Jura. The countryside is splendid and even the
smallest village contains something of beauty and interest.

ARBOIS
This is an attractive small town. There is
a small wine museum in the cellars of the
Hôtel de Ville. A wine festival is held in
the second half of Jul and another on the
1st Sun of Sep.

Vin jaune *is sold in special, small, stumpy
62cl* clavelin *bottles.*

BAUME-LES-MESSIEURS
The impressive remains of an old abbey
lie in a beautiful steep-sided valley called
the **Cirque de Baume** (there are many
of these *cirques* or horseshoe-shaped cliffs
in Jura). There is a small museum of local
Jura crafts in the abbey.

LONS-LE-SAUNIER
A spa town as far back as the Romans,
Lons-le-Saunier is today the prefecture
of the Jura. The 11th-century crypt of
the **Eglise St Désiré** is one of the oldest
in the Jura. Attractive arcaded buildings
line both sides of the **r. de Commerce**,
most dating from the late 16th and 17th
centuries and there are pleasant gardens
surrounding the thermal baths.

Hotels and Restaurants

Few Frenchmen can name a single specialty from the Jura other than cheese and wine.
The delicious smoked and dried beef (*brési*) rarely leaves the region, and dishes such as
the famous *poulet au vin jaune* can be made only where this golden wine is plentiful. The
mountain lakes and streams are full of fish and there are excellent smoked meats and
sausages, as well as a range of fine cheeses, including the solid, nutty Comté and the
velvety soft Vacherin.

ARBOIS (39600)
Le Paris (R,H), 9 r. de l'Hôtel de Ville.
Tel: 84.66.05.67. One Michelin star.
Closed Mon pm, Tue and mid-Nov–
mid-Mar. AE DC MC V
Jean-Paul Jeunet serves both *nouvelle*
and traditional fare. Wine-tasting can be
arranged. Excellent cellar.

LONS-LE-SAUNIER (39000)
Le Cheval Rouge (R,H), 47 r.
Lecourbe. Tel: 84.47.20.44. Closed Tue
Jul–Aug. DC MC V
Modest, family-run establishment. The
restaurant offers traditional and regional
dishes with a *nouvelle* touch. Good-value
menus.

COURLANS (39570)
Auberge de Chavannes (R). Tel:
84.47.05.52. One Michelin star. Reservations recommended. AE DC
Small, country establishment.

ST AMOUR (39160)
Hôtel Alliance (H,R), r. Ste Marie.
Tel: 84.48.74.94. DC MC V
Attractive small hotel in a 17th-century
monastery.

Four *départements* make up the region known as the Languedoc-Roussillon or the Midi – Gard, Hérault, Aude and Pyrénées-Orientales. It is an historic part of France which has seen much coming and going by passing armies – from Hannibal and his elephants, and the Romans, who founded great cities such as Arles and Nîmes, to the Catalans who ruled the Roussillon in the early Middle Ages as part of the Kingdom of Catalonia.

Everywhere you look in this region there are vines, down on the arid plains and up on the hillsides too and after traveling in the region it comes as no surprise to learn that over 40 per cent of all French wine is produced here. For far too long, however, the wines of the Midi were thought of as uninteresting or even as downright poor and fit only to add to Europe's "wine lake." The fortune, but not the fame, of winegrowers in the Midi was made in the 19th century when railroads made the shipping of cheap southern wines to Paris and the north possible. Massive planting of vines took place which turned the productive coastal plains into a vast vineyard supplying *vin ordinaire* to the thirsty northern market.

The Wines of the Languedoc-Roussillon

What has happened in this region to make its wines some of the most exciting and interesting in the whole of France today? In the late 1960s there were only a few *appellations* and a handful of VDQS in the region and *vin de pays* did not exist at all. Then the system of *vin de pays* was brought in with the intention of encouraging producers to make regional wines to satisfy the consumer's demand for better quality instead of making mediocre stuff destined entirely for the blending vats. The flexibility of the *vin de pays* regulations has encouraged an upgrading of grape varieties to suit specific soils and microclimates; grape varieties not normally indigenous to the area are permitted and there are increased plantings of varieties from farther

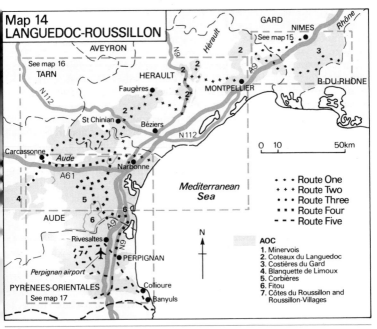

north, such as Syrah, Mourvèdre, Cabernet Sauvignon and Merlot; this fact alone has opened the gates to some exciting wines. The indigenous Carignan grape, with its high alcohol and big yield, is still predominant but the Aramon grape which produced oceans of mediocre wine is being grubbed up all over the region. Updating equipment and vinification methods has also played an important part; modern refrigeration allows for cool fermentation of the juice, even in the scorching heat of the Mediterranean sun, and carbonic maceration – the Beaujolais method of fermentation – has increased the freshness and fruitiness of the wines.

In 1977 there were only a few *appellations* in the whole of the Languedoc-Roussillon and now there are over 20, with more wines being promoted from VDQS each year. This is a region of co-operatives who handle an enormous range of wines, from *appellation* through to *vin de pays*, and with over 80,000 growers cultivating less than 5 hectares or so they play an important part in making wines that are improving each year.

An understanding of the wines of Languedoc-Roussillon must include a brief look at its four *départements* as each is a wine-growing entity with a specific personality. The Gard, the Hérault, and Aude make up the Languedoc, which begins south of Avignon on the west bank of the Rhône and extends along the coast to Fitou and inland to Quillan in the foothills of the Pyrenees. From here the Roussillon, officially the *département* of Pyrénées-Orientales, extends south to the Pyrenees themselves and the Spanish border and west to Andorra. The Aude and the Hérault still produce vast quantities of *vin de pays* whereas AOC and VDQS wines are proportionally more important in the Gard to the east and in the Roussillon to the west.

Traveling from the east the first *appellation* is the Costières du Gard, south and east of Nîmes. These wines are often compared to their neighbors in the southern Rhône but they generally have less body. Then comes the Hérault, which has the most vineyards of any *département* in France. Virtually all the wines here are grouped together under the newly created *appellation* Coteaux du Languedoc. This was formed out of 13 individual VDQS and these 13 areas can now add their name to the overall regional name Coteaux du Languedoc. The best are the light St Saturnin red and the fuller St Georges-d'Orques. The other two *appellations* in the Hérault are St Chinian and Faugères. Faugères makes good ripe reds and St Chinian makes lighter ones, with a scented bouquet.

Further west is the Aude, a massive producer like the Hérault, but making perhaps the best wines in the Midi today. The red wines of Corbières, like those from neighboring Fitou, go well with regional dishes such as *cassoulet* and are becoming very popular in the late 1980s. However, the real star in this area is Minervois. The wines are lighter than Fitou and Corbières and are usually reliable and often elegant reds. The increased use of carbonic maceration for all three wines has greatly improved their quality. At Limoux a champagne-method sparkling wine, Blanquette de Limoux, is made from the Mauzac grape with a little Clairette and Chardonnay and it can easily match its rivals in the Loire and Burgundy for quality.

The Roussillon is best known for its dark red wines made under the *appellations*, Côtes du Roussillon and Côtes du Roussillon-Villages. Most of the wines are made by the co-operatives but there is a growing tendency for producers to bottle their own wines. The rosés are also delicious. Collioure is a tiny coastal *appellation* almost on the border with Spain which produces hefty reds.

Languedoc-Roussillon is also the home of most of France's *vins doux naturels* or fortified wines made from either the red Grenache or the white Muscat grape. Good ones include red Banyuls and Maury and white Muscat de Frontignan.

Visiting the Vineyards

The Languedoc-Roussillon is the hottest area in France, particularly in the coastal plains, and even in winter the dry ground and vegetation give off a feeling of warmth when traveling in this often arid expanse of land. Rainy days are few and far between, hence the tendency to insist that "good" and "bad" years do not exist. The roads used by Hannibal and his elephants on their way to Italy in the 3rd century BC are now part of the French autoroute system leading invaders of another kind the other way to the Iberian coast; even inland Carcassone and Nîmes are thick with traffic when the summer vacations begin in July. It is therefore better to visit this area in the spring or early summer if you prefer leisurely touring without the crowds.

Route One

Costières du Gard, from Arles to Nîmes: 100km

The greater part of this route covers the Costières du Gard, but it also passes through the Clairette de Bellegarde vineyards south-east of Nîmes and the Muscat de Lunel *appellation* south-west of Nîmes where a fortified Muscat is made. The route also takes you into the Coteaux du Languedoc and their solid red and fruity rosés that are best drunk young and slightly chilled.

The Itinerary:
Leave **Arles** in the direction of Nîmes on N113. Vineyards, orchards and fields cover the low-lying plain. As you approach **Bellegarde** signs proudly proclaim the *Capital de la Clairette* and the vineyards spread out in all directions. Watch for the left-hand turnoff to enter Bellegarde. In the center of town, bear right away from Beaucaire to pick up D38 which heads toward **St Gilles** through vineyards, fields and woods. In the town follow the signs for **Vauvert** on N572. The vines are mixed with orchards here (asparagus, strawberries and peaches are sold from roadside stands in season), but soon spread out once again to cover the surrounding hills; signs announce the *Vignoble de Gallician* and the *Costières du Gard*.

Continue on N572 through **Aimargues**, then turn left on N113 to **Lunel**. Bear right on N113 coming into Lunel, then turn onto D34 to go to Sommières. Approaching **Saturargues**, the Côteaux du Languedoc begins; either continue straight on to Sommières on D34 and N110 or turn left opposite the Saturargues access road to visit **Vérargues**, **St Christol** and **St Drézéry**, all former individual VDQS areas and now part of the Coteaux du Languedoc *appellation*.

In **Sommières**, a beautiful medieval town dominated by a fortified château, bear right to cross the Vidourle river, then watch for a right turn onto D40 in the direction of Nîmes. From here to **Langlade** is a wonderful drive through rugged, beautiful countryside where olive trees mix with the vines among the stony hills. Soon the plain widens and is covered with vines again. The road runs toward a ring of low-lying hills surrounding Langlade; **Nîmes**, with its famous Roman temple and arena, is only minutes away.

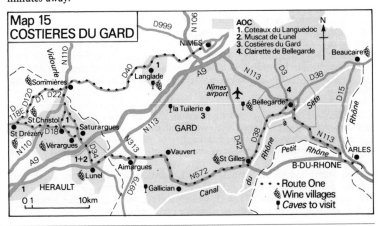

103

Route Two

Coteaux du Languedoc, from Montpellier to Narbonne: 180km

Most of the Coteaux du Languedoc vineyards lie between Montpellier and Narbonne. There is also an *appellation* Clairette du Languedoc, a fairly dull white wine, which lies just west of the Hérault around Aspiran and Cabrières. This route runs through almost uninterrupted vineyards and though the small roads can be difficult at times, the beauty of the scenery more than makes up for the effort involved in navigating them.

The beautiful Valmagne abbey is now an estate making good Coteaux du Languedoc.

The Itinerary:

From **Montpellier** head west in the direction of Lodève and Millau on N109. Continue on N109 through **Juvignac** to **Gignac**. The vineyards begin just outside Montpellier, alternating with patches of *garrigue* – a scrub brush common in this part of the country. Mas de Daumas Gassac, one of the great success stories of the Midi in recent years, is only 4km north of Gignac. At Gignac continue on N109 to **St André-de-Sangonis** or visit the Montpeyroux and St Saturnin vineyards by turning right on D9 to **Arboras**, left on D130E to **St Saturnin**, then left again on D130 for St André.

In St André, the beginning of the Clairette du Languedoc *appellation*, watch for a left-hand turnoff to **Clermont-l'Hérault** on D908, then follow the signs for **Pézenas** left on N9. Just after the access road to **Clermont**, the plain gives way to rolling hills covered with vines. If you wish to visit the abbey of Valmagne, a 12th-century Cistercian abbey and now a beautiful wine property, turn left before Pézenas onto N113 to **Montagnac** and then the abbey is 6km east on D5.

In Pézenas signs proclaim the *vins de Molière*, a reminder that the great French playwright lived in the town. Turn right on D13 through the wine villages of **Roujan** and **Gabian**. About 7km down the road from Gabian, where the Faugères vineyards begin, watch for a left turn to the small town of **Laurens** on D136, a road that provides magnificent views over the vineyards to the distant mountains. Continue through Laurens on D136, then turn right onto D909; just before **Faugères** is a left-hand turnoff onto D154, a twisting mountain road that leads through forest and vines through **Caussiniojouls**, **Cabrerolles**, and **la Liquière** to **Lenthéric**; at the junction turn right onto D136 to **St Nazaire-de-Ladarez**, in the St Chinian vineyards. The views are striking, with steep vineyards climbing the nearby mountains. From St Nazaire continue on D136 for 4km in the direction of Béziers; then, bear right to cross the bridge and take D19 to **Roquebrun**.

As the road winds along the slopes next to the river Orb, you catch your first sight of Roquebrun, a beautiful town dominated by the ruins of a medieval tower. In the center of Roquebrun turn left onto D14 toward Cessenon-sur-Orb and Béziers. Old olive trees are mixed with the vineyards here. At the stop sign turn right onto D20 to go to **St Chinian**.

In St Chinian, turn left onto N112 toward Béziers, watching for the right-hand turnoff to Narbonne on D36, just after passing through Cébazan. Continue on D36 (which then becomes D13 when it crosses D5) all the way through the vineyards and orchards to **Narbonne**, the ancient capital of the Roman province of *Gallia Narbonensis* and today's commercial center for the wines of the Minervois and Corbières.

A detour may be made to visit the la Clape vineyards, between Narbonne and the sea, by turning left at Cuxac d'Aude on D118 to Coursan, and continuing on D31 to Salles d'Aude, and D118 to Fleury. The villages around the Montagne de la Clape have a good reputation for white and rosé Coteaux du Languedoc.

Route Three

The Minervois, from Narbonne to Carcassonne: 110km

The Minervois in the Aude is a small area compared to its southern neighbor, Corbières, but has attracted much attention in recent years for its improving quality. Wine-growing in the Minervois is not easy – the climate is very hot and very dry and most of the terrain is difficult to cultivate, except in the south-east where the hills give way to coastal plain.

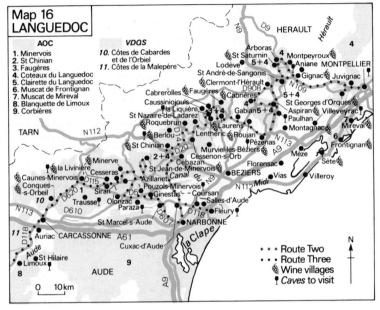

The Itinerary:

Leave **Narbonne** on D607 in the direction of St Pons; bear right at the large fork upon leaving town. The vineyards begin at the edge of the city, covering the plain. At **St Marcel-d'Aude** follow the signs for **Ginestas** on D607, but watch for the left-hand turn off on D926. Bear left in Ginestas, following the signs indicating *Commerces*; in the center of town turn left to **Ventanac-en-Minervois** on D26. Just over the Canal du Midi turn right onto D124 to **Paraza**. In Paraza turn left onto D167. This road takes you past Château de Paraza, an estate making fine Minervois wines. Continue north on D167 to D5 and turn left and then after a short way turn right onto D52 to **Olonzac** where the local wine brotherhood is based. Just before Olonzac, turn right onto D910 in the direction of **Aigues-Vives**.

This is an arid region with small but regular plots of vines. Just before Aigues-Vives turn left at the T-junction toward Minerve on D907 and D10 (or turn right to make a detour to **St Jean-de-Minervois** where an excellent Muscat is produced). On D10 the town of **Minerve** suddenly appears on a rise in the middle of a deep gorge. The sight is breathtaking.

Just before the bridge, take the left-hand fork (although it is not indicated, this is the road to **Azillanet**). In Azillanet, follow the signs right on D168 through **Cesseras** and **Siran** to **la Livinière**. The countryside is very different here, lush and green with stands of trees planted among the vines. From la Livinière, follow the signs on D52 and D115 to **Caunes-Minervois** across a vine-covered plain studded with lovely old houses and glowing with poppy fields. As you approach Caunes follow the *Toutes Directions* signs, then drive straight ahead to **Carcassonne** on D620 rather than turning into Caunes, unless seeing growers there. The drive to Carcassonne is a very pleasant one, often shaded by trees; near Carcassonne is a spectacular view of *la Cité*, a magical medieval village perfectly preserved on its own hill above the town.

If you wish to visit Limoux and its good sparkling wine take D118 south from Carcassone.

Route Four

Corbières and Fitou, from Carcassonne to Perpignan: 150km

The wines of Corbières cover a huge area of the Aude. The region is fairly mountainous and it is exciting countryside to tour.

The Itinerary:
Leave **Carcassonne** on N113 in the direction of Narbonne. Leave the highway at **Lézignan-Corbières**, following the signs to *Lézignan Centre* and Durban-Corbières, then turn left through **Cruscades** to **Ornaisons** on D24; in Ornaisons turn right onto D123 to **Gasparets**.

The road heads toward distant mountains through a patchwork of vineyards. Continue through Gasparets; at the T-junction turn right; labeled *Route des Corbières*, this is D613 heading for St Laurent-de-la-Cabrerisse. At the stop sign, turn right toward St Laurent; continue straight ahead at the next intersection and then turn left at the roundabout to go to **Durban-Corbières** on D611. The landscape is hilly with huge rocky outcrops in places; the road begins to twist and turn through the crags. There are just a few vines but, nearing Durban, grapes once again cover the hillsides and signs announce: *Ici commence le vignoble de Fitou.*

Continue on D611 to **Villeneuve-les-Corbières**. Bear left on D205 through **Embres-et-Castelmaure**, where there is a good wine co-operative, to **St Jean-de-Barrou**. Turn right onto D27 through **Treilles** to N9. The Mediterranean can now be seen stretching across the horizon in the distance. Turn right on N9, driving past **Fitou** with sand dunes on your left, past the magnificent fortified château at **Salses** on your right, and through a wide, vine-covered plain past **Rivesaltes** to **Perpignan**.

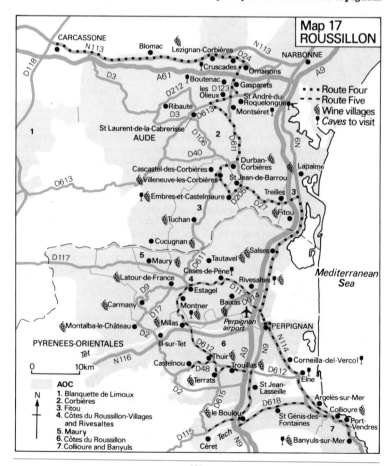

From Perpignan to Banyuls, to Estagel and back to Perpignan: 150km

Perpignan is the capital of the Roussillon and also the center of the local wine trade. It is an excellent base for touring the Pyrénées-Orientales, the most southern region of mainland France, with its strong feeling of Catalan Spain.

The Itinerary:

In **Perpignan**, follow the signs indicating N114 and **Argelès-sur-Mer**; continue through Argelès to **Collioure**, an attractive seaside town. The vineyards begin outside the town, perched precariously on steep slopes, and the scenery becomes quite spectacular as the road twists and turns between the sea and the hills. At Collioure newly built vacation cottages are overshadowed by two fortified hilltop châteaux and the magnificent port with its fortified church and Château Royal.

Drive through Collioure and **Port-Vendres** to **Banyuls-sur-Mer**. Port-Vendres is an important center for the anchovy trade and large fishing boats are moored in the harbor. On the outskirts of Banyuls the hills are entirely covered with a patchwork of terraced vines. The town itself, just 14km from Spain, is rather touristy and is packed with roadside stands offering Banyuls wine for sale, with posters depicting a stocky *vigneron*, a glass of Banyuls in hand, proclaiming *A ta santé, touriste*.

N114 is the only road leading down to Banyuls, so drive back along it and take the left-hand fork by-passing Argelès after Collioure; turn left on D618 to **le Boulou**. At the junction with N9, turn right through le Boulou toward Perpignan. At the intersection with D612, turn left through **Trouillas** and **Thuir**; from Thuir follow D612 through **Millas** to **Estagel** through lush vineyards. After Millas the road begins to climb, winding along the edge of a precipice, with magnificent views all along the route.

In Estagel follow the signs right on D117 to Perpignan. On the hills outside Estagel patches of bright orange earth in the grey rocks contrast sharply with the lush green carpet of vines covering the valley floor and nearing **Rivesaltes** orchards mix with the vines in the plain surrounding Perpignan.

Caves and Vineyards to Visit

Once an area known almost exclusively for inexpensive table wines and sweet aperitifs, the Languedoc-Roussillon is now a beehive of activity with many growers striving to improve the quality of their wines and the image of the region. Many of the *vins de pays* are every bit as good to drink as their AOC neighbors down the road and the wisest thing is to taste as extensively as possible, without regard to official status – these wines are improving faster than their labeling reveals.

ANIANE, map 16
Mas de Daumas Gassac (G),
Aniane,
34150 Gignac.
Tel: 67.57.71.28.

Mas de Daumas Gassac has achieved great fame in its short history. Aimé Guibert bought the property in 1970 as a family home and with no specific intention of planting vines. Helped by two friends eminent in the field of viticulture he discovered that the soil on his land was very rare and had the potential to produce great wine. The vineyards were reclaimed from scrub and planted mainly with Cabernet Sauvignon but also with other red and white grape varieties from Bordeaux, Burgundy and the Rhône.

The first red wines began to appear in 1981 to rave reviews and comparisons have been made with the best classed growths of Bordeaux. A white wine is also made, at present from Viognier and Chardonnay with a small amount of Muscat. Not entitled to the Coteaux du Languedoc *appellation*, the Daumas Gassac wines can only call themselves Vin de Pays de l'Hérault.
Visiting hours: (Cellars and tasting) mid-Jun–mid-Sep Fri, 10–12, 2.30–7; and Mar 20–end Dec Sat, 10–12, 2.30–7; (sales) Mon–Fri 2–7.
Location: 2km off D32 between Gignac and Aniane.

BANYULS-SUR-MER, map 17

Cellier des Templiers (C), rte du Mas-Reig, 66650 Banyuls-sur-Mer. Tel: 68.88.31.59.

This co-operative in the Collioure and Banyuls *appellations* is an outstanding one, in a region where there are many good examples. The members cultivate a total of 2,400 hectares of vines on steep terraces overhanging the sea. The soil is thin and poor and production is, therefore, extremely limited.

The co-operative is magnificently housed in carefully restored cellars that once belonged to the Knights Templar and produces a wide range of wines.

Visiting hours: Daily 9–7.
Location: 1km W of Banyuls on D86.

CASES-DE-PENE, map 17

Château de Jau (G), Cases-de-Pène, 66600 Rivesaltes. Tel: 68.54.51.67.

Château de Jau

Château de Jau overlooks the river Agly in the heart of the Côtes du Roussillon vineyards. Bernard Dauré who owns the estate is one of the most forward-looking winemakers in the Roussillon and he believes strongly that the area can produce wines of far better quality than normally associated with the *appellation*.

The Daurés bought the run-down estate in 1974 and have replanted the vineyards, now totaling 200 hectares, with classic varieties; Syrah, Mourvèdre and Muscat in the hot valleys, and Grenache and Cinsaut on the more exposed hillsides. The red and white Côtes du Roussillon wines are excellent and the *négociant* side of the business makes two good fortified wines, a rich Muscat de Rivesaltes and a straight Rivesaltes.

Château de Jau is also becoming known as an important center of modern art, with a gallery presenting regular exhibitions of works by noted contemporary artists. In the summer there is a pleasant restaurant serving simple regional dishes, with tables set outdoors under a mulberry tree, a survivor of the days when the Roussillon was a major producer of silk.

Visiting hours: (Cellars and sales) Daily 9–7. (Restaurant) mid-Jun–mid-Sep daily from 12.30; remainder of year Sat–Sun only. Reservations necessary. Tel: 68.64.11.38.
Location: Signposted in the village.

The handsome 17th-century Château de Jau just north of Perpignan.

CRUSCADES, map 17

Château l'Etang des Colombes (G), Cruscades, 11200 Lézignan-Corbières. Tel: 68.27.00.03.

This Corbières domaine is worth visiting not only for its highly regarded wines but also because of the small but fascinating Musée de la Vigne et du Vin created by its owner, Henri Gualco. The Cuvée Spéciale is a classy red Corbières redolent of wild fruits and spices.

Visiting hours: Daily 8–12.30, 2–8.
Location: 1km W of Cruscades on D24.

ELNE, map 17

Mas Chichet (G),
Chemin de
Charlemagne,
66200 Elne.
Tel: 68.22.16.78.

Jacques Chichet, proprietor of the 30-hectare domaine, is one of several innovative winemakers in the Roussillon today and his experiments with his wines have attracted widespread praise. Chichet makes only *vins de pays*, since he is developing wines outside the traditional framework laid down in the strict *appellation* laws. His Vin de Pays Catalan rosé (from Merlot, Syrah and Grenache) and the red Cuvée Spéciale Cabernet (from Cabernet Sauvignon and Cabernet Franc and aged in wood for 9–12 months) are his best wines.
Visiting hours: Mon–Fri 8–12, 2–5; Sat 8–12.
Location: 1.5km from Elne on D11 going to Alénya.

LANGLADE, map 15

**Domaine de
Langlade (G),**
30980 Langlade.
Tel: 66.81.31.37.

Before the outbreak of phylloxera at the end of the 19th century, Langlade was considered one of the best wine villages in the Languedoc. Unfortunately production was virtually abandoned until Henri Arnal, an industrialist with a passion for wine, bought this particular property and began to restore it to its former luster, replanting the vineyards in the late 1970s. The red Coteaux du Languedoc is good.
Visiting hours: Daily 8–12, 2–8.
Location: In the center of the village and signposted.

LIMOUX, map 16

**Société des
Producteurs de
Blanquette de
Limoux (C),**
av. du Mauzac,
11300 Limoux.
Tel: 68.31.14.59.

Blanquette de Limoux is the only *appellation* devoted to sparkling wines in the Languedoc-Roussillon and production now amounts to a respectable 5 million bottles a year. The largest producer is the co-operative based in Limoux, whose members cultivate a total of 2,000 hectares of vines. The co-operative uses very modern equipment in an impressive and well-laid out winery.
Visiting hours: Mon–Fri 8–12, 2–6.
Location: In the center of Limoux.

MONTPELLIER, map 16

**Domaines
Viticoles des
Salins du Midi
(G/M),**
68 cours Gambetta,
34063 Montpellier.
Tel: 66.58.23.77.

The Domaines Viticoles des Salins du Midi are part of the Compagnie des Salins du Midi, one of France's largest land owners with a virtual monopoly of the country's salt production. Most of their land is on the coastal strip of the Golfe du Lion at the Rhône estuary between the walled town of Aigues-Mortes in the east and the mouth of the river Aude in the west. Its viticultural importance began when it was discovered that the phylloxera louse did not attack vines planted on sandbanks. After World War II the vineyards were replanted and the company was the first to plant Cabernet Sauvignon and Merlot in the Midi.

The wines are sold under the brand name of Listel and the vineyards total more than 2,500 hectares. The wines are made with great skill and in the most "natural" way possible; no chemical products on the soil and no pasteurization.

The main properties in the Midi are Domaine de Jarras near Aigues-Mortes and Château du Villeroy south of Sète. Jarras is well organized for visitors with a splendidly decorated *caveau*. The business office is in Montpellier.
Visiting hours: (Domaine de Jarras) Apr–Sep daily, 9–6; Oct–Mar Mon–Fri, 9–6. To visit Château du Villeroy contact the office in Montpellier.
Location: (Jarras) 2km SW of Aigues-Mortes on D979.

MONTSERET, map 17

Château les Ollieux (G),
Montséret,
11200 Lézignan-Corbières.
Tel: 68.43.32.61.

The area where the château was built, initially as a Cistercian abbey for women in 1153, was apparently named by the Romans for its numerous olive trees. Since 1311, when the vineyard was first planted, the property has been primarily associated with wine-making. Mme Françoise Surbezy-Cartier, is noted for her hospitality and the enthusiasm and knowledge with which she presents her wines. The red Corbières has an elegant nose and good length. There is also an interesting Corbières rosé.
Visiting hours: Daily 8–12, 2–6.
Location: On D613 2km N of Montséret at les Ollieux.

PARAZA, map 16

Château de Paraza (G),
Paraza,
11200 Lézignan.
Tel: 68.43.20.88.

This is one of the leading estates in the Minervois. The château is a fine 17th-century building with terraces on the south side leading down to the Canal du Midi. The estate has about 140 hectares of vines, 10 of which have been recently planted with Bourboulenc to produce a fine white Minervois by 1990. For the moment, Château de Paraza is known for its good red and rosé wines.
Visiting hours: Daily 8–12, 2–6, by appt.
Location: On D167 just over the bridge from Paraza.

TRAUSSE-MINERVOIS, map 16

Domaine Daniel Domergue (G),
Paulignan, Trausse-Minervois,
11160 Caunes.
Tel: 68.78.32.37.

This small 5-hectare estate in the Minervois is owned by Daniel and Hélène Domergue and their wines have attracted much attention in recent years. The vineyards are planted only with non-indigenous grape varietes, such as Mourvèdre, Grenache and Cinsaut. The wines made by traditional methods are exciting and made for aging, especially the Cuvée des Clos du Bosc.
Visiting hours: Daily 10–12, 2–7, by appt; Sun by appt.
Location: On D55 between Trausse and Félines.

La TUILERIE, map 15

Château de la Tuilerie (G),
rte de St Gilles,
30900 Nîmes.
Tel: 66.70.07.52.

The château was once a stopping place for the Knights of Malta and it is still an attractive and hospitable domaine, with 70 hectares of vineyards, and is now owned by Mmes Guy Serres and Chantal Comte. Within the Costières du Gard *appellation* it produces all three versions, red, white and rosé, and there is also a highly respectable red Vin de Pays des Coteaux Flaviens.
Visiting hours: Mon–Sat 8–12, 2–6.
Location: 10km S of Nîmes off rte de St Gilles (D42).

VILLEVEYRAC, map 16

Abbaye de Valmagne (G),
Villeveyrac,
34140 Mèze.
Tel: 67.78.06.09.

The abbey of Valmagne was one of the richest in the south of France during the 12th and 13th centuries. Many of the abbey buildings remain, including a beautiful cloister and chapter house. The refectory is now used as a concert hall. Since the Revolution the church nave has been used for maturing the wines and is an ideal place because of its low temperature and lack of light. The wines made are Coteaux du Languedoc and Vin de Pays Collines de la Moure.
Visiting hours: Jun 15–Sep 15 Wed–Mon 2·30–6·30; remainder of year Sun 2–6.
Location: 6km E of Montagnac on D5.

Further *Caves* and Vineyards to Visit

BANYULS-SUR-MER, map 17
Domaine du Mas Blanc (G), 9 av. du
Gén.-de-Gaulle, 66650 Banyuls-sur-
Mer. Tel : 68.88.32.12. Visiting hours : By
appt.
This is an outstanding producer of
Banyuls and Collioure wines and the
reputation of the Parcé family far exceeds
the small output from just 12 hectares.

BELLEGARDE, map 15
Domaine St Louis-la-Perdrix (G),
30127 Bellegarde. Tel : 66.01.18.13. Visiting hours : By appt.
The domaine is owned by Mme Geneviève Lamour and makes good red and
rosé Costières du Gard. It is one of the few
producers of the white Clairette de
Bellegarde.

BERLOU, map 16
**Cave Co-opérative Coteaux du
Rieu-Berlou (C)**, av. des Vignerons,
Berlou, 34360 St Chinian. Tel :
67.38.03.19. Visiting hours : Mon–Sat ;
appt preferred ; closed hols.
This is one of the best co-operatives in the
Midi and is very well equipped. It makes
a wide range of wines within the St
Chinian *appellation*.

BOUTENAC, map 17
**Domaine de la Voulte-Gasparets
(G)**, Boutenac, 11200 Lézignan-
Corbières. Tel : 68.27.07.86. Visiting
hours : Daily 9–12, 2–7.
This old Corbières property of 50 hectares is owned by Jacques Berges-Reverdy
who is a knowledgeable president of the
local association of growers.

La CLAPE, map 16
Château de Pech Redon (G), la Clape,
11100 Narbonne. Tel : 68.90.41.22. Visiting hours : Mon–Fri 9–12, 2–6.
This is an attractive estate high on the la
Clape hills between Narbonne and the
sea. The 15 hectares of vines make a good
rosé Coteaux du Languedoc.

CORNEILLA-DEL-VERCOL,
map 17
Château de Corneilla (G), 66200
Corneilla-del-Vercol. Tel : 68.22.12.56.
Visiting hours : By appt.
Château de Corneilla was built at the end
of the 12th century by the Knights

Templar and stands in a commanding
position between the Pyrenees and the
sea just south of Perpignan. The large
estate produces top-quality red and
white Côtes du Roussillon and Muscat de
Rivesaltes. The estate is also used for
cattle and horse breeding.

EMBRES-ET-CASTELMAURE,
map 17
**Cave Co-opérative Castelmaure
(C)**, Embres-et-Castelmaure, 11360
Durban-Corbières. Tel : 68.45.91.83.
Visiting hours : Mon–Fri 8–12, 2–6.
This is the leading co-operative in the
Corbières region and all the wines are
made by carbonic maceration.

FLEURY, map 16
Domaine de Rivière-la-Haut (G),
11560 Fleury-d'Aude. Tel : 68.33.61.33.
Visiting hours : Daily 7–8.
The domaine is owned by Jean Ségura
who practices organic viticulture. He
makes a very good traditional white
Coteaux du Languedoc la Clape.

GALLICIAN, map 15
Mas Aupellière (G), Gallician, 30600
Vauvert. Tel : 66.73.30.75. Visiting
hours : Mon–Sat 8–6.
Léo Grootemaat has 22 hectares of vines
planted around his ancient *mas* or
farmhouse and makes good, sturdy red
Costières du Gard.

La LIQUIERE, map 16
Bernard et Claudie Vidal (G), la
Liquière, Cabrerolles, 34480 Magalas.
Tel : 67.90.29.20. Visiting hours : Mon–
Sat 8–12, 2–6.
The Vidals were the pioneers of carbonic
maceration in the Faugères region and
they use this method for all their wines.
There is no aging in wood at all. They
make a range of red and rosés within the
Faugères *appellation* as well as a Vin de
Pays de l'Hérault Rouge.

La LIVINIERE, map 16
Château de Gourgazaud (G), la
Livinière, 34210 Olonzac. Tel :
68.78.10.02. Visiting hours : Daily 8–12,
2–6.
The 68-hectare domaine, owned by
Roger Piquet, produces a good, rich and
aromatic red Minervois.

MONTNER, map 17
Cave Co-opérative de Montner (C), Cellier St Jacques, 66720 Montner. Tel: 68.29.11.91. Visiting hours: Daily 9–7; appt for groups.

Montner is one of the best villages in the Côtes du Roussillon-Villages *appellation* and lies high up overlooking the river Agly with spectacular views of the mountains in the distance. The good wine co-operative makes a fine red that ages well as well as some red Rivesaltes and a Muscat de Rivesaltes.

PAULHAN, map 16
Château de la Condamine-Bertrand (G), 34230 Paulhan. Tel: 67.24.46.00. Visiting hours: Daily 8–7. The Janys are an old Languedoc family and enthusiastic winemakers. The estate has an elegant château. Their Clairette du Languedoc is a very individual wine made only from the Clairette grape.

PEZENAS, map 16
Domaine de St Jean-de-Bébian (G), 34120 Pézenas. Tel: 67.98.13.60. Visiting hours: By appt.

The 25-hectare domaine just north of Pézenas is owned by Alain Roux who makes interesting red Coteaux du Languedoc.

POUZOLS-MINERVOIS, map 16
Domaine Jacques Mayzonnier (G), Pouzols-Minervois, 11120 Ginestas. Tel: 68.46.13.88. Visiting hours: Mon–Sat appt preferred.

This is a small 7-hectare property making Minervois wines. Carbonic maceration is used extensively.

RIVESALTES, map 17
Cazès Frères (G), 4 r. Francisco Ferrer, 66600 Rivesaltes. Tel: 68.64.08.26. Visiting hours: Daily 8–12, 2–6; appt preferred.

André and Bernard Cazès are leading winemakers in the Rivesaltes area and make a wide range of wines in their well-equipped cellars.

ST ANDRE-DE-ROQUELONGUE, map 17
Domaine de Villemajou (G), St André-de-Roquelongue, 11200 Lézignan-Corbières. Tel: 68.45.10.43. Visiting hours: Mon–Fri by appt.

Georges Bertrand is one of the talented new winemakers of Corbières. On his 63 hectares of vines he grows Grenache, Syrah and Cinsaut as well as the more traditional Carignan and all his wines are made by carbonic maceration.

Sights

The beaches of the Languedoc-Roussillon have become as popular as those of Provence and the Côte d'Azur and for this reason the coastal stretches should be avoided during July and August. Visiting the coast at any other time of year is highly recommended; in the far south, near Spain, the terraced vineyards tumble down steep hillsides to the sea around fishing villages where the colorful custom of auctioning the catch has not changed for centuries. Inland cities such as Nîmes and Carcassonne provide insights into Roman and medieval France while villages in the Minervois or Corbières are as striking in their isolation.

ARLES
The Roman amphitheater in Arles is one of the oldest known and is used today for bullfights and other events. The **Musée Arlaten**, with displays of everyday life in Provence is one of the most interesting museums of its type in France.

BEZIERS
Béziers is a bustling center of the local wine trade. The **Musée du Vieux Biterrois et du Vin**, housed in a former Dominican church, contains some fascinating exhibits. The **Musée des** Beaux-Arts has paintings by Géricault, Delacroix, Dufy, Utrillo and Corot. A festival of the new wine is held in Oct.

CARCASSONNE
La Cité, a walled and turreted town, is one of the wonders of France and has survived miraculously intact from the Middle Ages. It is worth taking a guided tour and a stroll around the ramparts to appreciate fully this old fortress-city.

The **Château Comtal**, built by the Counts of Toulouse in the 12th century, stands on its own and contains a local

# LANGUEDOC-ROUSSILLON

istory museum of life in Carcassonne and the Aude. The **Basilique St Nazaire** has superb stained-glass windows from the 13th–14th centuries.

COLLIOURE

Collioure is a fishing port so picturesque that it inspired artists such as Braque, Derain and Matisse, and now acts as a magnet to tourists. The impressive **Château Royal** was once the residence of the Kings of Majorca. The **Eglise St Vincent**, built on the edge of the old port in the 17th century, has a bell tower that was once used as a lighthouse.

The Maison Carrée *in Nîmes.*

MONTPELLIER

Montpellier grew to become an important city in the early Middle Ages as a result of the spice trade. Spices were extensively used in medicines and an ancient medical tradition led to the foundation of the medical school and university in the 13th century. Rabelais was one of the more illustrious graduates.

The **promenade du Peyrou**, designed in 1688, has two levels of terraces, the upper one providing superb views of the surrounding countryside. An interesting **Château d'eau** supplies Montpellier with water from the Lez by way of a two-tiered aqueduct resembling the famous Pont du Gard.

An International Fair of the Vine and of Wine is held in Oct and in Nov the city is host to the International Salon of Vinicultural Techniques and Equipment.

NARBONNE

Founded in 118BC by a decree of the Roman Senate, Narbonne became one of the leading cities of Gaul and was a flourishing port until it silted up in the 17th century.

Most of its impressive buildings are clustered around the **pl. de l'Hôtel de Ville**. The **Palais des Archevêques** is fronted by two medieval keeps and between them runs an attractive fortified street, the **Passade de l'Ancre**. North of the cathedral is the **Maison Vigneronne**, a wine museum. The **Musée Lapidaire** has one of the richest collections of ancient and medieval sculpture in France.

Narbonne holds a wine festival on the first Fri and Sat after Aug 15.

NIMES

Nîmes was capital of a Gallic tribe when the Romans imposed their rule in the 2nd century BC. Veterans of Augustus' campaign against Antony and Cleopatra in Egypt were given lands around the town. Today, Nîmes is a lively city whose prime attraction is the famous arena, the twin of that of nearby Arles and the best preserved Roman arena in the world today. Bullfights are now staged in the arena during the summer season.

Half a kilometer to the north is the **Maison Carrée**, a Roman temple built in the time of Augustus and now the **Musée des Antiques**. A wine harvest festival is held at the end of Sep.

PERPIGNAN

In the 13th century the Balearic Islands and the Roussillon formed the Kingdom of Majorca, ruled by a son of the Aragonese monarch, with Perpignan as its capital. The former royal palace, the **Palais des Rois de Majorque**, has a splendid courtyard where concerts are given throughout the summer season. Perpignan has a food and wine fair in Jun.

PEZENAS

Once a center of the wool trade, with three annual fairs and the residence of the governors of Languedoc, Pézenas has retained much of its ancient charm. The old town is compact and the only way to see and savor everything is on foot.

SALSES

The brick and stone fortress just north of Perpignan, built by Ferdinand of Aragon in 1497, is one of the finest examples of military architecture of the period and is generally well preserved. Restoration carried out in recent years has done much to make good the losses.

Hotels, Restaurants and Where to Buy Wine

The Languedoc-Roussillon has a varied *cuisine*. Even along the coast specialties differ but there are some common themes. Olive oil is the cooking medium of choice from Nîmes to Perpignan, and hints of garlic can be found in many a dish. Thyme, rosemary, sage and basil are also common. But the often spicy *cuisine* of the Catalans, with their predilection for squid, aubergine, tomatoes and anchovies, has relatively little in common with that of Carcassonne, proud of its version of *cassoulet*, a famous white bean stew. Farther north, Nîmes boasts its celebrated *brandade*, a salt cod purée, while Sète has its locally farmed oysters. Goat cheeses are made throughout the area and the celebrated *fromage des Pyrénées* is generally made from ewe's milk.

From Nîmes to Perpignan there is no shortage of red wines to serve with these dishes; if they lack elegance on occasion, they often compensate with a heady grapiness that perfectly suits the kind of rustic fare you will be sampling here. Do not overlook the *vins doux naturels*. Those made from the Muscat grape have an intense flavor of fruit and are perfect as an apéritif, while the dark Banyuls goes with blue cheese, *foie gras* and rich chocolate.

No one restaurant in the Languedoc-Roussillon boasts an extensive selection of wines from throughout the region. There are, however, a few restaurants that have decided to promote the wines of their specific "corner" of this vast area.

For the Costières du Gard
Les Vendanges (R), 1 r. de la Violette, 30000 Nîmes. Tel: 66.21.09.09. Closed Sun, 3 weeks Feb and 1 week Aug. AE DC MC V
The owner of this elegant wine bar has assembled a fine list of both reds and whites from the local Costières du Gard *appellation*. Though hot food is limited to two *plats du jour* (well prepared, with a *nouvelle* touch), there is also a good selection of ham, sausage, or cheese platters, making this a perfect place for a light lunch in Nîmes.

For the Wines of the Hérault
Hôtel Montpelliérain des Vins du Languedoc (W,R), 7 r. Jacques Coeur, 34000 Montpellier. Tel: 67.60.42.41. Closed Sun–Mon. (W) open only 10–1. (R) reservations necessary. MC V
The owners display a crusading fervor in their promotion of quality wines from the Hérault. Over 80 wines have been selected for sale in the shop on the ground floor of this magnificent medieval *hôtel*. Downstairs in the former cellars is a simple dining-room where regional specialties are served.

The wine list covers the entire Coteaux du Languedoc and the *sommelier* will organize a tasting of different wines from the region.

For the Wines of the Aude
Domaine d'Auriac (H,R), rte de St Hilaire, 11000 Carcassonne. Tel: 68.25.72.22. Closed 2 weeks Jan. AE DC V
This beautiful old château is now an elegant restaurant and hotel belonging to the prestigious Relais et Châteaux group. The owner and chef, Bernard Rigaudis, is an avid supporter of both regional dishes and wines. His wine list, though not lacking in wines of other regions, has many fine bottles from the nearby *appellations* of Corbières, Minervois and Fitou.

For the Wines of the Roussillon
Le Relais St Jean (R), pl. de la Cathédrale, 66000 Perpignan. Closed Sun and Mon lunch, and 3 weeks Feb. Tel: 68.51.22.25. AE DC MC V
Marie-Louis Banyols is a great promoter of the wines of Banyuls from south of Perpignan. Fight the temptation to choose one of the fine Bordeaux, Burgundy or Rhône wines and pick (with her help) from among the 30 fine Roussillon wines on offer.

Mme Banyols will guide you through a tasting menu that provides a sampling of the region's best wines, starting, perhaps, with an excellent Muscat de Rivesaltes and ending with a fine Banyuls. The food, for the most part, perfectly complements the wines.

BANYULS-SUR-MER (66650)
Le Catalan (H,R), rte. de Cerbère. Tel: 68.88.02.80. Closed mid-Oct–mid-Apr. AE DC MC V
Quiet, modern hotel overlooking the bay and with fine views of the mountains and the sea.

Le Sardinal (R), 4 pl. Paul-Reig. Tel: 68.88.30.07. Closed Sun pm–Mon. MC V
Regional specialties, friendly service and a pleasant atmosphere in this large restaurant. Live music, with the owner on the saxophone. Good selection of local wines.

Le BOULOU (66160)
Relais des Chartreuses (H,R), rte d'Argelès-sur-Mer (4.5km SE on D618). Tel: 68.83.15.88. No cards.
An old stone *mas* or farmhouse has been become an elegant hotel and restaurant with views over the mountains. Traditional French and Moroccan *haute cuisine* and interesting Roussillon wines.

CARCASSONNE (11000)
Auberge Pont Levis (R), près de la Porte Narbonnaise. Tel: 68.25.55.23. Closed Sun pm–Mon, 2 weeks Feb and Sep. AE DC MC V
Classic and regional *cuisine* with cheerful service and reasonable prices.

Cité (H,R), pl. Eglise. Tel: 68.25.03.34. Closed Oct. AE DC MC V
Quiet, elegant hotel surrounded by gardens in the heart of the old city. Large rooms with a medieval feel.

COLLIOURE (66190)
La Balette (R), 114 rte de Port-Vendres. Tel: 68.82.05.07. One Michelin star. Closed Nov–Apr Sun pm–Mon and Jan. MC V
One of the best known restaurants in Roussillon and in a wonderful position between the mountains and the sea. Classic and regional *cuisine* and good local wines.

GIGNAC (34150)
Hôtel Capion (R,H), 3 bd de l'Esplanade. Tel: 67.57.50.83. Closed Sun pm–Mon in winter and Feb. AE DC MC V
Well-established restaurant with a few rooms. Excellent cellar.

MONTPELLIER (34000)
Altea-Antigone (H) and **Lou Pairol (R)**, 218 r. du Bastion-Ventadour. Tel: 67.64.65.66. (R) closed Sat lunch and Sun. AE DC MC V
In the town center with comfortable, quiet rooms. Light, imaginative *cuisine* and good local wines.

Chandelier (R), 3 r. Leenhardt. Tel: 67.92.61.62. One Michelin star. Closed Sun, Mon lunch, 2 weeks Feb and 3 weeks Aug. AE DC V
Charming, small restaurant with classic *cuisine*.

Réserve Rimbaud (R), 820 av. de St Maur. Tel: 67.72.52.53. Closed Sun pm–Mon, and Jan. AE DC V
A rendezvous for the locals since 1875, this charming restaurant on the bank of the river Lez serves good reliable dishes, using fresh, local produce.

NARBONNE (11100)
Languedoc (H,R), 22 bd Gambetta. Tel: 68.65.14.74. Closed Sun pm–Mon and Jan. AE DC MC V
Handsome, comfortable, old hotel in the center of town. Inexpensive restaurant.

Réverbère (R), 4 pl. des Jacobins. Tel: 68.32.29.18. One Michelin star. Closed Sun pm–Mon, 2 weeks mid-Jan and mid-Sep and 1st week of Jun. AE DC V
Perfect service, a good cellar and fine food in an elegant dining-room.

NIMES (30000)
Imperator (H) and **L'Enclos de la Fontaine (R)**, quai de la Fontaine, pl. A.-Briand. Tel: 66.21.90.30. One Michelin star. Closed Feb. AE DC MC V
A well-kept hotel with its own garden. Large, beautiful dining-room and terrace. Classic *cuisine* and good Costières du Gard wines.

La Vinothèque (W), 6 pl. de la Révolution. Tel: 66.67.04.82. Closed Sun–Mon. MC V
Good shop for wines of the Gard region.

ORNAISONS (11200, Lézignan-Corbières)
Relais du Val d'Orbieu (H,R). Tel: 68.27.10.27. AE DC MC V
In the heart of the Corbières vineyards this is a delightful base for touring the region. Peaceful gardens with swimming-pool. Reasonable prices.

PERPIGNAN (66000)
Le Mas des Arcades (H,R), av. d'Espagne (2km N on N9). Tel: 68.85.11.11. Closed Dec. MC
Spacious, bright and well-decorated rooms. Swimming pool and garden.

Festin de Pierre (R), 7 r. Théâtre. Tel: 68.51.28.74. Closed Tue pm–Wed, and Feb. AE DC V
In an elegant 15th-century building. Classic *cuisine* and excellent wine list.

THE LOIRE VALLEY

From its source in the mountains of the Massif Central in southern central France scarcely 150km north of the Mediterranean, the river Loire glides on its way northward and then westward for over 1,000km to the Atlantic Ocean in southern Brittany. The river passes through some of the lushest agricultural countryside in France and has been described as the French Nile, a river passing through a "Valley of the Kings" lined with monumental reminders of a glorious past. Like the pyramids, the fairy-tale castles of the Loire were built in a fertile valley, much favored by the kings of France for its temperate climate. The Loire valley offers much to the curious tourist willing to explore: cave dwellers still live in the shadows of these magnificent châteaux, windmills and orchards line the roads and vineyards produce every imaginable type of wine. Today this sleepy rural region is being stirred up, as new farming methods replace the old and modern industries move in; but for the visitor with time to leave the highways and travel leisurely through the countryside the old world of the peasant is still to be found.

Even when the Loire is out of sight the traveler is constantly crossing smaller rivers and streams that feed into it and for centuries these rivers were the best means of communication within the area and with the sea and the wider world beyond. Now only navigable in limited stretches, the Loire is still the unifying element in this varied region. Although now divided into 15 separate *départements*, all named after the rivers that flow through them, the older provincial boundaries reflect a much truer division of the region. In the east is Berry, the heart of provincial France with its old capital, Bourges; Touraine is the "garden of France", richest of all these rich provinces, whose vineyards, orchards and châteaux, with their memories of courts and kings, line the banks of the rivers. Anjou has its associations with the Plantagenets, the medieval kings of England who ruled here for several centuries, while nearer the Atlantic, the white-washed cottages south of Nantes are a reminder of nearby Brittany.

The Wines of the Loire Valley

The wines of the Loire were once among the most famous in France. As was the case in Burgundy and Champagne they were known by the name of the town whence they were exported, and during the Middle Ages the *vins d'Orléans* were considered equal to the wines of Beaune and Reims. This

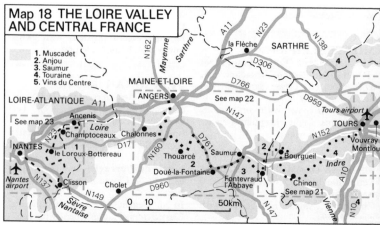

Map 18 THE LOIRE VALLEY AND CENTRAL FRANCE

1. Muscadet
2. Anjou
3. Saumur
4. Touraine
5. Vins du Centre

situation changed dramatically in the 17th century as a demand for brandy by the Dutch meant that more and more wines were distilled for this profitable market; then a law was passed obliging Parisian *cabarets* or bistros to purchase wine made at least *vingts lieues* (88km) from the capital – both factors combined to provide an incentive for growers in the region to plant more productive grape varieties and to concentrate on quantity rather than quality. The decline in quality was spectacular and continued throughout the 18th century. Finally, when the vineyards were devastated by the phylloxera plague in the late 19th century, many farmers turned to planting apple and pear trees, and the area devoted to vineyards declined.

Today the wines of the Loire valley are divided into four main growing areas – *vins du centre* (wines from central France), *vins de Touraine* (wines from the region of Tours), *vins d'Anjou* (wines from the region of Angers) and *vins du pays nantais* (wines from the region of Nantes). Generally speaking, the better reds are found in western Touraine between Tours and Saumur, and the finest dry white wines (Sancerre and Pouilly-Fumé) in the extreme east of the region. Champagne-method sparkling wines are also made, particularly around Saumur, and Anjou rosé is renowned worldwide, though it is not the most interesting of Anjou wines. The more everyday wines (with the exception of Muscadet) are often sold as varietals; Cabernet Franc (usually labeled simply Cabernet) or Gamay for the reds of Touraine and Sauvignon Blanc for the whites. Chenin Blanc, called here Pineau de la Loire, is found widely in Anjou and can make some wonderful sweet wines, especially in the Layon valley south of Angers. Muscadet, also known as Melon de Bourgogne, is the white grape used for Muscadet and almost exclusively found in the Pays Nantais bordering the Atlantic. These are the main styles of wine in the Loire valley and the many individual *appellations* are described in detail in the following pages.

In the 20th century, the Loire wines have regained much of their former prestige and, although none are considered as great as they were in the Middle Ages, they have become today's "country wines" *par excellence*. Like dark bread and country sausages, the wines of Muscadet, Sancerre and Chinon are fashionable. They are also reliable and modestly priced (though prices are rising) and many a Parisian has a *cubitainer* of St Nicolas-de-Bourgueil or Chinon wine shipped up once a year to bottle himself and drink young and chilled, never suspecting that the better vintages are worth laying down or that he is re-establishing the link, broken for over 300 years, between these wines and the best Parisian tables.

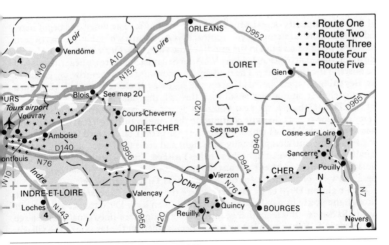

Route One

From Cosne-sur-Loire to Reuilly: 150km

This route covers the *appellations* of the Upper Loire or Central France and is, without doubt, the most scenic drive in all the Loire valley. The region is hilly and the vineyards, often covered with white stones which reflect the sun, are mixed with attractive farmland. In the east near Sancerre the traveler will criss-cross what is locally called the *Route du crottin* (*crottin* is a popular goat cheese made in and around Chavignol). This is the perfect opportunity to discover one of the "classic" wine and cheese combinations – Sancerre with *crottin*.

Sancerre and Pouilly-Fumé are the most famous *appellations* and have now become chic restaurant wines. Made from Sauvignon Blanc, the vineyard areas for these wines are relatively small and prices are accordingly high. Pinot Noir is used to make small amounts of Sancerre red and rosé wines. Reuilly, Quincy and Menetou-Salon are three *appellations* in the west of the region for dry, fruity whites made mainly from Sauvignon Blanc. The Coteaux du Giennois are VDQS wines from around Gien and Cosne-sur-Loire. These light reds, whites and rosés are mostly consumed locally.

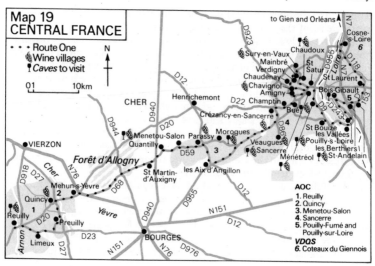

The Itinerary:

Cosne-sur-Loire is easily reached from Gien or Orléans by the highways that border the Loire. Leave N7 at Cosne and go south to **St Laurent** on D118, a bumpy and twisting road. In St Laurent turn left onto D4, then almost immediately right onto D153 toward **Pouilly-sur-Loire** and the *Route du Vin*. The vineyards begin here, and become more numerous as you approach **St Andelain** whose château can be seen from afar, perched on a hill in the middle of the vineyards. Drive around the church and follow the small road labeled *Vers N7*. After St Andelain, there is a beautiful view of the hills and the Loire valley. The road dips down toward the wine-growing village of **les Berthiers**; when the road meets the highway bear right on N7, then turn immediately left onto a very small road through the vineyards.

From **Bois Gibault**, the next village, a detour can be made to visit Château de Tracy near the river; otherwise continue on the route by turning left at the stop sign, then left again on D243 which runs along the bank of the Loire toward **Pouilly**. At the stop sign in the outskirts of Pouilly turn right and cross the Loire on a very narrow metal bridge, then drive straight ahead to **les Vallées**. Turn right onto D59 and follow the signs for Sancerre. After **Prévant** the road passes between rows of tall poplars and there is a view of the beautiful brick Château la Grange on the left.

Turn right on D920 to **St Bouize**, where the *région du Sancerrois* begins; drive through the pretty little village of **Ménétréol**, then leave D920 to take D9 straight toward **St Satur** – this is another beautiful drive along a tree-lined canal. At the large crossroads in St Satur, turn left toward Sancerre, then, at the far side of the village, turn right and almost immediately left on D134 which leads to **Verdigny**. From here you have an excellent view of the stony Sancerrois vineyards and a winding drive through the villages of Verdigny, **Chaudoux**, and **Sury-en-Vaux**. Entering Sury, follow the signs toward Menetou-Râtel, but before reaching the top of the hill and the Sury church, take a sharp left toward the hamlet of Chaudenay on the *Route du Chavignol et du Sancerrois*. In **Mainbré** follow the lefthand road through **Chaudenay**. Then, at the junction, turn left, and then right toward **Chavignol** where you should visit the *fromagerie* in the center of the village for a taste of the famous *crottin* cheese.

Continue along the main road to **Sancerre** – drive straight uphill into town, turning right at the top of the hill, then right again toward **Amigny** on D7. After Amigny take the first road to the left through the vineyards. At the junction turn left, then almost immediately right to **Bué**. Drive through the village, then turn left uphill on a very bumpy road through the vineyards toward **Champtin**. Continue straight ahead at the crossroads, then turn right at the stop sign onto D22 toward **Crézancy-en-Sancerre**.

At Crézancy, you will be leaving the Sancerrois vineyards. Turn left toward Veaugues on D86 then, at the intersection with D955, turn right toward **les Aix d'Angillon**. This is a straight highway passing through lush farmland and rolling hills. Drive into les Aix-d'Angillon, follow the signs to Bourges, then for Henrichemont on D955 and D12. Once on D12, watch for a small road off to the left indicating D59 and **Parassy**; follow this, bearing right at **les Faucards** to go into **Menetou-Salon** which has its own *appellation*. The next town on the route, **St Martin-d'Auxigny**, is well signposted from Menetou-Salon along D59.

The route now takes you through apple and pear orchards and past countless roadside fruit stands. From St Martin, head along D68 for **Mehun-sur-Yèvre**, passing through the edge of the Allogny forest. At the junction with D944, continue straight ahead on D68 into Mehun, following the signs for *Centre Ville*. Go through the impressive, fortress-like gate to the old city and take D20 to **Quincy**; after Quincy, follow the signs for Reuilly, then watch for the road to **Preuilly**, on D27 off to the left. In Preuilly, turn right along D228, then right again on D23 through **Limeux**, driving through scattered vineyards to reach **Reuilly**, a quiet provincial village which received its *appellation* as long ago as 1937.

To reach **Selles-sur-Cher**, the starting point of Route Two, head north to **Vierzon** on D918, then west on N76. Romorantin-Lanthenay, just north of N76, and Valençay, just south of N76, make good stopovers between the two routes.

Route Two

From Selles-sur-Cher to Tours: 175km

Selles-sur-Cher is a pretty town in eastern Touraine with a turreted château and claims to be "the goat cheese capital" of France. The ideal time to sample the cheeses is during the cheese and wine festival held every year on the weekend following Easter. On this route you will see numerous troglodyte dwellings, houses carved into the chalky stone embankments with their front doors and windows let into the side of the hills and their chimneys sticking up into the fields above!

Touraine is the regional *appellation* and covers red, white and rosé wines made from a variety of grapes, including Sauvignon and Gamay. These are fresh, young wines and often excellent value for money. Between Blois and Tours two places, Amboise and Mesland, can add their names to the Touraine *appellation*. (Azay-le-Rideau south-west of Tours can also do this.) The wines from these three places must have one degree more of alcohol than simple Touraine and hence they have a greater concentration of flavor.

Two VDQS wines, Valençay, between Valençay and Selles-sur-Cher, and Cheverny, from a small area south of Blois, are good examples of "Loire" wines – fresh, fruity and to be drunk young.

Farther downstream on the northern bank of the Loire, at the gates of Tours, is Vouvray and its highly regarded white wines which can be either still (sweet or dry) or sparkling and all made from Chenin Blanc; Montlouis on the opposite bank are similar wines. Both these wines can be aged in good years and are often kept for 20 or 30 years.

THE LOIRE VALLEY

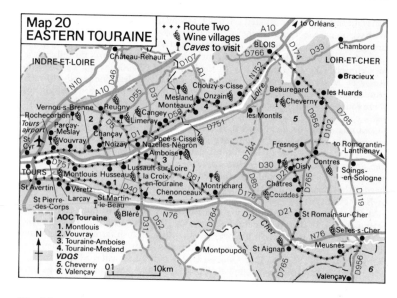

The Itinerary:

In **Selles-sur-Cher**, follow consecutively the signs *Toutes Directions*, Châteauroux, and **Meusnes**. On D956 watch for the righthand turnoff onto D17 to Meusnes. Continue through Meusnes to **St Aignan** and turn right on D675, crossing the Cher and passing through the orchards and vines between **St Romain** and **Couddes**. At Couddes, take the lefthand turnoff toward **Châtres** and **Oisly**; note the dark rich earth here, very different from the stony vineyards near Sancerre. After Châtres turn left at the junction with D21 – this road leads into Oisly, where signs indicate the way to **Fresnes**. Bear right toward Fresnes through a vast expanse of vineyards; at the next major crossroad, turn right onto D30 which will take you into **Contres**.

In Contres turn left on D956, then right on D102, heading for **Cheverny**, whose famous château can be seen at the end of a road bordered by fir trees. Bear right around the château into Cheverny, follow the signs *Toutes Directions* and then turn left on D765 toward **Blois**. After passing through woodlands, D765 becomes D956 and crosses the Loire, giving a lovely view of the old part of the town. Turn left onto N152, toward *Centre Ville* and Tours.

Follow this highway along the Loire past **Chouzy-sur-Cisse**; watch for a righthand turn to **Onzain** just before you approach the next bridge across the Loire. In Onzain bear left toward **Mesland** on D1, passing through woods, orchards and vines. In Mesland turn left and south to **Monteaux**. Turn right onto D58 and D1 through **Cangey**, **Limeray** and **Pocé-sur-Cisse**. Many troglodyte dwellings can be seen along this stretch as well as some beautiful stone houses and small châteaux.

Continue on D1 toward Vouvray and at **Nazelles-Négron** turn right on D5 to **Reugny**. In Reugny turn left on D46 south to **Chançay** where the *Route de Vouvray* begins; on the way out of Chançay watch for the lefthand turnoff to **Noizay** on D78. At the intersection in Noizay, turn right onto D1 toward **Vernou** and **Vouvray**. In Vernou, look for the lefthand turnoff to Vouvray on D46. After Vouvray turn right at the next junction and left uphill through the vineyards (toward the *centre de Sens*). At the junction head downhill to the left, then, at the bottom of the hill, right toward **Tours**, a city where the people are said to speak the purest French in France.

To visit the Montlouis area on the south bank of the Loire, take D751, signposted *Amboise par Montlouis*, which follows the Loire. After Montlouis turn right onto D40 toward **Bléré**, and then immediately left, following the signs for *Caves et vignobles* and **Husseau** on a narrow road, twisting through the vineyards. At the first main junction, turn left, then right to **Lussault-sur-Loire** to pick up D751 again in **Amboise**. After Amboise head south on D31 through the great forest until you reach **la Croix-en-Touraine**. From la Croix you can turn left on D61 to make a detour to Chenonceaux and its famous château. Return by way of D40 and D140, following the Cher to Tours.

Route Three

From Tours to Fontevraud-l'Abbaye: 110km

This route passes through the vineyards where the most famous red wines of the Loire valley are made and takes you to the western part of the Touraine and the beginning of the Anjou/Saumur region adjoining it to the west. Below Tours, on the south bank of the Loire, the first *appellation* is Touraine-Azay-le-Rideau, where Chenin Blanc grapes produce fresh, crisp white wines and Grolleau makes rosé wines. The neighboring *appellation* is Chinon, named after the fortress town a short distance away. These are mainly red wines, made usually from Cabernet Franc, which is called *le Breton* locally. On the northern bank of the Loire the red and rosé wines of Bourgueil and St Nicolas-de-Bourgueil rival those of Chinon for quality. These are also made from Cabernet Franc and all three can be superb wines.

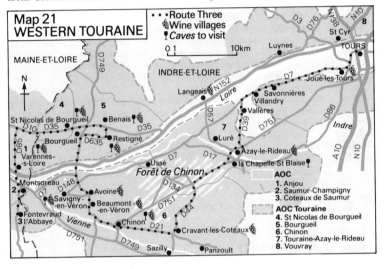

The Itinerary:

Leave the centre of **Tours** south on D86, following the signs for Chinon, then for Villandry. Immediately after the bridge across the Cher, watch for a right turn onto D7 toward **Savonnières** and Château de Villandry with its superb formal gardens. The road leads through lush farmland before passing in front of the château. Watch for the turnoff left onto D39 in the direction of **Vallères** and **Azay-le-Rideau**, taking you through neat orchards and vineyards. Follow the signs for Azay until you reach D751. Turn right and continue toward Chinon, bypassing the town of Azay unless you wish to visit its fairy-tale château on the bank of the river Indre. After Azay the road enters the large forest of Chinon. Watch for a lefthand turnoff to **Cravant-les-Coteaux**, a picturesque village where the older houses have sharply slanted roofs. Turn right on D21 to **Chinon** with its reminders of life in the Middle Ages.

In Chinon, ignore the *Centre Ville* signs in order to see some of the beautiful old town; turn left on r. Hoche, just before the church, then right at the next junction and bear left. Turn right at the next junction for a drive along the river past the statue of Rabelais. After following the signs for *Toutes Directions*, head for D749 and **Bourgueil** through orchards and vineyards dotted with pretty stone houses before crossing the Loire just after the oldest nuclear power plant in France.

In Bourgueil look for a small sign indicating *Toutes Directions* off to the right, followed by a sign indicating a right turn toward D635 and Restigné. Turn left just before Restigné, driving through the vineyards on D69 toward Benais. At the crossroads turn left on D35 and continue through **St Nicolas-de-Bourgueil**. Five kilometers from St Nicolas, in the middle of the vineyards, turn left onto D85, passing through farmland to **Varennes-sur-Loire**. Go straight through Varennes and across a bridge with a beautiful view of **Montsoreau** and its château. Turn left on D947 toward Montsoreau and continue on to **Fontevraud-l'Abbaye** with its magnificent abbey, which is being restored. You are now in Anjou.

121

Route Four

From Fontevraud l'Abbaye to Angers: 150km

The Anjou countryside is gentle and undulating and the vineyards here are interspersed with great expanses of wheatfield. Anjou is best known for its rosé, in fact, one of its *least* good wines, and a recent decline in its popularity has led many producers to switch to making a light red wine instead from Cabernet Franc. Perhaps the best of the Cabernet Franc reds are to be found in the Saumur-Champigny *appellation*, a group of nine villages upstream of Saumur.

The much larger area of Saumur is best known for its champagne-method sparkling wines which are often made and stored in vast caves hollowed out of the limestone cliffs just as in Champagne. Immediately south of Angers in the valley of the Aubance, a semi-sweet white wine is made from Chenin Blanc. However, Coteaux de l'Aubance is increasingly hard to find, as Cabernet Franc is being planted instead to make red wines and more dry Anjou Blanc is being made also.

The most interesting wines of the Anjou region are undoubtedly the sweet and fruity whites produced in the *appellations* of Quarts de Chaume, Coteaux du Layon, and Bonnezeaux. A much sought-after dry white from Chenin Blanc is made on the northern bank of the Loire in the small area covered by the Savennières la Roche-aux-Moines and Savennières Coulée-de-Serrant *appellations*; the Coulée vineyard is just 7 hectares and owned by a single proprietor.

All in all, the Anjou region offers a wide variety of whites and reds of fluctuating quality and some of the the most exciting and least appreciated sweet whites to be found anywhere in France.

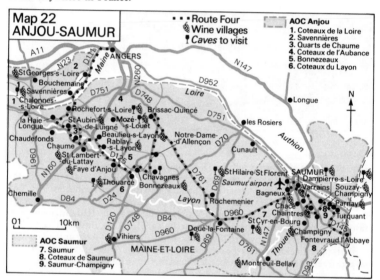

The Itinerary:

From **Fontevraud**, take D145 toward Champigny; turn off right at a crossroads onto a small bumpy road through the vineyards, following the signs for **Turquant**, then for **Parnay**. Go through Parnay onto D947, then turn left onto D205 to **Champigny**. Turn left into Champigny (signs indicate D145 and Fontevraud), then right onto D205 to Chacé, passing through woodlands and vineyards. Before Chacé, turn right on D93 toward **Varrains**, then right again to **Chaintres**; from there drive straight through the vineyards and left on D145 to **Saumur**. The villages here are in the Saumur-Champigny *appellation*.

In Saumur, follow the signs for *Centre Ville*, then signs indicating Angers and le Mans; take a left turn onto D161 toward **St Hilaire-St Florent** where there are several good Saumur producers and an interesting museum of mushroom-growing. Leave St Hilaire-St Florent on D751 in the direction of **Bagneux**, then, at the large intersection, bear right on D138. Turn right again toward **Doué-la-Fontaine** on D960, passing the massive Château de Pocé on the right shortly after Bagneux.

Approaching Doué you will see the first of many windmills in this area. From Doué, follow the signs for Angers along D761. If you are interested in seeing some troglodyte dwellings turn off right toward Rochemenier which has a small troglodyte museum. As the road approaches **Brissac-Quincé** the vineyards reappear. Drive past the first turnoff to Brissac. Take the second turnoff into the town which leads right past the château. Follow D748 south through the vineyards to **Chavagnes**, then just in the town, take the righthand turnoff for **Bonnezeaux** on D199. From here on to Angers the wine route is quite spectacular as it passes through rolling hills topped with windmills, once so common in this region.

From Bonnezeaux drive south on D24 to **Thouarcé**. In Thouarcé turn right on D125 and follow the signs to **Rablay-sur-Lyon**. From Rablay take D54 through **Beaulieu-sur-Layon**. Turn left onto N160 in the direction of **St Lambert-du-Lattay**. In St Lambert, turn right off N160 and then right again to take D209 toward Rochefort. Turn left at the junction with D54. Fork left, then left again at the second crossroads onto D106 and follow the signs to **St Aubin-de-Luigné**. At the bottom of the hill in St Aubin, follow the signs right toward Chaudefonds, going around the church. Then, at the junction, take the uphill road on the right, heading away from Chaudefonds; this is a beautiful drive through the vineyards.

Continue straight on, following the signs for **la Haie Longue**, then turn right on D751 to **Rochefort**. At Rochefort, turn left onto D106, crossing the Louet and the Loire to **Savennières**. Drive up to the Savennières church and turn right on D111 in the direction of **Bouchemaine** and **Angers**. This road passes in front of Château de Varennes and the famous Coulée de Serrant vineyards belonging to Château de la Roche aux Moines on the way to Angers.

Château de Goulaine where the Marquis de Goulaine makes excellent Muscadet.

Route Five

From Ancenis to Nantes: 135km

This route takes you through the best Muscadet vineyards in the western end of the Loire valley. The presence of the Atlantic can be felt strongly here; the sky seems brighter and the houses are whiter with orange-tiled roofs, giving an almost Mediterranean air to parts of the region.

Two wines dominate here, Muscadet and the VDQS wine of the region, Gros Plant, which is not nearly so well known outside France. Muscadet is produced throughout the region from the Muscadet or Melon de Bourgogne grape. The finest Muscadet is made east of Nantes in the rolling hills of the Sèvre et Maine district south of the Loire, between the Sèvre and Maine rivers. There is also a relatively limited production of Muscadet des Coteaux de la Loire from vineyards on both sides of the river above Nantes.

Upstream of Nantes, Ancenis is the production center of some interesting, light, pleasant VDQS wines. Here, reds, whites and rosés are made from single grape varieties such as Gamay, Cabernet Franc, Chenin and Malvoisie.

The Itinerary:

Ancenis is easily reached from Angers on N23. As the road approaches Ancenis there is a magnificent view of the suspension bridge spanning the Loire. Continue on N23 to **St Géréon**, turning sharp left on D23 back toward Ancenis. Drive straight along this road to the roundabout, then turn right, cross the bridge and take D763 toward Clisson; the vineyards begin as the road approaches **Liré**. Once in Liré, turn right on D751 to go through **Drain** and **Champtoceaux** to **la Varenne**. Here the road twists and turns through hills and valleys covered with farmland, forest, and vineyards, providing a lovely view of the la Varenne château off to the right. From la Varenne, drive through **la Chapelle-Basse-Mer** on D7, a road that climbs up onto a high plateau covered with fields and vineyards. Just before **le Loroux-Bottereau**, turn right at the crossroads and pick up D115 in the direction of Vertou; in only a few minutes you will come to the lefthand turnoff onto D74 toward **Haute-Goulaine**. Drive into the village, turn left at the church and left again on D74 toward la Haie-Fouassière, passing Château de Goulaine on your left just after leaving Haute-Goulaine.

From here on the route is quite beautiful, though extremely circuitous, as it passes through the Muscadet vineyards before arriving at last in Vertou and Nantes. At the junction with D756, turn left toward Vallet. Drive into the center of **la Chapelle-Heulin**, bear left at the church and take D7 in the direction of le Loroux-Bottereau and **le Landreau**. At the junction with D55 turn right toward le Landreau, enter the village and turn right at the church to go to **Vallet** on D37. At the stoplight in Vallet, turn right onto D763 toward Clisson, cross the highway and take the first turnoff to the right, following signs for D116 and **le Pallet**. At the junction with N149 turn right toward Nantes, then follow the signs to **Monnières** on D7. Continue south, then turn left at the crossroads onto D59 to **Clisson**.

As you approach Clisson turn right, following the signs to Aigrefeuille and D117 as far as **St Lumine-de-Clisson**. From St Lumine follow the signs to the right for D58 and **Maisdon**; in Maisdon follow the signs for **St Fiacre**, then watch for signs to **la Haie-Fouassière** on D74. At the church in la Haie, a village that claims fame as "the birthplace of Muscadet", turn left onto D359 toward **Vertou**, finally turning right onto D59 to bypass Vertou in the direction of **Nantes**.

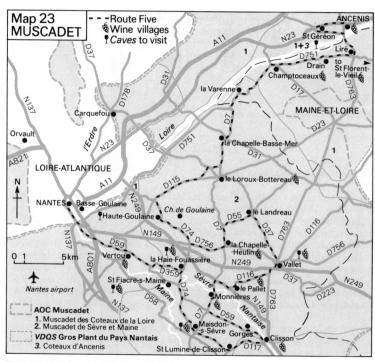

Map 23
MUSCADET

- - - Route Five
🍇 Wine villages
🍷 Caves to visit

Caves and Vineyards to Visit

Though the Loire valley has a great concentration of châteaux, most wines are produced in farmhouses by *vignerons* who live modestly in the villages. In recent years these growers have been making great efforts to promote and improve their wines and they have succeeded so admirably that some growers in popular regions, such as Sancerre and Chinon, can no longer satisfy the demand for their wines. Though the Parisian market remains important, many now export up to one third of their production.

Large merchants are the exception rather than the rule here and wine-making continues to be extremely small scale; what is more common are the "dynasties" found throughout the valley, families whose members all make the same wine (leading to some confusion if the buyer is only familiar with the grower's last name).

As in other wine regions, the trend here is toward making wines to be drunk relatively young, and many *vignerons* continue the tradition of selling the new wine by the barrel to be bottled by their customers and generally consumed within the year.

CHAVAGNES, map 22

Vincent Goizil (G),
Domaine du Petit-Val, Chavagnes, 49380 Thouarcé.
Tel: 41.54.31.14.

After a period of decline the great sweet wines of France are undergoing a revival and one of the best is Bonnezeaux. Production of this rich, heady wine is centered on the village of the same name, a few kilometers north-east of Thouarcé in Anjou.

A leading producer is Vincent Goizil, who makes his Bonnezeaux from 2 hectares of Chenin Blanc vines. The wine needs time to develop fully and M. Goizil proudly shows visitors a bottle of the 1893 vintage (not for sale). Altogether, he cultivates 17 hectares of vines and as well as Bonnezeaux, he makes other sweet and semi-sweet wines – Coteaux du Layon and Cabernet d'Anjou.
Visiting hours: Mon–Fri 8–8; Sat–Sun by appt.
Location: Just N of Chavagnes on the road to Angers.

CHINON, map 21

Domaine René Couly (G/M),
Couly-Dutheil Père et Fils,
12 r. Diderot,
37502 Chinon.
Tel: 47.93.05.84.

The author Rabelais lived at Chinon in the 16th century and his family owned property in the area, including the 17-hectare Clos de l'Echo vineyard, which is now owned by Couly-Dutheil, a family firm. The brothers, Pierre and Jacques Couly-Dutheil are now in charge.

As well as being *négociants*, Couly-Dutheil own 48 hectares of vineyards, all within the Chinon *appellation* and have contributed a great deal to the reputation of Chinon wines. The Clos de l'Echo is a full-bodied wine which requires long cask-aging. The Baronnie Madeleine is another excellent wine made by the family.
Visiting hours: Mon–Fri 8–12, 2–4.30, by appt.
Location: At the E edge of town on the road to Cravant-les-Coteaux.

HAUTE-GOULAINE, map 23

Marquis de Goulaine (G),
Château de Goulaine,
Haute-Goulaine,
44115 Basse-Goulaine.
Tel: 40.54.91.42.

The Château de Goulaine is one of the most splendid properties in the western end of the Loire valley. For over 1,000 years the Goulaine family has lived and made wines here. The present head of the family is Robert, the eleventh marquis, and he personally supervises all the wine-making on the estate. He has also played an important part in promoting Muscadet wines around the world.

As well as the excellent Muscadet de Sèvre et Maine *sur lie* and other Muscadets, there is a Domaine de la Grange Gros Plant *sur lie* from Château la Grange 20km away. This is also owned by the estate but cannot be visited. All the Goulaine wines are bottled at la Grange.

The present château was built in the 15th and 16th centuries and contains a superb collection of 17th-18th century art. The ground floor of the château has been well laid out for exhibitions and receptions. Light meals, buffets or gala dinners can be organized. There is also a tropical butterfly farm.

Visiting hours: Easter–Nov 1 Sat, Sun and hols, 2–5.30; Jun–Sep 15 Wed–Mon, 2–5.30.

Location: 2km S of Haute-Goulaine off D74.

MAISDON-SUR-SEVRE, map 23

GIE Louis Métaireau (G/M), la Févrie, Maisdon-sur-Sèvre, 44690 la Haie-Fouassière. Tel: 40.54.81.92.

Louis Métaireau is one of the best-known *négociants* in the Muscadet de Sèvre et Maine region. The firm is an association of nine independent growers who select their best wines each year to sell under the name Coupe Louis Métaireau. They also own the Grand Mouton estate at St Fiacre, one of the best villages in the Muscadet *appellation*.

Visiting hours: Mon–Fri 8.30–12, 2–6.

Location: In the village center.

MENETOU-SALON, map 19

Cave Clément (G), Domaine de Châtenoy, 18510 Menetou-Salon. Tel: 48.64.80.25.

Menetou-Salon is a small *appellation* which is rapidly growing in reputation and size and the wines are good value compared to those of nearby Sancerre. Domaine de Châtenoy is a leading Menetou estate and is owned by Bernard and Pierre Clément, who are descended from the family who has owned the estate since 1733. Their wine-making is highly modern and the wines fresh and fruity. As well as white Menetou-Salon made from Sauvignon there is a small amount of red from Pinot Noir.

Visiting hours: Mon–Sat 9–12, 2–7.

Location: 1km S of Menetou-Salon on the road to les Aix d'Angillon.

MONTRICHARD, map 20

SA J.-M. Monmousseau (G/M), 71 rte de Vierzon, BP 25, 41401 Montrichard. Tel: 54.32.07.04.

Montrichard is a pleasant town on the northern bank of the Cher and the limestone cliffs above the town are honeycombed with quarried caves, which are now used by mushroom growers as well as by firms making sparkling wine. One of these is Monmousseau, founded in 1886 and now owned by Taittinger, the champagne firm. Monmousseau also own 50 hectares of vines in the Touraine and Vouvray *appellations* which supply 25 per cent of their needs.

Visiting hours: Easter–Nov 1 daily, 9–11.30, 2–6.

Location: At the E side of Montrichard on the road to Vierzon.

MOZE-SUR-LOUET, map 22

Domaine Richou Père et Fils (G), Chauvigné, Mozé-sur-Louet, 49190 Rochefort-sur-Loire. Tel: 41.78.72.13.

The Richou family has records of its wine-making activity dating back to the 16th century and in the 18th century supplied wines to the royal table. The family now owns 30 hectares which are planted with several varieties, including old Chenin vines for its semi-sweet Coteaux de l'Aubance wines made by traditional methods. There is also an excellent Anjou Rouge, and an Anjou Blanc from Chenin softened by the addition of Chardonnay.

Visiting hours: Mon–Sat 8–7.

Location: Chauvigné is between Mozé-sur-Louet and Denée.

OISLY, map 20

Confrérie des Vignerons de Oisly et Thesée (C), Cédex 112, Oisly, 41700 Contres. Tel: 54.79.52.88.

The Confrérie des Vignerons de Oisly et Thésée was set up in 1961 to bottle and market the wines made by individual growers in the region around Oisly. There are now 53 members who cultivate a total of 300 hectares of vineyards and production is fairly substantial.

Most of the wines made come under the Touraine *appellation*, and there is a tiny amount of Vin de Pays du Jardin de la France. The Confrérie has a particular reputation for Sauvignon de Touraine, a wine to be drunk young, preferably within the first year. The Baronnie d'Aignan, both red and white, is another leading wine from this co-operative.

Visiting hours: Daily 9–12, 2–5; no groups.
Location: In the village center.

POUILLY-SUR-LOIRE, map 19

Château de Nozet (G), 58150 Pouilly-sur-Loire. Tel: 86.39.10.76. Paris office tel: 47.20.66.62.

Château du Nozet has been owned by the Ladoucette family since 1785 and is a wonderful turreted building in beautiful gardens above Pouilly. The estate is one of the largest in the Pouilly-Fumé *appellation*, and includes a single holding of 52 hectares. The present owner is the energetic Baron Patrick de Ladoucette who took over the estate in the early 1970s as a young man. He has invested heavily in the best up-to-date equipment for the cellars as well as restoring the château to its former glory and it is now used for banquets and receptions.

To supplement their own grapes must is bought in from local growers and the whole is vinified together. There is no wood aging. The top *cuvée* is the Baron de "L", a top quality Pouilly-Fumé made from specially selected lots of wine. Sancerre is also made at the château from must bought in from growers in Sancerre across the river and these wines are sold under the name of Comte Lafond Sancerre.

Visiting hours: By appt with the Paris office. No visits in Aug or Christmas and New Year.
Location: 1km N of Pouilly-sur-Loire on N7.

ROCHECORBON, map 20

Ets. Marc Brédif (M), 87 quai de la Loire, Rochecorbon, 37210 Vouvray. Tel: 47.52.50.07.

An old firm of *négociants*, Marc Brédif has no vineyards of its own. The grapes are supplied by growers in the Vouvray area with whom the firm has dealt for generations. There is a wide range of still and sparkling wines, including a Vouvray Pétillant, a slightly sparkling wine. The limestone cellars are one of the largest and most interesting in the Vouvray area. In 1980 the firm was sold to Baron Patrick de Ladoucette, the well-known Pouilly producer (see above).

Visiting hours: Mon–Fri at 10.30 and 4, by appt.
Location: Between Vouvray and Rochecorbon on N152.

ST CYR-EN-BOURG, map 22

Cave des Vignerons de Saumur (C), St Cyr-en-Bourg, 49260 Montreuil-Bellay. Tel: 41.51.61.09.

The Saumur co-operative is based at St Cyr and the cellars are in quarries hewn out of the limestone cliffs. These are over 4km in length and visitors drive in by car! The co-operative has 260 members who cultivate 820 hectares of vines between them. There is a wide range of both still and sparkling wines, including Saumur and Crémant de Loire.

Visiting hours: May 1–Sep 30 daily, 9–11.30, 2–5.30; Oct–Apr by appt.
Location: Signposted from the village center.

ST FIACRE-SUR-MAINE, map 23

Ets. Chéreau Carré (G/M),
Domaine de Chasseloir,
St Fiacre-sur-Maine,
44690 la Haie-Fouassière.
Tel: 40.54.81.15.

Chéreau Carré's headquarters are in an aristocratic 15th-century building, Château de Chasseloir, in one of the best Muscadet villages. The firm is a joint venture between the Chéreau and Carré families, and owns six estates in the Sèvre et Maine region. All the wines are bottled *sur lie* at the individual estates. Chasseloir, run by Mme Edmonde Chéreau, is an old property and has a fine cellar with painted and carved beams which is well organized for visitors.

Other Chéreau Carré estates include Château de Coing at St Fiacre, Château de l'Oiselinière at Vertou, Grand Fief de la Cormeraie at Monnières, Moulin de Gravelle at Gorges, and Domaine du Bois Bruley at Basse-Goulaine. Chéreau Carré is also experimenting with wood-aging Muscadet made from older vines.

Visiting hours: Mon–Sat 8–6:30.
Location: Signposted in the village.

The beautiful cellar with painted beams at Château de Chasseloir.

ST HILAIRE-ST FLORENT, map 22

Ackerman-Laurance (M),
r. Léopold-Palustre,
BP 1, St Hilaire-St Florent,
49416 Saumur.
Tel: 41.50.25.33.

St Hilaire-St Florent is a suburb of Saumur squeezed between steep hills and the Thouet, a minor tributary of the Loire, which it joins just below the town. The rivers have cut away the hills leaving chalk cliffs which have been quarried over the centuries. The caves left by the quarrying are ideal places for maturing wine, with a constant temperature of 13°C throughout the year.

Ackerman-Laurance is the oldest and one of the best-known makers of champagne-method sparkling Saumur or Saumur Mousseux. A Belgian, Jean Ackerman learned the art of making sparkling wines in Champagne and married a girl from Saumur, hence the name of his firm which he founded in 1811. For nearly 40 years he was the only person in the region to make use of the local caves for his sparkling wines. There are now over 10 firms making sparkling Saumur but Ackerman-Laurance is the largest with over 3 million bottles of champagne-method wines produced annually. There is a range of styles of Saumur Mousseux as well as some Crémant de Loire.

Visiting hours: May 1–Sep 30 9–12, 3–5.30.
Location: 3km W of Saumur on D751 and signposted.

Bouvet-Ladubay S.A. (M),
r. Jean Ackerman,
St Hilaire-St Florent,
49400 Saumur.
Tel: 41.50.11.12.

Bouvet-Ladubay, owned by Monmousseau which in turn has been owned by Taittinger, the champagne house, since 1984, is a leading Saumur firm. Bouvet-Ladubay do not own any vineyards of their own and buy in grapes from at least 150 different growers in the region. The firm has expanded in recent years under the guiding hand of Patrice Monmousseau, with a target of 2.5 million bottles a year. Quality is high and these are the most expensive

sparkling Saumurs. Bouvet-Ladubay use only white grapes, mainly Chenin Blanc, for their sparkling wines, except for the rosé which is a blend of Cabernet Franc and Grollot.
Visiting hours: Mon–Fri 9–12, 2–6.
Location: 3km W of Saumur at the entrance to St Hilaire.

The interesting remuage *system developed by Patrice Monmousseau.*

SAUMUR, map 22

Gratien et Meyer (G/M), Château de Beaulieu, BP 22, rte. de Montsoreau, 49100 Saumur.
Tel: 41.51.01.54.

Gratien, Meyer, Seydoux is the name of the firm that owns Alfred Gratien, the champagne house and Gratien et Meyer, a leading maker of sparkling Saumur. Founded in 1864 by Alfred Gratien, Gratien et Meyer is on the eastern side of the Saumur, high up on the hillside with fine views over the Loire. The firm now owns 20 hectares of vineyards planted with Chenin Blanc and Cabernet Franc, as well as buying in grapes from over 200 local growers. Gratien et Meyer make a wide range of Saumur and Crémant de Loire wines, as well as some Anjou rosé. Their Crémant de Loire is excellent.
Visiting hours: Daily 9–12, 2–5.
Location: 2km E of Saumur on D947.

SAVENNIERES, map 22

Vignoble de la Coulée de Serrant (G), Château de la Roche aux Moines, 49170 Savennières.
Tel: 41.72.22.32.

Château de la Roche aux Moines is a charming, rambling country house in the narrow valley of the river Serrant between D111 and the Loire. The estate was founded by monks in the 12th century and an avenue of cypress trees on the estate is known as the Cimitière des Anglais because King John of England lost a battle on the site in 1214. The château and small estate are owned by Mme Joly who is one of the few people in France to own an entire *appellation*, Savennières-Coulée de Serrant. This is one of the finest dry white wines in all France and made entirely from Chenin Blanc. The vineyard on the steep slopes above the Loire is only 7 hectares and production is deliberately limited, partly because of the terrain where work has to be done either by hand or by horses, and partly to achieve higher quality. Since 1985 organic viticulture has been practised, with no chemicals, and vinification methods are as natural as possible.

In addition, Mme Joly owns a small amount of land in the neighbouring *appellation* of Savennières la Roche-aux-Moines. Yields for this dry white wine, also made from Chenin Blanc, are higher than from the Coulée de Serrant vineyard as the slopes are less steep. There is also a small amount of red Anjou made from Cabernet Franc and sold under the label Château de la Roche. An estate that enjoys such status might be expected to actively discourage visits by the general public; however, Mme Joly quite willingly receives guests without prior notice.
Visiting hours: (Tasting only) Mon–Sat 8.30–12, 2–5.30; closed hols.
Location: 3km N of Savennières on D111 and signposted.

VALLET, map 23

Sauvion et Fils (G/M), Château du Cléray, BP 3, 44330 Vallet. Tel: 40.36.22.55.

Château du Cléray was once part of an important feudal estate and the present elegant 18th-century château was restored after the Revolution. The vaulted cellars are magnificent. The firm is one of the leading *négociants* in the Muscadet region and exports throughout the world. Sauvion also owns a total of 30 hectares of vineyards.

The best wines are the Cuvée Cardinal Richard, named after a former archbishop of Paris who once owned the estate, and les Decouvertes range, an interesting range of single-vineyard Muscadets, selected each year from the dozen estates looked after by Sauvion.

Visiting hours: Apr–Sep daily 8–12, 2–5.30.

Location: Just off D375 S of Vallet.

Further *Caves* and Vineyards to Visit

AMBOISE, map 20

Girault-Artois (G), Domaine d'Artois, 7 quai des Violettes, 37400 Amboise. Tel: 47.57.07.71. Visiting hours: By appt.

François Girault's firm is based in Amboise but the vineyards and cellars are in the heart of the Touraine-Mesland *appellation* across the Loire.

BENAIS, map 21

Robert Caslot-Galbrun (G), Domaine Hubert, la Hurolaie, Benais, 37140 Bourgueil. Tel: 47.97.30.59. Visiting hours: By appt.

Robert Caslot-Galbrun makes a good, classic Bourgueil that ages well.

BOIS-GIBAULT, map 19

GAEC Roger Pabiot et ses Fils (G), 13 rte de Pouilly, Bois-Gibault, Tracy-sur-Loire, 58150 Pouilly-sur-Loire. Tel: 86.39.12.41. Visiting hours: By appt.

The hills slant steeply down to the Loire around Bois-Gibault just north-west of Pouilly. Roger Pabiot's vineyards are south of the village and he and his sons make a highly regarded Pouilly-Fumé Coteau des Girarmes.

BOURGUEIL, map 21

Maison Audebert et Fils (G/M), Domaine du Grand Clos, av. Jean-Causeret, 37140 Bourgueil. Tel: 47.97.70.06. Visiting hours: Mon–Fri 8–12, 2–7; Sat–Sun by appt.

The Domaine du Grand-Clos owned by the Audebert family consists of 28 hectares planted entirely in Cabernet Franc. Their Bourgueil has a fine bouquet and lingering flavor.

BUE, map 19

GAEC B. Bailly-Reverdy et Fils (G), la Croix St Laurent, Bué, 18300 Sancerre. Tel: 48.54.18.38. Visiting hours: By appt.

Bué is a thriving wine-making village in the Sancerre *appellation*. Bailly-Reverdy is a respected family firm, making good Sancerre whites, including the Clos du Chêne Marchand from an important Bué vineyard, and Domaine de la Mercy Dieu.

La CHAPELLE-ST-BLAISE, map 21

Robert Denis (G), 11 r. de la Rabière, la Chapelle-St Blaise, 37190 Azay-le-Rideau. Tel: 47.45.46.57. Visiting hours: By appt.

La Chapelle is across the Indre from Azay-le-Rideau and its fairy-tale château. Robert Denis owns a modest 4 hectares of vines and makes good Touraine-Azay-le-Rideau.

CHAUDOUX-VERDIGNY, map 19

Bernard Reverdy et Fils (G), Chaudoux-Verdigny, 18300 Sancerre. Tel: 48.79.34.76. Visiting hours: By appt.

The domaine makes fine white Sancerre as well as interesting rosé.

CHEVERNY, map 20

Gendrier (G), les Huards, Cour-Cheverny, 41700 Contres. Tel: 54.79.97.90. Visiting hours: Mon–Sat 8–8.

Wine-making is a tradition in the Gendrier family that extends back six generations and they make a wide variety of wines within the Cheverny VDQS *appellation*. About a quarter of their vineyards are planted with Romorantin, a rare white grape variety.

DAMPIERRE-SUR-LOIRE, map 22

Paul Filliatreau (G), Chaintres, Dampierre-sur-Loire, 49400 Saumur. Tel: 41.52.90.84. Visiting hours: Daily 8–12, 2–6.

Paul Filliatreau is a leading maker of Saumur-Champigny, including a superb wine from old vines.

Domaine Vinicole de Chaintres (G), Dampierre-sur-Loire, 49400 Saumur. Tel: 41.52.90.54. Visiting hours: Mon–Fri, by appt.

The Château de Chaintres belongs to the de Tigny family and the immense cellars contain an impressive array of oak casks in which an excellent Saumur-Champigny is aged.

DOUE-LA-FONTAINE, map 22

Vignobles Touchais SCA (G), 25 av. Gén.-Leclerc, 49700 Doué-la-Fontaine. Tel: 41.59.12.14. Visiting hours: By appt.

Coteaux du Layon wines can be aged for an extraordinary length of time and the Moulin Touchais has a superb collection of old bottles that are proudly shown to visitors – the oldest is dated 1870. All the sweet wines are kept for at least 10 years before being released for sale. The family also make other Loire wines, including some Anjou Blanc.

La HAIE-FOUASSIERE, map 23

Robert Brosseau (G), Domaine des Mortiers-Gobin, 44690 la Haie-Fouassière. Tel: 40.54.80.66. Visiting hours: By appt; closed Aug.

Robert Brosseau makes an elegant Muscadet de Sèvre et Maine *sur lie* and some Gros Plant, also *sur lie*.

LIMERAY, map 20

Dutertre et Fils (G), 20 r. d'Enfer, pl. du Tertre, Limeray, 37530 Amboise. Tel: 47.30.10.69. Visiting hours: Daily 8–7.

Another good producer of Touraine-Amboise wines is the Dutertre family who have made wine in Limeray for many generations. As well as red and white wines, there is a good rosé. There are fine cellars carved out of rock.

MENETREOL-SOUS-SANCERRE, map 19

Gitton Père et Fils S.A. (G), 18300 Ménétréol - sous - Sancerre. Tel: 48.54.38.84. Visiting hours: By appt.

Marcel Gitton and his son Pascal make interesting Sancerre and Pouilly-Fumé from 30 hectares. The grapes are vinified in separate batches according to soil type for maximum individuality.

MESLAND, map 20

Philippe Brossillon (G), Domaine de Lusqueneau, Mesland, 41150 Onzain. Tel: 54.70.28.23. Visiting hours: Daily 8–8.

Philippe Brossillon makes good red and rosé Touraine-Mesland wines.

MEUSNES, map 20

Hubert Sinson (G), le Muza, Meusnes, 41130 Selles-sur-Cher. Tel: 54.71.00.26. Visiting hours: By appt.

This is a reliable producer in the Valençay area of eastern Touraine, making mainly Gamay wines.

MOROGUES, map 19

Domaine Henry Pellé (G), pl. de l'Eglise, Morogues, 18220 les-Aix-d'Angillon. Tel: 48.64.42.48. Visiting hours: Daily 9–12, 2–6; Sun and hols by appt.

Morogues is a leading wine village in the Menetou-Salon *appellation*, and Henry Pellé makes good wines, as well as being mayor of the village.

OISLY, map 20

Maurice Barbou (G), les Corbillières, Oisly, 41700 Contres. Tel: 54.79.52.75. Visiting hours: Mon–Sat 8–12, 2–6.30; Sun by appt.

The Barbou family have made wine in the Oisly area for three generations. Maurice Barbou's grandfather introduced the Sauvignon grape to Touraine. As well as the fresh-tasting Sauvignon de Touraine there is a fruity Cabernet Franc and a good Pinot Noir.

RESTIGNE, map 21

Paul Caslot-Jamet (G), Domaine de la Chevalerie, Restigné, 37140 Bourgueil. Tel: 47.97.32.11. Visiting hours: Daily by appt.

Paul Caslot-Jamet's Bourgueil estate

is 12 hectares of Cabernet Franc, and the wines are of good quality.

REUILLY, map 19
Gérard Cordier (G), la Ferté, 36260 Reuilly. Tel : 54.49.28.98. Visiting hours : By appt.
Reuilly received its *appellation* as long ago as 1937. Gérard Cordier is an enthusiastic winemaker with a small vineyard of less than 5 hectares. His Reuilly Blanc is light and fragrant.

ROCHEFORT-S-LOIRE, map 22
Jacques Lalanne (G), Château Bellerive, 49190 Rochefort-sur-Loire. Tel : 41.78.33.66. Visiting hours : By appt ; closed 3 weeks Sep.
Quarts-de-Chaume is a tiny *appellation* in the Layon valley for noble-rotted sweet wines and Jacques Lalannes's 17-hectare estate is one of the largest. He makes excellent Quarts de Chaume and has spent much time and money restoring the château.

ST ANDELAIN, map 19
Didier Dagueneau et Fils (G), les Berthiers, St Andelain, 58150 Pouilly-sur-Loire. Tel : 86.39.15.62. Visiting hours : By appt.
Didier Dagueneau is an enthusiastic winemaker, one of Pouilly-Fumé's best and most innovative. He hand picks his 7 hectares of vineyards several times over and experiments with aging in new oak barrels.

ST GÉRÉON, map 23
Jacques Guindon (G/M), la Couleu-verdière, St Géréon, 44150 Ancenis. Tel : 40.83.18.96. Visiting hours : Mon–Sat 9–12, 2–7.
The family firm has established a good reputation for its wines, including a Muscadet des Coteaux de la Loire *sur lie*, and a Gros-Plant du Pays Nantais.

ST MARTIN-LE-BEAU, map 20
Guy Delétang et Fils (G), 19 rte d'Amboise, St Martin-le-Beau, 37270 Mountlouis-sur-Loire. Tel : 47.50.67.25. Visiting hours : Mon–Sat 8–12, 2–6.30.
St Martin is on the north bank of the Cher, near Tours, and is one of the three villages in the Montlouis *appellation*. The Delétangs make good sparkling

Montlouis from Chenin Blanc, as well as an interesting still Montlouis.

ST NICOLAS-DE-BOURGUEIL, map 21
Claude et Thierry Amirault (G), le Clos des Quarterons-Amirault, 37140 St Nicolas-de-Bourgueil. Tel : 47.97.75.25. Visiting hours : Mon–Sat 8–12.30, 1.30–7.
The Amiraults make good St Nicolas-de-Bourgueil.

SANCERRE, map 19
Alphonse Mellot (G/M), 3 r. pte César, 18300 Sancerre. Tel : 48.54.07.41. Visiting hours : (Sales only) by appt.
Alphonse Mellot is an enterprising winemaker and *négociant* who has the biggest wine business in Sancerre and an attractive shop in the town center.

SAVIGNY-EN-VERON, map 21
Raymond Raffault (G), Domaine du Raifault, 23-25 rte de Candes, Savigny-en-Véron, 37420 Avoine. Tel : 47.58.44.01. Visiting hours : Mon–Sat 8–12, 2–6, by appt.
Raymond Raffault sells his Chinon wines under the name Domaine du Raifault as there are many Raffaults around Chinon. The 17 hectares of vines surround an attractive 16th-century manor house.

THOUARCE, map 22
Jacques Boivin (G), Château de Fesles, 49380 Thouarcé. Tel : 41.54.14.32. Visiting hours : Mon–Sat, by appt.
Jacques Boivin makes an excellent Bonnezeaux wine.

René Renou (G), Domaine de Terre Brune, pl. du Champ-de-Foire, 49380 Thouarcé. Tel : 41.54.04.05. Visiting hours : By appt.
René Renou is a staunch supporter of Anjou wines and his range is headed by a good Bonnezeaux.

VOUVRAY, map 20
Société Huet (G), Domaine du Haut-Lieu and Clos du Bourg, 37210 Vouvray. Tel : 47.52.78.87. Visiting hours : By appt.
Gaston Huet, the mayor of Vouvray, makes excellent classic wines, including a dry Vouvray from the Haut-Lieu vineyard.

Though châteaux and fortresses exist throughout France, nowhere are they as concentrated or as well preserved as in the Loire valley. This is also the land where Rabelais and Ronsard were born and monumental abbeys and cathedrals such as those of Fontevraud and Tours are reminders of the valley's importance in the Middle Ages. Fields of flowers and fruit trees make the valley bright with color in the late spring and early summer.

AMBOISE
In a picturesque setting on the banks of the Loire, Amboise is famous chiefly for its **château** high above the river. Also in Amboise is the **Manoir du Clos-Lucé**, the house where Leonardo da Vinci spent the last three years of his life until his death in 1519. The room where he died has been restored and can be visited. There is also a small museum displaying models made from his drawings.

Two annual wine fairs are held in Amboise, at the beginning of Apr, and in mid-Aug.

ANGERS
Angers, the ancient capital of Anjou, is an important market for the local wines, fruits and vegetables. There are fine buildings in the old town at the foot of the château, including the **Hôtel du Croissant**, the **Maison d'Adam**, and the **Tour St Aubin**, the belfry of the old abbey.

The **château** is a vast 13th-century fortress overlooking the city center and the river Maine. The 17 round towers are linked by walls more than 1km long.

AZAY-LE-RIDEAU
The Renaissance **château**, on a small, wooded island in the Indre, is one of the most beautiful sights in all the region. Inside are fine Renaissance paintings, furniture and tapestries and a sound and light show (*Son et Lumière*) is held in summer.

A wine fair is held in the town in Jan and an apple fair at the end of Oct.

The château of Azay-le-Rideau.

BLOIS
Originally a 13th-century fortress, the **château** has been rebuilt as a royal residence and is a marvelous mixture of medieval and Renaissance styles. Most famous of all is the ornate octagonal staircase built during the reign of François I. The view of the town and river below alone makes a visit worthwhile. In summer, there is a sound and light show (*Son et Lumière*).

The old town between the château and the river is worth exploring and has many fine picturesque houses.

BRISSAC-QUINCE
The **château**, framed by two round towers, was once part of a medieval castle and there is a rich collection of tapestries inside.

CHENONCEAUX
One of the most remarkable and graceful buildings in the world, the **château de Chenonceau** is magnificent (note that the village itself is spelt 'Chenonceaux'). Built between 1513 and 1521, it was later owned by Diane de Poitiers, Henri II's famous mistress, who was responsible for the construction of the gallery across the Cher, and then by Catherine de Médicis, the King's widow. The apartments occupied by these two ladies can be visited as well as the gallery, kitchens and chapel. There are delightful gardens.

CHEVERNY
The **château**, built between 1604 and 1634, is one of the few in the Loire valley still belonging to the same family. The apartments are splendidly furnished and decorated, especially the Chambre du Roi. Set in a large park, the château has a fascinating hunting museum, the **Musée de Vénerie**.

CHINON
On the banks of the river Vienne, Chinon is dominated by its vast ruined **château**. It was here in 1429 that Joan of Arc first met the Dauphin, going on to help

liberate France from the English. A sound and light show (*Son et Lumière*) is held in summer.

The oldest part of the town, the **Grand Carroi**, is a warren of narrow lanes and fine old buildings. The **Musée du Vin et de la Tonnellerie** explains the making of wine and wine barrels and a free tasting of the local wines is included. The feast of St Vincent, patron of winemakers, is also ceremonially observed in Chinon in Jan and there is a wine fair in mid-Mar.

FONTEVRAUD-L'ABBAYE

Founded in 1099, the **abbey** is a superb Romanesque building and contains the tombs of several Plantagenet kings. Plundered during the Revolution, it was turned into a prison by Napoleon, and remained one until 1963. It is now being restored.

LANGEAIS

The 15th-century feudal **fortress** has been restored recently and the medieval apartments contain a magnificent collection of tapestries.

MONTRICHARD

Above Montrichard on the right bank of the Cher is an 11th-century keep from which there is a fine view of the surrounding countryside. The cliffs along the river bank are used as wine cellars and for cultivating mushrooms.

NANTES

For a long time the capital of Brittany, Nantes is a busy seaport at the mouth of the Loire. This formidable castle was begun in 1466 by Duke François II and continued by his daughter, Anne of Brittany. Within its spacious courtyard are several fine buildings which now house the **Musée d'Art Populaire Régional** and the **Musée des Salorges**, a maritime museum.

The **Cathédrale de St Pierre-et-St Paul**, built between 1434 and 1893, is rather severe, but has a breathtaking lofty interior, over 35m high. The **Musée Jules-Verne** contains mementos of the famous author who was a native of Nantes and the **Musée des Beaux-Arts** has a fine collection of Renaissance and 20th-century paintings.

A wine fair is held in mid-Nov.

ST AIGNAN

Surrounded by forests and vineyards, this little town has an attractive church with a Romanesque crypt decorated with medieval frescoes. There is also a pleasant Renaissance château (access to the terrace only).

SANCERRE

On the summit of a ridge, Sancerre was occupied as early as Gallo-Roman times. The old town, with its quiet squares and steep, narrow streets, is dominated by an enormous 14th-century keep, the **Tour des Fiefs**. A wine fair is held at the beginning of Jun.

SAUMUR

Saumur, famous for its sparkling wines, lies between the Loire and the Thouet. It is a lively and prosperous town with an interesting château which today houses two museums, the **Musée des Arts Décoratifs**, and the **Musée du Cheval**. The famous cavalry school was founded in 1763. Today, it teaches armored warfare but also maintains a cavalry unit, with a celebrated squadron of riders, the Cadre Noir.

There is a curious **Musée du Champignon** at St Hilaire-St Florent (3km W by D751), showing how mushrooms are cultivated locally. Saumur also hosts a wine fair in mid-Feb.

TOURS

Tours has been a rich and bustling university city for many centuries and its position between the Loire and the Cher makes it an ideal starting point for exploring the region. The center of the old city has many attractive old buildings and the **Cathédrale St Gatien** has famous 13th–15th-century stained-glass windows.

The **Musée des Beaux-Arts**, in the former archbishop's palace, boasts a fine collection of paintings. The **Musée des Vins de Touraine** is a wine museum in the 12th-century vaulted cellars of the **Eglise St Julien**.

VILLANDRY

The 16th-century **château** has magnificent formal gardens in a series of terraces descending to the Loire. The château itself contains a series of paintings of the 16th–17th century Spanish school.

Hotels, Restaurants and Where to Buy Wine

The Loire valley is rich in gastronomic associations: a statue of Rabelais graces his native Chinon; a square in Angers honors Curnonsky (Maurice Sailland), the 20th-century's "prince of gastronomes;" *tarte tatin* (hot upside-down apple tart) and *beurre blanc* (foamy butter sauce) are both said to have been created here, and the *rillettes* and *rillons* of Tours are now found throughout France. Naturally enough, the region is also famous for fish. Both *matelote d'anguilles* (eels stewed in red wine) and poached pike (*brochet*) with *beurre blanc* are memorable dishes.

Caves hollowed out of the hillsides along the rivers, particularly at Saumur and Montrichard, proved to be ideal places for the large-scale cultivation of mushrooms (*champignons de Paris*). The over-production of low-quality wines in the 18th and 19th centuries gave birth to an important vinegar industry in Orléans (the Cointreau family began making their famous liqueur in Angers in 1849 for much the same reason).

More recently, a humble goat cheese made in Chavignol near Sancerre, the *crottin*, has become all the rage with *nouvelle cuisine* chefs who serve it hot with salad, adding yet another Loire valley product to the list of national favorites. Like the wines, the food is varied and without pretension, sure to please and closer to what one thinks of as typically "French" than that of any other province.

The wines of the Loire offer endless possiblities for orchestrating a meal. The hardest to serve are the sweet white wines, which can be quite astonishing – try a Coteaux du Layon or Vouvray as an aperitif or with dessert and be sure not to overlook certain "logical" but perfect combinations such as white Sancerre with *crottin de Chavignol* or Muscadet with shellfish.

Charles Barrier (R), 101 av. Tranchée, 37000 Tours. Tel: 47.54.20.39. Two Michelin stars. Reservations essential for Fri–Sat. Closed Sun pm–Mon, and 10 days Feb. MC V
Barrier is back! After having closed his restaurant because of tax problems, Charles Barrier has started anew and, now in his 70s, is showing the sort of enthusiasm and talent one notes in a "rising star." Still in the same location, he now serves only 35 to 40 people, and has decided to emphasize regional dishes and, of course, wines of the Loire valley.

Selection of the wine list was made with an eye toward wines with personalities rather than of great repute. There is an exceptional collection of Vouvrays, both dry and sweet, and including some older vintages ('33, '45, and '47) and the reds from Bourgueil and Chinon are varied, reflecting the different small producers Barrier has chosen.

Barrier smokes his own salmon (delicious), and claims to be the creator of the cold fish *terrine* which has become a *nouvelle cuisine* classic (his version remains unrivaled). Rarely will one find a great restaurant serving foods more in tune with the regional wines: his superb version of the famous *rillons* and *rillettes* of Tours go well with either a dry white or red, while a Chinon is the perfect choice to accompany a spectacular *matelote* of eel stewed in Chinon with prunes. The cheeses offered are local goat cheeses.

A meal at Barrier should end with either a glass of an interesting (though rough) *marc* or the excellent pear *eau de vie* made by Maurice Raffault in Chinon.

AMBOISE (37400)
Le Choiseul (H,R), 36 quai Ch.-Guinot. Tel: 47.30.45.45. Closed Jan 5–Mar 15. MC V
An old, but comfortable hotel with Italian-style terraced gardens down to the Loire.

Le Mail St Thomas (R), pl. Richelieu. Tel: 47.57.22.52. One Michelin star. Closed Tue and Jan. AE DC MC V
Recently moved to an attractive Renaissance house with a garden, François le Coz prepares classic *cuisine*, including *foie confit au Vouvray*.

ANCENIS (44150)
Auberge de Bel Air (R), St Herblon (7.5km NE by N23 and D112). Tel: 40.83.02.87. Closed Sun pm–Mon. MC V
Attractive dining-room and imaginative *cuisine*.

ANGERS (49000)
Anjou (H) and **Salamandre (R)**, 1 bd Mar.-Foch. Tel: 41.88.24.82. Closed Sun. AE DC MC V
A comfortable hotel with large rooms. Restaurant is popular with local Angevins and serves fine fish dishes.

Les Caves du Roy (W), 8 r. Montault, 49100 Angers. Tel: 41.88.25.23. Closed Sun–Mon. AE MC V
A good selection of regional wines.

Le Quéré (R), 9 pl. du Ralliement. Tel: 41.87.64.94. Reservations recommended. Closed Fri pm–Sat, and 3 weeks Jul. AE DC V
Refined, inventive *nouvelle cuisine* served in a luxurious and elegant dining-room. Long list of Anjou wines.

AZAY-LE-RIDEAU (37190)
Le Grand Monarque (H,R), pl. République. Tel: 47.45.40.08. Closed mid-Nov–mid-Mar. AE MC V
Pleasant, quiet atmosphere. Regional cooking and reasonable prices.

BEAUMONT-EN-VERON
(37420, Avoine)
La Giraudière (H), rte Savigny. Tel: 47.58.40.36. Closed Jan–Feb. AE DC MC V
Elegant 17th-century country mansion.

BLOIS (41000)
Le Bocca d'Or (R), 15 r. Haute. Tel: 54.78.04.74. Closed Feb. AE V
Elegant dining-room in a beautiful 14th-century cellar.

Hostellerie de la Loire (R,H), 8 r. Mar.-de-Lattre-de-Tassigny. Tel: 54.74.26.60. Closed Sun in winter. AE DC MC V
A restaurant with rooms. Fine views of the old bridge across the Loire.

BRACIEUX (41250)
Le Relais (R), 1 av. Chambord. Tel: 54.46.41.22. Two Michelin stars. Reservations essential. Closed Tue pm–Wed, and Jan. MC V
Near the forest of Chambord this is one of the best restaurants in the Loire valley. Light, imaginative *cuisine* with a wide choice of Loire wines and served in an elegant dining-room.

CHINON (37500)
Au Plaisir Gourmand (R), 2 r. Parmentier. Tel: 47.93.20.48. One Michelin star. Reservations recommended. Closed Sun pm–Mon. V
The best restaurant in Chinon with an excellent list of local wines.

Château de Marçay (H,R), Marçay (7km S by D749 and D116). Tel: 47.93.03.47. One Michelin star. AE V
Traditional, comfortable rooms and good food in an attractive 15th-century château complete with turrets and surrounded by a park. Relais et Châteaux.

Vinothèque Charles-VII (W), 40 quai Charles-VII. Tel: 47.93.23.64. Closed Sun pm–Mon. MC V
Local wines including good Chinon.

CLISSON (44190)
La Bonne Auberge (R), 1 r. O.-de-Clisson. Tel: 40.54.01.90. One Michelin star. V
Small establishment with local specialties and good wines.

COSNE-SUR-LOIRE (58200)
Le Sévigné (R), 16 r. du 14 Juillet. Tel: 86.28.27.50. Closed Sun pm–Mon. AE DC MC V
Pleasant, small restaurant with good-value menus in this pretty town.

COUR-CHEVERNY (41700)
St Hubert (H,R), r. Nationale. Tel: 54.79.96.60. Closed Tue pm, and Dec-Jan. MC V
Comfortable hotel and good regional restaurant.

JOUE-LES-TOURS (37300)
Château de Beaulieu (H,R), rte de l'Epand. Tel: 47.53.20.26. MC V
A delightful, small 18th-century château surrounded by a magnificent park. Traditional *cuisine*.

LUYNES (37230)
Domaine de Beauvois (H,R), rte de Cléré (4km NW by D49). Tel: 47.55.50.11. One Michelin star. Closed mid-Jan–mid-Mar. AE DC MC V
A beautiful manor house surrounded by lawns and woods. Large, comfortable rooms and a good selection of local Touraine wines. Relais et Châteaux.

MONTRICHARD (41400)
Le Bellevue (H,R), quai du Cher. Tel: 54.32.06.17. Closed Mon pm–Tue. DC MC V
Good views of the Cher and the château with modern, comfortable rooms.

NANTES (44000)

Abbaye de Villeneuve (H,R), rte des Sables d'Olonne, 44400 les Sorinières (12km S by N137 and D178). Tel: 40.04.40.25. AE DC V
A former Cistercian abbey now makes a pleasant base for touring the region. Friendly welcome and service with traditional *cuisine*. Relais et Châteaux.

Le Fief de Vigne (W), 16 r. Marceau. Tel: 40.47.58.75. Closed Sun–Mon. AE MC V
Good wines from all regions and an outstanding selection of Muscadet.

Manoir de la Comète (R), 21 r. de la Libération, 44230 St Sébastien-sur-Loire (6km E by D751). Tel: 40.34.15.93. One Michelin star. Reservations recommended. Closed Sat lunch, Sun, 1 week Feb and 3 weeks end Jul. MC V
Country restaurant with reasonably priced menus.

Les Maraîchers (R), 21 r. Fouré. Tel: 40.47.06.51. One Michelin star. Reservations recommended. Closed Sat lunch and Sun. AE DC MC V
Charming establishment offering *nouvelle cuisine*. Good list of Muscadet and Anjou wines.

POUILLY-SUR-LOIRE (58150)

L'Espérance (R,H), 17 r. René-Couard. Tel: 86.39.10.68. One Michelin star. Closed Sun pm–Mon, and Dec–Jan. AE DC MC V
A large, family-run hotel facing the vineyards and serving traditional fare. Good Sancerre and Pouilly Fumé wines.

ROMORANTIN-LANTHENAY (41200)

Le Lion d'Or (R,H), 69 r. Clemenceau. Tel: 54.76.00.28. Two Michelin stars. Reservations essential. Closed Jan 5–mid-Feb. AE DC V
This is a well-known establishment in a beautiful setting. Didier Clément serves imaginative dishes in the *nouvelle* style. Fine list of Loire wines.

ST AIGNAN (41110)

Grand Hôtel St Aignan (H,R), 7-9 quai Jean-Jacques Delorme. Tel: 54.75.18.04. Closed Mon. MC V
Comfortable and inexpensive restaurant on the banks of the Cher.

SANCERRE (18300)

L'Etoile (R,H), 2 quai de la Loire, St Thibault (3km NE by D955 and D4). Tel: 48.54.12.15. Closed Wed, except Jul–Aug, and Dec–Feb. No cards.
Views of the Loire from the dining-room. Simple rooms.

La Tasse d'Argent (R), 18 rempart des Augustins. Tel: 48.54.01.44. Closed Wed in winter and Jan. AE DC MC V
Good regional cooking.

SAUMUR (49400)

Le Prieuré (R,H), Chênehutte-les-Tuffeaux, 49350 Gennes. (7km W by D751). Tel: 41.67.90.14. One Michelin star. V
This pretty Renaissance manor house is on the banks of the Loire. Large, comfortable rooms. Excellent food and service. Relais et Châteaux.

TOURS (37000)

Bardet (R,H), 57 r. Groison. Tel: 47.41.41.11. Reservations necessary. AE DC MC V
Formerly in Châteauroux, Bardet's restaurant now rivals Barrier for the title of "Best Restaurant in Tours." *Nouvelle* with strong regional overtones, Bardet's cooking has attracted much attention. His wife, Sophie, is in charge of the cellars and she has assembled an outstanding collection of Loire wines.

Caves du Serpent Volant (W), 44 r. du Grand Marché. Tel: 47.64.30.01. MC V
A wide range of Anjou-Touraine wines.

VALENCAY (36600)

Hôtel d'Espagne (H,R), 9 r. Château. Tel: 54.00.00.02. One Michelin star. Reservations necessary. Closed Jan–Feb. AE V
An old, comfortable inn run by the same family since 1875 and an excellent stopover between Routes One and Two. Good food and service. Relais et Châteaux.

VILLANDRY (37510, Joué-les-Tours)

Le Cheval Rouge (R,H), near the château. Tel: 47.50.02.07. One Michelin star. Closed Nov 11–mid-Mar. V
A well known traditional hotel and restaurant with modern facilities.

PROVENCE

There is a moment on the autoroute driving south, somewhere around Orange, when the atmosphere subtly changes and you know that you have reached the warm south of Provence. The sun is stronger, the light brighter, and there are warm scents of lavender, thyme and pine trees. Soon before Aix-en-Provence the Mont Ste Victoire looms into view, conjuring up the bold colors of Cézanne. This is also the land of the mistral, which blows viciously on an otherwise hot summer's day.

If you have ever vacationed on the Côte d'Azur, sat at a café in St Tropez, eaten *bouillabaisse* in Marseille and sipped the local wine, the chances were that you drank a rosé Côtes de Provence in a funny amphora-shaped bottle. Rosé wine is part of the vacation atmosphere, with which Provence is readily associated; it is for picnics on the beach, a light wine for sipping in the sunshine with the turquoise Mediterranean and sparkling white cliffs never far away. Rosé Côtes de Provence caters for the many sun-worshipping tourists who flock each year to the Mediterranean but to judge the wines of Provence on this wine alone is to ignore a myriad of other tastes and flavors.

The Wines of Provence

The largest *appellation* of the region is Côtes de Provence, but as well as rosé, there is white and, much better than either, red. These wines have improved enormously in recent years; the ubiquitous Carignan that makes indifferent wine is being supplanted by Syrah, Mourvèdre and even Cabernet Sauvignon. Vinification methods have improved too; the red wines are aged in oak and fermentation temperatures are carefully controlled to make crisp fresh whites and rosés. You occasionally see the mention *cru classé* on a Côtes de Provence label. Back in 1955 about 20 estates were recognized as *cru classé*; at the time they were the best wines of the area, and in particular were those that bottled their own wine. Since 1955 the fortunes of these estates have fluctuated; some indeed have disappeared and only a few merit any distinction today.

The vineyards around the town of Aix-en-Provence go under a separate recent *appellation*, Coteaux d'Aix-en-Provence, with a sub-region Coteaux des Baux-en-Provence with vineyards in the dramatic lunarscape of the foothills of the Alpilles. The *appellation* is for red, rosé and white and the area has been known for its red wines for some time, unlike neighboring Côtes de Provence. Pioneering estates such as Château Vignelaure and Domaine de Trévallon are making good examples of red Coteaux d'Aix.

Between these two large areas is the recently promoted VDQS of the Coteaux Varois, with the town of Brignoles at its center. Production regulations are much less strict for a *vin de pays*, with greater flexibility for grape varieties and so on and consequently more adventurous producers have been achieving interesting wines here, notably at Domaine St Jean de Villecroze.

Within these larger areas are four smaller, more prestigious *appellations*. Cassis, which has a reputation for its white wine, but also produces some rosé and red, is a small *appellation* with vineyards behind this attractive sailing resort. Sadly the vineyards are more valuable as building land and are being eaten up by the growing town. Palette is a tiny *appellation* outside Aix-en-Provence, where one estate, Château Simone, maintains the reputation of this wine, in a superbly traditional and individual way. Bellet is rather isolated from the rest of Provence, as the vineyards are almost lost in the suburbs behind Nice. Here the Rolle grape makes some delicious white wine, and there is red and rosé too.

The most important red *appellation* of the region is Bandol, a serious wine, made from a minimum of 50 per cent Mourvèdre, but often more, with Grenache and Cinsaut. The *appellation* regulations demand a minimum of 18 months aging in wood and often it is longer, for Mourvèdre yields a substantial, meaty wine that needs time to mellow and mature. There is a little white and rosé Bandol too; however the reputation of the *appellation* stands upon its red wine. The vineyards are planted on steep terraces behind the town and share the slopes with olive trees.

Organic viticulture is widespread in Provence and here the mistral proves a great asset. The hard drying winds are the best treatment against rot and vine diseases originating from excess humidity. There is less need to spray the vines, and more thoughtful growers use natural manure to fertilize them and keep sulphur dioxide to a minimum. Domaines Ott is one of several estates to keep a flock of sheep to provide manure for its vineyards.

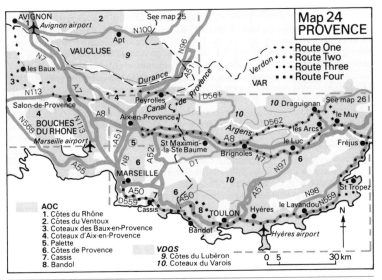

Visiting the Vineyards

A region where olive groves and lavender fields line the roads makes for memorable touring, especially in the lush weeks of early summer – and yet for many visitors the attraction of Provence can be summed up in one word: sunshine. In July and August the peaceful atmosphere of spring or autumn is replaced by a "boom town" climate where anything goes. Avoid Provence when the rush is on or be prepared for headaches and traffic jams that can spoil a visit to even this idyllic corner of France.

Route One

Coteaux d'Aix, from Avignon to Aix: 180 km

There is no end to beautiful scenery and astounding rock formations in this part of Provence. The countryside around St Rémy-de-Provence was immortalized in the paintings of Van Gogh, and Paul Cézanne made his home in later years in the stark countryside of Mont Ste Victoire outside Aix which features in many of his paintings. The vineyards of the Coteaux d'Aix begin just east of St Rémy-de-Provence and spread out to the north-east and south-west of Aix-en-Provence, mainly in the *département* of the Bouches-du-Rhône.

PROVENCE

The Itinerary:

In **Avignon,** follow the *Toutes Directions* signs and then those for Arles. After crossing the bridge on N570 turn left toward **St Rémy-de-Provence**; from St Rémy, follow the signs south on D5 for **les Baux-de-Provence**. Stark, rocky hills rise on both sides of the road as it climbs toward les Baux perched on a high spur of les Alpilles. Watch for a right turn into les Baux on D27e. Vineyards and olive groves appear just before the town where spectacular rock formations make a fabulous tableau. From les Baux, follow the signs to **Maussane-les-Alpilles** on D27, then turn left on D17 and follow the signs to **Salon-de-Provence** toward Aix on D572.

Occasional vineyards reappear just after **Pélissanne** (note Château de la Barben on the hill to the left). Continue on D572 to **St Cannat,** driving into the center of town, then turn left just after the statue of Suffren, taking the road opposite the sign indicating D18 and Eguilles. This narrow twisty road is D18 heading in the direction of **Rognes** through vineyards and woods. At the junction, turn right to enter Rognes, then follow the signs indicating the *Route des vins* and **le Puy-Ste Réparade** on D15 (watch for a left-hand turnoff to le Puy shortly after leaving Rognes).

The road winds uphill through the vineyards, offering a beautiful view of dramatic pine-covered hills before dipping down again into the valley of the Durance. At the junction turn left to take D15 into le Puy, then follow D561 to **Meyrargues**. Château Fonscolombe, one of the leading Coteaux d'Aix producers, is a few kilometers south of le Puy on D13. At the stop sign, turn left onto N96 to **Peyrolles-en-Provence,** then bear right to **Jouques** and **Rians** on D561. Although vineyards are only intermittently visible, roadside signs point out nearby wine domaines or châteaux, while pale rocky outcrops and reddish-purple soil contrast strikingly with the lush green fields lining the road. Along the road is Château Vignelaure, an interesting domaine to visit for its collection of modern art as well as for its excellent wines.

Just before Rians, turn right onto D3 in the direction of St Maximin-la-Ste Baume, then follow the signs right to **Pourrières** on D23. This is a narrow, winding road through scrubland mixed with wild thyme and umbrella pines. As the road winds downhill toward Pourrières, huge rocky outcrops loom up before giving way to vineyards in the plain surrounding the town.

Drive through Pourrières, following the signs for N7 and **Aix-en-Provence**; at the intersection with the highway, turn right – signs will later indicate that the road is indeed N7. This is another magnificent drive, through a vine-covered plain with a backdrop of red hills and cliffs with strata of colored rock. Aix, one of the most beautiful cities in all of Provence, makes a fitting end to the journey.

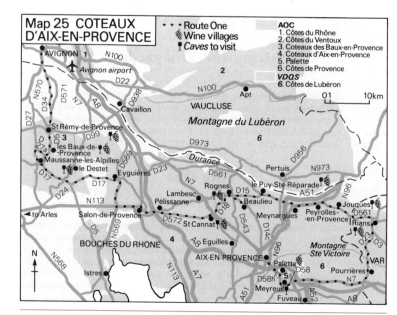

Route Two

Coteaux Varois and inland Côtes de Provence, from Aix to Fréjus: 150 km

From Aix-en-Provence east to Cannes most of the vineyards are either AOC Côtes de Provence or VDQS Coteaux Varois, promoted only in 1984. Coteaux Varois extends to the north-east and south-west of St Maximin-la-Ste Baume and Brignoles. The red and rosé wines, made from Carignan, Cinsaut, Grenache, Mourvèdre and Syrah, are best drunk young and slightly chilled.

The inland Côtes de Provence vineyards are more dispersed than those along the coast and often vie for space with olive groves, especially around Lorgues and Draguignan.

The Itinerary:

From **Aix** take A8 toward Fréjus. Leave the autoroute at the **Brignoles** exit and follow the signs to the town, site of the medieval palace of the counts of Provence and famous for its plums and olives. In Brignoles, take N7 toward Fréjus or, alternatively, visit the wine towns of **le Val, Carcès**, and **Lorgues** by turning north at the autoroute exit, turning right at le Val and continuing on D562 to Draguignan to pick up the main route.

Vineyards cover the plain on both sides of N7, rising up to the treeline on the neighboring hills. Just before **Flassans-sur-Issole** the Côtes de Provence vineyards begin. Just east of Flassans you pass the Commanderie de Peyrassol, a Côtes de Provence property now making good red Côtes de Provence as well as rosé. Continue on N7, following the signs to Draguignan and Fréjus. About 5km down the road after **Vidauban**, watch for the left-hand turnoff for Draguignan on D555. In **Trans-en-Provence**, turn left away from Fréjus on N555 and continue to **Draguignan** through the olive groves.

In Draguignan, follow the signs *Centre Ville* and *Autres Directions*, turning right toward Castellane and Grasse on D562. As the road twists uphill there is a magnificent view of old Draguignan overlooking the valley. After winding through woods, the road once again passes through vineyards and olive groves above the vine-covered valley floor. At the crossroads, turn right, following the signs for **la Motte** on D54; as the road begins a very wide curve to the right, watch for the turnoff leading into la Motte that appears suddenly on the left.

Drive through la Motte, then follow the signs for **le Muy** on D54 through the vineyards in the direction of the distant rocky hills – the combination of grey stone, red earth and green vines is strikingly beautiful. At the junction with N7 turn left toward Nice, then follow the signs for **Fréjus**. The vineyards give way to gaudy signs as you near Fréjus on this busy road – a reminder that you are now on the Côte d'Azur.

Route Three

Coastal Côtes de Provence from Fréjus to Toulon: 135 km

The most extensive vineyards of the Côtes de Provence lie between St Raphael and Toulon, along the coast at the foot of the Maures mountains. Umbrella pines, cacti, palms and cork trees line the road between the mountains and the sea.

The Itinerary:

From **Fréjus**, follow the signs for **Ste Maxime** and **St Tropez** on N98 and D98a. Souvenir stands abound, but with the notable exception of Ste Maxime, this part of the coastline is relatively free of ungainly large hotels though the road is lined with many summer homes. The vineyards begin between Ste Maxime and St Tropez and there are unforgettable views of the Mediterranean, alternately turquoise and ultramarine against the distant mountains.

In St Tropez, turn right on D93 to **Ramatuelle**. The vineyards extend virtually down to the water's edge and inland as far as the eye can see. Before Ramatuelle, begin following the signs to **Gassin** on a small narrow road through pine forests, then opening up to provide a splendid view of the surrounding countryside. Continue uphill toward Gassin, a hilltop town surrounded by vineyards; just before Gassin take a sharp left-hand turn downhill through the vines to **la Croix-Valmer**. Cork trees with neat strips of bark cut from each trunk line the road. At the junction, turn left onto D559.

The road follows the cliff at the water's edge between **le Rayol** and **Cavalière**, where eucalyptus trees perfume the air.

Approaching **St Clair**, terraces can be seen on the surrounding hills and from **le Lavandou** a blanket of vines and occasional palms cover the plain which continues almost all the way to **Toulon**, a large naval port at the foot of Mt Faron. D559 leads on to N98 which takes you direct to Toulon. If you want to prolong the tour, turn right on D12 just before **Hyères** and follow it north to **Puget-Ville** where a left turn on to N97 takes you back to Toulon.

Route Four

Bandol and Cassis, from Toulon to Marseille: 75 km

Bandol and Cassis are two small *appellations* on the coast between Toulon and Marseille and complement one another well, Bandol being renowned for its red wines, Cassis for its whites. Production is small, with only about 50 *vignerons* working 1,000 hectares in Bandol and 13 working 195 hectares in Cassis. Bandol reds, made essentially from Mourvèdre, Cinsaut, and Grenache, are fruity and spicy; aged in wood for 18 months, many can be kept for up to 20 years.

Cassis is known mainly for its fresh aromatic white wines which are the perfect partner for the local *bouillabaisse*, especially when eaten in the little restaurants around the harbor. They are made principally from Ugni Blanc, Clairette, Marsanne and a little Sauvignon.

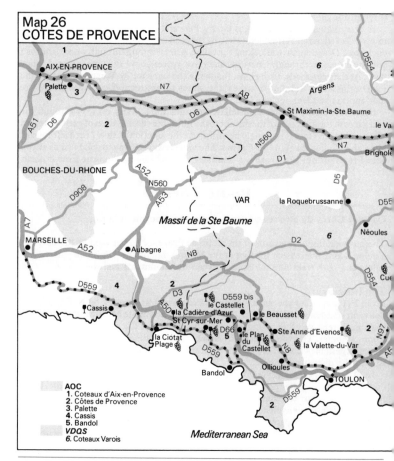

Map 26
COTES DE PROVENCE

AOC
1. Coteaux d'Aix-en-Provence
2. Côtes de Provence
3. Palette
4. Cassis
5. Bandol
VDQS
6. Coteaux Varois

The Itinerary:
From **Toulon,** follow the signs on N8 for Marseille, then for Aubagne, past a rocky ridge and the town of **Ollioules** before crossing the Gorges d'Ollioules on a switchback road between high rocky hills. Continue on N8 to **le Beausset,** then turn left and go through **le Plan de Castellet** on D559bis, where beautiful terraced hills covered with vines line the road. A detour can be made to la Cadière-d'Azur by turning right on D66 before reaching le Plan. These villages contain many good Bandol properties such as Château Romassan, one of the Domaines Ott estates, and Domaine Tempier. Otherwise continue on D559bis to Bandol.

Bandol is a tourist resort and port whose little harbor is always full of yachts. In town, follow the signs indicating Marseille on D559, to **St Cyr-sur-Mer.** As the road dips downhill there is a beautiful view of the Bandol vineyards to the left. In St Cyr, drive past the bright gold replica of the Statue of Liberty, following the blue signs indicating the autoroute to Marseille, then follow the signs for Marseille on D559, which goes along the sea but is very busy in summer. Alternatively take A50 direct to the Cassis exit. If you decide to follow the coastal route, follow the signs for Cassis and Marseille *par le R.N.* once you reach **la Ciotat Plage.**

D559 climbs again through rocky pine-covered hills, then, after passing the autoroute at the **Cassis** exit, it rises above the vineyards which slope down into the valley while white cliffs rise up on the left.

Continue following the white signs to **Marseille.** After leaving Cassis, a bustling fishing port, D559 climbs up onto a high, barren plateau. From here to the outskirts of Marseille the drive is breathtaking but the magic ends as the road dips down and the first billboards appear, sure signs that you are now entering a large, cosmopolitan city.

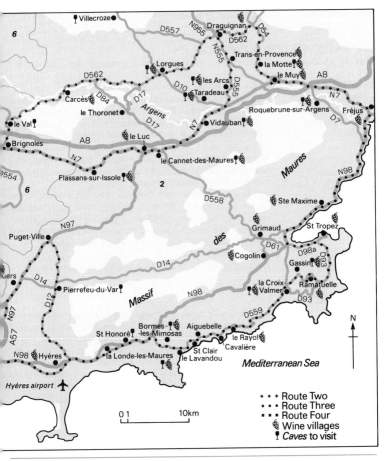

Caves and Vineyards to Visit

For the wine enthusiast, Provence is an area in transition: vinification methods are improving and grape varieties are changing. There are some large co-operatives, but it is the pioneering small growers, often newcomers to the area, who are making the most exciting wines. For most of the serious producers of Provence wines, it is the name of their estate that matters, rather than that of the *appellation*.

ANTIBES

Domaines Ott (G), (Office) 22 bd d'Aiguillon, 06600 Antibes. Tel: 93.34.08.91.
Château de Selle, map 26, Taradeau, 83460 les Arcs. Tel: 94.68.86.86.
Château Romassan, map 26, le Castellet, 83330 le Beausset. Tel: 94.98.71.91.
Clos Mireille, map 26, 83250 la Londe-les-Maures. Tel: 94.66.80.26.

Marcel Ott came to Provence from Alsace at the end of the 19th century and began making wine at a Côtes de Provence property, Château de Selle. There are now three excellent properties in the group, all of which can be visited.

The two Côtes de Provence properties, both *crus classés*, are Château de Selle, a beautiful 18th-century residence formerly used by the counts of Provence, and Clos Mireille whose vineyards have a stunning location right beside the Mediterranean and which makes particularly good but expensive Blanc des Blancs. The third property, Château Romassan, is in the Bandol *appellation* and the vineyards are on steep terraces locally called *restanques*. This is the most recent arrival in the Ott empire. All three properties practice organic viticulture with no chemical fertilizers.

Visiting hours: By appt with the individual properties.
Location: Château de Selle – on D73 3km N of Taradeau. Clos Mireille – 5km SE of la Londe-les-Maures on the road to Brégançon. Château Romassan – on D66 between la Cadière d'Azur and le Beausset.

Les BAUX-DE-PROVENCE, map 25

Mas de La Dame (G), rte de St Rémy, les Baux-de-Provence, 13520 Maussane. Tel: 90.54.32.24.

mas de la dame

Vincent Van Gogh sought inspiration for some of his paintings on this well-known Provençal property which lies at the foot of the Alpilles and in 1889 he painted the 15th-century house, once an old mill. The striking rocky outcrops which reflect the hot Mediterranean sun help both the vines and olive trees to ripen. Now owned by M. and Mme Jacques Chatin, the 60-hectare domaine was replanted in the early 1930s by M. Chatin's father-in-law, Robert Faye. A Burgundian *négociant*, M. Faye made an important contribution to the development of the Coteaux des Baux wines by planting better grape varieties.

There is a good red Coteaux des Baux made from Grenache, Cabernet Sauvignon, Syrah and Carignan and the Cuvée Spéciale, based on a careful selection in the vineyard and winery, is aged in wood for several months. There is also an elegant rosé with a pretty color.

Visiting hours: Daily 8–7.
Location: Off D5 8km S of St Rémy-de-Provence

Le DESTET, map 25

Mas de Gourgonnier (G), le Destet, 13890 Mouriès. Tel: 90.47.50.45.

mas de gourgonnier

Mas de Gourgonnier is a domaine of 40 hectares of vines in a very pretty area near les Baux. The owner, Nicolas Cartier, practices organic viticulture, one of many estates in the south to do so. He also grows almonds, apricots and olives by organic methods. Traditional methods of vinification are followed to make good white and rosé and two red wines, including the Reserve du Mas which is aged for 12 to 18 months in oak and keeps for 6 to 10 years. Cabernet Sauvignon accounts for much of its finesse but there is a substantial proportion of Syrah and Grenache.

Visiting hours: Daily 8–12, 2–6.
Location: 5km N of Mouriès on D24.

PROVENCE

FLASSANS-SUR-ISSOLE, map 26

Commanderie de Peyrassol (G),
Flassans-sur-Issole,
83340 le Luc.
Tel: 94.69.71.02.

This Côtes de Provence property was producing grapes for wine-making as far back as 1204 and the Rigord family bought Commanderie de Peyrassol in 1870. Today, it is run by Yves and Françoise Rigord, and the domaine has become a model establishment making good wines. Yves Rigord inherited the 60 hectares of vineyards in 1967 and has replanted with better grape varieties such as Cabernet Sauvignon.

Côtes de Provence is best known for its rosé but the red wines of the *appellation* are the ones attracting attention today. Commanderie de Peyrassol began making red wine only when it started bottling its own wine in the late 1970s and a considerable investment in cellar equipment was needed. Traditional methods of vinification are used for the red wines. There is an attractive old Provençal farmhouse.

Visiting hours: Daily; appt preferred.
Location: 2.5km E of Flassans on N7.

GASSIN, map 26

Château Minuty (G), Gassin,
83990 St Tropez.
Tel: 94.56.12.09.

Château Minuty was one of the 20 *crus classés* created in 1955 and the oldest estate of the area. The domaine was taken over by Gabriel Farnet in 1936 and he runs it today with his daughter Mme Matton, who designed the typical Côtes de Provence bottle that is used by the local growers' *syndicat*. Château Minuty makes good red, rosé and white Côtes de Provence from its 45 hectares and also from grapes grown on 30 hectares of the nearby Domaine Farnet. The beautiful château built in the reign of Napoleon III cannot be visited but the vineyards and cellars can. The tiny chapel featured on the labels of the red Cuvée de l'Oratoire was built to commemorate a son of the then owners who was killed in the Franco-Prussian war of 1870.

Visiting hours: Easter–mid-Oct daily, 9–8; remainder of year Mon–Fri 9–12, 2–6.
Location: 2km N of Gassin on D61.

Les Maitres Vignerons de la Presqu'Ile de St Tropez (C),
Carrefour de la Foux, Gassin,
83990 St Tropez.
Tel: 94.56.32.04.

Each grower in this co-operative makes his own wine and the co-operative deals with the bottling and marketing. The dozen growers have 150 hectares of vines between them on the mountainous peninsula behind St Tropez. Life along the beach at St Tropez may be frivolous but the growers take their wine seriously, producing a good range of Côtes de Provence wines in all three styles. Best of all is probably the red Cuvée de la Chasse, which is sold under 14 different labels, each with an attractive drawing and the name of a different game animal or bird. In most vintages the wine can be kept for three or four years. Other wines include the Carte Noire, a fresh rosé best drunk within two years, a Cuvée Prestige de la Pêche, both white and rosé, and the Château de Pampelonne Rouge, an impressive red that can usually be aged for a few years. There is a pleasant tasting room.

Visiting hours: Mon–Thu 8–12, 2–6; Fri 8–12, 2–5.
Location: Carrefour de la Foux is 4km W of St Tropez on D98.

LORGUES, map 26

Castel Roubine (G), BP 117,
83510 Lorgues.
Tel: 94.73.71.55.

Castel Roubine is an ancient property and has been producing wine since 1307. There is an attractive château surrounded by pine trees. Today the estate covers only 110 hectares of which half are given over to vines. Castel Roubine is one of 14 estates left entitled to use the term *cru classé* for its Côtes de Provence wines. It is owned by Ojivind Hallgren and since the mid-1970s improvements have been made to the grape varieties planted. As well as the local Provençal varieties there is also some Cabernet Sauvignon, Sémillon and Syrah. The new plantings have all been on land previously covered by forest and scrubland. The pine forests and undulating hills around the estate give good protection to the vines from the mistral.

Visiting hours: Mon–Fri 8–12, 2–6; groups by appt.
Location: 4km E of Lorgues on D562.

Castel Roubine has been making wine since 1307.

MEYREUIL, map 25

Château Simone (G),
13590 Meyreuil.
Tel: 42.28.92.58.

Palette is a tiny *appellation* for red, white and rosé wines outside Aix-en-Provence. Nearly all of the Palette wines are made by Château Simone, a small estate of 15 hectares which has been owned by the Rougier family since the time of Louis XVI. Vinification methods are traditional – for instance, the red wines are fined with real egg whites.

However, the estate broke with tradition when they were the first growers to bottle their own wines in 1921. This created their reputation and also that of the *appellation*. The domaine makes all three Palette wines, red, white and rosé. The red, made mainly from Grenache, Mourvèdre and Cinsaut with other local grape varieties, is particularly good. It is aged in oak and can be kept for five years or more. There are two styles of white made from Clairette, Ugni Blanc and Muscat; one is bottled after one year's aging and the second after two years.

Visiting hours: Mon–Sat 8–12, 2–6.
Location: 2km off A8 at exit "Aix-Est".

Le PLAN-DU-CASTELLET, map 26

Domaine Tempier (G),
83330 le Plan-du-Castellet.
Tel: 94.98.70.21.

This excellent estate with 25 hectares of vines has belonged to the same family since 1834. It is now directed by Lucien Peyraud who married Mlle Tempier, and he takes most of the credit for the great improvement in the quality of the Bandol wines. M. Peyraud recognized the value of the Mourvèdre grape, which today, thanks to his efforts, must constitute a minimum of 50 per cent of Bandol.

The grapes are grown on steep terraced hillsides which benefit from cooling sea breezes during the day and the mountain air at night. The estate's red wine is one of the best of the *appellation* and is relatively long-lived.

Visiting hours: Mon–Fri 9–12, 2–6; Sat 9–12.
Location: Between le Plan-du-Castellet and la Cadière.

Le PUY-STE-REPARADE, map 25

Château de Fonscolombe (G),
13610 le Puy-Ste
Réparade.
Tel: 42.61.89.62.

This is one of the leading Coteaux d'Aix estates. The domaine was granted to the Fonscolombe family in the 15th century when King René was lord of Provence and the region was a prosperous cultural centre. In 1810, the estate was acquired through marriage by a Spanish noble, the Marquis de Saporta, whose family still own it. There is a fine château and a park where visitors may walk.

The domaine is a large one with 170 hectares of vines on the southern banks of the river Durance. The present Marquis de Saporta took over Fonscolombe in 1963 and with the help of his son-in-law has made it into one of the most modern wine-making properties of the south of France. It was one of the first to plant Cabernet Sauvignon in the Coteaux d'Aix area which now makes up 15 per cent of the planting on the estate. The white wine is especially good, made from a mixture of Ugni Blanc, Clairette, Grenache and Sauvignon, and has a lovely scent of spring flowers.

Château Fonscolombe also owns the nearby Domaine de la Crémade, and Domaine de la Boullery and Domaine du Temps Perdu are part of the Fonscolombe estate. These wines are sold under individual domaine names.

Visiting hours: Mon–Fri 8–12, 2–6; Sat 9–12, 2–5.
Location: 3km S of le Puy on D13.

The fine Renaissance château at Fonscolombe.

QUARTIER ST HONORE, map 26

Domaine St André-de-Figuière (G),
Quartier St Honoré,
83250 la Londe-les-Maures.
Tel: 94.66.92.10.

The 15-hectare domaine has been owned since 1979 by a father and son, André and André-Daniel Connesson. They practice strict organic viticulture and avoid chemicals in vinification, even sulphur dioxide if possible. This approach has borne fruit since the wines are among the best in the Côtes de Provence *appellation*. There are fine new underground cellars.

Visiting hours: Mon–Sat 9–12, 2–6.
Location: Signposted in la Londe-les-Maures.

RIANS, map 25

Château Vignelaure (G),
83560 Rians.
Tel: 94.80.31.93.

Georges Brunet has proved himself an imaginative and innovative winemaker in two regions of France, for in addition to Château Vignelaure in Provence, he has revived the fortunes of Château la Lagune in the Médoc and produced claret to justify its classification. When M. Brunet came to Provence in the mid-1960s he was looking for conditions suitable for the vine and he found the perfect place in the Haut-Var near Rians, an attractive Provençal town.

Château Vignelaure was a country farmhouse in much need of restoration but it had the attraction of magnificent cool cellars. The soil was perfect for vines, with large stones to

retain the heat at night, and the first vines planted are now more than 20 years old. Vinification methods are meticulous and the underground cellars a showpiece, with not a barrel out of place. There is also a fascinating collection of original art by contemporary French artists, sculptors and photographers, who have donated pieces in return for Château Vignelaure wine.

Château Vignelaure's red Côteaux d'Aix-en-Provence is made from a high proportion of Cabernet Sauvignon with some Syrah and a little Grenache. It is a full-bodied wine that many regard as closer to Bordeaux than Provence in taste. Visiting hours: Mon–Sat 8.30–12.30, 2.30–6.30.
Location: 5km W of Rians and signposted.

VIDAUBAN, map 26

Domaine des Féraud (G), rte de la Garde-Freinet, 83550 Vidauban. Tel: 94.73.03.12.

The red wine of the domaine, made from grapes grown on 40 hectares of vines, has been compared with those of Bordeaux but there is still a scent of the Mediterranean south, a combination of vanilla, cassis and raspberries. There is also a distinctive Blanc de Blancs – also Bordelais in style since it is made from Sémillon as well as Ugni Blanc.
Visiting hours: Mon–Fri 8–12, 2–6 (Jul–Sep 3–7); Sat 9–12.
Location: 5km S of Vidauban on D48.

Further *Caves* and Vineyards to Visit

Les ARCS-SUR-ARGENS, map 26

Château St Pierre (G), 83460 les Arcs-sur-Argens. Tel: 94.47.41.47. Visiting hours: Mon–Sat 8–12, 2–6.
This Côtes de Provence estate has 35 hectares of vineyards. There is an excellent red Côtes de Provence, as well as good rosé and white.

Château Ste Roseline (G), 83460 les Arcs-sur-Argens. Tel: 94.73.32.57. Visiting hours: Daily by appt.
The 53-hectare domaine, belonging to Baron Henri de Rasque de Laval, is one of the *crus classés* of the Côtes de Provence and makes red, rosé and white wines. It is a traditional estate and aging takes place in old wooden barrels. Until the Revolution the estate was an abbey and the 12th century cloisters are still there today.

BORMES-LES-MIMOSAS, map 26

Domaine de la Malherbe (G), 83230 Bormes-les-Mimosas. Tel: 94.64.80.40. Visiting hours: Daily 9–12, 2–6.
The small vineyards, virtually next door to the summer retreat of the presidents of France at Brégançon, produce a Pointe du Diable rosé and white as well as red Côtes de Provence.

La CADIERE-D'AZUR, map 26

Château Vannières (G), 83740 la Cadière-d'Azur. Tel: 94.90.08.08. Visiting hours: By appt.
This old property has been owned by the Boisseaux family for 30 years and is one of the leading makers of Bandol. The family have entirely replanted the vineyards. There is also good red, white and rosé Côtes de Provence. The 19th-century château is of unusual design.

Moulin des Costes (G), 83740 la Cadière-d'Azur. Tel: 94.98.72.76. Visiting hours: Jul–Sep daily; Oct–Jun Mon-Sat.
Pierre and Paul Bunan own altogether about 60 hectares of vines on two estates, Moulin des Costes and Mas de la Rouvière, and both are within the *appellation* of Bandol. Vinification takes place at Moulin des Costes. Although both labels are used the wines are identical.

Le CANNET-DES-MAURES, map 26

Domaine la Bastide Neuve (G), 83340 le Cannet-des-Maures. Tel: 94.60.73.30. Visiting hours: Daily by appt.
The 12-hectare domaine, owned by René Brochier, has won many awards for its

wines, especially for the rosé made from the Tibouren grape, a variety indigenous to Provence. However, the varietal wines are even more interesting and include a well-rounded Grenache, a Mourvèdre with great character, and a Syrah.

CASSIS, map 26
Clos Boudard (G), 7 rte de la Ciotat, 13260 Cassis. Tel: 42.01.72.66. Visiting hours: Daily 8–12, 1–6.
The domaine, owned by Pierre Marchand, is small and all the work is done by members of the family. The level of quality is high and there is a good aromatic white Cassis.

Clos Ste Magdeleine (G), av. du Revestel, 13260 Cassis. Tel: 42.01.70.28. Visiting hours: Daily 10–12, 3–6; closed hols.
Cassis owes its reputation to its white wines and this domaine is no exception. The white wine comes from 11 hectares of vines right on the Mediterranean and has a honeyed taste with a touch of acidity. It is best drunk young with the local fish. The lesser known reds and rosés of the *appellation* are easy, undemanding wines.

La CROIX-VALMER, map 26
Domaine de la Croix (G), 83420 la Croix-Valmer. Tel: 94.79.60.02. Visiting hours: By appt.
The domaine is one of the oldest vineyards in Provence and was one of the original Côtes de Provence *crus classés*. It still has an excellent reputation for its red Côtes de Provence which is produced in substantial quantity.

GASSIN, map 26
Château Barbeyrolles (G), 83990 Gassin-St Tropez. Tel: 94.56.33.58. Visiting hours: By appt (tasting only and no cellar visits).
The young proprietor, Mlle Régine Sumeire, is a serious winemaker who has succeeded in producing a rich red Côtes de Provence with nuances of vanilla and peppery fruit. Her red Cuvée Spéciale from Grenache, Syrah, Mourvèdre and a little Cabernet Sauvignon is aged in new oak barrels for a few months. She also makes a small amount of Pétale de Rosé, which is a richly perfumed wine that visitors to nearby St Tropez love to quaff in the summer.

JOUQUES, map 25
Domaine de la Boulangère (G), 13490 Jouques. Tel: 42.67.60.87. Visiting hours: By appt.
This Coteaux d'Aix estate and the neighboring Domaine de la Grande Séouve are both owned by the Bordonado family but, while the grape varieties and the vinification techniques are the same, the wines are distinctive.

La MOTTE, map 26
Domaine de Clastron (G), 83920 la Motte. Tel: 94.70.24.57. Visiting hours: Mon–Sat 8–12, 2–6.
This estate was once a *bastide* or fortified farm and has been carefully rebuilt after damage suffered in World War II. The vineyards also have been renewed and now produce well-regarded red and rosé Côtes de Provence.

PIERREFEU-DU-VAR, map 26
Domaine François Ravel (G), Château Montaud, Pierrefeu-du-Var, 83390 Cuers. Tel: 94.28.20.30. Visiting hours: By appt.
The domaine, which was reorganized in 1958, makes an attractive Vin de Pays des Maures from Cabernet Sauvignon as well as Côtes de Provence wines.

ROGNES, map 25
Château de Beaulieu (G), 13840 Rognes. Tel: 42.50.24.07. Visiting hours: By appt.
The domaine makes the traditional varieties in the Coteaux-d'Aix *appellation*, including a good red, and has 275 hectares of vineyards planted in the crater of an extinct volcano.

ROQUEBRUNE-SUR-ARGENS, map 26
Domaine des Planes (G), 83520 Roquebrune - sur - Argens. Tel: 94.45.70.49. Visiting hours: Mon–Sat 8–12, 2–6; closed hols.
Ilse and Christophe Rieder are a German couple who trained as agronomists and enologists at Geisenheim and Montpellier. They have settled in Provence to apply their theoretical knowledge. Their 25-hectare estate makes red Côtes de Provence, a rosé from the indigenous Tibouren grape, a Blanc de Blancs from Sauvignon and Rolle and a dry Blanc de Blancs Muscat Vin de Pays du Var.

ST CANNAT, map 25
Commanderie de la Bargemone (G), N7, 13760 St Cannat. Tel: 42.28.22.44. Visiting hours: Mon–Sat 8–12, 2–6.
The domaine is a former property of the Knights Templars dating back to the 13th century. The abandoned estate was bought by Jean-Pierre Rozan at the end of the 1960s and replanted. The wines have a sound reputation, especially the red and rosé Coteaux-d'Aix.

ST CYR-SUR-MER, map 26
Domaine du Cagueloup (G), 83270 St Cyr-sur-Mer. Tel: 94.26.15.70. Visiting hours: Mon–Sat 9–12, 2–6.
The domaine's wines have established an enviable reputation and its red Bandol was chosen to represent the *appellation* in celebrations marking the INAO's (Institut National des Appellations d'Origine) 50th anniversary in 1985. The 25 hectares of vineyards are owned by Gaston Prébost who also makes a supple rosé and elegant white Bandol.

ST ETIENNE DU GRES,
just off map 25
Domaine de Trévallon (G), 13150 St Etienne du Grès. Tel: 90.49.06.00. Visiting hours: By appt.
Domaine de Trévallon is an innovative estate between St Rémy and Tarascon owned by Eloi Durrbach, who has only Syrah and Cabernet Sauvignon on his 16 hectares of vineyards, with no indigenous Provençal varieties. The results are interesting as well as being good.

ST REMY-DE-PROVENCE,
map 25
Domaine des Terres Blanches (G), 13210 St Rémy - de - Provence. Tel: 90.95.91.66. Visiting hours: Mon–Sat 8–12, 2–6.
This domaine at the foot of the Alpilles is owned by Noel Michelin and has 35 hectares of vines. There is a good red Coteaux des Baux-en-Provence which includes some Cabernet Sauvignon, a rosé and a fresh Blanc de Blancs.

STE ANNE-D'EVENOS, map 26
Domaine de la Laidière (G), Ste Anne-d'Evenos, 83330 le Beausset. Tel: 94.90.37.07. Visiting hours: Mon–Fri 8–12, 1–5; Sat 8–12.

Jules and Freddy Estienne, whose family has owned the 18-hectare estate for four generations, make a red Bandol, the Carte Noire, that has been praised for its complex bouquet and flavor and which is capable of considerable aging. There is also a good rosé.

TARADEAU, map 26
Château St Martin (G), Taradeau, 83460 les Arcs-sur-Argens. Tel: 94.73.02.01. Visiting hours: Mon–Fri 8–12, 2–6. Sat–Sun by appt.
This 60-hectare property was one of the original Côtes de Provence *crus classés* and is owned by Comtesse Thérèse de Gasquet. The Cuvée Spéciale red Côtes de Provence is highly rated, as are the rosé and white.

Le VAL, map 26
Château Réal Martin (G), 83143 le Val. Tel: 94.86.40.90. Visiting hours: Daily 8–12, 2–6.
Jacques Clotilde's domaine produces all three versions of the Côtes de Provence *appellation*. The red is an elegant wine with a bouquet of vanilla and tobacco.

VIDAUBAN, map 26
Domaine de Peissonnel (G), rte de la Garde-Freinet, 83550 Vidauban. Tel: 94.73.02.96. Visiting hours: Daily 8–12, 3–6.30.
The 15-hectare estate owned by Pierre Lemaitre exports much of its Côtes de Provence wine so that it may be easier to find its wines abroad than in France. The same family has owned the domaine since the days of Napoleon III. The red Côtes de Provence has a superb bouquet and can age well. There is also a rosé and an interesting Vin de Pays made from Merlot, an unusual variety in Provence.

VILLECROZE, map 26
Domaine de St Jean de Villecroze (G), 83690 Villecroze. Tel: 94.70.63.07. and 94.70.74.30. Visiting hours: Mon–Sat 9–12, 2–6.
One of the most innovative estates of the Coteaux Varois is Domaine de St Jean de Villecroze in beautiful Provençal countryside. A Franco-American couple, Allan and Denise Hirsch, make excellent red and rosé wines, including pure Cabernet Sauvignon and Syrah. Organic viticulture is practiced.

For most people Provence means beaches, fancy hotels and traffic jams, but there is much more to the region than that. This is an ancient province and many of its cities were Greek or Roman trading towns which passed from one conquerer to another. Over the centuries a specific Provençal culture emerged, leaving behind the artistic and architectural legacy we admire today.

Two painters, Cézanne and Van Gogh, immortalized the landscape while others, such as Picasso and Matisse, found an atmosphere and a light that fed their imaginations. Museums throughout the area are devoted to the works of the many artists that have lived in Provence and musical, dramatic or film festivals attract visitors who may never see the sands of the nearby beaches.

AIX-EN-PROVENCE

Aix was founded in 122BC by the Romans on the site of therapeutic hot springs which are still in use today and it became the capital of the counts of Provence. Aix combines the charm of a small town and the sophistication normally associated with larger cities. Many of its streets remain exactly as they were during the 17th and 18th centuries and, thanks to the influx of students and Parisian designers, it has regained much of its former prestige as a center of the arts. The heart of the city is the **Cours Mirabeau**, a shady avenue lined with mansions, which was laid out in the 17th century.

Inside the **Cathédrale St Sauveur**, begun in the 5th century, is a collection of Flemish tapestries originally created for Canterbury cathedral in England. The **Musée Granet**, housed in a former 17th-century priory, has a fine collection of paintings by European masters.

The most famous "son" of Aix is Paul Cézanne, who often spent time at his family's country home at Jas de Bouffan on the outskirts of the city. The studio he installed at Aix is now a museum devoted to his life and work.

BANDOL

This little port, with its three fine beaches, is popular with tourists and sailing enthusiasts. There is an interesting **Musée International des Vins** at the Domaine de Paul Ricard on the nearby **Ile de Bendor** (Tel: 94.29.44.34.) where 8,000 bottles of wine and other drinks from 50 countries are on display. The Fête des Vins de Bandol is held on the first Sun of Dec.

Les BAUX-DE-PROVENCE

The old village and fortress of Baux are in ruins but the setting is magnificent and one of the most breathtaking in Provence. The lords of Baux were extremely powerful in the Middle Ages, domi-nating a vast territory from their eyrie atop a huge peak in the southern Alpilles.

Little is now left of the château itself, but the 17th-century former **Hôtel de Ville** has three period rooms with fine vaulting, and the Renaissance **Eglise St Vincent** has a lovely bell tower and Romanesque aisles.

BORMES-LES-MIMOSAS

This attractive village has three beaches and a yacht harbor. The **Chapelle St François**, set amid the cypresses, dates from the 16th century. The château, formerly owned by the lords of Fos, has been restored and is again inhabited. A nearby terrace gives superb views out over the Mediterranean.

BRIGNOLES

The 12th-century **Eglise St Sauveur** dominates the center of the old town where the narrow streets are best ex-plored on foot. A **Musée du Pays Brignolais**, in the former summer palace of the counts of Provence, con-tains displays of local history and folklore. At the center of the Coteaux Varois, Brignoles has a wine fair in early Apr.

CASSIS

This is a typical Provençal fishing village which has been depicted by many artists, including Matisse and Dufy. To the west of the town is Cap Canaille, the highest cliff in France. There is a wine festival on the first Sunday of Sep.

DRAGUIGNAN

Part of the prosperous fortified medieval town still exists. The well-shaded main square is surrounded by narrow streets and intriguing old houses. The **Musée-Bibliothèque**, formerly an Ursuline convent, houses a small but interesting collection of archeological finds and paintings. There is an olive fair in Jul.

FREJUS

Founded by Julius Caesar in 49BC, Fréjus (*Forum Julii*) was an important port with a large artificial harbor joined to the Mediterranean by a canal, but the sea has since receded. Fréjus later became a bishopric and there are many fine Roman ruins and medieval buildings, especially in the **quartier episcopal**.

Bullfights are staged during the summer in the large amphitheater on the edge of the town. There is a wine fair in Aug.

The 10th-century cathedral and Roman baptistry at Fréjus.

HYERES

Hyères is a popular resort, both in summer and winter, and is surrounded by market gardens cultivating flowers. Immediately around the **Eglise St Paul** is a maze of attractive old streets. In the **pl. Massillon** there is a picturesque daily market, and in Aug there is a garlic fair in the town.

It is worth considering an excursion to the nearby **Iles d'Hyères**, three wild and lovely islands which are largely unspoilt.

MARSEILLE

Marseille has been a cosmopolitan port since the days of the Greeks and Romans and Eastern Mediterranean sailors still fill the streets near the waterfront. The center of activity is the old port which is best seen from one of the boats moored along the **quai des Belges**. **Château d'If**, a former prison on an offshore island, served as the setting for Alexandre Dumas' *The Count of Monte-Cristo* and can be visited.

Severely damaged during World War II, Marseille lacks much of the charm of other southern French cities and it is, above all, a trading center. However, a walk down its famous avenue, the **Canebière**, or a climb to the **Basilique de Notre-Dame-de-la-Garde** will show that there is more to this bustling metropolis than immediately meets the eye. There are many excellent museums.

ST MAXIMIN-LA-STE-BAUME

This small town with attractive arcaded streets has a fine Gothic basilica where concerts are held in summer.

ST REMY-DE-PROVENCE

This is a charming Provençal town and an important center for market gardening. The **Musée des Alpilles**, in an attractive 16th-century residence, contains displays of Provençal folk art. The 15th–16th-century **Hôtel de Sade** houses a collection of Greek and Roman finds from Glanum just outside St Rémy.

ST TROPEZ

Now a popular beach resort on one of the most beautiful bays along this coast, artists and writers have been attracted to this little fishing port since its "discovery" at the beginning of the 20th century. Today in high summer the fashionable flock to St Tropez to see and be seen. The **Musée de l'Annonciade** contains works by famous artists such as Matisse, Braque and Signac who all painted at St Tropez. The 16th-century **Citadelle** is now the site of a music festival in summer.

SALON-DE-PROVENCE

Surrounded by olive groves, Salon is one of the main centers for the production of olive oil. The **Château de l'Empéri**, a fortress crowning the hill upon which the old town was built, was once the residence of the archbishops of Arles and now contains a military museum. The **Eglise St Laurent**, built in the 14th–15th centuries, contains the tomb of Nostradamus, the famous 16th-century physician-astrologer and his recently restored house can be visited too.

TOULON

Toulon has long been France's main naval port. The colorful old town has been much restored following damage in World War II and there are lively fish and flower and vegetable markets held each morning. Among the city's museums is the **Musée de la Marine**, devoted to Toulon's maritime history.

Hotels, Restaurants and Where to Buy Wine

Few regional *cuisines* are as misunderstood as that of Provence. If a chef sprinkles a mixture of rosemary and thyme (*herbes de Provence*) over a dish, has a heavy hand with garlic and prefers olive oil to butter, he lays claim to being "Provençal." This is a travesty; not only are these ingredients sparingly used in many Provençal recipes, but others, such as bitter orange peel, basil, chickpeas and sage, that are rarely associated with it, are more typically Provençal. Salt cod served with boiled vegetables is hardly what most people consider Provençal and yet this (*le grand aïoli*), beef stewed in red wine (*daube*), lambs' feet and tripe (*pieds et paquets*) or baby artichokes simmered with bacon, olive oil and garlic (*artichauts à la barigoule*) are typically Provençal.

Each corner of Provence has its own specialties: Marseille and *bouillabaisse*, Grasse and stuffed cabbage (*fassoum*), and Sète and its *bourride* (a fish soup), to name but a few and unfortunately many tourists seem intent only on sampling grilled fish at one of the many seaside restaurants and paying astronomical prices for the privilege. With a small effort, however, the visitor will discover another *cuisine provençale* richer and more varied than the one exported around the world.

Drinking Provençal wine with Provençal food may not be as easy as it seems. The whites are well suited to the spicy and highly aromatic fish stews, and the reds are perfect with straightforward meat dishes. As for rosé, which some consider *the* wine of Provence, it is more likely to replace white than red, and has become so associated with summer that one hesitates to order it at any other time of year. Generally speaking, the wines are discreet companions to food and, like many of the dishes, infinitely better *sur place* than when they are served several thousand kilometers away in the dead of winter.

La Riboto de Taven (R), Val d'Enfer, les Baux - de - Provence, 13520 Maussane - les - Alpilles. Tel: 90.97.34.23. One Michelin star. Closed Sun pm, except during the season, Mon, and Jan–Feb. AE DC V

Strangely enough most people are unable to name a restaurant in Provence that has an exceptional collection of fine wines from the region. Indeed, some would protest that "fine" wines don't exist here but the chef of this attractive inn owned by the Theme family in the shadow of one of Provence's most famous sites (and restaurants) would not agree.

Philippe Theme believes in the wines of his region and is particularly active in promoting those from the Coteaux des Baux. His list includes 20 local wines (all red), mostly recent vintages but some over 10 years old. Other Provençal wines are more selectively represented:

there is a list of Provençal rosés, whites including Cassis, Bandol, and a rare white from Palette, and some well-chosen reds from elsewhere in the Coteaux d'Aix. The restaurant also has an exceptional collection of fine wines from Château Rayas in Châteauneuf-du-Pape (the owner is a faithful friend).

The pleasures of these "simple" wines (Rayas aside) is increased if one chooses the "simpler" dishes: a suberb plate of baby vegetables served warm with the outstanding olive oil made in les Baux is a perfect dish, as is the rack of Alpilles lamb roasted and discreetly garnished with snow peas, eggplant, and garlic or the *papetton de volaille* (stuffed chicken leg) served with fresh spinach and a light cream sauce. All in all, the palate will be satisfied and, if lunching outdoors beneath the cliffs of les Baux, the eye will be as well.

AIGUEBELLE (83980)
Roche Fleuries (H,R), 1 av. des Trois-Dauphins. Tel: 94.71.05.07. closed Nov–mid-Mar. AE DC MC V
Luxurious rooms with a good view over the sea. Swimming pool.

AIX-EN-PROVENCE (13100)
Les Augustins (H), 3 r. de la Masse. Tel: 42.27.28.59. AE DC MC V
Small, comfortable hotel in the former Augustine convent in the center of town near the cours Mirabeau.

Clos de la Violette (R), 10 av. de la Violette. Tel: 42.23.30.71. One Michelin star. Reservations necessary. Closed 2 weeks Mar and Nov. AE MC V
By far the best restaurant in Aix and now in a new location, in an old town house with an attractive garden. Jean-Marco Banzo prepares both regional cooking and *nouvelle* specialties. Regional wines, particularly Coteaux d'Aix and Bandol.

Grand Hôtel Nègre Coste (H), 33 cours Mirabeau. Tel: 42.27.74.22. AE DC MC V

An 18th-century building in the heart of town. All the modern comforts, but reasonably priced.

Paul Cézanne (H), 40 av. Victor-Hugo. Tel: 42.26.34.73. Closed 3 weeks end Dec. AE
Beautiful old Aix house recently converted into a comfortable hotel.

BANDOL (83150)
Pullman-Ile Rousse (H) and **les Oliviers (R)**, 17 bd L.-Lumière. Tel: 94.29.46.86. AE DC MC V
Comfortable, modern hotel with excellent service and tastefully decorated rooms. Swimming pool, terrace and private beach.

Les BAUX-DE-PROVENCE (13520)
La Cabro d'Or (R,H), au Val d'Enfer. Tel: 90.54.33.21. One Michelin star. Closed Nov 16–Dec 20. AE DC MC V
Exceptional views over the countryside. Creative cooking with an excellent choice of local wines. Swimming pool, tennis and riding. Relais et Châteaux and same management as L'Oustau de Baumanière but less expensive!

L'Oustau de Baumanière (R,H), au Val d'Enfer. Tel: 90.54.33.07. Closed mid-Jan–Feb. Three Michelin stars. Reservations necessary. AE DC MC V
One of the finest restaurants in France, luxurious and elegant and expensive too. Exceptional service and *cuisine* and with a superb cellar. Charming rooms in beautifully restored Provençal buildings. Swimming pool, tennis and riding. Relais et Châteaux.

CASSIS (13260)
La Presqu'île (R), quartier Port-Miou (2km SW in the direction of les Calanques). Tel: 42.01.03.77. AE DC V
Charming restaurant with romantic décor in a stunning situation. Excellent fish specialties, good-value menus and pleasant service.

Roches Blanches (H,R), rte de Port-Miou (1km SW). Tel: 42.01.09.30. Closed Dec–Jan. AE DC MC V
Overlooking the sea on a rocky promontory. Rooms have views of the bay over terraced gardens to the sea. Restaurant for residents only.

Le CASTELLET (83330, le Beausset)
Castel Lumière (R,H), le Porche. Tel: 94.32.62.20. Closed Tue (open dinner only Jul–Sep 15) and Nov. AE DC V
A charming, comfortable restaurant with six rooms in the medieval village of le Castellet in the heart of the Bandol vineyards. Magnificent views over the old Provençal houses in the village. Reasonable prices.

CAVALAIRE-SUR-MER (83240)
Hôtel de la Calanque (H,R), r. Calanque. Tel: 94.64.04.27. DC V
This superb, modern hotel is surrounded by rocks and lush vegetation. Cheerful, large rooms. Swimming pool and tennis courts.

DRAGUIGNAN (83300)
Les Deux Cochers (R), 7 bd G.-Péri. Tel: 94.68.13.97. Closed Mon. DC MC V
Good, simple cooking and reasonable prices.

Col de l'Ange (H,R), rte de Lorgues. Tel: 94.68.23.01. (H,R) closed Jan. (R) closed Sat. AE DC MC V
A modern hotel set amid pine trees with good views. Classic *cuisine*.

FREJUS (83600)
Le Vieux Four (R,H), 57 r. Grisolle. Tel: 94.51.56.38. Closed Sep 20–Oct 20. DC MC V
Pleasant restaurant with a small menu, including good seafood and generous helpings. Local wines.

GRIMAUD (83360)
Les Santons (R), rte Nationale. Tel: 94.43.21.02. One Michelin star. Closed Wed (open dinner only Jul–Aug), and Nov–Easter. DC V
Pleasant Provençal décor. Very good but expensive and crowded in high summer.

HYERES (83400)
La Vieille Auberge (R,H), N98, quartier St Nicolas. Tel: 94.66.40.01. (R) closed Mon (in winter only) and Jan. (H) closed Jan. V
Charming friendly establishment with Provençal furniture. Straightforward cooking.

MARSEILLE (13000)

Le Sommelier (W), 69 r. de la Palud, 13006 Marseille. Tel: 91.33.77.87. Closed Sun–Mon and Aug. MC V
An extensive collection of wines from the region and elsewhere.

Miramar (R), 12 quai du Port, 13002 Marseille. Tel: 91.91.10.40. Closed Sun and Aug. AE DC MC V
Traditional dishes of Marseille including the famous *bouillabaisse*. The fish specialties are a favorite with the locals.

Petit Louvre (H,R), 19 la Canebière, 13001 Marseille. Tel: 91.90.13.78. (R) closed Nov–Apr Sun. AE DC MC V
Well-run hotel in a lively part of Marseille, near the old port.

ST TROPEZ (83990)

Bistrot des Lices (R), 3 pl. des Lices. Tel: 94.97.29.00. DC MC V
Pleasant bistro with piano bar and terrace in a garden. Very popular in high season.

Byblos (H) and **La Braiserie (R)**, av. Paul-Signac. Tel: 94.97.00.04. One Michelin star. Closed mid-Oct–mid-March. AE DC V
Luxurious hotel-village of Provençal houses arranged around the swimming pool. Fashionable and expensive. The restaurant serves simple dishes at the pool side.

Leï Mouscardins (R), 16 r. Portalet. Tel: 94.97.01.53. Closed Nov–Jan. V
Comfortable dining-room has a good view over the colorful harbor.

Résidence de la Pinède (H,R), la plage de la Bouillabaisse (1km E). Tel: 94.97.04.21. Closed Nov–Easter. AE DC MC V
Quiet hotel bordering the sea with large rooms. Private beach and swimming pool.

Yaca (H), 1 bd d'Aumale. Tel: 94.97.11.79. Closed mid-Oct–Mar. AE DC MC V
Charming, quiet hotel in the center of town. Swimming pool and garden.

STE MAXIME (83120)

Belle Aurore (H,R), 4 bd Jean-Moulin, La Croisette (2km W by N98). Tel: 94.96.02.45. Closed mid-Oct–mid-Mar. AE V
On the sea with a private beach.

SALON-DE-PROVENCE (13300)

Abbaye de Ste Croix (H,R), 3km NE by D16 (Val du Cuèche) and private road. Tel: 90.56.24.55. Closed Nov–Mar. AE DC MC V
Perfectly restored 12th-century abbey with fine views of the mountains. Antique furniture and modern comforts. Park, terrace and swimming pool. Regional *cuisine* and good service.

Robin (R), 1 bd G.-Clemenceau. Tel: 90.56.06.53. One Michelin star. Closed Sun pm, Mon and Feb. AE DC MC V
A wide choice of *nouvelle* specialties and a good cellar.

Le THORONET (83340, le Luc)

Relais de l'Abbaye (R,H), 3km N on D84. Tel: 94.73.87.59. (R) closed Mon pm and Tue except for residents. No cards.
In peaceful countryside near the Abbaye du Thoronet, this is a charming, small inn with friendly service.

Many Côtes de Provence wines are sold in distinctive amphora-shaped bottles.

TOULON (83000)

Corniche (H,R), 1 littoral F.-Mistral, le Mourillon. Tel: 94.41.39.53. (R) closed Mon. AE DC MC V
Small hotel facing the sea. Seafood specialties in restaurant.

Le Dauphin (R), 21 bis r. Jean-Jaurès. Tel: 94.93.12.07. Closed Sat lunch, Sun and Jul.
This charming Provençal restaurant is the best in Toulon.

Le Lutrin (R), 8 littoral F.-Mistral, le Mourillon. Tel: 94.42.43.43. Closed Sat. AE DC MC V
In a 19th-century villa facing the port. Light dishes served in an elegant Louis XV-style dining-room. Excellent cellar.

THE RHONE VALLEY

Rising high in the Swiss Alps, the Rhône makes its way south through varied countryside to join the Saône at Lyon where it then turns south to the Mediterranean, emerging at flat marshlands near Marseille. The central stretch of the Rhône valley, from Lyon to Avignon, is considered the heart of the river and where the most important vineyards lie. Once south of the industrial suburbs of Lyon the traveler passes perceptibly from the cooler rational atmosphere of the north into the warm exuberance of the south, dominated by the hot Mediterranean sun and harsh mistral wind. The vine-covered hillsides start just outside Vienne and plunge down into the narrow valley; the Romans built these steep terraces in an early and successful attempt to prevent erosion of the soil. Some of the terraces are now abandoned and the hillsides have been bulldozed and landscaped to provide easier means of cultivation. The mulberries that fed the silkworms and the silk industry of Lyon have gone, but heavy industry keeps barges busy on the Rhône, making it a fluvial rival to the nearby autoroute. Few holidaymakers in the 1980s stop to admire the ancient monuments or the natural beauty of the Rhône on their yearly pilgrimage south to the sun; for them, the valley is but a long corridor linking Lyon with Marseille, but those who explore it will be richly rewarded and the wines made here are as varied as the dramatic landscape.

The Wines of the Rhône

The wines are divided broadly into northern and southern Rhône: the northern vineyards stretch from the Côte Rôtie, just outside Vienne, to Cornas and St Péray, near Valence. These vineyards form a narrow strip, clinging mainly to the west bank of the Rhône. The terraced vineyards are dramatically steep and looking after the vines here is very hard work indeed. Mechanization is nearly impossible. Between Valence and Montélimar there is little of importance on the banks of the Rhône, except the Drôme valley to the east where an interesting sparkling wine, Clairette de Die, is made. The southern vineyards cover a large area between Montélimar and Avignon and lie on both sides of the Rhône. The land here is much flatter and provides a stark contrast to the precariously steep hillsides north of Valence. The vineyards cover enormous expanses, broken up by long rows of cypresses to protect the vines and other crops from the mistral. The climate of the northern Rhône is continental, with considerable rainfall and brisk winters; the southern area is strongly influenced by the Mediterranean with long, hot, dry summers and relatively mild winters.

The northern Rhône is made up of several small *appellations*, including France's smallest, Château Grillet, and the world-famous Hermitage on steep slopes overlooking the Rhône above Tain. In contrast, the southern vineyards account for over 85 per cent of the overall regional *appellation* Côtes du Rhône. In the north, the vineyards are dominated by the Syrah, which is at its most brilliant in the highly perfumed red wines of Côte Rotie and Hermitage. These tough, tannic wines are made for lengthy aging. In contrast, the varied terrain in the southern Rhône accounts for many different grape varieties and forward-looking wine growers, particularly in Châteauneuf du Pape where 13 varieties are permitted, are beginning to realize that this wide range gives them enormous scope to experiment. The predominant red grape in the southern Rhône is the Grenache, which gives a high-alcohol wine, quick to mature.

The white varieties are even more varied than the reds. In the north the rare and fragile Viognier grape makes the expensive Condrieu and Château

Grillet, and the Marsanne and Roussanne are used to make the dry whites of Hermitage and Crozes-Hermitage. In the isolated Drôme valley Muscat and Clairette grapes make a flavorsome sparkling white wine, Clairette de Die, that is well worth seeking out. The most interesting white grape in the southern Rhône is the Muscat, which is at its best in the delicious *vin doux naturel* Muscat de Beaumes de Venise.

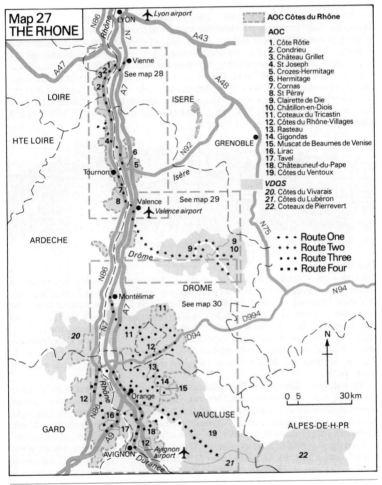

Visiting the Vineyards

Until fairly near its delta on the Mediterranean, the Rhône is a fast-moving river that carves its way through limestone ridges creating occasional stretches of fertile lowland. In general, however, the valley is narrow and the slopes of the hills rise fairly close to the river's bank. The soil on the slopes is usually thin and will not support intensive cultivation of other crops but their exposure to the sun is ideal for grapes.

Just as the Rhône dominates river traffic in France, the A7 that links Lyon and Marseille is one of the busiest autoroutes in the country. Visiting the vineyards will mean taking the less busy national roads that wind through the valley and up to the hill villages but in the height of summer even these can become congested and, as elsewhere in the south, it is best to avoid touring the region when the holiday rush is at its height in July and August.

Route One

The northern Rhône, from Vienne to Valence: 100km

Immediately outside Vienne at Ampuis are the vineyards of the Côte Rôtie. The sheer steepness of the terraced slopes explains both the limited yields and high price of this famous red wine. A white wine made in neighboring Condrieu from Viognier is even more of a rarity. The Condrieu vineyards cover only 10 hectares while a minuscule 3-hectare *appellation*, Château Grillet, produces one of the most famous whites in France. These northern wines are, without a doubt, the most powerfully fragrant wines produced in the whole Rhône valley and are justifiably famous.

Farther south, on the left bank, are the vineyards of Hermitage and Crozes-Hermitage. Red Hermitage is formidable, tannic and aromatic, requiring 5 to 10 years of aging in normal vintages and lasting a couple of decades or more in exceptional vintages. The wines of the larger neighboring *appellation* of Crozes-Hermitage are more supple and light, though they too often age well. Back on the right bank the vineyards of St Joseph and Cornas are not as well known but the wines are underrated and often prove excellent value. St Joseph can be a light and subtle red or a delicately fragrant white, while the wines of Cornas are more substantial: only red, they are fruity with a spicy bouquet. St Péray is best known for its white wines, both still and sparkling, which are fairly acidic and dry.

The tiny chapel on the Hermitage hillside which is owned by the négociant *Jaboulet.*

The Itinerary:

Vienne is easily reached from Lyon on the A7 autoroute. From Vienne, there is a beautiful view of the Rhône, and the city contains many Roman ruins. Leave the center of Vienne following the signs to **Ste Colombe** and **St Etienne**. After crossing the river, turn left toward Tournon on N86, a busy road going straight down the valley with rounded, vine-covered hills looming on either side. At **Ampuis**, the terraced vineyards of the Côte Rotie are an impressive sight while farther on at **Condrieu** the vines are less obvious and mixed with woods. At **St Pierre-de-Boeuf** there is a lovely view of the river and distant hills as the vineyards give way to orchards and lush countryside.

Drive through **Serrières**, **Peyraud** and **Champagne**, then watch for a right-hand turn onto D291 toward **St Désirat**. Continue on D291 in the direction of Annonay, then at the T-junction turn left on D82 to **Andance**, where you turn right onto D370, following the signs to **Talencieux** on a winding climb through the forest. At the entrance to the village, follow the signs left on D370b, for N86 and St Vallier.

Turn right on N86 to **Sarras**, where you turn left to cross the river (in front of the Louis Vuitton factory). Across the river in **St Vallier**, turn right onto N7, following the signs to Valence. There are no vineyards visible at this point, but the terraced hills on both sides of the river are dramatic; approaching **Serves** the vineyards of Crozes-Hermitage begin. Crozes-Hermitage is the largest *appellation* in the northern Rhône and the vineyards surround the smaller but more famous Hermitage *appellation* on the north, east and south sides. From Serves N7 passes through **Gervans** where the steepest and best slopes in the *appellation* are found. As N7 nears **Tain-l'Hermitage** the vines cover the great hill of Hermitage all the way into town. The Hermitage hill is supposed to be the oldest vineyard in France.

From Tain, take N95 across the river to **Tournon**, where there are good views back across the Rhône of the Hermitage vineyards. Then turn left on N86. Here, the St Joseph vineyards blanket the hills and the scenery is magnificent all the way to Valence. Before reaching Valence you pass through the small *appellations* of Cornas and St Péray, which are the last vineyards in the northern Rhône. The high point of this part of the route is the Château de Crussol whose ruins seem to grow out of the craggy cliffs as you cross the Rhône from **St Péray** to **Valence** on N532.

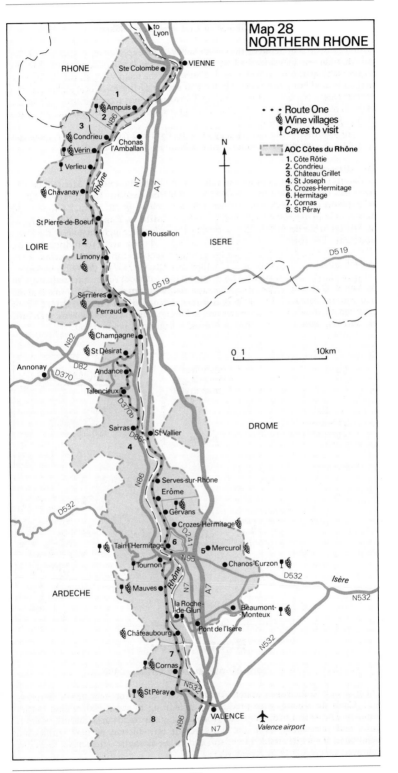

Map 28
NORTHERN RHONE

• • • Route One
🍇 Wine villages
❢ *Caves* to visit
▨ AOC Côtes du Rhône
1. Côte Rôtie
2. Condrieu
3. Château Grillet
4. St Joseph
5. Crozes-Hermitage
6. Hermitage
7. Cornas
8. St Péray

N

0   1   10km

Route Two

Clairette de Die, from Valence to Luc-en-Diois: 95km

To the east of the Rhône, along the Drôme valley, are the *appellations* of Clairette de Die and Châtillon-en-Diois. In the first, which is also the larger, Clairette and Muscat grapes make sparkling white wines. If Clairette is the main varietal, the champagne method is used but when there is at least 50 per cent Muscat, a local technique, the *méthode Dioise*, is used in which the second fermentation is accomplished without the addition of sugar and yeasts; the distinctive bouquet of the Muscat is lost when the champagne method is used.

Slightly farther to the east, Gamay provides light and fruity reds and Aligoté and Chardonnay give pleasant whites in the Châtillon-en-Diois *appellation*.

The Itinerary:

In **Valence** follow the signs for the autoroute A7 in the direction of Montélimar and Marseille, then bear left to take D111 through **Beauvallon**, **Etoile-sur-Rhône**, **Montoison** and **Crest**. From Crest, D93 leads through all the major towns and villages of both *appellations* (**Aouste-sur-Sye**, **Saillans**, **Pontaix**, **Die**, and **Luc-en-Diois**) in the beautiful valley carved by the Drôme through the hills of the Diois mountains. Die itself was once a Roman colony and there are several Roman ruins.

If you have time, there are two interesting diversions into the mountains. After Saillans, look for a right turn on D135, then turn left on D357 up the valley to **Aurel**. Return along the same road, then turn right on D157 and look for another right turn, to **Barsac** on D739. Again, return on the same road and turn right on D157 to rejoin the main route at Pontaix. To visit **Châtillon**, turn left on D539 at **Pont de Quart**. From Châtillon it is a spectacular drive to Luc-en-Diois; return on D539 for 2km, then turn left on D69, which winds through isolated villages to Luc-en-Diois.

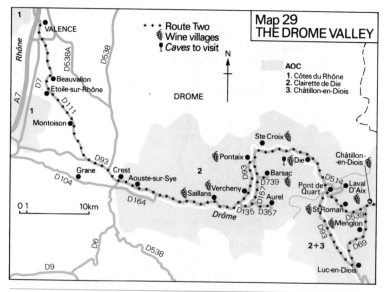

Route Three

The southern Rhône, from Montélimar to Orange: 180km

The area south from Montélimar to Avignon produces most of the wine sold simply as AOC Côtes du Rhône, with production amounting to about 250 million bottles annually. The wines can differ greatly; some are quite firm and tannic and others light, fruity and refreshing. Until the fairly recent introduction of new vinification techniques, the whites tended to be soft and rather alcoholic – they have, however, improved spectacularly in recent years.

Côtes du Rhône-Villages wines can only come from one of the 17 villages which have the right to attach their names to the wines they produce. Most of these villages lie east of Grignan in an arc that curves south to Orange. Several wines have their own *appellation* and are worth looking out for, specifically the reds from Gigondas, and the *vin doux naturel* made from Muscat at Beaumes-de-Venise.

Just south of Montélimar is a large area with its own *appellation*, the Coteaux du Tricastin, where spicy, aromatic reds are produced that are often very good value.

The Itinerary:

In Montélimar, follow the signs for Avignon and Nyons on N7; shortly after passing the turnoff to the autoroute, turn left onto D133 toward Nyons. This region is the Coteaux du Tricastin which extends south beyond St Paul-Trois-Châteaux. The vineyards here share parched, rocky soil with occasional fields of lavender. Near **Valaurie** where the D133 becomes D541, the vines grow up the sides of the rugged hills and the red soil can be seen in exposed areas.

From **Grignan**, a fortified town made famous by Mme de Sévigné, follow the signs to **Valréas** on D941. Nearing **Grillon**, a sign announces *Ici commence l'enclave des papes*, a medieval papal territority that comprised Grillon, Richerenches, Valréas, and Visan, and this is the beginning of the Côtes du Rhône. In Grillon, turn right onto D20 to **Richerenches**, which has a church with a fine wrought-iron belfry typical of the area. In the village, turn left onto D142, following the signs to **Valréas** through a vine-covered plain with magnificent vistas of the distant hills. In Valréas follow the signs for *Centre Ville*, then *Toutes Directions*, taking the turnoff to Nyons on D941. The countryside becomes very dramatic, with rugged hills and tall dark cypresses rising up out of the vineyards. Turn left to **St Pantaléon-les-Vignes**, bearing right in the village to **Rousset-les-Vignes**. These two villages are the most north-eastern in the Villages *appellation* and are set against a backdrop of steep mountains.

Rousset-les-Vignes is a beautiful village with reddish-gold houses and stunning views of the surrounding countryside. Watch for a hard right turn indicating D538, the road to **Nyons**. Continue on D538 to Nyons through vineyards uninterrupted save by olive trees, some of which are planted right among the vines. In Nyons, a charming town with houses tucked into the hill and a bustling Thursday morning market, follow the signs indicating *Toutes Directions*, then drive straight across the bridge, turn right and follow D538 along the Eygues valley to **Mirabel-aux-Baronnies**. In the valley, olive trees alternate with orchards and vineyards and the patchwork effect on the surrounding hills is beautiful. Just before Mirabel take the right-hand turnoff on D4 to **Vinsobres**; at the junction, turn left onto D94. The villages are much farther apart here than in the northern Rhône and occasional isolated houses are common.

Continue on D94 past the Vinsobres turnoff (unless seeing growers there), and through **St Maurice-sur-Eygues**; more and more winegrowers have signs out along the road inviting travelers to taste their wines. Turn right onto D20 to go into **Visan** (where there is a good co-operative), then follow the signs to **Bouchet** on D161, turning left, then right to **Suze-la-Rousse** on D251. Go through Suze, past the imposing château and the Université du Vin, turning right onto D94, then turn left onto D117, following the signs to Rochegude. Just before **Rochegude**, D117 crosses a major road, D8. Turn left here to **Ste Cécile-les-Vignes**.

Continue on D8 to **Cairanne**, a pretty village, from where there are good views of the enormous vine-covered plain, then follow the signs off left to **Rasteau**, famous for its fortified wine; there is a good view of the famous Dentelles de Montmirail, a jagged wall of white rock set on a ridge. Drive through Rasteau, then turn left to **Roaix** on D975. Once there, follow the signs for **Séguret** and **Sablet**. Before Séguret, a hill-top village, is the right-hand turnoff on D23 to Sablet. In Sablet, follow the *Route des Vins* (D7) toward **Vacqueyras**.

If you wish to visit **Gigondas**, which has its own *appellation*, watch for a left turn on D79, then return to the main route by following D80 out of the village and turning left back on D7. Turn right on D80 toward **Violès** or make a slight detour by continuing on D7 to Vacqueyras and **Beaumes-de-Venise**.

If going directly to Violès, turn right on D8, then left at the stop sign to go into Violès. In the village, turn right onto D67 to **Camaret-sur-Aigues** where you follow the signs for *Centre Ville* and *Autres Directions*, then for **Sérignan-du-Comtat** on D43. Turn right on D172 toward Piolenc past Château St Estève, a good Côtes du Rhône property, and return to Orange on D11.

Route Four

The southern Rhône from Orange to Avignon: 100km

Though the northern Rhône can claim to make the finest wines, some of those from the southern Rhône can be every bit as good: the best Châteauneuf-du-Pape is the equal of Côte Rôtie and Hermitage. Although deep in color and full-bodied, red Châteauneuf is quicker to mature than its northern rivals. White Châteauneuf is much rarer but can be very good with distinctive floral perfumes and flavors. Across the Rhône from Châteauneuf are Lirac and Tavel. Lirac whites and rosés are fruity while the reds are assertive and generous and Tavel claims to be the finest rosé in France. Côtes du Rhône-Villages comes from 17 villages traditionally thought of as making the finest wine and most of these are in the foothills of the Dentelles de Montmirail.

To the east of Châteauneuf, and extending roughly between Malaucène in the north and Apt in the south, is the *appellation* Côtes du Ventoux. On the slopes of Mt Ventoux the area has a slightly cooler climate so that Ventoux wines tend to be a little lower in alcohol than other Rhône wines, but if well made they are smooth and fruity.

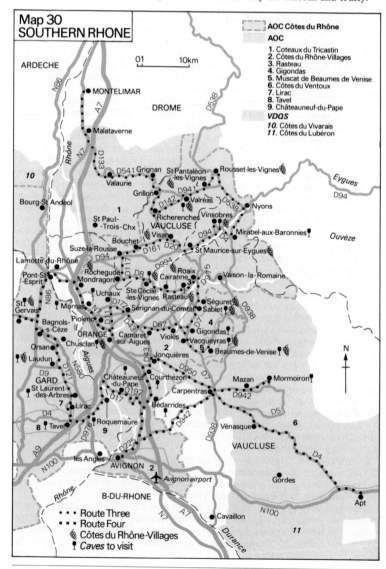

The Itinerary:

Leave **Orange** northward on N7; drive through **Mornas** (note Château de Mornas jutting out of the rocky hills to the right), then, as you approach **Mondragon**, watch for a left-hand turnoff indicating D44 and Lamotte-du-Rhône; cross the river and follow the signs for **Pont-St Esprit**. At the T-junction, turn left on D994 to Pont-St Esprit, a beautiful town dominated by three churches rising up on the western bank of the Rhône. From there, follow the signs to **Bagnols-sur-Cèze** on N86. Just before Bagnols you can turn right to St Gervais on D980 to visit a good Villages property at les Celettes. After Bagnols continue south on N580 before turning off right onto D138 to visit the villages of **Orsan** and **Laudun**.

Between Orsan and Laudun, cypresses and other trees give relief to the large expanses of vines. In Laudun, follow the signs to the left indicating l'Ardoise on D9, then bear right on D121, following the signs to Tavel through **St Laurent-des-Arbres** and **Lirac**. The Lirac vineyards begin just north of St Laurent, which has a stunning citadel, and Lirac itself has some lovely old houses.

In **Tavel**, follow the signs for **Roquemaure** on D4, turning left at the crossroads onto D976. A patchwork of vineyards interspersed with wildflowers covers the rugged hills around Roquemaure, a town with an extremely confusing system of roads. Drive straight into the center of Roquemaure, and follow the signs for *Toutes Directions*, then for Orange on D976, passing some stark, imposing cliffs on the way out of town. Cross the Rhône, then turn right and follow the signs for **Châteauneuf-du-Pape** on D17.

After passing through extensive red-earth orchards surrounded by rough black hills, the Châteauneuf vineyards begin. In Châteauneuf-du-Pape, follow the signs to Avignon, then turn left onto D192 toward **Bédarrides**, driving past the châteaux of les Fines Roches and la Nerte; note the large, smooth stones (or *galets*) covering the ground that are characteristic of the vineyards of Châteauneuf. These retain the midday heat, releasing it slowly at night. At the junction with N7, you can either turn right to drive directly to the enchanting city of Avignon, where the routes to the wines of Provence begin; or turn left to see growers in Bédarrides and **Courthézon**. From Courthézon, either return on N7 south to Avignon, or continue east to explore the Côtes du Ventoux, using the following suggestions.

Begin by following the signs to Vaison; bear left around the fountain to take the road with a sign hand-labeled *Passage à niveau*. Follow the signs to **Jonquières** on D43, then right on D950 to **Carpentras**, the strawberry capital of France and a bustling market town. Shortly before Carpentras, you enter the Côtes du Ventoux *appellation* (the vineyards themselves begin on the other side of the town). Follow the signs to *Centre Ville* through the imposing gate. From Carpentras, either continue to **Mazan** and **Mormoiron** on D942 or take D4 to **Apt**, famous for candied fruits, lavender and truffles; alternatively, return to Avignon on D942.

Caves and Vineyards to Visit

The Rhône valley is one of the most densely planted wine-growing regions in France. In the northern Rhône large houses such as Chapoutier, Jaboulet or Guigal are important. They not only make wine from their own vines but also buy grapes from the many small growers in the region. Each house has its specialty and quality is usually high. As elsewhere in France, however, an increasing number of small growers are bottling their own wines with exciting results. In the southern Rhône the co-operatives are important and provide much good to excellent wine at affordable prices.

AMPUIS, map 28
**Vidal-Fleury
(M/G)**, Ampuis,
69420 Condrieu.
Tel: 74.56.10.18.

This firm is one of the most important owners in the Côte Rôtie with 8 hectares of vines, all on the slopes. As *négociants* they are the oldest wine house of the northern Rhône, dating back to 1781, and also deal in all the principal *appellations* of the Rhône valley. Their reputation lies with their Côte Rôtie and Hermitage. In recent years Vidal-Fleury have undergone some modernization and are now owned by Maison Guigal, another top Côte Rôtie grower.
Visiting hours: Aug–Jun Mon–Thu, 8–12, 2–6.
Location: On N86 in the village.

CHATEAUNEUF-DU-PAPE, map 30

Château des Fines Roches (G),
84230 Châteauneuf-du-Pape.
Tel: 90.83.73.10.

This domaine, owned by Mme Catherine Mousset-Barrot, is one of the best-placed properties in the Châteauneuf *appellation*. There is a huge modern vinification plant next to the château, a turreted and crenellated 19th-century extravaganza which is now a splendid hotel (see page 172). The red wine, elegant and powerful, is a lighter Châteauneuf in the modern style, but still highly regarded.
Visiting hours: Mar–Dec daily, 9–8.
Location: On private road 3km S on D17.

Château des Fines Roches has fine views over the Châteauneuf-du-Pape vineyards.

CORNAS, map 28

Robert Michel (G), Grande-Rue,
07130 Cornas.
Tel: 75.40.38.70.

This domaine has been owned by the same family for two centuries. The vineyards cover 6 hectares, some on the steep slopes which give the best wines, and some at the foot of the hill, and the two are vinified separately. There is a very fine Cornas, la Geynale, which is the domaine's best wine and made from old vines on the terraced slopes. It can be aged for up to 20 years.
Visiting hours: Mon–Fri 8–12, 2–6; Sat 2–6; closed hols.
Location: In the center of the village near the church.

COURTHEZON, map 30

Château de Beaucastel (G),
84350 Courthézon.
Tel: 90.70.70.60.

Surrounded by vines on all sides, this attractive Châteauneuf property was mentioned in documents as early as the 17th century but suffered considerable setbacks before the vineyards were replanted beginning in 1909. Now run by François Perrin, the domaine has all 13 Châteauneuf grape varieties on its 250 hectares. Organic viticulture is practiced as far as possible. A specialty of Beaucastel's vinification is the unique flash-heating technique. Its red Châteauneuf-du-Pape has been repeatedly praised for its complexity of scents and flavors and is a wine that can be aged for a considerable time in most years.
Visiting hours: Mon–Fri 8–12, 2–5; closed hols.
Location: Signposted off N7 between Avignon and Courthézon.

DIE, map 29

Cave Co-opérative de la Clairette de Die (C), BP 79,
av. de la Clairette,
26150 Die.
Tel: 75.22.02.22.

The Clairette de Die *appellation* covers about 1,000 hectares of which 850 belong to members of the co-operative. Nearly all its Clairette de Die is made in the traditional way, not by the champagne method, and it has a delicious taste of Muscat. There is also a small amount of AOC Châtillon-en-Diois: the fruity red Cuvée du Reviron made from Gamay, to be drunk young, and two whites from Chardonnay and Aligoté of which the Chardonnay is generally considered the better.
Visiting hours: May–Sep daily, 8–7.30; Oct–Easter daily, 8–12, 1.30–6.
Location: At the entrance to Die.

GIGONDAS, map 30

Domaine les Pallières (G),
84190 Gigondas.
Tel: 90.65.85.07.

Domaine les Pallières is one of the leading estates in Gigondas, a pretty village in the hills below the Dentelles de Montmirail. The family of Hilarion Roux were the first growers in Gigondas to bottle their wine, as far back as the 1890s. Their wine is traditional Gigondas and released for sale only when three or four years old.
Visiting hours: Mon–Sat 8–12, 2–6.
Location: On D7 between Gigondas and Sablet.

MAUVES, map 28

Pierre Coursodon (G), pl. du Marché, Mauves,
07300 Tournon-sur-Rhône.
Tel: 75.08.29.27.

Mauves is the main village in the St Joseph *appellation*. The Coursodon family own 8 hectares of vines dotted throughout the *appellation* on steep, terraced hillsides. They are one of the few estates to make both red and white wine, and both benefit from some aging in bottle; the red spends some 18 months in barrel and is a solid, tannic mouthful.
Visiting hours: Mon–Sat 8–12, 2–7; closed hols.
Location: In the center of the village.

ST GERVAIS, map 30

Domaine Ste Anne (G), les Celettes, St Gervais,
30200 Bagnols-sur-Cèze.
Tel: 66.82.77.41.

The 27-hectare domaine, owned by Steinmaier et Fils, makes an excellent special *cuvée* Côtes du Rhône-Villages, Notre-Dame-des-Celettes, named after an ancient chapel that has been carefully restored and can be seen during a visit to the property. The Côtes du Rhône-Villages is also good. There is a simpler but no less appealing Côtes du Rhône Ste Anne.
Visiting hours: Mon–Sat 9–11, 3–7; closed hols.
Location: 3km N of St Gervais.

TAIN-l'HERMITAGE, map 28

Max Chapoutier (G/M), BP 38, 18 av. du Dr-Paul-Durand,
26600 Tain-l'Hermitage.
Tel: 75.08.28.65.

This famous house, which has established a reputation for quality, is mainly a *négociant* dealing with wines of the whole Rhône valley. It also owns some 70 hectares of vineyards, mostly in the northern part of the region. Its best wines are red and white Hermitage, especially the white Hermitage Chante Alouette. Their Hermitage Rouge Monier de la Sizeranne Grand Cuvée is rich and tannic and develops superbly with aging, while the Côte Rôtie Grande Cuvée can be magnificent. The Châteauneuf-du-Pape Grande Cuvée la Bernardine is also excellent.
Visiting hours: (Sales only) hours Mon–Fri 8–12, 2–6; Sat 9–12; cellar visits by appt.
Location: In the center of town, near the station.

TAVEL, map 30

Château d'Aquéria (G),
30126 Tavel.
Tel: 66.50.04.56.

Although the château is 18th-century, this excellent Tavel estate is itself much older and was given by the monks of Villeneuve-lès-Avignon to Louis-Joseph d'Aquéria in 1595. Since then it has gradually been reduced, reaching its present size of 55 hectares by 1920. Jean Olivier, who died in 1974, was the long-standing owner of Aquéria and he did much to make the rosé so popular in the United States. It is now run by Paul Debez, his son-in-law. There is also a small amount of red Lirac, with scents of ripe fruit.
Visiting hours: Mon–Fri 8–12, 2–6; closed Sep 20–Oct 15; groups by appt.
Location: Off N580 2km E of Tavel.

UCHAUX, map 30

Château St Estève (G), rte de Sérignan, Uchaux, 84100 Orange. Tel: 90.40.62.38.

Owned by the Français-Monier family, the domaine has established an outstanding reputation for quality. The property consists of 55 hectares of vines and has a charming château in an attractive setting just north of Orange. All three basic types of Côtes du Rhône, red, rosé and white are made by the domaine, and there are numerous special *cuvées*, the result of careful selection of grapes and wines. The top wine is a Grande Réserve, made only in the best years. It has a high proportion of Syrah and six months aging in barrel to give it structure and tannin, allowing it to develop in bottle for several years. The Muscat de Beaumes de Venise and Crème de Myrtilles are also good.

Visiting hours: Mon–Fri 8–12, 2–6; Sat 8–12; closed hols.

Location: Signposted from D172 between Uchaux and Sérignan.

Château St Estève is in attractive countryside just north of Orange.

VERIN, map 28

Château Grillet (G), 42410 Vérin. Tel: 74.59.51.56.

This famous property has a legendary reputation. It is an *appellation* in its own right, the smallest one in France with only 3 hectares of vines and there is only one owner, M. Neyret-Gachet. The wine, a full white, is made from the Viognier which is peculiar to the northern Rhône and gives rich perfumed wines with overtones of apricots. The property owes its individuality to the site of its vineyard, an amphitheater of terraced granite, protected from cold north winds and exposed to warm sunshine. The château itself is a mixture of architectural styles with a Renaissance façade. Needless to say, the limited output guarantees high prices.

Visiting hours: Daily by appt.

Location: Off N86 2km S of Condrieu next to the Rhône.

Further *Caves* and Vineyards to Visit

AMPUIS, map 28

Maison Guigal (G/M), rte Nationale, Ampuis, 69420 Condrieu. Tel: 74.56.10.22. Visiting hours: By appt.

An important Rhône *négociant* and also a leading grower in the Côte Rôtie, with 10 hectares on the slopes, Guigal believes in long aging in cask.

BEAUMES-DE-VENISE, map 30

Cave des Vignerons de Beaumes-de-Venise (C), 84190 Beaumes-de-Venise. Tel: 90.62.94.45. Visiting hours: (Sales only) Mon–Sat 8.30–12, 2–6; closed hols.

The co-operative is the largest producer

of the sweet Muscat de Beaumes de Venise, which is golden in color and deliciously grapy in flavor. This Muscat is easily the best of all the southern French fortified wines and the only one to have a small, enthusiastic market outside France.

Domaine des Bernardins (G), Quartier Ste Anne, 84190 Beaumes-de-Venise. Tel: 90.62.94.13. Visiting hours: Mon–Sat 8–12, 2–6; closed hols.

This is one of the few private estates making Muscat de Beaumes de Venise. The 20-hectare vineyard is owned by M. and Mme Castaud-Martin who also make a red Côtes du Rhône-Villages.

BEAUMONT-MONTEUX,
map 28

Cave des Clairmonts (C), Beaumont-Monteux, 26600 Tain l'Hermitage. Tel: 75.84.61.91. Visiting hours: Mon–Sat 8–12, 2–6; groups by appt.

This is a co-operative, although something of a family affair run by M and Mme Borja. It makes reliable red and white Crozes-Hermitage and a fruity Vin de Pays de la Drôme.

BEDARRIDES, map 30
Domaine du Vieux-Télégraphe (G), 3 rte de Châteauneuf-du-Pape, 84370 Bédarrides. Tel: 90.33.00.31. Visiting hours: Mon–Sat by appt; closed hols.

This is an important estate, owned by Henri Brunier et Fils, with an excellent reputation for its Châteauneuf-du-Pape. The cellars are modern and streamlined and the wine aged in oak for 12 months.

CAIRANNE, map 30
Domaine Rabasse-Charavin (G), Quartier St Martin, 84290 Cairanne. Tel: 90.30.70.05. and 90.30.85.27. Visiting hours: (Sales only) Mon–Sat 8–12, 2–7; closed hols; cellar visits by appt.

Cairanne is a pretty village and one of the best in the Villages *appellation*. This domaine is run by Mme Corinne Couturier who produces good wines.

CHANOS-CURSON, map 28
Domaine des Entrefaux (G), GAEC de la Syrah, Chanos-Curson, 26600 Tain-l'Hermitage. Tel: 75.07.33.38. Visiting hours: Mon–Sat 9–12, 2–6; appt preferred.

The domaine, owned by Charles Tardy and Bernard Ange, consists of 15 hectares of vines and produces respectable red and white Crozes-Hermitage.

CHATEAUNEUF-DU-PAPE,
map 30
Château Fortia (G), 84230 Châteauneuf-du-Pape. Tel: 90.83.70.06. Visiting hours: Mon–Sat 9–11, 2–5.

Château Fortia is the property of Baron Henri le Roy de Boiseaumarie whose father established the regulations for the production of Châteauneuf-du-Pape in 1923, the forerunners of the laws of *appellation contrôlée*. The 27.5 hectare estate continues to produce superb traditional Châteauneuf, both red and white.

Domaine de Mont-Redon (G), rte d'Orange, 84230 Châteauneuf-du-Pape. Tel: 90.83.72.75. Visiting hours: (Cellar visits) Mon–Fri 8–1, 1.30–8. (Sales and tasting) weekends and hols.

This is now the largest Châteauneuf estate with 95 hectares of vineyards, and has a good reputation for aromatic wine. Mont-Redon is the largest producer of white Châteauneuf.

Domaine du Clos des Papes (G), 13 rte de Sorgues, 84230 Châteauneuf-du-Pape. Tel: 90.83.70.13. Visiting hours: Mon–Fri 8–12, 2–6; closed hols.

This was once the old papal vineyard situated behind the château and is now owned by Paul Avril, a highly respected grower who makes good red Châteauneuf-du-Pape from 34 hectares of vines scattered throughout the *appellation*.

CHUSCLAN, map 30
Cave Co-opérative des Vignerons de Chusclan (C), Chusclan, 30200 Bagnols-sur-Cèze. Tel: 66.89.63.03. Visiting hours: Daily 8–12, 2–6.

This good, medium-sized co-operative makes careful wines, including an attractive Villages rosé.

CORNAS, map 28
Marcel Juge (G), pl. de la Salle-des-Fêtes, 07130 Cornas. Tel: 75.40.36.68. Visiting hours: Daily 8–8.

Marcel Juge has just 3 hectares of vines in Cornas and St Péray. His Cornas, aged for at least 18 months in oak barrels, is very good value.

GERVANS, map 28
Caves Fayolle Fils (G), GAEC Les Gamets, Gervans 26600. Tel: 75.03.33.74. Visiting hours: Mon–Fri 9–12; Sat 9–12.

This family-owned estate makes Hermitage and Crozes-Hermitage to last.

GIGONDAS, map 30
Domaine St Gayan (G/M), 84190 Gigondas. Tel: 90.65.86.33. Visiting hours: Mon–Sat 9–11.45, 2–7; Sun am and hols by appt.

Roger and Jean-Pierre Meffre make wines which are among the best in the region. Their Gigondas is a big wine with tannin, acidity and the flavor of cherries, violets and spices.

LAUDUN, map 30
Cave les Quatre Chemins (C), le Serre de Bernon, 30290 Laudun. Tel: 66.82.00.22. Visiting hours: Mon–Sat also Jun 1–Aug 30 Sun and hols 9–7.
This good co-operative makes a reliable, red Côtes du Rhône-Villages Laudun, as well as a small amount of white.

Domaine Rousseau (G), les Charmettes, 30290 Laudun. Tel: 66.50.01.19. Visiting hours: Sep–Jul Mon–Sat, 9–12, 2–6.
This domaine makes a fruity Lirac rosé, as well as a sound Côtes du Rhône-Villages Laudun. The vineyards were completely replanted in 1962, so the vines are now in full maturity.

MIRABEL-AUX-BARONNIES, map 30
Domaine de la Taurelle (G), Mirabel-aux-Baronnies, 26110 Nyons. Tel: 75.27.12.32. Visiting hours: Daily 8–7.
In the Eygues valley Mme Claude Roux and her son own the 20-hectare Domaine de la Taurelle and make a traditional red Côtes du Rhône.

MORNAS, map 30
Château du Grand Moulas (G), 84550 Mornas. Tel: 90.34.35.96. Visiting hours: Mon–Fri 7.30–12, 1.30–6.30; Sat and hols, by appt.
The Ryckwaert brothers make wine which is now ranked among the best Côtes du Rhône. Shrubland as recently as the late 1960s, the estate consists of 29 hectares of vines planted on south-facing slopes some 11 km from Mornas near Uchaux. The cellars are in Mornas itself.

MORMOIRON, map 30
Cave Co-opérative les Roches Blanches (C), 84570 Mormoiron. Tel: 90.61.80.07. Visiting hours: Mon–Sat 8–12, 2–6; Sun, hols and during the summer, 9.30–12, 4–7.
This village co-operative, with 850 hectares of vineyards, is an important producer of red, white and rosé Côtes du Ventoux.

La ROCHE-DE-GLUN, map 28
Paul Jaboulet Aîné (G/M), BP 46 les Jalets, la Roche-de-Glun, 26600 Tain-l'Hermitage. Tel: 75.84.68.93. Visiting hours: Sales only by appt.

Jaboulet are one of the leading *négociants* of the Rhône with a range of excellent wines. Their own vineyards are in Hermitage (their Hermitage la Chapelle is the most renowned wine from this famous vineyard) and Crozes-Hermitage, and Jaboulet own the tiny chapel on the Hermitage hillside.

ROQUEMAURE, map 30
Domaine de Castel Oualou (G), 30150 Roquemaure. Tel: 66.82.82.64. Visiting hours: Mon–Sat, 8–12, 2–5.45; closed hols.
When Charles and Marie Pons-Mure returned to France from Algeria they created their vineyard in Lirac by planting a wooded plateau near Roquemaure. Today, the 51-hectare estate produces excellent, fruity Lirac, both red and rosé. There is also a flinty dry white Lirac.

SABLET, map 30
Domaine de Verquière (G), 3 r. d'Orange, Sablet, 84110 Vaison-la-Romaine. Tel: 90.46.90.11. Visiting hours: Daily 8–12, 1–7.
The domaine consists of a 16th-century château surrounded by 40 hectares of vines. The Chamfort brothers are skilled in turning out long-lived Côtes du Rhône-Villages, Vacqueyras and Sablet. There is also a good rosé.

ST LAURENT-DES-ARBRES, map 30
Domaine du Devoy (G), N580, St Laurent-des-Arbres, 30126 Tavel. Tel: 66.50.01.23. Visiting hours: Mon–Sat 8–12, 2–6; closed hols.
The Lombardo brothers created the 40-hectare vineyard in the 1960s on their return from Tunisia and have an excellent reputation for red and rosé Lirac.

ST PERAY, map 28
Darona Père et Fils (G), les Faures, chemin des Putiers, 07130 St Péray. Tel: 75.40.34.11. Visiting hours: Daily 8–12, 1–9.
The Darona family owns 9 hectares of vineyards in St Péray and makes both still and sparkling whites from Marsanne and Roussanne. Their wines have more acidity and less alcohol than other northern Rhône whites because of the vineyards' particular microclimate.

TAIN-L'HERMITAGE, map 28
Marc Sorrel (G), 128 bis av. Jean-Jaurès, BP 69, 26600 Tain-l'Hermitage. Tel: 75.07.10.07. Visiting hours: Mon-Fri 10–12, 2–7.
This is a modest property, only 2.7 hectares, but on some of the best sites on the Hermitage hill. M. Sorrel makes good red Hermitage, called le Gréal, and a white Hermitage made from 50-year-old vines, les Rocoules.

TAVEL, map 30
Château de Trinquevedel (G), 30126 Tavel. Tel: 66.50.04.04. Visiting hours: Mon-Fri 8–11.30, 2–5; hols by appt.
The attractive Château de Trinquevedel is outside the village and has 26 hectares of vines which produce sound Tavel.

Domaine de la Genestière (G), 30126 Tavel. Tel: 66.50.07.03. Visiting hours: Mon-Fri 8–12, 1.30–5.30.
The 37-hectare domaine, owned by Mme André Bernard, is one of the outstanding producers of Tavel. The estate also makes some good Lirac.

Domaine Maby (G), 30126 Tavel. Tel: 66.50.03.40. Visiting hours: Mon-Sat 8–12, 2–6.
The Maby family has been making wine at Tavel for many generations and their wine has always been considered outstanding. In the last 20 years, they have also planted vineyards at Domaine de la Fermade in neighboring Lirac and their red wine from this property is a good example of the *appellation*.

TOURNON-SUR-RHONE, map 28
Jean-Louis Grippat (G), la Sauva, 07300 Tournon-sur-Rhône. Tel: 75.08.15.51. Visiting hours: By appt.
The small estate has land in both St Joseph and Hermitage. The wines are among the best in the *appellations*.

VACQUEYRAS, map 30
Château des Roques (G), BP 9, 84190 Vacqueyras. Tel: 90.65.85.16. Visiting hours: Mon-Fri 9–12, 2–6; closed Sun pm and hols.
The village has a long tradition of winemaking and the 40-hectare domaine, owned by Edouard Dusser-Beraud, makes a good Côtes du Rhône-Villages Vacqueyras, a substantial wine.

Domaine la Fourmone (G), rte de Bollène, Vacqueyras, 84190 Beaumes-de-Venise. Tel: 90.65.86.05. Visiting hours: Daily by appt.
Roger Combe makes a fine traditional Côtes du Rhône-Villages Vacqueyras, as well as some lighter Côtes du Rhône. He also owns l'Oustaou Fauquet, a 9-hectare vineyard first planted in the 18th century, which makes an excellent red Gigondas, Cru du Petit Montmirail.

Domaine le Clos des Cazaux (G), 84190 Vacqueyras. Tel: 90.65.85.83. Visiting hours: Sep–July Mon–Sat, 9–12, 2–6; closed hols.
This is another good property in Vacqueyras. The 35-hectare domaine, now owned by Maurice Vache, was once the property of the Chevaliers Templiers (Knights Templar), hence the name of a special *cuvée* of Côtes du Rhône-Villages.

VALREAS, map 30
Cellier de l'Enclave des Papes (C), BP 51, 11 av. Gén.-de-Gaulle, 84600 Valréas. Tel: 90.41.91.42. or 90.37.36.75. Visiting hours: Daily 8–12, 3–7.
This is a serious co-operative whose name recalls the area's association with the Avignon papacy. It makes a large quantity of Côtes du Rhône from 3,000 hectares of vines, as well as a fine Côtes du Rhône-Villages Valréas, and a spicy red Coteaux du Tricastin.

VERLIEU, map 28
Pierre et André Perret (G), Verlieu, 42410 Chavanay. Tel: 74.87.24.74. Visiting hours: By appt.
The Perrets make one of the best wines in the small Condrieu *appellation*. Rarity accounts perhaps for some of Condrieu's reputation, but it is still a superb white wine, made only from the Viognier, perfumed and flowery, and best drunk within four or five years.

VINSOBRES, map 30
Domaine du Coriançon (G), Vinsobres, 26110 Nyons. Tel: 75.26.03.24. Visiting hours: Mon–Sat 9–12, 2–7; closed hols.
The 60-hectare domaine, owned by François Vallot, makes a good range of wines, the best of which is the Côtes du Rhône-Villages Vinsobres Cuvée Claude Vallot, a firm, scented wine that requires some aging to reach its peak.

Sights

The Rhône valley is dominated by the two cities which act as its gateways, Lyon in the north and Avignon in the south. In between, the river winds between steep hills and through towns which have been important trading centers for centuries, but their development and prosperity generally dates from the Roman occupation of Gaul, of which the temple in Vienne and the theater in Orange are the most striking reminders.

There are many festivals in the region, including those of Avignon and Orange which attract thousands of visitors for their music, dance and theater performances. Throughout the valley more modest events are organized to celebrate the harvest or to promote the local wines.

APT
Originally a Roman town, Apt has a fine medieval cathedral and an excellent **Musée Archéologique Gallo-Romain** with displays of local Roman finds.

AVIGNON
The true "gateway to the South", Avignon marks the beginning of Provence. Most of its glory stems from the fact that throughout the 14th century it was the residence of the popes when it became one of the most important and wealthy cities in Europe. There are good views from the **Palais des Papes** and from the **Rocher des Doms** overlooking the Rhône.

The majestic city walls are another reminder of Avignon's former importance. It is possible to walk along the top around almost the entire perimeter of the city. The best known sight in Avignon is the 12th-century **Pont St Bénézet**, the Pont d'Avignon of the old French song.

A major festival of Côtes-du-Rhône *primeur*, with a parade of the various wine brotherhoods, takes place in Nov.

BAGNOLS-SUR-CEZE
The **Musée Impressioniste**, in the Hôtel de Ville, has works by Bonnard, Monet and others. There is a wine festival in early May.

CARPENTRAS
This is a bustling town with fine 18th-century buildings. On a clear day it is worth driving to the summit of the nearby Mt Ventoux (NE on D974) for spectacular views.

CHATEAUNEUF-DU-PAPE
One tower is all that remains of the powerful château, built by the Avignon popes to protect the city from the north. A Fête de la Véraison (when the grapes first begin to change color) is held at the beginning of Aug.

MONTELIMAR
Famous for its nougat, and infamous for the carnival atmosphere created by the road-side vendors (all selling *véritable nougat*) that has made the town synonymous with bad taste. This judgment is a bit excessive since Montélimar is not without charm.

NYONS
Nyons is famous both for its small black olives and olive oil. The **Vieux Pont** was built in the 15th century and is still in use. The oldest section of the town, the **quartier des Forts**, is built onto a hill and is well worth exploring on foot.

ORANGE
When the Romans occupied Provence, Orange (Arausio) was already a Celtic settlement. It expanded rapidly, becoming one of the principal cities of southeast Gaul and today is famous chiefly for its Roman buildings, which include a well-preserved **Théatre Antique** used for concerts and opera performances in the summer. The **Musée de la Ville** contains Roman artifacts and mementoes of old Orange. A wine fair is held in Jul and Aug.

The Roman triumphal arch in Orange.

SEGURET
With its steep streets this attractive hilltop village is worth exploring on foot. A wine fair and Provençal festival are held in mid-Oct.

TOURNON-SUR-RHONE

On the banks of the Rhône, Tournon is a bustling town with good views of Tain l'Hermitage and its world-famous vineyards on the opposite bank.

VAISON-LA-ROMAINE

Lying in wooded hills on the banks of the river Ouvèze, Vaison is famous for its Roman city which gives a marvelous feel of the way of life at the time. Across the river is the medieval quarter, **la Haute Ville**, where many old houses have been restored and are once again inhabited.

A fair and festival of *vin nouveau* is held in mid-Nov.

VIENNE

A city that once rivaled Lyon for importance, Vienne is now a quiet town on the banks of the Rhône, known primarily as the location of Fernand Point's celebrated restaurant, la Pyramide, where many of today's famous chefs perfected their art (see page 173).

The town has many Roman and medieval attractions; high on the list are the **Cathédrale St Maurice**, built between the 12th and 15th centuries and with a nave nearly 100m long, and the **Roman amphitheater**, the largest in Roman Gaul, which could seat 13,500 spectators. It is now used in summer for concerts and plays.

Hotels, Restaurants and Where to Buy Wine

The Rhône valley does not exist as one gastronomic region and it has long been both a gastronomic and cultural crossroads. Most of the right bank is in the Ardèche and the left bank in the Drôme, and both areas proclaim their culinary independence. To complicate matters, the extreme northern and southern ends of the valley are special cases, thought of either as a satellite of Lyon or as part of Provençe. There are a few common traits: olive oil is universally appreciated (the oil made near Nyons is the most famous), goat cheeses, truffles and wild mushrooms abound and the entire valley is one great orchard – when peaches are in season the roads are lined with producers selling perfect fruit at astonishingly low prices. The markets in the Rhône valley offer a dazzling display of color; south of Valence, the mood changes and the heat of the sun, the olives and herbs show that northern France is now far behind.

Although some local specialties, such as the tiny cheese-filled *ravioles* of Royans, are beginning to be exported, the characteristic peasant diet of chestnuts, potatoes, and pork has not inspired great gastronomic achievement. This should not imply that the Rhône valley is a culinary wasteland – far from it. Indeed, ever since la Pyramide restaurant in Vienne shot to fame as the birthplace of *nouvelle cuisine* under the guiding hand of Fernand Point, a growing number of creative young chefs have done honor to the region and the great wines of its vineyards.

La Beaugravière (R,H), rte N7, 84430 Mondragon. Tel: 90.40.82.54. Closed Sun pm and the last 2 weeks of Sep. MC V

Few people passing this modest inn on the busy N7 just north of Orange suspect that its cellar harbors the finest collection of Rhône wines in the region. No one has assembled as extensive and as carefully chosen a list as this establishment's young owner and chef, Guy Jullien. Logically enough, the *appellation* closest to Mondragon is the best represented of all: 67 different Châteauneuf-du-Pape wines, many 20 years old, are listed. However, the northern Rhône valley is by no means neglected with six growers in Hermitage supplying 20 different wines – all exceptional – and 22 different Côte Rôtie!

As if this were not enough, Guy

Jullien has another passion – truffles. The *département* of Vaucluse produces more truffles than Périgord and during the season M. Jullien has them delivered fresh to his door. He delights in experimenting and generously proposes truffles in a myriad of preparations from Oct–Apr.

Let the visitor be warned, however, that M. Jullien is often alone in the kitchen and he cannot always produce dishes as exceptional as his wines. One would be wise to order the simpler dishes à la carte or stick to the "little" menu which is astonishingly good value at less than 100 francs per person.

Above the restaurant there are six nicely furnished rooms. With M. Jullien's expert guidance, rewarding excursions to many of the surrounding vineyards are guaranteed.

Les ANGLES (30133)
Ermitage-Meissonnier (R,H), 32 av. de Verdun, rte de Nîmes. Tel: 90.25.41.68. One Michelin star. Closed Jan–Feb. AE DC V
Fine cooking in the *nouvelle* style with regional overtones. Excellent cellar with particularly interesting Châteauneuf-du-Pape. Beautiful garden.

APT (84400)
Luberon (R,H), 17 quai Léon-Sagy. Tel: 90.74.12.50. Closed Sun pm–Mon, and Dec 15–Jan 15. DC MC V
Reliable hotel and restaurant.

AVIGNON (84000)
Auberge de Cassagne (H,R), rte de Védene, 84130 le Pontet (Avignon-Nord exit from A7). Tel: 90.31.04.18. One Michelin star. AE MC V
Large, pretty rooms. Magnificent garden. Interesting *nouvelle* specialties and a good choice of Côtes du Rhône.

Auberge de France (R), 28 pl. de l'Horloge. Tel: 90.82.58.86. One Michelin star. Closed Wed pm–Thu, 3 weeks Jan and last 2 weeks Jun. AE DC MC V
In the heart of the old quarter of Avignon, this reasonably priced restaurant has been run by the same family since 1928. Classic *cuisine*.

Brunel (R), 46 r. Balance. Tel: 90.85.24.83. One Michelin star. Closed Sun–Mon (Sun only in summer), 3 weeks Feb, and 2 weeks Aug. AE MC V
Small, elegant, family-run restaurant with excellent Rhône wines.

Europe (H) and **Vieille Fontaine (R)**, 12 pl. Crillon. Tel: 90.82.66.92. AE DC MC V
A very comfortable hotel in a renovated 16th-century nobleman's residence. Attractive dining-room and courtyard.

Hiely Lucullus (R), 5 r. de la République. Tel: 90.86.17.07. Two Michelin stars. Reservations necessary. Closed Mon–Tue, 3 weeks Jan, and last 2 weeks Jun. AE MC V
Undoubtedly the best restaurant in Avignon, with both *nouvelle* and traditional dishes. Excellent cellar.

Hotel Mercure (H), r. de la Balance. Tel: 90.85.91.23. AE DC MC V
Modern, quiet, and in the center of town.

CARPENTRAS (84200)
Fiacre (H), 153 r. Vigne. Tel: 90.63.03.15. AE DC MC V
A small hotel in an 18th-century residence. Comfortable and quiet rooms.

L'Orangerie (R), 26 r. Duplessis. Tel: 90.67.27.23. Closed Sat lunch and Mon. AE DC MC V
Small restaurant with a good cellar and service. Seasonal dishes in the *nouvelle* style.

CAVAILLON (84300)
Nicolet (R), 13 pl. Gambetta. Tel: 90.78.01.56. One Michelin star. Closed Sun–Mon, 2 weeks in Feb and Jul. AE DC V
Alain Nicolet prepares interesting *nouvelle cuisine* dishes and there is a fine selection of regional wines.

CHATEAUNEUF-DU-PAPE (84230)
Host. du Château des Fines Roches (H,R), on private road 3km S on D17. Tel: 90.83.70.23. One Michelin star. Reservations recommended. MC V
Magnificent, luxurious 19th-century gothic château in the heart of the vineyards. *Nouvelle* specialties and, of course, wines from Châteauneuf.

CHATILLON-EN-DIOIS (26410)
Le Moulin (R). Tel: 75.21.10.73. Closed mid-Nov–Apr. MC V
Small restaurant with excellent selection of Côtes du Rhône and regional *cuisine*.

CONDRIEU (69420)
Hôtel Beau Rivage (H,R), 2 r. Beau Rivage. Tel: 74.59.52.24. Two Michelin stars. Closed Jan 5–Feb 15. AE DC MC V
Comfortable, old-fashioned rooms. The garden and terrace have wonderful views of the Rhône. The restaurant is a favorite in the northern Rhône with fine local wines. Relais et Châteaux.

GORDES (84220)
Les Bories (R,H), rte abbaye de Sénanque (2km N on D177). Tel: 90.72.00.51. One Michelin star. Reservations necessary. Closed Dec. No cards. Small inn, isolated among fields of thyme and lavender. Four rooms only. Fresh, seasonal *cuisine*.

GRANE (26400, Crest)
Giffon (H,R), pl de l'Eglise. Tel: 75.62.60.64. Closed Mon, and Nov 15–Dec 7. AE DC MC
Small, friendly hotel with good local *cuisine*.

MALATAVERNE (26780)
Domaine du Colombier (H,R). Tel: 75.51.65.86. One Michelin star. Closed Sun pm, Mon in winter, and Feb. AE DC V
Delightful establishment in the middle of a park with swimming pool.

MONTELIMAR (26200)
Parc Chabaud (H,R), 16 av. d'Aygu. Tel: 75.01.65.66. (H,R) closed Dec 25–Jan; (R) closed Sat–Sun. AE DC V
Luxurious and quiet hotel in a large garden in the center of town.

NYONS (26110)
Auberge du Vieux Village (H,R), Aubres (4km NE on D94). Tel: 75.26.12.89. (R) closed Wed lunch. AE DC MC V
Pleasant, secluded hotel with good views of the hills. Terrace and swimming pool.

ORANGE (84100)
Hôtel Arène (H), pl. de Langes. Tel: 90.34.10.95. Closed Nov–mid-Dec. AE DC MC V
Quiet hotel in the center of town.

Le Pigraillet (R), chemin de la Colline St-Eutrope. Tel: 75.84.60.09. Closed Sun pm–Mon and Dec–Feb. One Michelin star. AE DC
Pleasant restaurant overlooking Orange.

PONT-DE-L'ISERE (26600, Tain l'Hermitage)
Chabran (R,H), 29 av. du 45ème Parallèle. Tel: 75.84.60.09. Two Michelin stars. MC V
Family-run establishment and charmingly decorated. Good, creative cooking with some regional specialties. Excellent cellar. Relais et Châteaux.

ROCHEGUDE (26790)
Château de Rochegude (H,R). Tel: 75.04.81.88. (H/R) closed Jan–Mar. (R) closed Tue and Wed lunch in winter. AE DC MC V

The magnificent château has luxurious rooms, a garden, pool and tennis courts, all set in a beautiful park. Relais et Châteaux.

ROQUEMAURE (30150)
Château de Cubières (H,R), rte d'Avignon. Tel: (H) 66.82.64.28 and (R) 66.82.89.33. (R) closed Nov 15–30, and Feb–Mar Sun pm–Tue.
A magnificent 18th-century château in a garden. Regional dishes and good cellar. Popular with local winemakers.

SEGURET (84110, Vaison-la-Romaine)
La Table du Comtat (R,H). Tel: 90.46.91.49. One Michelin star. V
Beautiful surroundings and superb views of the vineyards. Good classic *cuisine*.

TAIN-L'HERMITAGE (26600)
Reynaud (R), 82 av. Pr. Roosevelt. Tel: 75.07.22.10. Closed Sun pm–Mon, and Jan. AE DC V
The best restaurant in Tain lies on the banks of the Rhône.

VALENCE (26000)
Pic (R,H), 285 av. Victor-Hugo. Tel: 75.44.15.32. Three Michelin stars. Reservations recommended on Sun. Closed 10 days in Feb and Aug. AE DC
One of France's best chefs, Jacques Pic, prepares *nouvelle cuisine* as it should be. Excellent wine list. A few comfortable rooms available, but reserve well in advance. Relais et Châteaux.

VIENNE (38200)
Magnard (R), 45 cours Brillier. Tel: 74.85.10.43. One Michelin star. Reservations recommended on Sun. Closed Tue pm–Wed, and 1 week in Feb. AE DC V
Pleasant restaurant with a superb collection of Hermitage wines.

La Pyramide (R), 14 bd Fernand-Point. Tel: 74.53.01.96. Two Michelin stars. Reservations recommended. AE DC MC
Once a must and now a monument, Fernand Point's restaurant is now run by Yves Berrier. This is where *nouvelle cuisine* is said to have begun. A sentimental favorite that still rates two Michelin stars.

SAVOIE

Savoie became French only in 1860 when, along with Nice, it was ceded by Italy. Despite its recent arrival the region is very French in character. Savoie has been making wine for centuries, though until recently there were few foreign outlets for it and most of it is consumed in the local ski resorts. Although there are some attractive towns such as Annecy and Chambéry, it is mostly a region of small villages and wooden houses set against the snow-capped splendor of the Alps.

The Wines of Savoie

The wines of Savoie can be either red, white, rosé, or sparkling, but the region is best known for its crisp whites, many of which are made from the local Jacquère grape. Vin de Savoie and Roussette de Savoie are regional *appellations* for wines made throughout the area. Crépy, on the shores of Lac Léman, and Seyssel on the Rhône are the other *appellations*. Certain villages can add their names to the *appellation* Vin de Savoie; among these are Chignin, Arbin, Cruet, Apremont, Montmélian, and the area of Abymes. The name of the grape variety may also appear on the label. To the west in the *département* of Ain is the VDQS Vin du Bugey. The wines are similar in style to their more mountainous neighbors in Savoie.

Savoie winemakers also produce a fair quantity of champagne-method dry sparkling wine. As for the reds, some Pinot Noir is grown but the most common varieties are Gamay and the indigenous Mondeuse which can produce formidable wines that require some aging to develop fully.

Recommended Route

From Chambéry to Geneva: 130km

The mountain climate of Savoie can prove as difficult to the visitor as to the *vigneron*. Most people visit the region during the winter months in order to ski in France's top resorts but the best time to tour the vineyards is late in the fall when days are warm, nights are cool and the weather is generally dry.

Geneva, although over the border in Switzerland, has been included here because of its proximity, its good communications by air and road and its wide choice of hotels and restaurants to suit all tastes.

The Itinerary:

From **Chambéry**, the historic Savoyard capital, take D201 south to **le Gaz**, then continue straight ahead on D12 to **St André** through the *appellations* of Apremont and Abymes. From St André take D12 and N90 to **les Marches**, where you turn right on D201 to **Montmélian**; from Montmélian, take N6 back toward Chambéry through the Chignin and **St Jeoire-Prieuré** vineyards. These villages south of Chambéry contain many good small winemakers.

Alternatively, if you have time, continue on D201 from Montmélian to see the vineyards of **Cruet** and **St Jean-de-la-Porte** before turning back toward Chambéry. Leave **Chambéry** north on N201, then, soon after the intersection with the autoroute, bear left on N504 to **le Bourget-du-Lac**. N54 goes through the Col du Chat tunnel which pierces the mountains separating Lac du Bourget from the Rhône valley to the west. On emerging from the tunnel, turn right on D210a, which winds through the hills and the wine villages of **Billième**, where it becomes D210, and **Jongieux**. At the junction with D921, turn right toward **Lucey**; from here a detour can be made via D37A and D107 to **Belley**, capital of the VDQS Vin du Bugey *appellation*. From Lucey continue on D921 until the junction with D904. Turn right to go to **Ruffieux**, where you turn left on D991 to **Seyssel** which has its own *appellation*. From Seyssel, D992 leads to **Frangy**, where the vineyards virtually stop and there is a choice of routes.

It is a considerable distance to the next major production area of Savoie wines on the southern shore of Lac Léman, and those pressed for time should turn left at the junction with N508 to pick up the autoroute A40 to Geneva at junction 11. Leave the autoroute at junction 14 and take N206 through **Annemasse** to **Machilly**.

The longer, more scenic, route continues on N508 from Frangy to the beautiful town of **Annecy**. It then joins A41 heading north toward Geneva. Leave the autoroute at the intersection with N203 and follow the signs east to **Bonneville**. Go into town and turn left on N205 toward Geneva. At Findrol turn right to pick up N503 to **Bonne**, then left on D903 and follow the signs to **Annemasse** and thence to **Machilly**. From Machilly, N206 leads north-west to **Douvaine** through the *appellation* of Crépy south of Douvaine around **Loisin** and **Ballaison**. Turn left on N5 to **Geneva**. Alternatively, you can make a detour to visit the vineyards of **Ripaille** near **Thonon-les-Bains** by continuing on N903 from Machilly to Thonon.

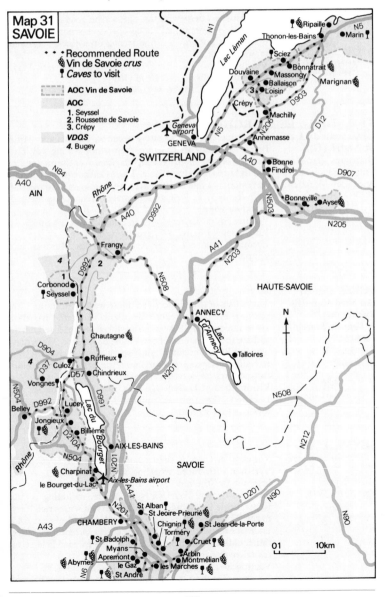

Caves and Vineyards to Visit

Until the 1960s, the production of wines in Savoie was experiencing a steady decline. Since then a small reversal has occurred, so that there are now about 1500 hectares of vineyards scattered over the region. Individual small estates are more important than co-operatives and there is a considerable diversity of methods and grape varieties.

APREMONT, map 31

Le Vigneron Savoyard (C), Société Co-opérative Vinicole, Apremont, 73190 Challes-lès-Eaux.
Tel: 79.28.33.23.

Properties are usually small in Savoie and growers often lack the funds needed for up-to-date equipment. One solution to this problem is the co-operative; this one was formed by several local growers in 1968 and vinifies grapes from a total of 40 hectares. The quality of both their red and white wines is high. The Apremont and Abymes are both whites made from the Jacquère, a traditional grape of the region. They also make a little Chardonnay, called locally Ste Marie. The red Mondeuse is a hefty wine that ages well in good vintages and there is some Gamay too. The co-operative is more utilitarian than smart but enjoys a fine setting on a thickly forested mountainside.
Visiting hours: Tue–Sat 8–12, 2–6; closed 1st week May, hols and usually at harvest in Oct.
Location: On D201 to Myans.

ST ANDRE-LES-MARCHES, map 31

Le Caveau du Lac St André (G), Domaines Vignes et Vins de Savoie, St André-lès-Marches, 73800 Montmélian.
Tel: 79.28.13.32. and 79.28.05.08.

The property is small, just 4 hectares, but M. and Mme Perret have gone about selling their wines in a big way. The *cave* and tasting room have superb views over the mountains and light snacks are available. Their Coteaux de la Redoute Apremont is a fine white. There is a Gamay in both red and rosé versions, as well as a pleasant, champagne-method sparkling wine.
Visiting hours: Easter–Jul 14 and Sep 15–Dec 20, Sun 3–7; Jul 15–Sep 14 daily, 3–7; groups by appt.
Location: Above Lac St André from les Marches and signposted.

SCIEZ, map 31

Bernard Canelli-Suchet (G), la Tour de Marignan, 74140 Sciez.
Tel: 50.72.70.30. and 50.72.60.05.

The cellars of this old fortified house were built in the 11th century. The 5 hectares of vines, all planted with Chasselas, are in the gentle hills overlooking the shores of Lac Léman and are the sole source of the Vin de Savoie *cru*, Marignan. The Vin Blanc Perlant, a lightly sparkling wine, is made by a technique perfected by the monks of the local abbey who used these cellars for several centuries.
Visiting hours: Daily 9–12, 2–7; by appt for groups.
Location: 1km from *mairie*; the domaine's tall medieval tower is easy to find.

SEYSSEL, map 31

Varichon et Clerc (G), les Séchallets, 01420 Seyssel.
Tel: 50.59.23.15.

Varichon et Clerc is the leading producer of Seyssel. M. Varichon introduced sparkling wine to the region at the beginning of the century. A Burgundian, Henri Gabet, is now the owner. Four wines are made, including a still Roussette de Seyssel aged in oak barrels and with a rich leafy flavor. Their best sparkling wine is a Seyssel Mousseux sold under the name Royal Seyssel. The cellars and equipment are rather old-fashioned, but M. Gabet's new mission in life is to revitalize the company.
Visiting hours: Sep–Jul Tue–Fri, 10–11.30, 3–4.30.
Location: On the Ain side of the village, over the new bridge.

Further *Caves* and Vineyards to Visit

CHIGNIN, map 31
Les Fils de René Quenard (G/M), les Tours, Chignin, 73800 Montmélian. Tel: 79.28.01.15. and 79.28.13.77. Visiting hours: Daily 8–12, 2–7 by appt.
Les Fils René Quénard – the family name is quite common in the village of Chignin – make white Chignin from two vineyards, Coteau de Mont-Ronjoux and Coteau de la Maréchale, and Chignin-Bergeron, a specialty of the village. The Bergeron grape is the same as the Roussanne of the Rhône valley.

Coteaux les Châteaux (G), les Tours, le Villard, Chignin, 73800 Montmélian. Tel: 79.28.01.46. Visiting hours: Mon–Sat 8–12, 2–6 by appt; closed during harvest in Oct.
Raymond Quénard has 7 hectares of vines, which is large by Savoie standards, and grows several varieties to make a good range of wines. His property is at the foot of several ruined towers that have survived from a medieval castle. He makes a fine Chignin-Bergeron, as well as white Jacquère and red Gamay and Mondeuse. These are all fruity, fresh wines that make for very pleasant drinking.

CRUET, map 31
Domaine de l'Idylle (G), Cruet, 73800 Montmélian. Tel: 79.84.30.58. Visiting hours: During school hols, Mon and Fri–Sat, 8–12, 2–6.30; during term time, Mon–Sat 8–12, 2–6.30; appt for groups of 10 or more.
The Tiollier brothers make both white and red wines on their 10-hectare property which lies in the shadow of the vast ridge above Montmélian. They have Jacquère and Roussette for the *cru* Cruet, as well as Gamay and Mondeuse.

JONGIEUX, map 31
Cave de Barcontian (G), Jongieux, 73170 Yenne. Tel: 79.36.82.08. Visiting hours: Daily 12–2; appt preferred.
Claudius and Jacques Barlet, who have 10 hectares of vines, are proudest of their rare *cru*, Roussette de Marestel. It is a rich wine and ages better than most Savoie wines. The *appellation* Roussette de Savoie covers the whole region and can be made from Chardonnay as well as from Roussette. The *crus* can be made only from Roussette. The Barlets also produce a lively white Jacquère and red Gamay, Mondeuse and Pinot Noir.

Les MARCHES, map 31
Domaine de la Violette (G), les Marches, 73800 Montmélian. Tel: 79.28.13.30. Visiting hours: Mon–Sat 8–12, 2–6; appt preferred.
The 7.5-hectare property, owned by Daniel Fustinoni, produces Abymes and Apremont as well as Roussette de Savoie, a red Mondeuse, and red and rosé Gamay.

MARIN, map 31
Claude Delalex (G), Marin, 74200 Thonon-les-Bains. Tel: 50.71.45.82. Visiting hours: By appt; closed 1st week Sep.
Claude Delalex is the principal producer of the small village of Marin, which is to become a *cru* of the Vin de Savoie *appellation* in 1988. His 5 hectares of vines are on steep slopes looking down on Lac Léman. Chasselas is the grape variety, giving a fresh fruity wine that nicely accompanies the fish from the lake.

RIPAILLE, map 31
G.F.A. Ripaille (G/M), Domaine du Château de Ripaille, 74200 Thonon-les-Bains. Tel: 50 71.75.12. Visiting hours: By appt.
Once a royal hunting lodge and Carthusian monastery, the 15th-century Château de Ripaille is surrounded by vineyards on one side and a magnificent wooded park and arboretum descending to the shores of Lac Léman on the other. Vines have prospered at Ripaille since Gallo-Roman times due to the gravelly soil and the milder climate of its lakeside situation; the Chasselas grapes make an excellent Vin de Savoie.

RUFFIEUX, map 31
Cave Co-opérative de Chautagne (C), Ruffieux, 73310 Chindrieux. Tel: 79.54.27.12. Visiting hours: Tue–Fri 2–6; Sat 8–12, 2–5; also Easter–harvest, Sun–Mon and hols, 9–12, 2–6.
The co-operative is built into a mountainside overlooking the marshy valley of the Rhône a few kilometers north of Lac du Bourget. Chautagne, unlike most Savoie *crus*, has a reputation for its red wines, made from Gamay, Pinot Noir and Mondeuse, either as separate varietal wines or blended to make le Chautagnard. Chautagne Blanc is a flowery wine made either from Jacquère or, unusually, Aligoté.

ST ANDRE-LES-MARCHES, map 31

Domaine les Rocailles (G/M), St Andrè-les-Marches, 73800 Montmélian. Tel: 79.28.14.50. Visiting hours: By appt. The domaine of 14 hectares, mostly within the *cru* of Apremont, produces a white Apremont of great finesse with a flavor of bitter almonds. The owner, Pierre Boniface, is one of the more dynamic growers in the region and is experimenting with aging his Mondeuse in oak barrels bought from Château Clarke in the Médoc.

ST ALBAN-LEYSSE, map 31

Château Monterminod (G), 73230 St Alban. Tel: 79.33.01.24. Visiting hours: By appt.

Château Monterminod is the only producer of the little-known *cru* Roussette de Monterminod, a white wine with a delicious hint of vanilla. A red wine is also made from Mondeuse, with enough tannin and fruit to develop with moderate aging.

ST BALDOPH, map 31

Le Cellier des Chênes (G), 616 rte d'Apremont, 73190 St Baldoph. Tel: 79.28.36.90. Visiting hours: Fri pm and Sat–Sun; appt for groups.

This small estate is owned by Gilbert Blanc, who makes both Apremont and Abymes as well as Gamay. The wines are light and fruity, and characteristic of the region.

TORMERY, map 31

André et Michel Quénard (G), Tormèry, Chignin, 73800 Montmélian. Tel: 79.28.12.75. Visiting hours: By appt. The Quénard family have 15 hectares of vines from which they produce a wide range of wines, including Chignin-Bergeron, Gamay and a white Chignin Coteaux de Tormèry with a bouquet of vanilla and hazelnuts.

VONGNES, map 31

Maison Eugène Monin et Fils (G), Vongnes, 01350 Culoz. Tel: 79.87.92.33. Visiting hours: Daily 8–12, 2–7; by appt for groups.

Monin are the principal producers of the little-known VDQS Vin du Bugey, just west of the Rhône over the border in the *département* of Ain. The family have 14 hectares planted with Chardonnay and Roussette for still white wines, as well as Jacquère, Aligoté and Molette for sparkling wines. Their best red wine, from Mondeuse, is a solid peppery wine which is kept in cement vats (wooden barrels have been abandoned here). They also have some Gamay and Pinot Noir.

Sights

Set against the backdrop of the Alps, Savoie is full of stunning scenery with lush valleys and mountain meadows, and the uncrowded roads make for leisurely traveling. There are several elegant towns which have a Victorian style and charm.

AIX-LES-BAINS

On the shores of **Lac du Bourget**, this is a perfect place for winter or summer vacations. Its great spa in the center of the town was once the site of Roman baths. The **Musée du Docteur Faure** has interesting collections, including Impressionist paintings and memorabilia of the poet Lamartine.

ANNECY

One of the most beautiful towns in Savoie, Annecy is beside a large lake surrounded by mountains. It has a carefully restored old town built on the banks of narrow canals, as well as a thriving modern center with many interesting shops and markets.

CHAMBERY

An elegant city with a well-preserved center, Chambéry was Savoie's capital when it was a separate kingdom. Visitors should explore the maze of passageways around the **r. Croix-d'Or** and admire the unusual fountain ornamented with the heads and forequarters of four elephants. The **Musée Savoisien** has a fine collection.

THONON-LES-BAINS

This is another spa town set high above Lac Léman. There are good views from **pl. du Château**. Nearby is a small port with a steamer service to various towns across and along the lake. A Fête du Petit Vin Blanc de Marin is held in mid-Sep.

Hotels, Restaurants and Where to Buy Wine

Savoie has some claims to gastronomic fame: lake fish, walnuts from around Grenoble, a little known truffle industry and, of course, the famous *gratin savoyard*. As with many mountainous regions there are excellent cheeses to be had; the fruity, hard Beaufort and the soft, creamy Reblochon are two of the best known.

AIX-LES-BAINS (73100)
Lille (R,H), Grand Port, 73100 Aix-les-Bains (3km NW by D991). Tel: 79.35.04.22. AE DC MC V
Regional specialties. Good-value menus.

Le Manoir (H,R), 37 r. Georges-1er. Tel: 79.61.44.00. DC MC V
Luxurious hotel with comfortable rooms. The restaurant is unexceptional.

ANNECY (74000)
Auberge de l'Eridan (R), 7 av. de Chavoires, Petit Port. Tel: 50.66.22.04. Two Michelin stars. Closed Wed, Sun pm, and 2 weeks mid-Aug. AE DC MC V
On the shores of Lac d'Annecy. *Nouvelle* specialties; consistently rated the best restaurant in Annecy, if not the region.

BONNATRAIT (74140, Douvaine)
Hôtellerie Château de Coudrée (H,R), Tel: 50.72.62.33. Closed Nov–Mar. AE DC MC V
A sumptuous medieval castle bordering Lac Léman. Heated swimming pool, tennis courts and private beach.

BONNEVILLE (74130)
Sapeur (H) and **Gill la Vivandière (R)**, pl. de l'Hôtel de Ville. Tel: 50.97.20.68. One Michelin star. AE DC V
Modern, comfortable hotel. *Nouvelle* specialties and regional wines.

Le BOURGET-DU-LAC (73370)
Bâteau Ivre (R). Tel: 79.25.02.66. Two Michelin stars. AE DC MC V
Nouvelle cuisine served in an elegant 17th-century dining-room. Good service.

Ombremont (H,R), 2km N by N504. Tel: 79.25.00.23. One Michelin star. AE DC MC V
Spectacular view of the lake and mountains. Luxurious rooms, exquisite dining-room and heated swimming pool.

CHAMBERY (73000)
La Cave Jeandet (W), 11 pl. de l'Hôtel de Ville. Tel: 79.85.61.65. AE MC V
A good selection of Savoie wines.

Roubatcheff (R), 6 r. du Théâtre. Tel: 79.33.24.91. One Michelin star. Reservations necessary. Closed mid-Jul–mid-Aug. AE DC MC V
Intimate and elegant ambience. Good-value menus.

GENEVA (SWITZERLAND)
Noga Hilton (H) and **le Cygne (R)**, 19 quai Mont Blanc, 1201 Geneva. Tel: (022) 31.98.11. Two Michelin stars. AE DC MC V
This elegant and modern complex with a view of Lac Léman has four restaurants; the most interesting is le Cygne, considered by many to be the best restaurant in Geneva. The *cuisine* is resolutely *nouvelle* and menus are moderately priced.

Le Richemond (H) and **le Gentilhomme (R)**, jardin Brunswick, 1201 Geneva. Tel: (022) 31.14.00. One Michelin star. AE DC MC V
Luxurious hotel with period furniture in the rooms and superb service. *Nouvelle* specialties.

MASSONGY (74140, Douvaine)
Auberge Gourmande (R). Tel: 50.94.16.97. AE DC MC V.
Friendly service with good classic *cuisine* and interesting wine list.

TALLOIRES (74290, Veyrier-du-Lac)
Auberge du Père Bise (R,H), rte du Port. Tel: 50.60.72.01. Three Michelin stars. Reservations recommended. Closed mid-Dec–mid-Feb; also 2 weeks end Apr. AE DC MC V
Beautifully situated, this restaurant was once ranked one of the best in France. Although it has lost some of its former prestige, it remains one of the finest in the region. *Nouvelle* specialties.

THONON-LES-BAINS (74200)
Le Prieuré (R), 68 Grand-Rue. Tel: 50.71.31.89. One Michelin star. Closed Sun pm and Mon. AE DC MC V
Nouvelle cuisine served in an 18th-century-style dining-room.

THE SOUTH-WEST

The South-West of France is a large area stretching from Bordeaux in the north to the Pyrenees and the Spanish border in the south; in the east of the region the Lot, the Tarn and the Aveyron rivers make their tortuous way westward through dramatic scenery. This region of rivers and green valleys once had a flourishing prehistoric civilization, shown by the numerous cave dwellings in the foothills of the Pyrenees and in the valleys of the Vézère and the Lot. When Caesar called this province *Aquitania* or "land of waters" he summed up one of its most striking features. Almost all the important towns in the South-West were inland ports at one time in their history and the great rivers, the Dordogne, the Garonne and their numerous tributaries, have made this a fertile region coveted by conquerors from an early date. Not only did the Romans leave their mark but the English, who ruled here for over 300 years in the Middle Ages, built many of the region's *bastides* or fortified towns as a means of defending their territorial gains.

Today, the South-West has been conquered by invading hordes that even the *bastides* cannot resist – tourists. After being considered a backwater for many centuries, the region has become a popular corner of rural France for Parisians and others (including many English) in search of an idyllic retreat. This upsurge of interest in the region, and particularly in its wines and *cuisine*, has helped preserve many local industries; the production of *foie gras* and *confit*, in particular, has soared in recent years and medieval hill villages such as Cordes, near Albi, have been restored and are now prosperous once more.

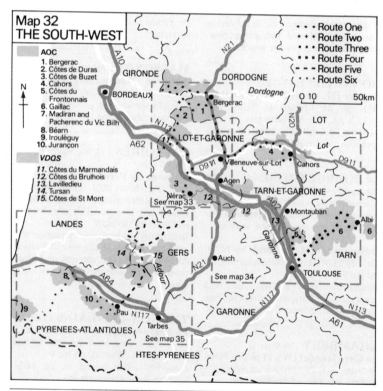

Map 32
THE SOUTH-WEST

	Route One
	Route Two
	Route Three
	Route Four
	Route Five
	Route Six

AOC
1. Bergerac
2. Côtes de Duras
3. Côtes de Buzet
4. Cahors
5. Côtes du Frontonnais
6. Gaillac
7. Madiran and Pacherenc du Vic Bilh
8. Béarn
9. Irouléguy
10. Jurançon

VDQS
11. Côtes du Marmandais
12. Côtes du Brulhois
13. Lavilledieu
14. Tursan
15. Côtes de St Mont

GIRONDE
DORDOGNE
BORDEAUX
Bergerac
Dordogne
LOT
LOT-ET-GARONNE
Villeneuve-sur-Lot
Cahors
Lot
Agen
TARN-ET-GARONNE
Nérac
See map 33
Montauban
Albi
LANDES
GERS
Auch
TARN
See map 34
TOULOUSE
Adour
Pau
Tarbes
GARONNE
PYRENEES-ATLANTIQUES
See map 35
HTES-PYRENEES

The Wines of the South-West

The South-West has some of the most interesting regional wines of France. Many of the old, respected but almost forgotten *appellations* are being revived, and several new exciting and original wines are to be found. Soils and microclimates in the region vary enormously, so much so that it is difficult to talk of one viticultural style. The climate is more temperate, and certainly less rainy than in the north of France, but variations in altitude and exposure to wind and sun fundamentally mark each wine. The techniques used by the growers are just as diversified. There are many grape varieties in the region; some are indigenous and found hardly anywhere else, and have wonderful names, such as Len de l'Elh, Baroque and Négrette.

A new spirit of enterprise and initiative has taken root in the South-West and has begun to show interesting results. Young growers and winemakers have taken a new look at the local traditions and have begun to adapt them to fit modern requirements, producing wines that are far more than rustic cousins to those of Bordeaux. By defending a certain *goût de terroir*, growers in the most famous *appellations* have regained much of the prestige their wines enjoyed in the past; many have not forgotten that as recently as the 19th century, some South-West wines (Jurançon, Monbazillac and Buzet) were cited just after the wines of Burgundy, Bordeaux, Hermitage and Champagne in a list of the finest in France.

Since the phylloxera plague in the late 19th century when many of the region's great vineyards disappeared, the *vignerons* of the South-West have had to fight an uphill battle. Some vineyards have come back to life in recent years, thanks to their having been granted *appellation* status and to the energy of some co-operatives in promoting the regional wines. Today, nearly every *appellation* can boast several growers making excellent wines.

Visiting the Vineyards

Such a large region necessarily has as many types of landscape and people as it does wine. As you drive through the South-West both the villages and the landscape are constantly changing: dense forests give way to heavily cultivated river valleys and old fortresses and villages stand high up on the hills keeping watch.

Route One

The Bergerac *appellations*, from Bergerac to St Michel-de-Montaigne and back: 130km

The market town of Bergerac, on the river Dordogne less than 70km east of St Emilion, would rather be called the gateway to Périgord than the outer limits of the Bordeaux region. The cluster of *appellations* around Bergerac have their own personality and some, like the sweet wine of Monbazillac, were once considered superior to their now more prestigious neighbors in Bordeaux.

The overall regional *appellation* Bergerac in fact covers 11 separate *appellations* for a wide range of wines. Bergerac reds and rosés, from Merlot, Cabernet Sauvignon and Cabernet Franc, come from the vineyards along the banks of the Dordogne and the reds can be exciting. Since the early 1970s much of the area has been changing over to red wines from the more unfashionable sweet wines which used to predominate. Bergerac Sec, a dry white, is made mainly from Sauvignon and Sémillon. Pécharmant from the right bank of the Dordogne is a sturdy red wine that ages well and the best red in the region. Monbazillac is a good dessert wine, which, when well made, has a characteristic scent of honey and flowers. Montravel, just 10km east of St Emilion, is a white wine, which can be dry, semi-sweet or sweet. Production of Rosette, a soft, semi-sweet wine from north of Bergerac, has now ceased.

The Itinerary:

Leave **Bergerac** on D32, r. du Pont St Jean, following the signs for **Prigonrieux**; do not go into the centre of Prigonrieux but continue on D32 through orchards, vineyards, and pastures to **le Fleix**. In le Fleix, turn left toward Port-Ste Foy, right onto D32 toward Villefranche-de-Lonchat, then almost immediately left again on a small country road D32e through the vineyards. From the top of the large, vine-covered plateau, there is a lovely view of the Dordogne valley.

Drive through **Fougueyrolles**, following the signs for Vélines and watching for a righthand turnoff to **Nastringues**, a very pretty town with old farmhouses amid the vineyards. In Nastringues go straight across the crossroads onto V4 which leads to **Vélines**.

After Nastringues the road twists and turns, offering some beautiful views. Continue into Vélines, turn right toward Pessac, then, at the stop sign, turn right again, following the signs indicating the *Route des vins* and le Soureau. Continue on the *Route des vins*, bearing right at the fork. In the next small village, turn right at the church toward Villefranche-de-Lonchat (although no signs indicate it, this is **Montcaret**, once the site of a large Gallo-Roman city). Drive to the top of the hill, and turn left onto V9 heading toward **St Michel-de-Montaigne**. From there, turn left toward **Lamothe-Montravel** on D9, and there, left again on D936 to the busy market town of **Ste Foy-la-Grande**, driving through an area rich in Gallo-Roman remains.

Cross the Dordogne into Ste Foy-la-Grande; just before leaving town, still on D936, watch for a righthand turnoff on av. Foch to D18 to Eymet and Monbazillac. This is a beautiful drive through vineyards, orchards and woods. Watch for a left turn into **Razac-de-Saussignac**. Drive toward the church, then follow the signs to **Saussignac**; from there, turn right onto D4 toward Couture, then left at the intersection with D4e into **Monestier**. Follow the signs toward Loubès-Bernac, watching for a lefthand turnoff to **Thénac** – the sign is only visible once the corner has been turned. After Thénac, bear right at the fork onto an unmarked road that leads to **Sigoulès**. At the T-junction, turn left onto D17, following the signs to Sigoulès, then to **Pomport** through the vineyards.

Continue on D17 toward Bergerac; turn left on D933, then right onto D107, following the signs left on D14e for the 16th-century Château de Monbazillac, owned by the local wine co-operative and which can be visited. Drive into **Monbazillac**, turn right on D13 toward Ribagnac, then left onto C2 following the signs for **Colombier**, past Château la Jaubertie. At the intersection with N21 turn left to return to **Bergerac** (from the road there is a beautiful view of Château de Monbazillac high on a hill to the left), or turn right to drive to Villeneuve-sur-Lot and explore the Cahors vineyards.

Route Two

Côtes de Duras, Côtes du Marmandais and Côtes de Buzet, from Ste Foy-la-Grande to Nérac: 110km

The small *appellation* of the Côtes de Duras is in a region with many independent growers who sell much of their wines to merchants. Sixty per cent of the wine is white, made from the Sauvignon grape, though more and more red is being produced from a blend of Cabernet Sauvignon, Cabernet Franc, Malbec and Merlot; both whites and reds are slowly gaining a reputation outside the area and are excellent value for money.

Growers in the Côtes du Marmandais, a high-ranking VDQS, would like to see their wines as well distributed and appreciated as those of Buzet, its neighbor to the south – they have made impressive progress and production has quadrupled since the late 1970s. These wines, which can be either red, white or rosé, are excellent value. For most French people, however, Marmande is more famous for another product – its tomatoes, a special variety considered by many to be the best in France.

Until the beginning of the 20th century and the delimitation of Bordeaux wines within the *département* of the Gironde, the wines from the Côtes de Buzet were sold as Bordeaux. Thereafter, like other South-West wines, they had to make a name for themselves and have, indeed, succeeded. Côtes de Buzet wines, red, white and rosé, became classified as AOC in 1970. Although there are a few individual growers, the co-operative is the largest and most dynamic producer in the *appellation*.

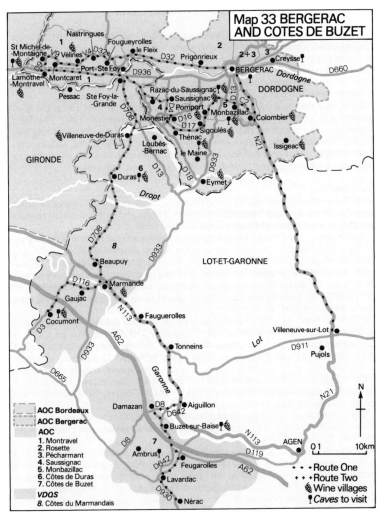

Map 33 BERGERAC AND COTES DE BUZET

The Itinerary:

From **Ste Foy-la-Grande** head south on D708. Just before **Villeneuve-de-Duras** the road passes out of the Gironde into the Lot-et-Garonne *département* and the beginning of the Côtes de Duras. Vineyards line the road all the way to **Duras**, an old town dominated by an imposing château. Continue south on D708 through the Marmandais vineyards to **Marmande**, a market town on a hill overlooking the Garonne. Drive toward *Centre Ville* and then follow the signs for N113 and Tonneins. You can make a detour from Marmande to Cocumont, where the best known wines of the Côtes du Marmandais are made. Turn left on D933 toward Casteljaloux, then turn off through **Gaujac** on D116 and then left to **Cocumont** on D3.

Back on the main route continue from Marmande on N113 to **Tonneins** and **Aiguillon**. From Aiguillon head west on D642 and D8 to Damazan. Just before the canal outside Damazan turn left onto a small road and continue to the junction with D642 where you turn right for **Buzet-sur-Baise**. Between Damazan and Buzet you pass through the Côtes de Buzet vineyards. Continue on D642 through Buzet, over the autoroute and turn left on D119 to **Feugarolles**. Leave Feugarolles south on D930 to **Lavardac**, passing between vineyards on the way. After Lavardac continue on D930 to **Nérac**, a pretty town and a former Huguenot citadel. From Nérac you can drive north-east to Agen and Villeneuve-sur-Lot to the Cahors and Gaillac vineyards.

Route Three

Cahors, from Villeneuve-sur-Lot to Cahors: 100km

This route includes some of the most tortuous driving in the South-West but the wines (and the views of the Lot valley) are well worth the effort. Vines were planted in the area as long ago as the first century AD and the wines they yield have long enjoyed an outstanding reputation. A severe frost in 1956 very nearly ended wine-making in the region; there has been much replanting since then and most of the vineyards are west of the medieval town of Cahors on the slopes above the river Lot.

Cahors is a dark and powerful wine generally meant to be aged and is the most exciting of the South-West wines; it was granted AOC status in 1971. The finest Cahors are well-structured, rich wines, often tannic when young but maturing into fine bottles which are the pride of many cellars in and out of the region. Cahors must contain at least 70 per cent Auxerrois (known in Bordeaux as Malbec), the rest being made up of varying proportions of Merlot, Tannat and Jurançon.

The Itinerary:
Leave **Villeneuve-sur-Lot**, following the signs to Cahors on D911 through **Fumel** along the Lot valley. After **Soturac** the vineyards begin and signs inform the traveler that this is the country of Quercy lamb and the wine of Cahors.

Continue on D911 through **Duravel**, which has beautiful old yellow stone houses, to **Puy-l'Evêque**, then bear right, downhill into town and over the bridge, following the signs indicating Tournon. Across the Lot, turn first left over the bridge on D44 and follow the signs to **Floressas** on a bumpy, twisting road that climbs up to the top of a plateau. At the *mairie* in the center of Floressas, turn left toward **Grézels**. The vineyards on the surrounding hills have an almost unearthly appearance with their neat rows and reddish earth amid the trees.

Follow the signs to Grézels, turning right on D8, then on to **Lagardelle** through a beautiful valley with vines on all sides. From Lagardelle continue on D237 to **Pescadoires**, then follow the signs to **Prayssac**. Cross the bridge back over the Lot and turn right through Prayssac on D911 to **Castelfranc**. Dolmens are scattered throughout this area and there are panoramic views of the vineyards. In Castelfranc, follow the signs on D9 to **Luzech**, with its Roman keep. Bear left and drive through town, following the signs for Douelle and Cahors on D8. Cross the Lot again, then turn left on D23 to **Parnac**.

The views along this road are spectacular, with vines in the valley extending right up to the cliffs. At the crossroads, turn right and continue on to Cahors. At the stop sign, turn left, following D8 to **Douelle**.

In Douelle turn right onto D12 in the direction of Villesèque; watch for a left-hand turnoff toward **Flottes** on a winding road with a magnificent view of the hills. There are fewer vineyards on the *causse*, as this high plateau is called, than down in the valley. Continue through Flottes to the junction with D27. Turn right and then bear left into **Trespoux-Rassiels**. Continue left through the village, then, on the outskirts, watch for a steep right turn down into the valley. At the T-junction turn left on D653, then left onto N20 which takes you to **Cahors**, an elegant medieval town with a famous fortified bridge, the Pont Valentré.

Route Four

The Gaillac vineyards, from Albi to Toulouse: 120km

Gaillac is the wine of Albi, a prosperous and bustling city and the home of Toulouse-Lautrec. Not only is this the second largest wine-making region in the South-West after Bergerac, but it also has the distinction of being famous for its sparkling wine long before Champagne (white Gaillac has a natural tendency to be *pétillant* or sparkling and was sought after and praised for this very reason). The white Gaillac wines, whether still or sparkling, are more interesting generally than the reds. The sparkling wines are still made according to the *méthode Gaillaçoise* which relies entirely on the natural sugar of the grapes to provoke bottle fermentation.

The Côtes du Frontonnais is a small *appellation* north of Toulouse. These delicious red and rosé wines are made mainly from a local grape, the Négrette, which is found almost exclusively between Albi and Toulouse.

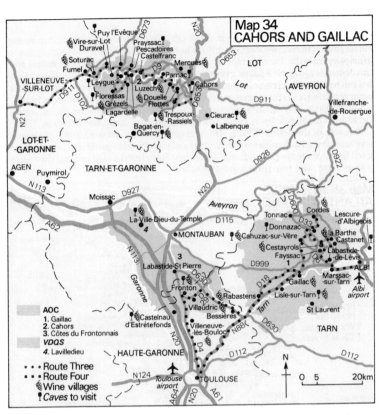

Map 34
CAHORS AND GAILLAC

AOC
1. Gaillac
2. Cahors
3. Côtes du Frontonnais

VDQS
4. Lavilledieu

• • • Route Three
• • • Route Four
🍇 Wine villages
❢ Caves to visit

N

0   5   20km

The Itinerary:

Leave Albi in the direction of Toulouse on N88. In **Marssac** cross the river, then watch for a right turn indicating the Caves Co-opératives de Labastide. As you approach **Labastide** either turn off to go into the town, or continue to **Fayssac** on D6 through a beautiful valley and large areas of vines. On the hill approaching Fayssac, turn right, away from Gaillac, and on turning the corner a sign indicates that this is D17. At the stop sign, continue straight ahead, following the signs to **Castanet**. The road rises and falls passing low, gnarled vines and stone houses with steep roofs. Bear right after the sign indicating the Domaine de Moussens, then bear left and take the next left into Castanet. Drive around the church and follow the signs to **la Barthe** on a small road that winds through woods and vines. At the T-junction, turn right and fork left almost immediately, then left again onto D3 in the direction of **Cestayrols**.

In Cestayrols, turn right toward Cahuzac, then immediately right again, following the signs for **Donnazac** on D33. The countryside here is dotted with old, picturesque villages. Drive into Donnazac, bearing right to go through the village; turn left on D33 in the direction of Tonnac, then, at the large intersection, turn left on D922, following the signs to **Cahuzac-sur-Vère**. You can make a short detour from Donnazac to Cordes, a medieval hill village only 7km to the north on D922.

The road south to Cahuzac, D922, climbs up onto a beautiful plateau and a sign proclaims that this is the *pays de Cocagne* – the land where all crops prosper and the vineyards are more than 1,000 years old. Drive through **Gaillac** and head south-west on the busy N88 which drops down into the plain on its way to Toulouse. An alternative route from Gaillac to **Rabastens** through the vineyards may be driven by taking D999 from Gaillac toward Montauban, then turning left following D18 toward Rabastens, where the Gaillac vineyards end.

To visit the Côtes du Frontonnais turn off N88 through **Bessières** toward Labastide-St Pierre on D630. In **Magnanac** turn left to **Villaudric** and **Fronton** on D29, then take D4 south to **Toulouse**.

Route Five

Madiran and Armagnac, from Condom to Pau: 180km

Though there are many fine wines in the South-West, Madiran is often said to be the *vrai vin gascon* (the real wine of Gascony). The best Madiran wine is traditionally made principally from the Tannat grape which, as it name implies, can be quite tannic and thus demands aging. Nowadays, even the better Madiran producers are making wines that can be consumed relatively young (8 to 10 years old). The wine has experienced a minor renaissance in recent years and production has risen from 700 hectoliters in 1955 to over 54,000 in 1987. Madiran is a red *appellation* but a dry white wine, Pacherenc du Vic Bilh, is made nearby in small quantities (less than 2,000 hectoliters in 1987).

This area of the South-West is also Armagnac country. As in Cognac, producers have experienced difficulties in recent years and found it more profitable to make wine or sell home-made *foie gras* and *confit* to tourists. Signs line the road inviting the visitor to stop, taste, and buy these local delicacies.

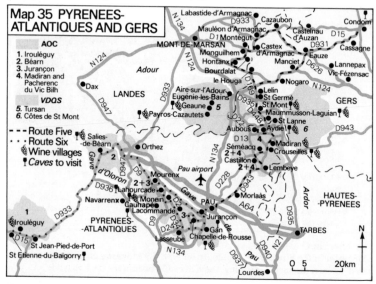

The Itinerary:

From **Condom** head south to **Eauze** on D931, a road surrounded by gnarled vines and orchards and bordered by signposts advertising Armagnac and home-made *foie gras*. From Eauze, which has a bustling market on Thursdays, you can either continue south on the main route or else make a detour to the west to visit the Armagnac area more thoroughly. To do this, turn right in Eauze onto D626 to **Cazaubon**. After Cazaubon head for **Mauléon d'Armagnac** on D154 and then south on D209 to **Castex d'Armagnac** where the château has an impressive *chai* lined with ancient casks. In Castex turn right on D1 to **Monguilhem** and then south on D125 to **le Houga**. In le Houga turn left on D6 to join highway N124 just south of Nogaro.

To follow the main route from Eauze drive south on D931 to **Manciet**, then south-west on N124 to **Nogaro** and on toward Aire-sur-l'Adour. Halfway between the two look out for the intersection with D169 where you turn left to **Lelin-Lapujolle** and on to **St Germé**. Cross over D935 onto D262 to **St Mont**, on the other side of the Adour river. In St Mont turn left on D946 and take the first right to **Maumusson-Laguian**. This road takes you through the heart of the Madiran vineyards. Continue south from Maumusson to D448 and on to the junction with D48 and D22. Turn right onto D22, left onto D292 and left again to D317 to **Aydie**. Go through Aydie onto D548 and then turn right onto D48 to go to **Madiran**. This stretch of road after Aydie has many growers' signs inviting you to taste their wines.

Leave Madiran south on D139 to **Crouseilles** and shortly afterward turn right on D228 to **Sémécaq** with its pretty church and palm trees. At the intersection with D13 turn left to **Lembeye**. The vineyards stop just after Lembeye and the road to Pau, D943, passes through farmland and woods.

Jurançon, from Pau to Mourenx and back to Pau: 95km

The snow-covered Pyrenees looming south of Pau are the most spectacular sight on this route. The mountains temper the otherwise tropical climate, though palm trees still grow in the shadow of the château at Pau where Henri IV of France was born.

Jurançon is one of France's most historic vineyard areas and after a period of perilous survival, vineyards are being expanded and an increasing amount of good wine made by small growers. The vineyards are spread out over the foothills of the Pyrenees; more than half the wine is produced by the local co-opérative. Fine Jurançon is extremely aromatic, even floral, and worth seeking out. Though it is often served with *foie gras* and desserts, the people here prefer it with the local sheep's cheese, *fromage de brebis*. Other Béarn wines are made around Orthez and Salies-de-Béarn. If you have time, make a detour to the Basque country near St Jean-Pied-de-Port and visit the vineyards where Irouléguy is made. Though somewhat of a curiosity, the better reds and rosés are worth looking out for.

The Itinerary:

Leave Pau southward on N134 until signs indicate the *Circuit des coteaux du Jurançon* (and Spain!). From here you can either take the "easy" route by continuing straight to **Gan** on N134, then turning right to **Lasseube** on D24; or take the "scenic" route to Lasseube via **Chapelle de Rousse**, which involves some difficult driving on narrow winding roads – and some spectacular scenery.

If you opt for the scenic route, leave N134 at Rousset, turning right to follow the *Route du Jurançon*. A steep winding road takes you to the top of a hill and turn left here toward Chapelle de Rousse. There is a magnificent view of the mountains as the road plunges downhill through fields and woods. The vineyards are visible on the hills ahead. Turn right toward Chapelle de Rousse, then follow the signs indicating the *Circuit du Jurançon*. This road passes through high-growing vines overlooking the valley, and vineyards plunge down the steep hills only inches away from the road. Take a sharp right turn on D230 through Chapelle, bear left past the château, then turn left and left again to take D217 through the little hamlets of **Crabès** and **Mouhous**. At the T-junction turn right toward Lasseube and Oloron on D24 which meanders through pastures and scattered vineyards to Lasseube.

In Lasseube bear right, then turn right onto D34 to Monein. The vineyards are more numerous near **Lacommande**, almost covering the hillsides, and there is a wonderful view approaching **Monein**. Follow the signs toward Monein *Centre Ville*, then *Autres Directions*, and finally **Lahourcade** and **Mourenx** on D9.

From Mourenx, this route can be extended to include other *vins de Béarn* by driving toward **Orthez** and **Salies-de-Béarn**, and even on to **Irouléguy** if a trip to Bayonne or Biarritz is envisaged. Otherwise, follow the signs back to Pau on D281, D33 and D2, entering the city through the suburbs of **Jurançon**.

Caves and Vineyards to Visit

Despite their growing fame, most of the South-West wines are still mainly for local consumption. Few restaurants in the region boast an extensive selection and some even avoid serving them for fear of "downgrading" their wine list. Fortunately, this situation is changing and the last 20 years have seen dramatic improvements in wine-making with the prestige of certains *appellations* (mainly the reds) on the rise.

The area, though vast, produces less than 5 per cent of all wine made in France and most growers work less than four hectares. Few rely strictly on wine for their income and in most areas vineyards take second place to farming. Despite this, there are over 25 *appellations* (AOC, VDQS, and Vin de Pays) in the South-West. The majority of these wines are produced by co-operatives, but there is a trend toward producing more and more quality wines and fewer *vins de consommation courante* (table wines). Although the overall amount of land devoted to vineyards continues to shrink, the amount of AOC vineyards is on the rise and, little by little, the powerful co-operatives are seeing their members turn to making their own wines. Such competition should encourage a continued rise in quality in years to come, and the fact that producers are replanting traditional grape varieties augurs well for the future, ensuring that the individual character of the region's wines will not be allowed to die out.

BERGERAC, map 33

Château de Corbiac (G),
24100 Bergerac.
Tel: 53.57.20.75.

The château has belonged to the same family since 1560. Bruno Durand de Corbiac has 11 hectares of vines in the Pécharmant area, a tiny *appellation* on the right bank of the Dordogne north of Bergerac. In most years, the wine is tannic, requiring a few years' bottle aging.
Visiting hours: Daily 8–8.
Location: 3km N of Bergerac off N21 and on the right.

The attractive Château de Corbiac.

BUZET-SUR-BAISE, map 33

Baise Vignerons Réunis des Côtes-de-Buzet (C),
47160 Damazan.
Tel: 53.84.74.30.

This large co-operative dominates the area and is the largest producer of Côtes de Buzet wines, its members cultivating a total of 1,170 hectares. Their basic Côtes de Buzet is a fruity and generous wine and the Cuvée Napoléon, made from selected grapes from vines at least 10 years old, is a complex and spicy wine that needs several years of bottle aging.

The co-operative also vinifies separately the wines of individual estates, such as Château de Gueyze and Château du Bouchet, aged in oak for six months, and perhaps its best wine. All the co-operative's AOC wines are aged in wood and there is a large aging cellar holding over 4,000 oak barrels. As part of its search for quality the co-operative even has its own cooper, who makes between 500-600 barrels a year. Visitors are shown an interesting film about in the area.
Visiting hours: Mon–Fri 9–12, 2–6.
Location: Just S of Buzet in the direction of Agen.

CAHUZAC-SUR-VERE, map 34

Vignoble Jean Cros (G), Cahuzac-sur-Vère,
81140 Castelnau-de-Montmiral.
Tel: 63.33.92.62.

The Cros family have two separate vineyard areas, the Domaine Jean Cros which surrounds the family's home, the Mas des Vignes at Cahuzac, and Château Larroze in the Côtes de Gaillac. Jean Cros and his two sons make a wide range of wines and his English son-in-law looks after exports. The Château Larroze wines are an elegant white from 100 per cent Mauzac and a fruity, medium-bodied red, from Duras, Merlot and Cabernet Sauvignon.

The Domaine Jean Cros wines are typical of the Gaillac *appellation* and include a Gaillac Perlé, a specialty of the area with a slight sparkle, made from Mauzac and Len de l'Elh, and Gaillac Crémant, made by the traditional rural method or *méthode Gaillaçoise*.

The family offers a hospitable welcome to visitors and takes great pride in the individuality of its wines. Even the very *parcelles* in their vineyards are named after family events.
Visiting hours: Mon–Sat 9–7, Sun 3–6 by appt.
Location: 4km E of Cahuzac on D1.

THE SOUTH-WEST

CASTANET, map 34

Domaine de Labarthe (G), Castanet, 81150 Marssac-sur-Tarn. Tel: 63.56.80.14.

The Albert family have been winemakers here for over 300 years and their domaine of 22 hectares shows the diversity of wines made in Gaillac. The vineyards are planted mainly with local varieties, such as Len de l'Elh, and many of the vines are over 20 years old. The wines include champagne-method Gaillac Mousseux from Len de l'Elh, and an interesting, elegant Gaillac Blanc Moelleux from Mauzac. The Gaillac Rouge combines the local grapes, Braucol and Duras, with Bordeaux varieties such as Merlot and Cabernet. Visiting hours: Mon–Fri 8–12, 2–6; Sat–Sun by appt. Location: 1km N of Castanet and signposted.

CASTELNAU-D'ESTRETEFONDS, map 34

Château Flotis (G), Castelnau-d'Estrétefonds, 31620 Fronton. *Caves* tel: 61.35.12.04. Office tel: 61.35.10.03.

The Küntz family originated on the opposite side of France, in Alsace, but is now firmly established on hills overlooking the Fronton plateau, north of Toulouse, where they bought Château Flotis, an old property, in 1973.

Roger Küntz looks after the vinification while his son, Philippe, is in charge of the 35 hectares of vineyards. These are the oldest in the area, and are mostly planted in older vines, although replanting is being carried out. The *chais* were originally built in 1777. The main grape variety is the indigenous Négrette which accounts for 60 per cent of the vineyard. Château Flotis' Côtes du Frontonnais is a fine, fruity wine made from the finest grapes (50 per cent Négrette, 25 per cent Syrah and 25 per cent Cabernet Franc), and is surprisingly soft for a red wine. Visiting hours: Daily 8–12, 2–6, by appt. Location: 2km N of Castelnau on D87 to Fronton and just past the autoroute.

CAUHAPE, map 35

Domaine Cauhapé (G), Henri Ramonteu, Cauhapé, 64360 Monein. Tel: 59.21.33.02.

The late 19th-century outbreak of phylloxera virtually destroyed the Jurançon vineyards. However, much replanting has now been carried out and a new generation of winemakers is going a step further to perfect the tradition. Henri Ramonteu makes some of the best wines in the *appellation*. His 10-hectare domaine produces a sweet Jurançon that is matured in new oak and then requires further bottle aging to bring out all its qualities. The Jurançon Sec owes its character to a short period of skin contact with the juice and is full of flavor. Visiting hours: Daily 8–12, 2–7; appt necessary during harvest. Location: 3km W of Monein on the road to Navarrenx.

DURAS, map 33

Cave Co-opérative Berticot de Duras (C), 47120 Duras. Tel: 53.83.71.12.

This small co-operative is the major producer of Côtes de Duras wines. Its members cultivate a total of 417 hectares of vines, two-thirds of which are red (Cabernet Sauvignon, Cabernet Franc, Merlot and Malbec) and one-third white (Sauvignon, Sémillon and Muscadelle). The co-operative uses the label Berticot for some of its wines, including some varietals such as a fruity Sauvignon, a light Merlot and an elegant Cabernet Sauvignon. These varietal wines are fairly unusual in the South-West. Visiting hours: Mon–Sat 8–12, 2–6; Jul–Aug daily. Location: 1km N of Duras on D708.

MAUMUSSON-LAGUIAN, map 35

Domaine du
Bouscassé (G),
Maumusson-
Laguian, 32400
Riscle.
Tel: 62.69.74.67.

The Brumont family have been winemakers at Maumusson
for 150 years. Alain Brumont took over the 30-hectare estate
from his father in 1978 and he has since bought another
property, Château de Montus, on the hills around Castelnau
Rivière-Basse, with 29 hectares of vineyards.

M. Brumont has established a considerable reputation for
aging his Madiran wines in wood. He also makes the rare
white Pacherenc du Vic-Bilh, both the dry wine and the more
traditional sweeter style which will develop with bottle age.
Visiting hours: Mon–Fri 8–7; Sat by appt.
Location: 4km S of Riscle on the road to Maumusson.

MONBAZILLAC, map 33

Château de
Monbazillac (C),
Cave Co-opérative
de Monbazillac,
Monbazillac,
24240 Sigoulès. Co-
operative
tel: 53.57.06.38.
Château de
Monbazillac
tel: 53.58.30.27.
Restaurant
tel: 53.58.38.93.

The large Monbazillac co-operative, with a total of over
1,000 hectares of vines, uses up-to-date equipment to make a
range of interesting wines, including a fine sweet Château
Monbazillac from 22 hectares of vines in the Dordogne
valley. These vineyards surround the co-operative's
showpiece, the 16th-century Château de Monbazillac, a
pleasant spot to while away a few hours. Inside the château
are several small collections, including a museum of wine,
and the former *chais* have been turned into an attractive
restaurant serving regional dishes at lunchtime in the
summer months. The wines made by the co-operative
(Monbazillac, Bergerac and Pécharmant) can also be bought
at the château.

As well as the Château Monbazillac sweet wines the co-
operative makes Château Septy, another Monbazillac wine
from a 17-hectare estate overlooking the town of Bergerac. A
fruity Pécharmant, Château la Renaudie, is made from
another small property on the right bank of the Dordogne.
Visiting hours: (Co-operative) Mon–Fri by appt; (Château
de Monbazillac) Daily 9–12, 2–6; (Restaurant) Jun–Sep
lunch only, dinner by arrangement; remainder of year open
for banquets and parties by arrangement.
Location: (Co-operative) 5km S of Bergerac on D933;
(Château) 6km S of Bergerac on D13.

Château de Monbazillac in the valley of the Dordogne.

PRAYSSAC, map 34

Clos de Gamot
(G), Jean Jouffreau,
46220 Prayssac.
Tel: 65.22.40.26.

Jean Jouffreau owns two properties in the Cahors region, the
Clos de Gamot and the Château de Cayrou. Clos de Gamot is
the Jouffreau family home and the Clos de Gamot Cuvée
Centenaire is made from Auxerrois vines planted 100 years
ago shortly after the phylloxera outbreak.

In 1971 the Jouffreaus bought Château de Cayrou, a short
distance downstream in another horseshoe bend of the river

Lot. This is a beautiful château, a 12th-century manor house that was extended in the 14th and 16th centuries. The gravelly soil at Château de Cayrou was a clear indication that the surrounding land had excellent viticultural potential and the vines do indeed benefit from the heat accumulated during the day by the large quantity of pebbles in the soil, and released at night. The Cayrou vineyards are planted with four different red grape varieties: Auxerrois, Merlot, Tannat and Jurançon. All four are vinified separately to make smooth, elegant wines. A new underground cellar was built at Cayrou in 1986 to enable the wines to benefit from some bottle age before being released for sale.

Visiting hours: (For both properties) daily 9–8, by appt.
Location: (Clos de Gamot) S of Prayssac on D67; (Château de Cayrou) S of Puy l'Evêque on D28.

RAZAC-DE-SAUSSIGNAC, map 33

Château Court-les-Mûts (G),
Razac-de-Saussignac,
24240 Sigoulès.
Tel: 53.27.92.17.

Jean-Pierre and Bernadette Sadoux own 54 hectares of vines and make a wide range of Bergerac wines. Jean-Pierre's father, Pierre, bought the estate on his return from Algeria in 1960. Although well known for its wines in the 19th century, the estate's 14 hectares of vines were in ruin and had to be replanted. Jean-Pierre is an enologist by training and the Sadoux make some interesting wines, including a sweet Côtes de Saussignac from very ripe Sémillon grapes. As well as the red, white and rosé Bergerac wines, there is also a champagne-method sparkling wine from Ugni Blanc. Jean-Pierre was one of the first winemakers in the Bergerac region to use oak barrels again for aging wines. There is an attractive tasting room.

Visiting hours: Mon–Fri 9–11.30, 2–5.30; Sat by appt.
Location: Signposted from the village.

ST MONT, map 35

Union des Producteurs de Plaimont (C),
32400 St Mont.
Tel: 62.69.62.87.

The Côtes de St Mont was only established as a VDQS *appellation* in 1981 although the area has always made wine. It is, in a sense, a continuation of the Madiran region and the local co-operative is a dynamic organization that has done much to improve the image and quality of the St Mont wines. The co-operative makes both wines, as well as Vin de Pays Côtes de Gascogne, made from Colombard, and Pacherenc du Vic Bilh.

Visiting hours: Mon–Sat 8–12, 2–6.
Location: In the center of the village.

TRESPOUX-RASSIELS, map 34

Domaine des Savarines (G),
46090 Tréspoux-Rassiels.
Tel: 65.35.50.55.

The small domaine of only 4 hectares makes a Cahors wine of good reputation. The vines were replanted in the mid-1970s by the owner, Mme Danielle Biesbrouck-Borde, an energetic lady who does most of the work in the vineyards and cellar herself, although she also has an enologist to advise her. Mme Biesbrouck-Borde even designs her own labels.

The vineyard is planted mainly in Malbec with small amounts of Merlot and Jurançon and the wines are aged in new casks of Allier oak.

Visiting hours: Jul–Sep daily; remainder of year by appt.
Location: Take D27 from Cahors to Tréspoux; leave Tréspoux and the Relais Hertzien on the left and take the 1st road on the right. The domaine is 4km down here.

Further *Caves* and Vineyards to Visit

AMBRUS, map 33
Château de Padère (G), Ambrus, 47160 Damazan. Tel: 53.84.77.11. Visiting hours: Mon–Sat 8–6.
The estate makes a splendid Côtes de Buzet.

AYDIE, map 35
Château d'Aydie (G), Aydie, 64330 Garlin. Tel: 59.04.01.17. Visiting hours: Daily 8–1, 2–9.
The Laplace family have been making wine since 1759 and make good Madiran and Pacherenc du Vic Bilh. Some of the vines on the estate are 200 years old.

BAGAT-EN-QUERCY, map 34
Domaine de Quattre (G), Bagat-en-Quercy, 46800 Montcuq. Tel: 65.36.91.04. Visiting hours: Daily by appt.
Philippe Heilbronner and Hervé de Portes are partners in an operation involving three Cahors estates. Domaine de Quattre is the largest with 18.5 hectares, Domaine de Treilles has 16 hectares and Domaine de Guingal is the smallest with only 11 hectares. The two partners have been replanting the vineyards since 1976 and the results are already encouraging. The differences between the wines of the three properties are carefully maintained.

BERGERAC, map 33
Château du Haut-Pécharmant (G), 24100 Bergerac. Tel: 53.57.29.50. Visiting hours: Daily 8–12, 2–7.
The domaine of 24 hectares is owned by the Roches family and is one of the leading estates in the Pécharmant *appellation*. Traditional vinification methods are used but no aging in oak.

CHAPELLE-DE-ROUSSE, map 33
Cru Lamouroux (G), Chapelle-de-Rousse, 64110 Jurançon. Tel: 59.21.74.41. Visiting hours: Daily 8–12, 2–7.
Jean Chigé makes sweet Jurançon on his small 7-hectare domaine. He harvests his grapes (60 per cent Petit Manseng and 40 per cent Gros Manseng) in mid-November when the grapes have been dried by the autumn winds in a process called *passerillage* so that the juice is rich and concentrated.

CIEURAC, map 34
Château de Haute-Serre (G), Cieurac, 46230 Lalbenque. Tel: 65.38.70.30. Visiting hours: Daily 9–7.
Georges Vigouroux spent five years in the early 1970s converting 62 hectares of shrubland to vines and restoring the attractive 18th-century château. The main grape variety is Auxerrois with some Merlot and Tannat. The grapes are harvested as late as possible and vinified slowly to make a richly perfumed Cahors.

COCUMONT, map 33
Cave Co-opérative de Cocumont (C), Cocumont, 47250 Bouglon. Tel: 53.94.50.21. Visiting hours: By appt.
Production of Côtes du Marmandais is dominated by this small, modern co-operative and one other.

COLOMBIER, map 33
Château la Jaubertie (G), Colombier, 24560 Issigeac. Tel: 53.58.32.11. Visiting hours: By appt.
The area around Bergerac is swarming with English people who have bought old homes on abandoned farms or in depopulated villages as summer or retirement residences.

Nick Ryman at Château la Jaubertie is an Englishman who has established a fine reputation for his wines, including outstanding red and white Bergerac and an oak-aged Réserve wine.

CONDOM, map 35
Janneau Fils (G/M), 50 ave. d'Aquitaine, 32100 Condom. Tel: 62.28.24.77. Visiting hours: Mon–Sat 10–12, 2–6; Jul 1–Sep 15 daily.
Janneau is the largest exporter of Armagnac.

CREYSSE, map 33
Château de Tiregand (G), Creysse, 24100 Bergerac. Tel: 53.23.21.08. Visiting hours: By appt.
The large 400-hectare estate has belonged to the St Exupéry family since 1831. François Xavier de St Exupéry is now in charge of wine-making. There is an attractive château and *chai*. There are 35 hectares of vineyards and the château's reputation is mainly based on its Pécharmant, a rich, well-balanced wine that ages gracefully. There is also an excellent Bergerac Blanc Sec.

CROUSEILLES, map 35
Vignerons Réunis du Vic-Bilh-Madiran (C), Crouseilles, 64350 Lembeye. Tel: 59.68.10.93. Visiting hours: Mon–Fri 8–12, 2–6, preferably by appt.
The co-operative has established a good reputation for its wines. The red Rôt-du-Roy Madiran can be aged for several years, as can another individual estate wine, Château-Guyon, which is extraordinarily well-balanced..

DONNAZAC, map 34
Mas d'Aurel (G), Donnazac, 81170 Cordes. Tel: 63.56.06.39. Visiting hours: Daily 8–8.
Albert Ribot's Mas d'Aurel Gaillac Rouge combines Braucol, Syrah, Merlot and Cabernet in a wine that can be aged. The white is made from Len-de-l'Elh, Mauzac and Sauvignon. The rosé is a blend of Duras and Syrah, vinified partly on the skins.

FLORESSAS, map 34
Domaine de Paillas (G), Floressas, 46700 Puy-l'Evêque. Tel: 65.21.34.42. Visiting hours: Mon–Fri 8–12, 1–5.30.
The estate makes the softer, lighter style of Cahors.

FRONTON, map 34
Château Bellevue-la-Forêt (G), D49, 31620 Fronton. Tel: 61.82.43.21. Visiting hours: Mon–Sat 9–12, 2–6.
All the vineyards have been planted since 1974 and the domaine makes red and rosé Côtes du Frontonnais, as well as Cuvées Spéciales Rouge and Rosé, both of which are exceptionally good.

GAN, map 35
Cave des Producteurs de Jurançon (C), 53 av. Henri IV, 64290 Gan. Tel: 59.21.57.03. Visiting hours: Daily 9–12, 2–6.30.
This is a good place to try the interesting sweet Jurançon wines, including Château les Astous made mainly from old Petit Manseng vines.

GEAUNE, map 35
Les Vignerons du Tursan (C), 40320 Geaune. Tel: 58.44.51.25. Visiting hours: Mon–Fri 9–12, 2–5; Sat 8–12, 2–5; appt essential.

Tursan is traditionally a white wine from the local Baroque grape and the modern co-operative makes a good example. Red wine was introduced to the region in 1960 and is now more important. The Cuvée de l'Impératrice is a light, pleasant red.

LAHOURCADE, map 35
Clos Cancaillau (G), Lahourcade, 64150 Mourenx. Tel: 59.60.08.15. Visiting hours: Mon–Sat 8–12, 2–6.
The 16-hectare domaine is owned by GAEC Barrère who make a good range of Jurançon wines.

LEYGUE, map 34
Domaine de la Pineraie (G), Leygue, 46700 Puy-l'Evêque. Tel: 65.30.82.07. Visiting hours: Mon–Sat 8–12, 2–7; closed hols.
The 25-hectare vineyard is owned by the Burc family who make firm, full-bodied Cahors by traditional methods.

LISLE-SUR-TARN, map 34
GAEC Boyals et Fils (G), 10 r. St Louis, 81310 Lisle-sur-Tarn. Tel: 63.33.37.80. Visiting hours: Daily 9–12, 2–7.
The Boyals cultivate 30 hectares of vines on the right bank of the Tarn and their dry white Gaillac is one of the best in the region.

MAUMUSSON-LAGUIAN, map 35
Domaine de Barréjat (G), Maumusson-Laguian, 32400 Riscle. Tel: 62.69.74.92. Visiting hours: Mon–Sat 8–12, 2–8; Sun by appt.
The 16-hectare domaine makes a fine Madiran and a dry white Pacherenc du Vil-Bilh.

MONBAZILLAC, map 33
Château la Borderie, and **Château Treuil-de-Nailhac (G)**, Monbazillac, 24240 Sigoulès. Tel: 53.57.00.36. Visiting hours: Mon–Sat 8–12, 2–6.
The two adjoining properties are owned by the Vidal-Hurmic family. La Borderie is the larger estate with 55 hectares, and Treuil-de-Nailhac is only 9 hectares. The Monbazillacs of both properties are excellent, especially the Treuil-de-Nailhac. There is also a good dry Sauvignon and various styles of Bergerac.

Repaire du Haut-Theulet (G), Monbazillac, 24240 Sigoulès. Tel: 53.58.30.30. Visiting hours: Daily by appt.

Mme Bardin makes a good, rich Monbazillac, as well as red and white Bergerac wines. There is an attractive tasting room with fine views of the Dordogne valley below.

MONEIN, map 35
Clos Uroulat (G), 64360 Monein. Tel: 59.21.46.19. Visiting hours: By appt.

The owner, Charles Hours, is a young enologist, who bought the small 6-hectare estate in the Jurançon *appellation*, with the intention of putting theory into practise. He is now one of the leading winemakers and one of the few producers in the region to age his sweet wine in new oak.

PARNAC, map 34
Les Côtes-d'Olt (C), Parnac, 46140 Luzech. Tel: 65.30.71.86. Visiting hours: Mon–Fri 8–12, 1.30–5.30.

This co-operative accounts for 40 per cent of all Cahors wine and the quality is improving. As well as its own wines the co-operative vinifies the wines of several individual estates, including Comte André de Montpezat, a classic Cahors that requires long aging.

PAYROS-CAZAUTETS, map 35
Dulucq et Fils (G), Payros-Cazautets, 40320 Geaune. Tel: 58.44.50.68. Visiting hours: By appt.

The Dulucq family cultivate 12 hectares in the Tursan area. Baroque and some Sauvignon are used to make white wines and Tannat and Cabernet Franc produce red and rosé wines.

PUY-L'EVEQUE, map 34
Clos Triguedina (G), 46700 Puy-l'Evêque. Tel: 65.21.30.81. Visiting hours: Mon–Fri 9–12, 2–6; Sat–Sun by appt.

The domaine of approximately 40 hectares has an attractive old house with cellars around the courtyard. The Baldès family firmly believe in aging their traditional Cahors and the top wine, the Cuvée Prince Probus, spends 9–15 months in new oak, giving the wine plenty of character and definition.

ST ETIENNE-DE-BAIGORRY, map 35
Cave Co-opérative d'Irouléguy (C), 64430 St Etienne-de-Baïgorry. Tel: 59.37.41.33. Visiting hours: (Shop) Mon–Fri 9–12, 2–6.30; Tasting and cellar visits by appt.

The whole production of the Irouléguy *appellation* is in the competent hands of the co-operative at St Etienne, an attractive town tucked into a narrow valley in the Pyrenees. Both the reds and rosés are made from Tannat, Cabernet Franc and Cabernet Sauvignon. Their red Cuvée Spéciale is a deliciously perfumed, peppery wine.

ST MICHEL-DE-MONTAIGNE, map 33
Domaine de Perreau (G), St Michel-de-Montaigne, 24230 Vélines. Tel: 53.58.60.55. Visiting hours: Daily 8–12, 2–8.

Jean-Yves Renou and his family produce a full red Bergerac that benefits from moderate aging.

SALIES-DE-BEARN, map 35
Co-opérative Vinicole de Bellocq (C), 64270 Salies-de-Béarn. Tel: 59.65.10.71. Visiting hours: Mon–Fri 9–12, 2–7.

The *appellation* of Béarn is very spread out and this co-operative makes nearly all the wine from this isolated western region. It is best known for its red and rosé wines.

THENAC, map 33
Château de Panisseau (G), Thénac, 24240 Sigoulès. Tel: 53.58.40.03. Visiting hours: Mon–Fri 8–12, 2–6.

The attractive estate makes good white Bergerac, including one made entirely from Sauvignon, and some red.

La VILLE-DIEU-DU-TEMPLE, map 34
Cave Co-opérative de la-Ville-Dieu-du-Temple (C), 82290 la-Ville-Dieu-du-Temple. Tel: 63.31.60.05. Visiting hours: Mon–Fri 8–12, 2–5.

Lavilledieu is one of the unknown, neglected wines of South-West France. The co-operative is the only producer and makes a successful, fruity Hugues de Verdalle with limited equipment and means.

Though the South-West has had more than its fair share of conflicts over the centuries, the visitor will discover today a peaceful region where fortified towns (*bastides*) have become charming villages and lost all of the menacing qualities they once possessed.

AGEN

The town of Agen is famous throughout France for its prunes; these are widely sold in the town and the larger and moister they are the better.

The **Musée** is housed in a group of Renaissance buildings, and has a fine collection of ceramics and some important Goya paintings.

ALBI

"Red Albi" derives its name from the profusion of brick buildings, among them the 14th-century **Cathédrale Ste Cécile** with its ornately painted interior and 14th–16th-century stained-glass windows. Next to the cathedral is the **Palais de la Berbie**, built between the 14th and the 16th centuries as the residence of the bishops of Albi. The reception rooms and terraced gardens can be visited but the major attraction is the museum containing the world's finest collection of the works of Toulouse-Lautrec, a native of Albi. His birthplace, the 18th-century **Hôtel du Bosc**, houses a collection of memorabilia.

From the **Pont du 22-Août** there is a splendid view of the town and of the 11th-century **Pont-Vieux** over the Tarn.

BERGERAC

Bergerac is a busy market town, and particularly lively during the winter months when one square is reserved for farmers selling *foie gras*, force-fed geese and ducks, and *cèpes* (*boletus* mushrooms) from the nearby forests – delicacies that bring out the best in the local wines. The old quarter has been restored in recent years.

The **Maison du Vin** is in the former Couvent des Récollets and has a fine galleried cloister. There is also an unusual **Musée du Tabac**, the only museum in France devoted to the processing and use of tobacco.

CAHORS

Cahors, the capital of Quercy, has retained much of its ancient charm, and holds a truffle market every Sat and on

Wed in winter in the square in front of the cathedral. The most famous landmark in Cahors is the medieval **Pont Valentré**, a bridge with three fortified towers over the Lot at the edge of the old quarter. The climb to Mont St Cyr to the south provides a fine view of the whole town, nestling in a loop of the Lot.

Pont Valentré at Cahors.

CONDOM

Condom, the heart of the Armagnac region, is a logical place for a **Musée d'Armagnac** to be created. The little museum, in a small house near the cathedral, illustrates the history of winemaking and distillation of the famous brandy.

CORDES

Cordes is a magnificent medieval village high up on a hill and an exceptional collection of 13th–14th-century sandstone houses makes it a living museum. With its surrounding ramparts and gate Cordes is also an excellent example of *bastide* architecture.

DURAS

This attractive little town, set on a spur above the valley of the Dropt, has narrow lanes and tiny, silent squares. The **château**, built in 1308, was converted into a residence for the dukes of Duras in 1680. The formal apartments can be visited and there is a small local museum. From the main tower there are good views of the valley and distant hills.

GAILLAC

An old town on the right bank of the river, Gaillac has many narrow streets of old houses. There is a wine fair in Aug.

MONTAUBAN

The painter Ingres was born in Montauban, a market town built originally almost entirely in soft pink brick which now sprawls rather unattractively across the plain. An unparalleled collection of his work, and that of the sculptor Bourdelle, is displayed in the former episcopal palace.

PAU

Pau, the historic capital of Béarn, is a handsome town with fine views of the Pyrenees. The old part of Pau is dominated by its **château** where Henri IV of France was born.

ST MICHEL-DE-MONTAIGNE

The château where the 16th-century writer Montaigne was born, and where he passed the last 10 years of his life, was badly damaged by fire in 1885 but has been restored. The writer's room and library can be visited, and from the terrace is a beautiful view of the valley of the Lidoire.

TOULOUSE

Toulouse is a large bustling city, the fourth largest in France, with ancient red brick buildings that give the city a pink glow which changes with the light. Halfway between the Mediterranean and the Atlantic coasts, the city has been an important crossroads for many centuries and has fine examples of medieval religious art. The awe-inspiring brick and stone **Basilique St Sernin** is one of the largest (over 115m long) and most important buildings of the Romanesque period. From Charlemagne's time onward many relics were housed in the original church, making it a magnet for pilgrims.

Toulouse has the largest university in France after Paris and this helps to make the center a bustling place with a wide choice of restaurants at all prices.

Hotels, Restaurants and Where to Buy Wine

Ironically, some of France's most expensive delicacies are produced by modest farmers and peasants in one of the most underdeveloped areas of the country. Specialties such as truffles and *foie gras* are sold around the world and in recent years *confit* (duck salted and preserved in its own fat) and *magret* (fattened-duck steaks) have joined them. *Nouvelle cuisine* chefs, despite their emphasis on lighter dishes, have promoted the *magret* and *foie gras* in particular. Hand in hand with the success of this peasant fare has gone the promotion of Armagnac, the local brandy of the region, which has now replaced Cognac as *the* after-dinner drink in top restaurants throughout the country.

Most of the region's wines are seen as "hearty" country wines destined to accompany the local dishes. However, the best reds can be subtle and the sweet whites are astonishingly floral; both are improving yearly in the hands of producers rediscovering the potential of their ancient *terroir*.

La Tantina de Burgos (R) and **Oenothèque Régionale (W)**, 27 av. de la Garonnette, 31000 Toulouse. Tel: 61.55.59.29. Closed Sat–Sun and Aug. MC V

This modest bistro boasts the most extensive list of South-West wines to be found anywhere in France. One would hardly expect such riches in a restaurant with virtually no décor, a 40-franc menu (tip and wine included) and waiters in T-shirts and jeans. Here, however, over 110 local wines (excluding Bordeaux) cover the wall behind the bar; and at the Oenothèque Régionale next door, over 300 wines from the South-West are on sale! The knowledgeable personnel in the shop and the restaurant have an evangelical zeal about the wines they sell and they probably do more to promote quality wines from the South-West than most official growers' organizations or government agencies.

The cooking, in the Basque style, is not the main attraction but is nevertheless quite good; cold dishes dominate at lunch. The problem here is choosing between sampling an obscure (and often quite exceptional) *vin de pays* or a fine wine from a little-known grower from the more famous South-West *appellations* such as Cahors or Madiran. The only solution is to return several times or to leave with a bag full of wines for tasting at home later on.

ALBI (81000)
La Réserve (H,R), rte de Cordes, Fonvialane (3km NW by D600). Tel: 63.60.79.79. Closed Oct–Apr. AE DC MC V
Magnificently situated in a park on the banks of the Tarn, this is a charming and comfortable hotel. Elegant restaurant with good cooking.

AUCH (32000)
Hôtel de France (H,R,W), 2 pl. de la Libération. Tel: 62.05.00.44. Two Michelin stars. Reservations recommended. (R) closed Jan. AE DC V
André Daguin has done much to promote regional cooking and Gascon products while earning a reputation as a creative *nouvelle cuisine* chef.

As well as the restaurant the building contains a small bistro serving regional specialties and a wine shop with an interesting selection of South-West wines, including an outstanding collection of Armagnacs.

BERGERAC (24100)
Le Bordeaux (H) and **Le Terroir (R)**, 38 pl. Gambetta. Tel: 53.57.12.83. Closed Dec 20–Jan 20. AE DC MC V
Comfortable, family establishment located in a quiet square. Good food and Bergerac wines served by the glass.

Le Cyrano (R,H), 2 bd Montaigne. Tel: 53.57.02.76. One Michelin star. Closed Mon and Dec. AE DC V
Two elegant, modern dining-rooms. Some regional specialties but generally *nouvelle*-style dishes.

CAHORS (46000)
Luc E. Reutenauer (W), le Pech d'Angely, BP194, 46004 Cahors. Tel: 65.35.26.47. Closed Sat–Sun. No cards. This *négociant*, in a southern Cahors suburb, has a superb range of local wines.

La Taverne (R), 1 r. J.-B.-Delpech. Tel: 65.35.28.66. AE DC V
Traditional *cuisine*. The cellar contains the largest choice of Cahors wines in France (71 different types).

Terminus (H) and **le Balandre (R)**, 5 av. Ch.-de-Freycinet. Tel: 65.35.24.50. MC V
Traditional, family-run hotel near the Pont Valentré. Good *cuisine* and a short but excellent wine list.

CORDES (81170)
Grand Ecuyer (H,R), r. Voltaire. Tel: 63.56.01.03. One Michelin star. Reservations recommended. Closed Nov–Easter. AE V
Yves Thuriès does the cooking here and oversees another restaurant, the Hostellerie du Vieux Cordes, also in Cordes. Both are in beautifully restored medieval buildings with fine views of the valley below. Thuriès is a master technician, whose desserts are famous.

EUGENIE-LES-BAINS (40320)
Les Prés d'Eugénie (H,R). Tel: 58.51.19.01. Three Michelin stars. Reservations recommended. Closed Dec–Feb. AE DC MC V
In an idyllic setting, Michel Guérard serves both his famous *cuisine minceur* to those here for a cure and his renowned *cuisine gourmande* to other guests. Considered by many to be the finest chef in France, Guérard uses only vegetables from his own garden and the finest local products (his *foie gras* is exceptional).

PUYMIROL (47270)
L'Aubergade (R), 52 r. Royale. Tel: 53.95.31.46. Two Michelin stars. Reservations essential in summer. Closed Mon except Jul–Aug. AE V
Michel Trama has made this restaurant one of the most popular "detours" in France today. Third generation *nouvelle cuisine* is served and regional products (duck and truffles) are often combined with exotic imports (ginger and mangoes). Mme Trama serves the wines.

ST JEAN-PIED-DE-PORT (64220)
Pyrénées (R,H), pl. Gén.-de-Gaulle. Tel: 59.37.01.01. Two Michelin stars. Reservations recommended. AE V
Small but comfortable rooms. The restaurant is one of the best in the region.

TOULOUSE (31000)
Vanel (R), 22 r. Maurice-Fontvieille. Tel: 61.21.51.82. Two Michelin stars. Reservations recommended. Closed Sun, Mon lunch and Aug. AE
In an unattractive modern building, but Lucien Vanel does not rely on his restaurant's façade to attract customers. A favorite with Toulousains, his cooking has a strong South-West accent.

GRAPE VARIETIES

Almost all of the world's great wine grapes are grown in France, where wine is made under many conditions, from the cool chalky hills of Champagne through the granite uplands of the Beaujolais to the roasted lowlands of the Midi. Centuries of tradition have matched grape types to environment, and many of these marriages, some happy, some not, have been enshrined in the *appellation* laws, which specify grape type along with alcohol levels, methods of pruning, yields and principles of vinification. The following is a short list of the best, most common, types.

CABERNET FRANC

Softer than Cabernet Sauvignon, Cabernet Franc is often overshadowed by its near namesake. In the Médoc it is planted as a softener to the Cabernet Sauvignon in more austere vintages; across the Gironde, its ability to stand cooler climates, to ripen earlier and subsist on ill-drained soils make it the preferred Cabernet partner for the dominant Merlot in St Emilion and Pomerol. Its other stronghold in France is the Loire valley where it achieves astonishing sharp blackcurrant flavors in Chinon and Bourgeuil.

CABERNET SAUVIGNON

The main red wine grape of Bordeaux is the most famous noble red variety in the world. Its woody, resistant vines yield small quantities of late-ripening small blue-black grapes that make wines with a deep color and formidable tannins. It is grown in the South-West, the Loire, Provence and the Languedoc as well, though rarely as the main grape, generally being used sparingly to add color, body, ageability and class to a blend. It is easy to grow and to harvest, provided there is enough warmth, sun and good drainage – a combination the gravel banks of the Médoc provide to perfection.

CARIGNAN

Although originating in Spain, the Carignan has found a home in the South of France. Its main use is as a workhorse grape, high-yielding and rot-resistant, that provides a strong base for grapes with a more delicate flavor, such as Grenache and Cinsaut. Interestingly, it reacts very well to the Beaujolais *macération carbonique* method and produces a very juicy red.

CHARDONNAY

France's most noble white grape, the Chardonnay prefers a light, chalky soil and relatively cool temperatures. Within these limits, however, it can produce the widest range of wine styles of any great grape. Though susceptible to spring frosts, it is easy to grow, ripens early and produces consistently high yields. In Burgundy, Chardonnay styles can vary from the crisp, fresh steel of Chablis to the fat, smoky wines of the Mâconnais and the brilliant, luscious yet dry wines of the Côte d'Or. The bouquet is always subtle, while the color can vary from delicate pale gold with green highlights to a deep amber with age. It is also an important grape in Champagne.

CHENIN BLANC

The Chenin is at its best in the Loire valley, where it is known as Pineau de la Loire. It is a high-yielding vine, though best when the yield is kept down by rigorous pruning, and it ripens late. Chenin wines should be fresh and thirst-quenching. There are a few sweeter Chenins made and these can be rich and exciting.

GAMAY

Although there is some Gamay in the Loire and in the Ardèche, it is very much a one-region grape. It thrives in the granite of the Beaujolais, where it makes up 98 per cent of the vineyards, and produces oceans of light, fruity, purplish wine, low in tannins, high in acid – and *very* high in fruit. Gamay wines rarely keep well; even the best Beaujolais *crus* seldom last more than a few years.

GEWURZTRAMINER

The pinkish-yellow grapes of the Gewürztraminer are very distinctive, and can be found all over Alsace. The wine, too, is easily recognized, deep golden in color, and scented with exotic fruits and spice.

GRENACHE

Grenache is the most widely planted red grape world-wide, though this is more a tribute to its ability to flourish in arid, windy climates than any great intrinsic quality. It is grown all over the south of France and in Corsica. It is basically a blending grape, adding body, warmth, alcohol and a broad raspberry fruit although in the Rhône valley it can make an exciting contribution to Châteauneuf-du-Pape, and makes some of France's most heady rosés. The grapes are very sweet, and are the basis of the Roussillon *vins doux naturels*.

MALBEC
The Malbec is a grape with many names that is grown in many places. Most important are Anjou where it is known as the Cot, St Emilion where it is the Pressac, and Cahors where it becomes the Auxerrois. It is going out of fashion in Bordeaux, where it adds color and body to blends, but it remains the principal ingredient of the smooth, dark, spicy wine of Cahors.

MERLOT
The main red grape of Bordeaux, in terms of quantity, the Merlot softens the Cabernet Sauvignon in the Médoc and the Graves, but comes into its own in St Emilion and Pomerol, where it produces some of the world's most complex wines. The Merlot adds a luscious, plummy fruit to blends.

MOURVEDRE
Mourvèdre is a small dry grape, difficult to ripen and to vinify, that is much valued in the south for its ability to produce high acid in relatively hot conditions and to add smoothness and body to blends. Bandol shows it off best.

MUSCADET
Muscadet or Melon de Bourgogne is very much a one-region grape, almost exclusively found in the Pays Nantais, where it produces a pale, neutral, bone-dry white.

MUSCAT
More of a family than an individual variety, small enclaves of Muscat produce very different wines all over France, such as *vins doux naturels* from the Roussillon, richly colored Muscat de Beaumes-de-Venise in the Rhône and dry wines in Alsace. Everywhere it is characterized by its sweet, floral scent and unmistakeably grapy taste.

PINOT NOIR
Indisputably great when it can be made to work, the Pinot Noir is heart-breakingly difficult to grow, susceptible to frosts in the spring and rot in the autumn. It has its greatest success in Champagne and its home territory of Burgundy.

RIESLING
Germany's great grape is excluded by France's *appellation* laws from every region but Alsace, where it thrives on poor, well-drained soils and cool conditions to produce a wide range of varietal wines. Golden in color and rich in body, Riesling wines have a heady bouquet of flowers, honey and spice. They are usually vinified full and dry, with plenty of fruit.

SAUVIGNON BLANC
Sauvignon Blanc is found in the South-West, Burgundy and the Midi. It comes into its own in the Loire valley, where it is the principal ingredient of Sancerre and Pouilly-Fumé, and in Bordeaux, where, together with Sémillon, it is responsible for much fine wine. It is the major grape in Bordeaux's dry wines; with cool fermentation it can provide a fresh, crisp, acid wine for early drinking.

SEMILLON
Sémillon is the major white wine grape in Bordeaux and is rarely seen elsewhere. High in alcohol but low in acid and lacking fragrance it is a fine complement to the tartness and strong grassy scent of the Sauvignon Blanc. The large, pale, thin-skinned grapes are particularly susceptible to rot, both the destructive grey rot and the sweetening noble rot. Noble-rotted Sémillon is the main ingredient of the sweet wines of Sauternes.

SYRAH
Syrah is a great grape in the northern Rhône while in the southern Rhône, Provence and the Midi it adds body and longevity to a wide range of wines. It is a dark grape that loves heat and flourishes on poor soils, even granite; more than most grapes it adheres to the maxim of low yield, high quality. It finds its perfect expression in Hermitage and Côte Rôtie, rich ruby-red wines which mature slowly into fruity, gamy mouthfuls.

VINTAGES

In a country as climatically varied as France, vintages can be critical to the success of a wine. In a cool summer the grapes will not ripen; in a wet autumn their flavor will be diluted, or they will rot on the vine; early summer rains will prevent the flowers from setting. Despite this, vintages are not everything. A good *vigneron* will make better wines in a poor year than an incompetent one in a good year, and in any year the bulk of the grape harvest goes toward everyday wines for quick drinking. Vintages in the South-West follow those of Bordeaux, generally, and everyday wines in the Jura and Savoie follow the vintages in Burgundy. Corsica, Provence, and Languedoc-Roussillon have uniformly hot summers and wines vary little year to year.

ALSACE

Most wines from Alsace are intended to be drunk young, but they can age well, particularly those made from Riesling, Pinot Gris-Tokay and, to a lesser extent, Gewürztraminer. The late-harvested *Vendange Tardive* and *Sélection de grains nobles* wines are always built to last, but their quality depends on a warm October.

1986 An average year, with a poor summer and a warm autumn.

1985 A great vintage for every style of wine-making in the region.

1984 Thin, tart wines were the product of a poor summer. Even those from the best producers have now lost any charm.

1983 A hot summer produced super-ripe grapes that were low in acidity. Basic wines are now flat but late-harvested wines are brilliant.

Other vintages 1976 was a brilliant year; some of the best late-harvested wines are only now at their peak.

BORDEAUX

With its wide variety of wine styles, grape varieties and *climats*, Bordeaux rarely enjoys a vintage that suits every grower. In the Médoc the late-ripening Cabernet Sauvignon requires warm dry summers; autumn rains can destroy a potentially great vintage. Over the river in Pomerol and St Emilion the Merlot ripens earlier and is unaffected by wet autumns, but is vulnerable to rains in June which hamper flowering, as happened in 1984. The sweet wines of Sauternes require hot humid days to encourage the development of noble rot. The majority of wines produced in Bordeaux, as everywhere else, are for quick drinking, but the top quality *crus* must be kept for upwards of 8–10 years in the best vintages.

1986 An unprecedentedly large harvest. Wines based on Cabernet have plenty of tannins and some acidity, those on Merlot are less successful. Whites are average; Sauternes are good.

1985 A good vintage for all, from the *crus* to the *petits châteaux*. Particular success in St Emilion and Pomerol. Dry whites were excellent for early drinking, but not enough noble rot for truly memorable Sauternes.

1984 The Merlot failed, and other reds were too light and grassy. The poor weather made for some fine acidic whites that have kept well, but most Sauternes is too light.

1983 Excellent, classic reds for long keeping. Dry whites a little past their best. Brilliant vintage for Sauternes, with masses of noble rot and strong, concentrated flavors.

1982 Hot summer and extra-ripe grapes. The reds will keep for some time, the whites are past their best. Some good Sauternes but no great quantity.

1981 Good, medium reds, under-rated in light of subsequent vintages. Sweet whites also reasonable.

Other vintages 1978 and '79 are good for red wines; '75 can be very good, though many wines are beginning to brown. 1970 is excellent. 1978 and '79 are also good for dry whites, while Sauternes are best from '67, '75 and '76.

BURGUNDY

It is perilous to generalize about Burgundy vintages. Rain is common at vintage time; those who pick early run the risk of having under-ripe grapes, those who pick late may find all the flavor diluted. Nonetheless, a good ripe year will produce reds that last from 8 to (exceptionally) 20 years. Top whites from the Côte d'Or and Chablis will keep for up to 10 years, but most is intended for early drinking, as is most Beaujolais, though the *crus* retain their fruit and freshness for three years before developing vegetal overtones.

1986 Large vintage with few good reds. Whites good, with high acidity and good fruit. Beaujolais lacks fruit.

1985 A great vintage for reds, fresh and fruity with good keeping properties; the same is true of Beaujolais. The whites too are rich and fruity, but without the acidity to keep them that way.

1984 A wet vintage that made for pale, rather dry reds and lean, steely whites from Chablis. Côte d'Or whites were likewise very dry.

1983 Summer hail and rot at vintage time made for much tough, harsh wine. The best wines are impressive, but too tannic to drink for a few years. Côte d'Or whites are similarly polarized between excellence and disaster, while Chablis enjoyed a fine, large vintage.

1982 Lots of delicate, well-balanced reds, now at their peak, good Côte d'Or whites, and above-average Chablis.

1981 A poor vintage all round, except in Chablis, where production was low, but quality was excellent.

1980 Underrated vintage now approaching its best. Some sound, acidic Chablis.

Other vintages 1978 was an excellent year for reds and whites alike, but most wines are now past their best.

CHAMPAGNE

Traditionally, vintages were only declared in Champagne in exceptional years, and wines were not released until they had been matured for 6–7 years. With increased demand, however, vintages are declared most years and released onto the market in 4–5 years. *Blanc de blancs* peaks earlier, but lasts as long as wines made with red grapes.

1986 A reasonably good vintage, somewhat affected by rot.

1985 Excellent, well-balanced vintage.

1984 Very poor.

1983 Rich and ripe, with good acid.

1982 Soft ripe wines, good quality and good quantity; coming to its peak.

1981 Mostly under-ripe, a little sour.

1980 A poor vintage, now faded.

1979 Good, soft, well-balanced vintage.

THE LOIRE VALLEY

Vintages are important in the Loire, though they vary along the river's length. Muscadet usually does well, though does not last, while Chenin will only ripen fully in the best years. Wines made from Sauvignon can be made dull by hot summers, but those made from Cabernet Franc need above-average sunshine to grow successfully. Most reds and dry whites are for early drinking, though good Vouvray and Savennières may last up to 10 years. Chinon and Bourgueil will last for 4–8 years and the best sweet wines will keep from 8–15.

1986 A good year for Muscadet, average for the central valley and excellent in Sancerre and Pouilly-Fumé. Sweet white wines do not have enough acidity to keep overlong.

1985 A hot summer and ripe grapes. Good reds and plenty of noble rot for the sweet whites. Sancerre and Pouilly promised much, but failed to deliver.

1984 A poor summer; hardly any worthwhile red but a few light, fresh whites and sweet wines with high acid.

1983 A little too hot for all but the best wines. Excellent sweet whites.

1982 Good red Sancerre, Chinon and Bourgueil.

Other vintages Best vintages for sweet white wines are '64, '69, '76 and '78.

THE RHONE VALLEY

Almost all the red wine from the northern Rhône is worth keeping; Hermitage can improve with 10–30 years' aging, and Côte Rôtie and Cornas with 8–20. Most whites should be drunk within 2–3 years, but white Hermitage may last for 10 years. Southern wines, and all rosés and whites, are for early drinking, though the best red Côtes du Rhône-Villages will last up to five years and good Châteauneuf up to 10 years.

1986 Generally good in the north, rather tough and tannic in the south.

1985 Very fine in the north, especially Côte Rôtie; well balanced in the south.

1984 Fair in the north, though under-ripe. The Grenache failed in the south, leaving all but the best reds short on delicacy and fruit.

1983 Dark ripe reds for long keeping in the north; excellent white Hermitage. Most southern reds past their best but there was good, fruity Châteauneuf.

1982 Fruity tannic reds, good for another year or two.

Other vintages 1969, '73, and especially '78 were excellent vintages.

WINE FAIRS AND FESTIVALS

France is a festive nation, and most wine villages have one or two festival days a year. The most popular dates are around the feast day of St Vincent, the winemaker's patron, on January 22, and at the end of the harvest. The regional Comités (see Useful Addresses) will provide details on request; there is only room here to list the most important ones.

Wine fairs are also occasions for rejoicing, though they have a more serious purpose, that of promoting and judging the region's wines. All those listed below are open to the public and offer an excellent opportunity to taste the best wines from a wide area. Some fairs are exclusively about wine, while others cover all the region's products.

CALENDAR OF FAIRS

January
Orange | Foire aux Vins
Le Mans | Foire aux Vins

February
Tours | Foire aux Vins

March
Paris | Salon International de l'Agriculture

April
Toulouse | Foire de Toulouse
Brignoles | Foire de Brignoles
Perpignan | Foire Internationale
Chambéry | Concours des Vins de Savoie
Paris | Foire de Paris

May
Mâcon | Foire National des Vins
Bordeaux | Foire du Mai
Grenoble | Foire de Grenoble

June
Troyes | Foire du Champagne
Reims | Foire du Champagne
Rivesaltes | Foire aux Vins du Roussillon

August
Colmar | Foire Régionale des Vins d'Alsace
Madiran | Foire des Vins

September
Strasbourg | Foire de Strasbourg
Dijon | Fêtes Internationales de la Vigne et du Vin
Bar-sur-Aube | Foire aux Vins de Champagne
Chambéry | Foire de Savoie

October
Dijon | Foire Gastronomique et des Vins

November
Beaune | Exposition Générale des Vins de Bourgogne
Nantes | Foire du Nantes

December
Villefranche-sur-Saône | Concours-Exposition des Vins
Paris | Salon National des Caves Particulières
Chablis | Exposition des Vins

TRADE BODIES

Every wine region in France has a trade body, or Comité Interprofessionel de Vins, which is an excellent source of information for the general public. They can supply lists of their members and calendars of wine-associated events, fairs and festivals.

ALSACE

C.I.V.A., 12 av. de la Foire aux Vins, 68003 Colmar. Tel: 89.41.06.21. There is also a Maison du Vin with tastings of Alsace wines.

BORDEAUX

(Bordeaux) **C.I.V.B.**, 1 cours du XXX Juillet, 33000 Bordeaux. Tel: 56.52.82.82.

(St Emilion) **Syndicat Viticole de St Emilion**, BP 15, 33330 Bordeaux. Tel: 56.24.72.17.

(Médoc) **G.I.E. des Vins du Médoc**, 1 cours du XXX Juillet, 33000 Bordeaux. Tel: 56.48.18.62.

BURGUNDY

(Burgundy/Mâcon) **C.I.B.M.**, Maison du Tourisme, av. du Mal.-du-Lattre-de-Tassigny, 71000 Mâcon. Tel: 85.38.20.15.

(Côte d'Or/Yonne) **C.I.B.**, r. Henri Dunant, 21200 Beaune. Tel: 80.22.21.35.

(Beaujolais) **U.I.V.B.**, 210 bd Vermorel, 69400 Villefranche-sur-Saône. Tel: 74.65.45.55.

CHAMPAGNE

C.I.V.C., BP 135, 51204 Epernay. Tel: 26.54.47.20.

CORSICA

Groupement Interprofessionnel des Vins de l'Ile de Corse, 6 r. Gabriel Péri, 20000 Bastia. Tel: 95.31.37.36.

JURA

Société de Viticulture du Jura, av. du 44ème R.I., 39016 Lons-le-Saunier. Tel: 84.24.21.07.

LANGUEDOC-ROUSSILLON

(Côtes du Roussillon) **Groupement Interprofessionnel de Promotion des Côtes du Roussillon**, 19 av. de Grande-Bretagne, 66000 Perpignan. Tel: 68.51.31.81.

(Coteaux du Languedoc) **Syndicat des Coteaux du Languedoc**, BP 1098, Maurin-Lattes, 34007 Montpellier.

(Aude) **S.U.A.P.**, Chambre d'Agriculture de l'Aude, 70 r. Aimé Ramon, 11000 Carcassone. Tel: 68.25.24.95.

(Fitou/Corbières/Minervois) **Conseil Interprofessionel des Vins**, RN 113, 11200 Lézignan-Corbières. Tel: 68.27.03.64.

(Minervois) **Syndicat du Cru Minervois**, bd Blazin, 34210 Olonzac. Tel: 68.43.21.66.

(Costieres du Gard) **Syndicat des Costières du Gard**, r. Porte de France, 30000 Nîmes. Tel: 66.57.51.63.

(Vins Doux Naturels) **C.I.V.D.N.**, 19 av. de la Grande Bretagne, 66000 Perpignan. Tel: 68.34.42.32.

THE LOIRE VALLEY

(Pays Nantais) **C.I.V.O.P.N.**, Maison des Vins, Bellevue, 44690 La Haie-Fouassière. Tel: 40.36.90.10.

(Touraine) **C.I.V.T.**, 19 square Prosper Mérimée, 37000 Tours. Tel: 47.05.40.01.

(Anjou-Saumur) **C.I.V.A.S.**, 73 r. Plantagenet, 49000 Angers. Tel: 47.87.62.57.

(Sancerre) **Union Viticole Sancerroise**, Mairie de St Satur, 18300 Sancerre. Tel: 48.54.04.07.

(Pouilly) **Syndicat Viticole du Pouilly**, les Loges, 58150 Pouilly-sur-Loire. Tel: 86.39.12.65.

PROVENCE

(Côtes de Provence) **C.I.V.C.P.**, Maison des Vins, RN 7, 83460 les Arcs-sur-Argens. Tel: 94.73.33.38.

THE RHONE VALLEY

(Côtes du Rhône) **Comité Interprofessionnel des Vins des Côtes du Rhône**, Maison du Tourisme et du Vin, 41 cours Jean-Jaurès, 84000 Avignon. Tel: 90.86.47.09.

SAVOIE

C.I.V.S., 3 r. du Château, 73000 Chambéry. Tel: 79.33.44.16.

THE SOUTH-WEST

(Bergerac) **C.I.V.R.B.**, 2 pl. du Dr Cayla, 24100 Bergerac. Tel: 53.57.12.57.

(Jurançon) **Syndicat du Défense des vins de Jurançon**, 33 bd Henri IV, 64290 Gan. Tel: 59.21.72.79.

(Madiran) **Syndicat de Défense et de Contrôle des Vins de Madiran et du Pacherenc du Vic-Bilh**, Château de Crouseilles, 64350 Lembeye. Tel: 59.68.10.93.

(Gaillac) **C.I.V.G.**, Maison de la Vigne et du Vin, Abbaye St Michel, 81600 Gaillac. Tel: 63.57.15.40.

(Armagnac) **B.N.I.A.**, pl. de la Liberté, 32800 Eauze. Tel: 62.09.82.83.

(Cahors) **Syndicat Interprofessionnel du Vin de Cahors**, Chambre d'Agriculture du Lot, av. Jean-Jaurès, 46001 Cahors. Tel: 65.22.55.30.

FOOD AND WINES FROM FRANCE

For general and specific information about the wine regions of France, contact the publicity organization **Food and Wines from France**.

USA

24 East 21st St, New York, New York 10010. Tel: (212) 477-9800.

2010 Century Business Center Boulevard, Suite 0, Irving, Texas 75062. Tel: (214) 438-1430.

5757 West Century Boulevard, Los Angeles, California 90045. Tel: (213) 641-9145.

UK

Nuffield House, 41-46 Piccadilly, London W1V 9AJ. Tel: 01-439 8371.

TOURIST OFFICES

The French Government Tourist Office provides a full travel information service.

USA

610 5th Avenue, Suite 222, New York, New York 10020. Tel: (212) 757-1125.

645 North Michigan Avenue, Suite 630, Chicago, Illinois 60611. Tel: (312) 337-6301.

9401 Wilshire Boulevard, Beverly Hills, California 90212. Tel: (213) 272-2661.

1 Halliday Plaza, Suite 250, San Francisco, California 94102. Tel: (415) 986-4174.

UK

178 Piccadilly, London W1V 0AL. Tel: 01-491 7622.

HOTELS

Relais et Châteaux A prestigious chain of hotels and restaurants, many of them in beautiful, peaceful surroundings.

USA

D. Mitchell and Co Ltd, 200 Madison Avenue, New York, New York 10016. Tel: (212) 431-0833.

UK

Interfrance Reservations Ltd, 3 Station Parade, London NW2 4NU. Tel: 01-450 9388.

Hostellerie du Vignobles Français, Z.A. de Pont de Joux, BP 40, 13360 Roquevaire. Tel: 42.04.41.97.
A small chain of hotels and restaurants in the wine regions of France with emphasis on serving good local wines. Visits to local producers can also be arranged.

GLOSSARY

cave, caveau a wine cellar; used loosely to describe any place where wine is kept. Wine shops are often referred to as "*caves de vin*".

cépage a grape variety; varietal.

chai a ground-level wine store, particularly in Bordeaux.

climat a specified vineyard site in Burgundy.

clos a walled or otherwise enclosed vineyard. These are found especially in Burgundy.

crémant semi-sparkling.

cru literally, growth; used to dignify the better sites, and the wines they produce, in some regions, particularly Bordeaux and Burgundy.

cuvée literally, the contents of a vat; in champagne, a blend. Elsewhere indicates a "special" wine.

dégustation tasting. *Caveau de dégustation* indicates a cellar where there are public tastings; you may be required to pay a small fee or to buy a bottle. *Vente dégustation* means sales and tasting.

domaine the total holdings of a vineyard proprietor.

mousseux fully sparkling.

négociant a blender or wholesaler of wines who may also act as a bottler and shipper.

perlant with a very slight sparkle.

pétillant having a little sparkle; between *perlant* and *crémant*.

vendange tardive late harvest; applied to wines where the grapes have been picked as late as possible to achieve maximum ripeness.

vigneron a vineyard worker; usually applied to a working proprietor.

vignoble a vineyard.

INDEX

INDEX